T0354781

आनन्द अनुभूति

आध्यात्मिक प्रबन्ध – मधु गीति

A'nanda Anubhu'ti

A'dhya'tmika Prabandha- Madhu Giiti

Perception of Bliss

Spiritual Management Poetry

गोपाल बघेल 'मधु'

Gopal Baghel 'Madhu'

रचियता : गोपाल बघेल ' मधु '

आनन्द अनुभूति, आध्यात्मिक प्रबन्ध– मधु गीति

रचियता संपर्क: AnandaAnubhuti@gmail.com;
www.GopalBaghelMadhu.com

मधु गीति का चल चित्र (विडिओ) लेने, पुस्तक को थोक भाव में क्रय करने, विचार आदान प्रदान एवं सुझाव देने हेतु रचयिता से सम्पर्क करने के लिये आपका हार्दिक स्वागत है।

हिन्दी, संस्कृत, ब्रज, बङ्गला, गुजराती, पञ्जाबी, उर्दू व अंग्रेजी
रोमन संस्कृत व अंग्रेजी स्वरूप सहित

Photography by Author, Graphic Design: Ms. Shweta Baghel

A'NANDA ANUBHU'TI; PERCEPTION OF BLISS
A'DHYA'TMIKA PRABANDHA- MADHU GIITI;
SPIRITUAL MANAGEMENT POETRY

Author Contact: PerceptionOfBliss@gmail.com;
www.GopalBaghelMadhu.com

You are heartily welcome to contact Author for Video and Bulk Purchases of book along with your valuable suggestions and exchange of ideas.

Hindi, Sanskrit, Braj, Bengali, Gujarati, Punjabi, Urdu and English with Roman Sanskrit and English versions.

Photography by Author, Graphic Design: Ms. Shweta Bag

iUniverse books may be ordered through booksellers or by contacting:

iUniverse
1663 Liberty Drive
Bloomington, IN 47403
www.iuniverse.com
1-800-Authors (1-800-288-4677)

ISBN: 978-1-5320-8246-7 (sc)
ISBN: 978-1-5320-8247-4 (e)

Print information available on the last page.

iUniverse rev. date: 12/23/2019

आनन्द अनुभूति

आध्यात्मिक प्रबन्ध – मधु गीति

A'NANDA   ANUBHU'TI
A'dhya'tmika Prabandha - Madhu Giiti

PERCEPTION OF BLISS
Spiritual Management Poetry

Gopal Baghel 'Madhu'
गोपाल बघेल ' मधु '

प्रथम भाग : हिन्दी
संस्कृत, ब्रज, बङ्गला, गुजराती,
पञ्जाबी, उर्दू व अंग्रेजी सहित

द्वितीय भाग : रोमन संस्कृत
तृतीय भाग : अंग्रेजी

Part 1 : Hindi
With Sanskrit, Braj, Bengali,
Gujarati, Punjabi, Urdu & English

Part 2 :   Roman Sanskrit
Part 3 : English

समर्पण

***

परम ब्रह्म परमात्मा

सभी सम्भूतियों, समस्त **सृष्टि चक्र**, प्रकृति, पञ्चभूत एवं चराचर जगत

आदिपिता व आदिगुरु **सदा शिव**, माँ **पार्वती,**
योगेश्वर श्री श्री **कृष्ण**, प्रेम स्वरूपिणी **राधा जी,**
परम पूज्य सद्गुरु श्री श्री **आनन्दमूर्ति जी**
इत्यादि के चरण कमलों में साष्टाङ्ग प्रणाम

पितृ व मातृ कुल, पितामह स्व. धर्म सिंह जी

(सुपुत्र स्व. सुखराम जी, पौत्र स्व. रामबल जी, प्रपौत्र स्व. खुशाला जी)

पिता स्व. डाल चन्द जी, माँ स्व. जय देवी जी,

नाना जी स्व. **सुख राम मिस्त्री जी**
ताऊजी स्व. **किशनलाल**, ताईजी स्व. **जगनी,**
श्वसुर स्व. **याद राम जी,** सासुमाँ स्व. **सावित्री जी**

प्रेरक स्नेही

सर्व स्व. जगन प्र. गुप्ता, बासुदेव, चरनसिंह,
छिद्दासिंह, मनोहर लाल, मुरारी लाल, इत्यादि

आध्यात्मिक व साहित्यिक

ऋषि गण, शोधकर्ता, आचार्य, वैज्ञानिक, अभियन्ता, व सद्ग्रन्थ, चतुर्वेद, तन्त्र,
श्रीमद्भगवद्गीता, श्री रामचरित मानस, योग वशिष्ठ, महाभारत, रवीन्द्र सङ्गीत,
सुभाषित संग्रह, प्रभात सङ्गीत, महर्षि वेदव्यास, पाणिनी मुनि, महर्षि पतञ्जलि,
आदि शंकाराचार्य, स्वामी विवेकानन्द, लक्ष्मीबाई, अहिल्याबाई, इत्यादि
आदि कवि महर्षि वाल्मीकि, मुशाना, गोस्वामी तुलसीदास,
सूरदास, कबीरदास, बिहारी, रहीम, मीरा बाई, इत्यादि

आभार

***

परिवार : पत्नी **आशा,** पुत्र **चैतन्य,**
पुत्रियाँ **श्वेता, ऋचा** व **प्रज्ञा;** धेवता **अरण्य** व पौत्र **रेयाँश**
ग्रही जीव: श्वान **ज़ैट** व स्व. **गूफी,** बिल्ली **मांऊँ,**
गिलहरी **गिल्लू,** पक्षी, वनस्पति, इत्यादि।

समस्त परिवारीय, रिश्तेदार, मूल ग्राम वासी जन
भाई स्व. भीकमसिंह, सर्व श्री सुनहरीलाल, ओमप्रकाश व हरदेव सिंह
जन्म, वास, प्रवास, दर्शित स्थान, भुक्ति, जिले, प्रदेश, देश, महाद्वीप,
विश्व ब्रह्माण्ड के वर्तमान, भूतकालीन व भविष्य में आने बाले समस्त प्राणी

जीवन सहयात्री, आचार्य गण व अनुरागी:
आचार्य व अध्यापक गण, साधक, ग्रही, सन्यासी, साधना सखा,
सह पाठी, सह कर्मी, सह व्यवसायी, सह यात्री व साक्षी जन

सर्वश्री गनपत राम मिस्त्री, उदयवीर सिंह रावत, रामजी लाल,
प्रमोद बघेल, पंकज बघेल, स्व. गोपाल प्र. गौड़, देवीदास,
श्री बालूलाल, श्रीमती लीलावती, इत्यादि

भूमिका लेखक, अभिमत व्यक्त कर्ता, पत्र लेखक व
संशोधन सुझाने बाले सभी आत्मीय जन
प्रेरक कवि गण, गायक एवं लेखक परिवार, मित्र, परिचित व श्रोता गण
प्रकाशक, वितरक व आयोजक

समाचार पत्र, पत्रिकाएं, पुस्तकें, आकाश वाणी, दूरदर्शन
व देश विदेश के सभी विश्व जन
सभी पाठक, गायक, श्रोता व मनन करने वाले सुजन
आनन्द लेने व देने वाले एवम् **सुझाव** देने वाले सभी सुहृद व सहद जन.

साधना मन्त्र

पितृ पुरुषेभ्यो नमः । ऋषि देवेभ्यो नमः । ब्रह्मार्पणं ब्रह्म हविःर्बह्माग्नौ ब्रह्मणा हुतम् । बृह्णेण तेन गन्तव्यं ब्रह्म कर्म समाधिनः ॥

गुरु वन्दना :

अखण्ड मण्डलाकारं व्याप्तं येन चराचरम् ।

तत्पदं दर्शितं येन, तस्मै श्रीगुरवे नमः ॥

अज्ञान तिमिरान्धस्य ज्ञानाञ्जन शलाकया ।

चक्षुरुन्मीलितं येन, तस्मै श्रीगुरुवे नमः ॥

गुरुर्बृह्मा गुरुर्विष्णुः गुरुर्देवो महेश्वरः। गुरुरेव परम बृह्म, तस्मै श्रीगुरुवे नमः॥

तव द्रव्यं जगत गुरु तुभ्यमेव समर्पये ।

मिलित साधना मन्त्र :

सङ्छछध्वं संबदध्वं सं वो मनांसि जानताम्,

देवा भागं यथा पूर्वे सञ्जानाना उपासते ।

समानी व आकुतिः समाना हृदयानि वः,

समानमस्तु वो मनो यथा वः सुसहासति ॥

ॐ मधु वाता ऋतायते मधु क्षरन्ति सिन्धवः। माध्वीर्नः सन्त्वोषधी ॥
मधुनक्तमुतषसो मधुमत्पार्थिवं रजः । मधु द्यौरस्तु नः पिता ॥
मधुमान्नो वनस्पतिर्मधुमान् अस्तु सूर्यः। माध्विर्गावो भवन्तु नः.॥
ॐ मधुः ॐ मधुः ॐ मधुः.

सर्वे भवन्तु सुखिनः सर्वे सन्तु निरामयाः
सर्वे भद्राणि पश्यन्तु न कश्चिद् दुःखमाप्नुयात्.
ॐ शान्तिः, ॐ शान्तिः, ॐ शान्तिः.

ॐ भूर्भुवः स्वः। तत्सवितुर्वरेण्यं भर्गो देवस्य धीमहि। धियो यो नः प्रचोदयात्।

* अथ श्री 'आनन्द अनुभूति' *

अनुक्रमणिका INDEX

(विषय सूची Contents)

कविता सं. व मधु–गीति तालिका
Poem No. (PN) & Madhu Giiti (MG) Index

कविता सं.– मधु– गीति PN-MG	कविता सं.– मधु– गीति PN-MG	कविता सं.– मधु गीति PN-MG	कविता सं.– मधु– गीति PN-MG	कविता सं.– मधु– गीति PN-MG	कविता सं.– मधु– गीति PN-MG	कविता सं.– मधु– गीति PN-MG
01- 601	34- 087	67- 566	100- 322	133- 175	166- 588	199- 031
02- 132	35- 088	68- 567	101- 320	134- 179	167- 062	200- 038
03- 286	36- 089	69- 006	102- 150	135- 178	168- 063	201- 557
04- 328	37- 117	70- 509	103- 118	136- 180	169- 065	202- 646
05- 330	38- 052	71- 026	104- 119	137- 183	170- 094	203- 647
06 -191	39- 123	72- 007	105- 127	138- 184	171- 097	204- 752
07- 192	40- 008	73- 027	106- 651	139- 162	172- 096	205- 136
08- 193	41- 116	74- 020	107- 126	140- 226	173- 098	206- 091
09- 195	42- 129	75- 045	108- 002	141- 236	174- 099	207- 440
10- 308	43- 130	76- 072	109- 003	142- 238	175- 095	208- 554
11- 312	44- 115	77- 073	110- 120	143- 319	176- 100	209- 508
12- 163	45- 131	78- 074	111- 004	144- 327	177- 142	210- 510
13- 028	46- 135	79- 092	112- 005	145- 260	178- 143	211- 168
14- 129	47- 050	80- 134	113- 017	146- 188	179- 189	212- 468
15- 053	48- 051	81- 075	114- 159	147- 015	180- 190	213- 461
16- 030	49- 058	82- 152	115- 018	148- 224	181- 194	214- 167
17- 586	50- 235	83- 141	116- 140	149- 022	182- 329	215- 463
18- 575	51- 049	84- 411	117- 025		183- 040	216- 464

19- 021	52- 060	85- 146	118- 055	150- 016	184- 281	217- 658
20- 042	53- 078	86- 147	119- 037	151- 043	185- 600	218- 465
				152- 044		
21- 011	54- 784	87- 148	120- 128		186- 263	219- 466
22- 056	55- 079	88- 149	121- 046	153- 048	187- 429	220- 467
23- 014	56- 071	89- 151	122- 047	154- 240	188- 239	221- 471
24- 057	57- 080	90- 155	123- 054	155- 081	189- 041	222- 661
25- 013	58- 133	91- 155	124- 137	156- 81A	190- 434	223- 666
26- 061	59- 122	92- 157	125- 160	157- 082	191- 645	224- 662
27- 012	60- 059	93- 158	126- 139	158- 82A	192- 656	225- 665
28- 068	61- 121	94- 185	127- 161	159- 083	193- 668	
29- 069	62- 225	95- 201	128- 164	160- 024	194- 669	
30- 070	63- 521	96- 203	129- 153	161- 144	195- 700	
				162- 258		
31- 076	64- 520	97- 186	130- 154		196- 701	
32- 077	65- 138	98- 202	131- 176	163- 093	197- 321	
33- 086	66- 001	99- 023	132- 182	164- 563	198- 323	
				165- 564		

प्रथम भाग – हिन्दी
Part 1 - Hindi

विषय सूची व अध्याय
Contents & Chapters

कवि परिचय

गोपाल बघेल 'मधु' का जन्म भारत में श्रावण वदी ४, सम्वत २००४ तदनुसार १९४७ में श्री कृष्ण के लीला स्थल गोवर्धन के निकट **रामपुर**, अड़ींग, मथुरा (उत्तर प्रदेश) में ब्रज भूमि में हुआ. राष्ट्रीय योग्यता छात्रवृत्ति व क्षेत्रीय गायन पुरुष्कार प्राप्त हुए. राष्ट्रीय तकनीकी संस्थान, दुर्गापुर, प. बङ्गाल से १९७० में यान्त्रिक अभियान्त्रिकी (B. E. Mech.) में विशेष योग्यता लिये स्नातक बने. अखिल भारतीय प्रबन्ध संस्थान, नई दिल्ली, से १९७८ में प्रबन्ध शास्त्र (AIMA Diploma in Management) किया ।

इंडस्ट्रियल इंजीनीयरिंग, मेटेरियल मेनेजमेंट, प्रिवेंटिव मेन्टीनेन्स, फाइनेंशियल मेनेजमेंट आदि में विशेष प्रशिक्षण लिया. पूर्व 'चार्टर्ड इंजीनीयर', इंस्टीट्यूशन ऑफ इंजीनीयर्स, भारत; पूर्व 'सर्वेयर व लॉस असेसर': भारत; पूर्व सदस्यः भारतीय प्रबन्ध संस्थान, दिल्ली प्रबन्ध संस्थान, दिल्ली उत्पादकता परिषद, भारतीय पल्प व पेपर संस्था (IPPTA), इत्यादि. २००७–२००८ में टोरोन्टो, कनाडा से सिस्टम्स एप्लीकेशन प्रोडक्ट– बिजनेस वेयर हाउस (SAP-BW) में व सं. रा. अमरीका से ऐप्लीकेशन सीक्यूरिटी में प्रशिक्षण लिया ।

व्यावसायिक (१९७०– १९९७) : भारत के विभिन्न उद्योगों (पेपर, प्रिन्टिंग, पैकेजिंग, कपड़ा, वनस्पति, ऊन, चीनी, आदि) में अभियन्ता, प्रबन्ध विश्लेषक, उत्पादन योजन व नियन्त्रक, कॉर्पोरेट मेटेरियल मैनेजर, विकास प्रबन्धक, महा प्रबन्धक, प्रबन्ध सलाहकार, मुख्य कार्यभारी, आदि पदों पर उत्तर प्रदेश, राजस्थान, प. बङ्गाल, पञ्जाब, उत्तराँचल, गुजरात, हरियाणा, दिल्ली, आदि में उद्योग प्रबन्धन किया. भारत में उत्तर, पूर्व, पश्चिम, मध्य, पूर्वाञ्चल एवं दक्षिण सर्वत्र जाने का अवसर मिला ।

व्यावसायिक वर्तमानः १९९७ उपरांत, टोरोन्टो में सपरिवार रहते हुए कागज, इस्पात आदि के क्रय विक्रय, उत्पादन, प्रबन्ध, प्रशासन, आयात निर्यात में प्रायः अमरीका जाते हुए विश्व भर से सम्पर्कित रहे. कनाडा व अमरीका के अनेक

उद्योगों, मार्केटिंग संस्थाओं, टेक्नीकल एसोसिएशन ऑफ पल्प एंड पेपर से संयुक्त रहे. वे 'ग्लोबल फ़ाइबर्स' नामक आयात निर्यात संस्था के अध्यक्ष हैं ।

आध्यात्मिक: बचपन से धार्मिक वातावरण, साधु जनों की प्रेरणा, प्रोत्साहन एवं आशीर्वाद का सुयोग प्राप्त हुआ. गुरु कृपा से १९६८ में आध्यात्मिक साधना सीखने का सुयोग मिला. १९८४ में गुरु दर्शन का सौभाग्य प्राप्त हुआ. १९८४–२००० आध्यात्मिक साधना, सत्सङ्कृति, कर्म व सेवा में सम्पृक्त रहा. २००० से एकाकी साधना का सुयोग हुआ. जागतिक, आध्यात्मिक, पारिवारिक, सामाजिक व साहित्यिक सरिता में प्रवृत गुरु, आचार्य, साहित्यकार व कवि जनों के विशेष आशीर्वाद के प्रसाद से जीवन धारा प्रवाहित रही.

साहित्यिक : १९८१–८४ में विज्ञान व अध्यात्म पर कुछ लेख व पद्य लिखे. प्रभु कृपा से २००८ से आध्यात्मिक प्रबन्ध, आध्यात्मिक प्रबन्ध विज्ञान शोध, भक्ति कृपा, करुणानुभूति, प्राकृतिक आदि विधाओं में मुख्यतः हिन्दी, ब्रज व बङ्गला में एवं संस्कृत, गुजराती, पञ्जाबी, उर्दू व अंग्रेजी में ७०००+ कविताओं का सृजन अब तक हुआ है जिनमें से २२५ कविताएं रोमन संस्कृत व अंग्रेजी स्वरूप सहित इस पुस्तक में प्रकाशित हैं. कविताएं गेय हैं और उनके वृत्त चित्र उपलब्ध हैं.

कवियों, मित्रों व जन साधारण ने उनकी कविताओं का खूब आनन्द लिया है व सराहा है. उनकी कविताओं का प्रकाशन कनाडा, सं. रा. अमरीका, भारत व विश्व भर के अनेक समाचार पत्रों, पत्रिकाओं एवं संकलन पुस्तकों में हुआ है. अनेक कविताएं कवि सम्मेलनों, साहित्यिक संस्थाओं की कवि गोष्ठियों, अखिल विश्व हिन्दी समिति न्यूयार्क, शिक्षा यतन न्यूयार्क, सं. रा. अ., टोरोन्टो स्थित भारतीय राज दूतावास में, हिन्दी मंच के 'हिन्दी दिवस' व हिन्दी राइटर्स गिल्ड के 'अन्तर्राष्ट्रीय हिन्दी महोत्सव' एवं अन्य अनेक आयोजनों में तथा यू-ट्यूब, आकाश वाणी व दूरदर्शन पर गायी गयीं हैं.

वे अखिल विश्व हिन्दी समिति एवं आध्यात्मिक प्रबन्ध पीठ, टोरोन्टो, ओंटारिओ, कनाडा के संस्थापक निदेशक व अध्यक्ष हैं। वे हिन्दी साहित्य सभा, कनाडा के महासचिव भी हैं व वे देश–विदेश की विभिन्न साहित्यिक संस्थाओं के सक्रिय सदस्य हैं।

विषय परिचय

सृष्टि चक्र व सृष्टि प्रबन्ध : ब्रह्माण्ड मूलतः निर्गुण सत्ता का प्रतिफलन है. निर्गुण ब्रह्म जब लीला भाव में आकर सगुण हो जाते हैं, तब त्रिगुणात्मक प्रकृति प्रकट होती है. त्रिगुणों (सत, रज व तम) में भार व स्थिति साम्य रहने तक साम्य स्थिति बनी रहती है. सन्तुलन असाम्य होने पर प्रकृति सञ्चर उन्मुख हो जाती है और महत अहम् चित्त प्रकट होजाते हैं. चित्त क्रमशः आकाश, वायु, आग्नि, जल एवं पृथ्वी बन उठता है परन्तु उनमें उपरोक्त सञ्चर अवस्थायें भी सूक्ष्म अवस्था में अन्तर्निहित रहती हैं ।

पृथ्वी के जड़ तत्व अतिशय संघर्ष रत होने पर उसमें अन्तर्निहित अव्यक्त चित्त एक कोशी और फिर बहु कोशीय वनस्पति की सृष्टि कर प्रतिसञ्चर उन्मुख, होजाता है. उत्तरोत्तर संघर्ष स्वरूप सृष्टि की प्रतिसञ्चर प्रक्रिया में जन्तु, मनुष्य, बुद्धिजीवी और आध्यात्मिक मानव का अविर्भाव होता है. अन्ततः आध्यात्मिक मानव इस सृष्टि चक्र से विलग हो सगुण में विलीन हो जाता है ।

सृष्टि प्रबन्ध अवस्था व प्रयोजनानुसार सगुण कभी निर्गुण हो जाता है और फिर कभी सगुण. उसका अपना स्वरूप भी उत्तरोत्तर विकसित होता चलता है और वह सृष्टि चक्र का प्रबन्ध सतत नियन्त्रित करता रहता है. इस सृष्टि चक्र की सञ्चर व प्रतिसञ्चर प्रक्रिया में प्रकट सब अवस्थायें सगुण के परोक्ष अपरोक्ष प्रबन्ध में अपना अस्तित्व रखते विलीन उत्थान करते हुए उत्तरोत्तर विकास करती चलती हैं. बृह्म चक्र/ सृष्टि चक्र का चित्र परिशिष्ट में देखें ।

सगुण बृह्म, गुरु, योग, तन्त्र, भक्ति एवम् कृपा : सगुण बृह्म ही सृष्टि में भक्ति और/ अथवा कृपा वश आवश्यकानुसार गुरु स्वरूप में प्रकट होते हैं. सृष्टि चक्र सृष्टा की भूमा संस्था है. सृष्ट अवयव उसके आयोजन हैं. देश काल पात्र उसके आयाम हैं. जीवों के भक्ति कर्म ज्ञान का मूल्याङ्कन, निर्देशन व नियन्त्रण होते हुए सृष्टि में उनकी उत्तरोत्तर पदोन्नति व प्रगति होती चलती है. सृष्टि के प्रबन्ध का ज्ञान और अनुभव ही योग है. योग में प्रवीण होने पर, सद्गति आने पर तन्त्र प्रतिष्ठित होता है. ज्ञान, भक्ति, कर्म, योग व तन्त्र के मूल्याङ्कन में उत्तीर्ण व प्रतिष्ठित होने पर और

भक्ति सुदृढ़ हो जाने पर सृष्टा कृपा कर सकते हैं. जीव का बृह्म की ओर चलने का प्रयास भक्ति है. बृह्म का जीव की ओर चलने का प्रयास कृपा है. सृष्टा का ध्येय है सृष्टि के प्रति अवयव (अणु जीवत्) को विकसित कर सृष्टि प्रबन्ध में प्रवीण कर देना और अन्ततः बृह्म अवस्था में ले आना. बृह्म अवस्था में ही विचरित प्राणी सृष्टि को भली भांति समझ पाता है और समुचित सृष्टि सेवा कर पाता है. सृष्टि में जो प्रबन्धन में बृहत्तम सत्ता हैं वे ही बृह्म हैं ।

आध्यात्मिक प्रबन्ध : सृष्टि नियन्त्रक सृष्टि में क्षुद्र एवम् सूक्ष्म के परस्पर विनियोग विनिमय से सृष्टि में जागतिक, मानसिक एवं आध्यात्मिक सृजन और विकास बढ़ाते चलते हैं. क्षुद्रतम को महत्तम बना देना, सृष्टि प्रबन्ध का ध्येय और कौशल है. योगः कर्मसु कौशलम्– कर्म का कौशल योग है. सृष्टा के सृष्टि प्रबन्ध का ज्ञान, विज्ञान, कला, भक्ति व कृपा भरा, योग व तन्त्र युक्त कर्म ही प्रबन्ध कौशल है।

देश काल पात्र : सृष्टि नियन्त्रक, सृष्टि के घटना क्रम का प्रबन्ध, देश काल पात्र को नियन्त्रित कर, करते हैं. यदि किसी सत्ता में देश काल पात्र को नियन्त्रित करने की अवस्था प्राप्त हो जावे तो वह सत्ता विश्व के घटनाक्रम को नियन्त्रित कर सकती है. देश काल पात्र में से किसी एक को भी बदल दें तो शेष दो भी स्वयमेव परिवर्तित हो जावेंगे – घटना व घटना चक्र भी परिवर्तित हो जावेगा. देश व्याप्त है सृष्टि व सृष्ट सत्ताओं की देह में. काल है देश में व्याप्त दूरियों की अनुभूति. पात्र हैं सृष्टि में व्याप्त सत्ताएं ।

सृष्टि में सृजन : सत्ता के, देश काल पात्र से स्वयं को समेट, सृष्टा में समर्पित होने से सृजन हो जाता है. जितना बृहत होगा शून्य, उतना ही बृहत होगा सृजन. नव जीव का सृजन, वैज्ञानिक आविष्कार, राजनैतिक परिवर्तन, प्रकृति की प्रक्रियाएं, संकल्पों का स्वरुपित होना, संस्कारों का उदय, सृष्टि परिवर्तन, आदि सभी कुछ देश काल पात्र की स्वर लहरियों के शून्य से जनित, प्रभावित या प्रतिफलित है ।

आनन्द अनुभूति : सृष्टा, सृष्ट जगत, सृष्टि प्रबन्ध, आध्यात्म एवं स्वयं को समझ लेने पर सृष्टि में रहना व सेवा करना, आनन्दमय होता है. साधना व्यक्ति को सृष्टा से जोड़ने की विधि, विज्ञान, कला, अभ्यास व अनुभूति है. गुरु स्वरूप में प्रकट

सगुण ब्रह्म की सद्कृपा से ही साधना सम्भव हो पाती है । गुरु ही अन्धकार (गु) से प्रकाश (रु) में ले चलते हैं. गुरु ही ज्ञात अज्ञात, प्रतक्ष अप्रतक्ष, हो कर जीव का मार्ग दर्शन करते हैं. गुरु ओत प्रोत भाव से प्रति पल, प्रति स्थान पर, प्रति पात्र के साथ रहते हैं. गुरु ही जीव को अपनी सृष्टि प्रबन्ध विधाओं से उत्तरोत्तर प्रबन्ध कौशलता में विकसित थिरकित स्पन्दित आनन्दित करते हुए चलते हैं. वे ही जीव को आध्यात्मिक प्रबन्ध के नन्दन विज्ञान में प्रतिष्ठित कर शुभमस्तु कहते हुए अद्भुत आनन्द अनुभूति लेते देते चलते हैं।

सृष्टा के सानिध्य में रहकर जो अनन्त सुख मिलता है वही है "आनन्द". यह आनन्द वे धरा पर सब को बाँट रहे हैं पर सब जीव सब समय आनन्द अनुभूति नहीं कर पाते. वे चाहते हैं कि उनके सब जीव इस आनन्द को यथाशीघ्र अनुभूत कर लें और उनकी सृष्टि को व स्वयं को आनन्दित करते हुए सृष्टि प्रबन्ध करें. आनन्द स्वयं ही अनुभव किये बिना आनन्दित नहीं कर पाता; अत: सृष्टा चाहते हैं कि हम सब अपने शरीर, मन व आत्मा को सतत परिष्कृत रखें, साधना द्वारा सृष्टा से सम्पर्कित हो जावें और जगत (ज= य= जो, गत= गतिशील है) को सृष्टा की दृष्टि से देखते, समझते, व्यबहार व प्रबन्धित करते हुए सतत व उत्तरोत्तर विकसित करते चलें. इस अवस्था में जो अनुभव होंगे, वही है 'आनन्द अनुभूति'।

हम सब अपनी आनन्द अनुभूतियों को परस्पर बाँटे तो और अधिक आनन्द अनुभूति होगी और सृष्टा भी आनन्दित होंगे. सृष्टा आनन्दित हों, हम सब पर और कृपा करें और हम सब उनकी सृष्टि की और उत्तम सेवा करे; यही तो है सर्व वाँछित अपेक्षित लक्ष. आनन्द अनन्त हो, "आनन्द अनुभूति" सतत हो समस्त विश्व में तरङ्गित हो. समस्त सृष्टि, सृष्टा, सृष्ट जीव, प्रकृति, पञ्च भूत एवं ब्राह्मी मन, इस ब्राह्मी आनन्द अनुभूति से तरङ्गित, थिरकित एवम् आनन्दित हो जावें यही सृष्टा के अन्तर्मन की अभिलाषा एवं संयोजना है. क्यों न हम उनकी इस एषणा को अपने ऊपर कृपा समझ भक्ति व आनन्द की वर्षा करालें और "आनन्द अनुभूतियों" में डूब जायें एवं सबको डुबा डालें ।

जब हम उनके आनन्द रस को अनुभूत कर रहे होते हैं, वे भी हमारे सर पर हाथ रखे हमारा हृदय सहला रहे होते हैं. हमारी समस्त व्यथा, व्यवधान, बाधाएं एवं ब्याकुलता यथा शीघ्र उनकी प्रकृति हमसे दूर हटा देती है. निकट नजर आती है

भक्ति, कृपा, ज्ञान, कर्म, ऐश्वर्य एवं "आनन्द अनुभूति". सहृदय व सानुराग शाश्वत सृष्टि प्रेम में सरावोर मानव हृदय आनन्द अनुभूति की मधु विधा में मधु विद्या पा गा उठता है उसके सूक्ष्म प्रेम की अनुभुतियां. थिरक उठता है उसके अनादि आनन्द में; विश्व नाच उठता है उसके उर में और वह संगोपन में गा उठता है सृष्टि की सर्वाङ्गी हृदय वीणा पर अनादि अनन्त स्वर भरी 'आनन्द अनुभूति' ।

आनन्द परम पुरुष व जीव के अन्तः मिलन से स्फुरित है. उसका उद्गम सृष्टि की भावधारा में है. जीव का परम शिव से सम्पर्क व मिलन सृष्टि में एक अद्भुत तरङ्ग सृवित करता है. स्वयं परम पुरुष, जीव व सृष्टि इस परम मिलन से तरङ्गित हो जाते हैं. इस भावातीत अवस्था में जो अनुभूतियां होती हैं वे ही हैं 'आनन्द अनुभूति'. आसान नहीं है उनको प्रकट करना, आसान नहीं है बिना अनुभव किये उनका आनन्द ले पाना. परन्तु हर जीव को उनका अहसास है. कभी न कभी सृष्टि चक्र की अपनी यात्रा में उसने इस रस का स्वाद चखा है. कभी न कभी परम पुरुष के अनन्त स्वरूप की अप्रतिम झलक उसे भायी है. वह अन्तर्मन में इच्छुक है इस परम आनन्द को सतत पाने के लिये ।

सृष्टि की अन्तर्मुखी व वहिर्मुखी क्रीड़ाओं की लीला, जाने अनजाने जीव को व्यस्त रखती है, सृष्टि के प्रबन्ध प्रवाह में. उत्तरोत्तर अनन्त मुखी सृष्टि व जीव विकास चिर चरैवति रखना परम पुरुष का कर्म व धर्म है. वे चाहते हैं कि उनके इस सृष्टि प्रबन्धन में प्रति जीव का अधिकतम योगदान हो. वे चाहते हैं देना यह प्रबन्ध आनन्द अधिकतम जीवों को. यह आनन्द ही उन्हें कर्म व धर्म में और प्रतिष्ठित करता है. यही उन्हें और पूर्ण करता है. यही सृष्टि के हर कण हर जीव को उत्तिष्ठ व प्रतिष्ठित करता है. यही सृष्टि के प्रति देश काल पात्र में विकास व आनन्द की गङ्गा बहाता है. 'आनन्द अनुभूति' बहे, बढ़े, थिरके व आनन्द मय रहे यही तो परम पुरुष, सृष्टि व प्रति अणु जीवत की आन्तरिक इच्छा है ।

●●

अखिल विश्व हिन्दी समिति, न्यूयार्क

108- 15 68 Drive, Forest Hills, New York 11375, USA
(संस्थापक अध्यक्ष : स्व. रामेश्वर अशान्त)

अन्तर्राष्ट्रीय अध्यक्ष   अध्यक्ष
डा. दाऊजी गुप्त   डा. विजय कुमार मेहता

भूमिका

जीवन का अनवरत प्रवाह गङ्गा की निरन्तर बहती धारा है, ठीक इसी प्रकार कविता मनोवेग की सहज अभिव्यक्ति है. इसका प्रस्फुटन स्वाभाविक है और कवि के कर-कमल से कविता-कमल की पंखुड़ियों को आकार प्राप्त होता है. श्री गोपाल बघेल 'मधु' आस्थाओं से आस्तिक एवं उनके दर्शन के अनुसार सृजन का सूत्र एकमेव परम बृह्म परमेश्वर है.

काव्य सृजन में कवि की अपनी अवधारणा एवं अपना व्यक्तित्व महत्वपूर्ण होता है. कवि और लेखक तो साधन-मात्र है, जिसके माध्यम से भाव को आकार प्राप्त होता है.

'श्रीमद् भगवद् गीता' में श्री कृष्ण ने अर्जुन से कहा–

"कर्मण्येवाधिकारस्ते मा फलेषु कदाचन,
मा कर्मफल हेतुर्भूमा ते सङ्गोऽस्त्वकर्मणि"

जनकवि गोपाल बघेल 'मधु' ने काव्य-रचना में अर्जुन का रूप ग्रहण किया और श्री कृष्ण ने प्रेरक रूप से उन्हें माध्यम बनाया. जैसे-जैसे निर्देश मिलते रहे, वैसे-वैसे रचना होती रही. चूँकि जनकवि गोपाल 'मधु' सृष्टि की रचना करने वाले प्रभु के अनुयायी हैं, इसलिये उनकी रचनाओं से क्या फलित होगा, इसकी उन्हें चिन्ता नहीं है. न तो उन्हें कर्म का फल चाहिये और न वह निष्क्रिय होना चाहते हैं, वरन् प्रभु के साथ एकाकार होना चाहते हैं–

"कविर्मनीषी परिभू स्वयंभू"

जनकवि ने कर्म (रचना) का फल पाने के लिये जन्म नहीं लिया है और न वह कर्महीन होकर बैठना चाहते हैं. वह तो रचना–कर्म पर अपना अधिकार मानते हैं और लेखनी के माध्यम से जो कुछ भी सृजित होता है, उसे प्रभु को समर्पित करते हैं क्योंकि कवि और मनीषी परिभू हैं और स्वयंभू के साथ एकाकार हो जाते हैं.

श्री गोपाल बघेल 'मधु' का रचना – संसार सीमित नहीं, विस्तृत है. उनकी कविताओं को ७ खण्डों में विभाजित किया गया है–

१. आध्यात्मिक प्रबन्ध, २. आध्यात्मिक प्रबन्ध विज्ञान व शोध,
३. भक्ति व कृपा ४. करुणानुभूति ५. कवि अनुभूति, ६. प्राकृतिक,
७. विविध भाषा साहित्य.

जिस कवि का जन्म मथुरा में हुआ वह श्री कृष्ण की अत्मानुभूति के रूप में सामने आया. मीरा ने कहा था– "मेरे तो गिरिधर गोपाल दूसरा न कोई" और ये गिरिधर कौन हैं? वह हैं श्री कृष्ण, जिन्होंने अपनी अंगुलि पर गिरि गोवर्ध्दन को धारण कर प्रलयंकारी, मूसलाधार वर्षा से सृष्टि की रक्षा की और इस प्रकार इन्द्र को पराजित किया. गोवर्ध्दन गिरि की छाया में जो लोग सुरक्षित रहे, उनको 'आनन्द-अनुभूति' हुई. वही श्री कृष्ण (गोपाल) अपनी छत्रछाया में जनकवि गोपाल 'मधु' की 'आनन्द अनुभूति' के रस को स्वर देते हुए मथुरा ही नहीं वरन् विश्व की धरती को ब्रज बना कविताओं के माध्यम से जनजन को आनन्द की अनुभूति करा रहे हैं.

जब परतंत्रता की बेड़ियों से मुक्त होकर स्वतंत्र 'भारत' का अभ्युदय हुआ, उसी वर्ष सन् १९४७ में गोपाल बघेल ' मधु' का जन्म हुआ. गोपाल स्वयं 'भारत' (अर्जुन) बने गोपाल (श्री कृष्ण) भी बने, एकाकार हुए. श्री कृष्ण ने गायों का पालन किया और गोपाल कहलाये. गोपाल 'मधु' ने कविताओं के रूप में जन्मी गायों का पालन किया, तो गोपाल बनकर उन कविता – रूपी गायों के दूध में 'मधु' घोल दिया, जिसकी मिठास से आनन्द की अनुभूति तो होनी ही है. इसलिये–
" मधु तुम आ जाओ तो रंग भरें जीवन में;
राग भरें, छन्द भरें, गीत भरें त्रिभुवन में.
रूप भरें, रस भर दें, गन्ध भरें हर मन में;

कर्म करें, ध्यान धरें, भक्ति भरें जीवन में. "

जनकवि गोपाल 'मधु' वाचिक परम्परा के कवि बन गये. वह केवल पुस्तक और पाठक के कवि नहीं हैं. जो कुछ लिखते हैं, सीधे कहते हैं, कविता में घुमाव फिराव नहीं लाते. तभी तो जनता के कवि बनकर कहते हैं :

" मानवता शोषित, विचलित है; आतंकित, शंकित, भयमय है.
ताण्डव जग में प्रभु कम कर दो, आनन्दित जन गण मन कर दो."

समय का वैज्ञानिक विश्लेषण करते हुए कवि प्रश्न करता है–

" समय क्या सृष्टि का आपेक्षिक आयाम है?
समय क्या देश काल पात्र का सहोदर है?
समय क्या सम्भावना की पथ तरङ्ग है? समय क्या अनादि अनन्त की रेखा है?

इन सभी प्रश्नों और जीवन की अनेकानेक समस्याओं का उत्तर हैं जनकवि गोपाल 'मधु' की समय – सापेक्ष कविताएं. उनमें कवि का आवेग और आत्माभिव्यक्ति का प्रवाह काव्य – प्रेमियों को सहज ही प्रभावित करेगा, इसमें कोई सन्देह नहीं है.

डा. दाऊजी गुप्त

एम. कॉम., एल. एल. बी., पी. एच. डी. अध्यक्ष : पी. ई. एन., भारत
पूर्व महापौर, एम.एल.सी., पैनल चेयरमैन, उत्तर प्रदेश विधान परिषद, भारत

लखनऊ, भारत

पद्मश्री, डा. श्याम सिंह शशि

पी. एच. डी. (समाज शास्त्र), डी. लिट.(नृविज्ञान एवम् साहित्य),
पी.जी., प्रबन्ध शास्त्र, इंग्लैंड

वरिष्ठ साहित्यकार व नृ–वैज्ञानिक

महा निदेशक, अंतर्राष्ट्रीय शोध संस्थान,
शिक्षा भवन, रोहिणी, सेक्टर ९, दिल्ली–११००८५, भारत
विजिटिंग प्रोफेसर, इन्दिरा गांधी नेशनल ओपिन यूनीवर्सिटी, नई दिल्ली.
पूर्व महा निदेशक, भारत सरकार– प्रकाशन विभाग, सूचना व प्रसारण

Safdarjung Encl., New Delhi- 110029, India

स्वस्ति पंथाः

परम सत्ता का प्रतिफलन प्रमुखतः दो स्वरूपों में है– निर्गुण और सगुण. उसके सगुण स्वरूप में सृष्टि के दृश्य जगत का विकास अथवा विवर्त होता है. किंतु वास्तविक नियंत्रक सत्ता मूलतः निर्गुण ही होती है. गुणों के आधार पर उसका सर्वांग्रीण निर्वचन होना आसान नहीं है. सम्पूर्ण जगत में अन्तर्यामी होते हुए भी वह तात्विक दृष्टि से अतिरेकी और निर्गुण ही रहता है. वह राम–रहीम के दो रुपों में प्रतिष्ठित होते हुए भी एक ओंकार अथवा एकेश्वरवाद की आस्था में रूहानी रोशनी पाता है. इसी एक मात्र सत्य को संतों की वाणी मनसा–वाचा–कर्मणा जीती जनाती रही है. कबीर, दादू, रैदास, मलूकदास और बाबा फ़रीद आदि संत–कवि गुरु नानक को भी भाये थे. फलतः वे गुरु ग्रंथ साहिब में स्थान पा गये. हिन्दी संत साहित्य में सूर, तुलसी तथा सगुण सन्त कवियों पर जितना लिखा गया उतना निर्गुण विचार धारा के संतों पर नहीं. कबीर अपवाद हैं, जिनकी वाणी को डा. हज़ारी प्रसाद द्विवेदी ने पूरी तरह पहचाना और कबीर वाणी का विशद मूल्याङ्कन किया. सूफ़ी मत अल्लाह तथा राम का समकेतिक स्वरूप है अतः हिन्दू मुसलमान दोनों वर्गों ने उसे अपनाया.

कनाडा वासी भारतीय मूल के रचनाकार गोपाल बघेल 'मधु' की आध्यात्मिक

रचनाओं का आनन्द लेते हुए ऐसा लगा कि जहाँ सार्वभौमिक भारतीय संस्कृति कभी कभी, कहीं कहीं भारत में पराई हो रही प्रतीत होती है, वहीं कुछेक भारतीय मूल के कलमगार वसुधा पर अन्यत्र जाकर उसे अपनी आत्मा में न केवल समाये, विकसित व प्रकटित किये हुए हैं वरन उसे विश्व भर में प्रस्फुट, पल्लवित और तरङ्गित कर रहे हैं।

मैंने यूरोप, यू. एस. ए., कनाडा, दक्षिण अमेरिका, मारीशस, सुरिनाम, गुवाना, फिजी, ट्रिनीडाड सहित अपनी विश्व यात्राओं में भारतवंशियों व अन्य प्रवासियों के सुख दुख व आनन्द अनुभूतियों को निकट से अनुभव किया है एवम् उनकी साहित्यिक कृतियां को देखा व सुना है. मुझे उनका वह सुर कभी उस भारतवंशी रोमा समुदाय के शोक भींगे आनन्द संगीत में सुनाई पड़ा जिसके पूर्वज एक हजार वर्ष पूर्व भारत छोड़कर मिश्र तथा अन्य देशों की ओर चल पड़े थे. उनके वंशज आज भी भारत को 'बारोथान' कहते हुए नहीं अघाते हैं. उनकी मात्रभाषा रोमानी है जिसका साहित्य मानवीय संघर्ष का दर्दीला दस्तावेज़ है. 'होलोकास्ट' की यातना झेलने के बाद भी उनका 'पैगानिज्म' जीवित रहा जो कहीं ऋग्वेद की प्रकृति पूजा से जुड़ा तो कहीं ईसाई, मुस्लिम तथा अन्य मत मतान्तरों में पल्लवित हुआ. वह 'वसुधैव कुटुम्बकम' के शान्ति सन्देश में अपना अस्तित्व बनाये हुए है. रोमा यद्यपि पश्चिमी संस्कृति में पूरी तरह घुलमिल गये हैं फिर भी उनकी रोमानी भाषा में अनेक शब्द हिन्दी, पंजाबी, मराठी, गुजराती, मारवाड़ी आदि के आज भी सुनने को मिलते हैं.

विश्व हिन्दी समिति, न्यूयार्क व लंदन, गीतांजली विर्मिंघम, आदि के आमन्त्रण पर आयोजित वर्ष २००३ की मेरी साहित्यिक यात्राओं में भी मैंने भरतवंशियों को भारतीय संस्कारों, भारतीय जन मानस व अपनों के आत्मीय प्रेम की याद में आतुर एवं सरावोर पाया. वे अपनी आत्मा में भूमा की भाषा लिये, नये परिवेश में अपने को ढालते संवारते हुए, उत्तरोत्तर अपनी जीवन आत्मा को विकशित, संशोधित करते हुए व विश्व मानव संस्कृति से समायोजन करते हुए, उसे कुछ भारतीय व भूमा स्वर और सुर देते हुए, आगे बढ़ने का सतत प्रयास करते रहे हैं. प्रवासियों के भूमा मानस की टीस बार–बार उनकी लेखनी से निसृत होकर विश्व व्यापी व्यथा, व्यवस्था, विविधता व अनुभवों को 'आनन्द अनुभूति' बना देती है. कोई रचनाकार छायाबादी शब्दावली से बंधा लगता है तो कोई प्रगतिवाद से जुड़ा हुआ.

जिसे जो भी भाता है, उसके सृजन का अङ्ग बन जाता है. अपने संस्कारों को तुकान्त अतुकान्त छन्दों में ढालते हुए वे अभिनव साहित्य सृजन करते चलते हैं.

मथुरा (उ. प्र.) में जन्मे, दुर्गापुर (प. बङ्गाल) व नई दिल्ली में पढ़े, भारत में पले, फले फूले, कनाडा के कवि गोपाल बघेल 'मधु' की रचनाओं में उनके धार्मिक व अध्यात्मिक संस्कारों, अनुभवों एवं अनुभूतियों को रसात्मक आनन्द प्रवाह मिला है. उन्होंने इसके लिये तत्सम शब्दावली का प्रश्रय लिया है. अपनी कविताओं में वे अपनी अटूट भारतीय संस्कृति व संस्कारों को भूमा भाव की आकाश गङ्गा में उतराते, डुबाते व रसमय करते या तरङ्गित व झंकृत करते प्रतीत होते हैं. उनका यह गेयाँश उनके सृजन का साराँश प्रतीत होता है:

" आनन्द उमङ्गों में भरकर, मैं तुमरा गीत सुना जाऊँ;
मैं तारक बृह्म लिये मन में, तरता जाऊँ, वरता जाऊँ."

'मधु' की लेखनी को स्नेहाशीश देते हुए, मैं आशा करता हूँ कि अध्यात्मिक कविता प्रवाह के साथ साथ, यदि वे विशुद्ध साहित्य सृजन की भाव विधा में काव्य या गद्य रचना करें तो उसमें भी निश्चय ही उनकी लेखनी भारतीय संस्कृति के संरक्षण–परिरक्षण में और अधिक सहायक सिद्ध होगी. स्वाभाविक रूप से उनकी लेखनी अपना पथ स्वयं पावेगी और अगले संकलनों में और भी अधिक ऊर्जा, अनुभूति, आनन्द व प्रभु कृपा के साथ प्रष्फुटित हो वैचारिक और आध्यात्मिक प्रबन्ध की क्रांति का पथ प्रशस्त करेगी. स्वस्ति पन्था:

डॉ. श्याम सिंह शशि

रचियता – ४००+ पुस्तकें– हिन्दी, अंग्रेजी, आदि भाषाओं में:
सामाजिक विज्ञान हिन्दी शब्दकोश, महाकाव्य अग्निसार, शिलानगर में, आदि

डॉ. हरी सिंह पाल

कवि, व्यंगकार, समीक्षक, वाल साहित्यकार व लोक साहित्य समीक्षक

पी. एच. डी (लोक साहित्य), एम. एड., पी. जी. डी.,

एम. ए. (हिन्दी), एम. ए. (समाज शास्त्र),

बी. एस. सी. (मेडीकल), बी. एस. सी., बी. एडूकेशन, सी. एल. सी.

विद्या वाचस्पति, साहित्य मार्तण्ड, साहित्य भूषण,

काव्य गौरव, साहित्य श्री, प्रतिभा श्री, इत्यादि.

भूतपूर्व कार्यक्रम अधिशासी, आकाश वाणी, सूचना एवं प्रसारण मंत्रालय, भारत सरकार, नई दिल्ली, ११००१, भारत

काव्य समीक्षा

भारतीय जीवन दर्शन में धर्म और अध्यात्म, आचरण और मानवीय चिन्तन के रूप में स्वीकृत रहे हैं. प्रकृति और ईश्वरीय सत्ता की विवेचना विद्वान लोग अपने अपने तरीके से करते रहे हैं. एक संवेदनशील रचनाकार कवि अपनी भावनात्मक अनुभूतियों की अभिव्यक्ति अपनी रचना में सहज ही कर लेता है । श्री गोपाल बघेल 'मधु' ऐसे ही सहृदय सफल एवम् सशक्त रचनाकार हैं जिन्होंने अपनी आध्यात्मिक अनुभूतियों का प्रष्फुटन 'आनन्द अनुभूति' नामक काव्य संकलन में किया है. बहुभाषी कविताओं का यह अनूठा काव्य संकलन पाठकों को एक अलग ही भाव भूमि में ले जाता है ।

कनाडा वासी कवि गोपाल बघेल 'मधु' मूलतः भारतीय हैं, ब्रजवासी हैं. आनन्द और उल्लास प्रत्येक कण कण में व्याप्त है, इसकी प्रतीति इस काव्य संग्रह में सहज ही की जा सकती है । 'मधु' जी की कविताओं की विशेषता यह है कि ये एक गीतात्मक शैली में लिखी हुई हैं इसलिये इन्हें गुनगुनाकर गाया जा सकता है और तब इनका आनन्द अलग ही आता है । मुझे इन कविताओं को पढ़ने का सुयोग मिला. फोन पर इन गीतों को 'मधु' जी से सुनने का सुअवसर भी मिला. इनकी आनन्द अनुभूति ने मुझे भाव विभोर कर दिया है । आशा है कि पाठक इन गीतों को इसी भाव स्वरूप में स्वीकार कर आनन्द मग्न हो सकेंगे ।

श्री गोपाल बघेल 'मधु' ने अभियान्त्रिकी व प्रबन्ध शास्त्र की कर्म भूमि से उत्तिष्ठ हो साहित्य में जो अजस्र आध्यात्मिक काव्य सरिता बहाई है वह अद्वितीय है । उन्होने अल्प काल में उत्तरी अमरीका, यूरोप, भारत व विश्व भर के हिन्दी साहित्य जगत में सबका मन मोह लिया है । उन्होने अब तक ७००० कवितायें हिन्दी, ब्रज, बंगाली, उर्दू, अंग्रेजी, इत्यादि में लिख कर सराहनीय कीर्तिमान स्थापित किया है ।

इस पुस्तक में प्रस्तुत २२५ कवितायें अपने रोमन संस्कृत व अंग्रेजी स्वरूप सहित प्रकाशित हैं। हिन्दी की देवनागरी लिपि को अच्छी प्रकार न जानने वाले भारत, नेपाल, बङ्गलादेश, पाकिस्तान, फ़िज़ी, गयाना, मौरीशिस, सूरीनाम, ट्रिनीडाड, टोबागो, दक्षिणी अफ्रीका, यमन, युगांडा, अमरीका, कनाडा, यू. के., जर्मनी, न्यूजीलेंड, सिंगापुर, मलेशिया, यू. ए. ई., इत्यादि में बसे आध्यात्मिक व हिन्दी कविता प्रेमियों के लिये यह प्रयास अभिनव अमृत वर्षा तुल्य है ।

सुकवि 'मधु' जी की काव्य शैली अपनी है और शब्दावली व प्रस्तुति भी उनकी अपनी निजी है। उन्होंने इन्हें किसी से उधार नहीं लिया है और न किसी की नकल करने का प्रयास किया है। इसीलिये कथ्य में और शैली तथा प्रस्तुतीकरण में अभिनवता विद्यमान है । इस सफल एवं सार्थक काव्य प्रणयन के लिये 'मधु' जी को विशेष वधाई और आशा है कि उनकी इस कृति का हिन्दी व अन्य सभी भाषाओं के साहित्य संसार में भरपूर स्वागत होगा ।

डॉ. हरि सिंह पाल

इन्द्रा पार्क, नई दिल्ली– ११००४५

डॉ. जगन्नाथ प्रसाद बघेल

एम. एस. सी., एम. ए., पी. एच. डी., पीजीडी पत्रकारिता
वरिष्ठ कवि एवं साहित्यकार
मुम्बई, महाराष्ट्र, भारत

सेवानिवृत उपमहाप्रबन्धक, दूरसंचार (एम. टी. एन. एल.), मुम्बई

प्रस्तावना

श्री गोपाल बघेल 'मधु' की काव्य–कृति 'आनन्द अनुभूति – आध्यात्मिक प्रबन्ध' की कवितायें पढ़ीं. मेरे बचपन के प्रेरक गोपाल जी एक उत्कृष्ट कोटि के कवि भी हैं, यह उनकी कविताओं की मन्दाकिनी में डुबकी लगाने पर ही जाना. उनका जन्म श्री कृष्ण की लीलास्थली ब्रज वसुन्धरा के पावन क्षेत्र गोवर्द्धन की तलहटी में रामपुर में किसान परिवार में हुआ. आपके जन्म के लगभग ८ माह में ही आपके पिताश्री पञ्च तत्व का शरीर त्याग परलोक चले गये. लालन पालन आपकी देवी तुल्य माँ ने भरपूर वात्सल्य से किया. धार्मिक स्वभाव के सामाजिक रूप से प्रतिष्ठित पितामह आपके प्रेरक व संरक्षक रहे.

आपकी प्रतिभा ने बचपन में ही अपनी पहचान दिखानी शुरू कर दी थी. उस जमाने में जब पढ़ने लिखने का माहौल भी नहीं था, आपने अत्यन्त मेधावी छात्र के रूप में ख्याति प्राप्त की. समुचित जानकारी व पर्याप्त मार्ग दर्शन के अभाव के बावजूद आपने आई. आई. टी., कानपुर द्वारा हुए चयन में एन. आई. टी., दुर्गापुर (पश्चिम बङ्गाल) में यान्त्रिक अभियान्त्रिकी में प्रवेश लिया और विशेष योग्यता लिये यान्त्रिक अभियन्ता बने. जिन्दगी के आपके अनुभव हर सामान्य व्यक्ति से नितान्त अलग और विशिष्ट रहे हैं. जिन्दगी के अनेक खट्टे मीठे अनुभवों से गुजरते हुये आप कनाडा में जा कर बस गये. इस तरह भारत से लेकर विश्व भर को आपने कवि की दृष्टि से अनुभव किया है; जिसका प्रतिफलन आपकी कविताओं में स्पष्ट रूप से देखने को मिलता है.

आप कर्म से अभियन्ता, प्रबन्धक व बिजनैस ऐक्जीक्यूटिव हैं तथा व्यवहार से आध्यात्मिक सद्पुरुष हैं. इसीलिये आपकी कविताओं में विज्ञान और अध्यात्म का

अद्भुत सामंजस्य दिखायी पड़ता है. आपने अध्यात्म को वैज्ञानिक दृष्टि से देखते हुये उसके रूपों को कहीं परिभाषित किया है तो कहीं उसका ईमानदार अनुसन्धान करने का प्रयास किया है.

आपके इस प्रयास का परिणाम यह हुआ है कि आपकी कविता एक ऐसे काव्य गुण से समृद्ध हो गयी है जिसकी किसी पारम्परिक काव्य गुण से तुलना नहीं की जा सकती. वैज्ञानिक दृष्टि संपृक्त तथा अध्यात्म रस से सराबोर इन कविताओं में ऐसी आनन्द की छटा बिखरी हुयी है जो इन कविताओं को समकालीन काव्य से पूरी तरह अलग इसे ऊँचे पायेदानों पर स्थापित कर देती है.

आपकी कविताओं में जिन्दगी के ऐसे विरल पहलुओं की झलक देखी जा सकती है जो अन्य किसी कवि की कविताओं में देखने को नहीं मिलेगी. आपकी भाषा सरल और प्रवाहमय है. आपने खड़ी बोली और ब्रज भाषा से शब्द–सम्पदा प्राप्त की है इसलिये आपके काव्य में मधुरता का प्राचुर्य है. इसमें आपके व्यक्तित्व पर बंगाली संस्कृति के प्रभाव को भी देखा जा सकता है. आपकी काव्य भाषा शुद्ध और तत्सम शब्दावली युक्त है. सभी कवितायें गेय तत्व से भरी हुयी हैं जिन्हें साज बाज के साथ गाय जा सकता है.

शिल्प की दृष्टि से मधु जी की कवितायें गीत छन्द के प्राय: सभी मानदंडों को पूरा करती हैं. आपकी काव्य शैली पाठक के मन पर प्रभाव छोड़ती है. अलङ्कारों के मोह में आप नहीं पड़े हैं फ़िर भी आपकी कवितायें काव्यत्व की हर कसौटी पर खरी उतरती हें. विषय वस्तु की दृष्टि से आपकी कवितायें गम्भीर और विचार प्रधान हैं. इनमें उच्च स्तरीय दर्शन और अध्यात्म की सर्वत्र व्याप्ति देखी जा सकती है. भक्ति, विज्ञान, जिज्ञासा, अनुसन्धान और सत्य के प्रति असीम आसक्ति के सम्यक संयोग ने इन कविताओं को असीम ऊँचाई प्रदान कर दी हैं. गोपाल जी की कविता आज के भौतिकवादी युग में भटके हुये मन को विशाल वट वृक्ष की छाया के समान शान्ति और शीतलता प्रदान करने वाली हैं.

डॉ. जगन्नाथ प्रसाद बघेल

प्रोफ़ेसर देवेन्द्र मिश्र

एम. ए., पीएच. डी.

वरिष्ट साहित्यकार

कनाडा के गवर्नर जनरल द्वारा
'सोवरीन मैडल फ़ॉर वोलंटीयर्स' से सम्मानित

मारखम, टोरोंटो, ओन्टारियो, कनाडा
devendramishra1963@gmail.com

शुभाशीष

मैं व्यक्तिगत रूप से श्री गोपाल बघेल 'मधु' जी को पिछले २० वर्षों से जानता हूँ । उनकी हिन्दी के प्रचार और प्रसार में की गई सेवाएँ उत्कृष्ट व अनुकरणीय हैं और वे सभी हिन्दी प्रेमियों को प्रोत्साहित करती हैं ।

वे तन-मन-धन से भारत की संस्कृति के स्तम्भ हैं और हिन्दी भाषा और साहित्य के लिए सदैव तत्पर हैं । एक कवि के रूप में श्री बघेल जी को देश विदेशों में उनकी रचनाओं के लिए विशेष सम्मान प्रदान किया गया है ।

'अखिल विश्व हिन्दी समिति, कनाडा' के अध्यक्ष के रूप में गोपाल जी पिछले १० वर्षों से लगातार प्रति वर्ष भव्य 'विश्व हिन्दी सम्मेलन' आयोजित करते आ रहे हैं जिसमें भारत, अमरीका व कनाडा के जाने माने साहित्यकार भाग लेते हैं ।

'हिन्दी साहित्य सभा, कनाडा' के महा- सचिव के रूप में भी उनकी सेवाएँ सम्मान योग्य हैं । भारतीय कोंसलावाल, टोरोंटो में भी वे 'हिन्दी दिवस' को होने वाले 'कवि सम्मेलन' का आयोजन व संचालन करते हैं ।

मूल रूप से बघेल जी की कविताएँ हृदय स्पर्शी, संदेश वाहक और हृदय को ओत- प्रोत करने वाली हैं । उनकी रचनाओं में हिन्दी साहित्य के विभिन्न रूप दृष्टि-गोचर होते हैं जिनमें कहीं छायावाद तो कहीं रहस्यवाद और आध्यात्मवाद तो प्रायः भरपूर देखने को मिलता ही है ।

उनकी रचनाएँ निस्सन्देह आपको एक ऐसे तार से जोड़ देती हैं जिसका अन्दाज़ आत्मा और परमात्मा के मिलन का अद्भुत संयोग है ।

उनकी असंख्य कविताओं की अनेक पुस्तकें हैं तथा 'आनन्द अनुभूति' उनमें वास्तव में एक अत्यन्त महत्वपूर्ण योगदान है ।

डॉ. देवेन्द्र मिश्र

श्याम त्रिपाठी

वरिष्ठ साहित्यकार व सम्पादक

प्रमुख सम्पादक, हिन्दी चेतना
अध्यक्ष, हिन्दी प्रचारिणी सभा, कनाडा

मारखम, टोरोंटो, ओंटारियो, कनाडा
ShiamTripathi@gmail.com

अभिमत

यह मेरे लिए सौभाग्य की बात है कि मैं कवि गोपाल बघेल 'मधु' जी के विषय में कुछ शब्द लिखूँ | गोपाल जी को मैं लगभग २० वर्षों से जानता हूँ | आप एक मँजे हुए साहित्यकार और सहृदय काव्य प्रेमी हैं | आप अखिल विश्व हिन्दी समित कैनेडा के अध्यक्ष हैं और साथ में हिन्दी साहित्य सभा कैनेडा के प्रमुख सचिव हैं | आप हिन्दी भाषा और भारतीय संस्कृति के लिए तन-मन-धन से कार्य करते रहते हैं |

विशेषकर हिन्दी भाषा के प्रति आपका समर्पण सराहनीय है | बघेल जी टोरंटो के सुप्रसिद्ध कवियों में अपना स्थान रखते है और हिन्दी मंच के जाने-माने कवि हैं | मंच पर अपनी कविताओं से श्रोताओं को मन्त्र मुग्ध कर देते हैं | आपकी वाणी बड़ी सरस और मधुमयी है | आपकी कविताएँ भावपूर्ण एवं काव्य के नियमों पर आधारित हैं | रचनाओं को पढ़कर भक्ति काव्य के कवियों की स्मृति सुगंध मिलती है |

आपकी शैली में आपके व्यक्तित्व की छाप है | जो भी लिखते हैं हृदय से लिखते हैं, जिससे सब आनन्दित होते हैं व मंच पर अपनी मौलिक रचनाएँ सस्वर सुनाकर श्री बघेल जी श्रोताओं को भाव विभोर कर देते हैं | आपकी रचनाओं में आध्यात्मिकता पदे पदे दृष्टिगोचर होती है | आपकी काव्य कला अन्तःकरण को कुछ ऐसे संस्पर्श करती है कि मन मयूर मग्न हो नाच उठता है | आपकी 'आनन्द अनुभूति' व अन्य पुस्तकें यथा आनन्द गंगा, आनन्द सुधा व मधुगीति पठनीय और मननशील होने के साथ संकलनीय हैं |

आपकी पुस्तकें पढने के उपरान्त मैं इस निष्कर्ष पर पहुँचा हूँ कि बघेल जी एक आध्यात्मिक कवि हैं और इनकी कविताओं में अनुभूति की गहराई के साथ- साथ भाषा का भव्यस्वरूप भी भावानुकूल ही अभिव्यक्त हुआ है | आपने जीवन के कई पक्षों पर गम्भीरता से विचार किया है और एक संवेदनशील रचनाकार व कमनीय काव्य-चित्रकार के रूप में उन विचारों को नयी वाणी प्रदान की है | आपके काव्य में भारतीय दर्शन की गहरी झलक है |

बघेल जी अनुशासित व्यक्तित्व वाले साधक कवि हैं | आपकी सर्व प्रियता, सुहृदयता, निष्कपटता, ओजस्विता व गरिमामयता आपको विशिष्ट श्रेणी का गुणोपेत मानव बनाती हैं | यही तो वे मूल्य हैं जो व्यक्ति को सितारों की भीड़ में भी चमकता सु-तारा बना देते हैं | आपके विषय में कुछ कहना या आपके व्यक्तित्व पर कलम उठाना मेरे लिए सूर्य को दीपक दिखाने के समान ही होगा | बंधुवर श्रीयुत गोपाल बघेल 'मधु' जी! मैं आपके उज्ज्वल भविष्य की हार्दिक कामना करता हूँ | आध्यात्मिक, सामाजिक एवं साहित्य के क्षेत्र में आपकी अप्रतिम सेवा सदैव स्मरणीय रहेगी |

श्याम त्रिपाठी

आपसे भावोन्मुख

हमारी जीवन धारा परम पुरुष कैसे बहाते हैं, ये वे ही जानते हैं. उन्हें जानने का प्रयास कर, हम स्वयं को कुछ समझ पाने योग्य होने लगते हैं. वे हमें सृष्टि में कब, कहाँ, कैसे, क्यों, किस परिवार, समाज, धर्म, देश, महाद्वीप, ग्रह, तारे व निहारिका पर जीवन दे हमारी जीवन यात्रा आरम्भ करावेंगे, वे ही जानते हैं. कब हमें कहीं और उपयोग करना चाहें, वे ही जानें. हम उनकी लीला, प्रयोजन, आयोजन व अभिप्राय के जाने अनजाने भागीदार हैं.

यदि हम उनकी योजना समझ कर उनके आयोजन में आनन्द लेते हुए कर्म रत रह सकें तो प्रति देश काल पात्र का सौन्दर्य हमें भाने लगता है. उनकी प्रति प्रक्रिया, प्रति प्रतिक्रिया, प्रति जीव की अठखेलियां, प्रकृति के रूप स्वरूप, प्रति देश या स्थान की खूबियां, प्रति पल की थाप, समय की ताल, व्यक्तियों व जीवों का व्यवहार, सब उनके आयोजन का प्रयोजन लगता है. उस अवस्था में भाषा, भाव, विचार, व्यवहार, अनुभव, मन, शरीर व सृष्टि का स्वरूप सब 'आनन्द अनुभूति' में मग्न हो गया प्रतीत होता है.

प्रस्तुत कविताओं का सृजन, सुख दुख की दहलीज पर, कर्म श्रृंखलाओं की डोर में बंधे जीवन के हवाई अड्डे पर, स्वजनों से मिलते बिछुड़ते हृदयों के सुख दुख आनन्द की भाव छाया में, जीवन में प्रस्तुत उड़ान की उत्कण्ठा में, पृथ्वी व आकाश के मध्य आते जाते भाव – यानों के त्वरित प्रवाह के सुरों में जीवन धारा से तरंज्जित भाव लहरों में अनायास आरम्भ हुआ.

प्रभु की इस भाव सम्पदा को प्रभु जनों को समर्पित करने का जो प्रयास अनेक प्रबुद्ध कवियों, श्रोताओं, समालोचकों, परामर्श दाताओं, परिवारीय जनों, अभिमत लेखकों आदि के अनन्त सहयोग से हुआ, वह आप की सेवा में समर्पित है. मेरी अनेक सीमाओं के कारण इस प्रयास में अनेक त्रुटियाँ व कमियां रह गयी होंगी. आप वात्सल्य भाव से मुझे क्षमा करते हुए कृपा कर कमियों को इङ्गित करें जिससे कि इन्हें सुधार कर और भी अधिक अच्छा प्रस्तुतीकरण हो सके.

अब तक रचित ७०००+ 'मधु गीति' में से २२५ मधु गीति, अपने मूल स्वरूप, रोमन संस्कृत व अंग्रेजी स्वरूप सहित इस पुस्तक में संकलित हैं. शेष मधु गीति आने बाले अगले संकलनों में यथा शीघ्र प्रकाशित होंगी. इच्छुक जन नयी कविताओं के लिये रचियता से संपर्क कर सकते हैं.

देवनागरी लिपि (हिन्दी) या अन्य प्रयुक्त लिपियां व भाषायें न जानने बालों को मूल भाषा का आनन्द देने के प्रयास में रोमन संस्कृत स्वरूप प्रकाशित किया गया है. हिन्दी न जानने बाले पाठकों के लिये अंग्रेजी स्वरूप सुविधा जनक होगा. हिन्दी भाषी भी अंग्रेजी भाव में मधु गीति पढ़ कर और अधिक आनन्द ले सकेंगे. प्रयास रहा है कि अंग्रेजी स्वरूप भी मूल रूप जैसा मधु मय लगे.

कविताओं के साथ चित्र व 'मधु छन्द' या 'मधु कप्लैट' दिये गये हैं जो बाद में रचित कविताओं या शायरियों के अँश हैं. पुस्तक में 'ब्रह्म चक्र' का चित्र परिशिष्ट में चक्रों व सृष्टि के आयामों के साथ दिया गया है.

मधु गीति की रचना की क्रम सं. व दिनाङ्क प्रति कविता के साथ दिन माह वर्ष के क्रम में अङ्कित है. प्रायः सभी मधु गीति गेय हैं और इनका विडिओ स्वरूप रचियता से सम्पर्क कर प्राप्त किया जा सकता है.

मार्ग दर्शन व सुधार के लिये आप के सुझावों व विचारों का सदैव स्वागत है. आप सभी का हृदय से साधुवाद.

गोपाल बघेल 'मधु'
AnandaAnubhuti@gmail.com
www.GopalBaghelMadhu.com

टोरोन्टो, ओन्टारिओ, कनाडा

आनन्द अनुभूति

अध्याय 1 – आध्यात्मिक प्रबन्ध

1. विश्व की आनन्द भूमि में
* 601/15.09.09

विश्व की आनन्द भूमि में रचा था एक हिया,
सरसता सा मचलता सा प्रज्ज्वलित सा वह हिया;
विचरते बृह्माण्ड में वह मधुरता ढाला किया,
सिहरता सुषमा लिये वह जीव को भाया किया।

मनुज को यम नियम दे वह प्रीति में बाँधा किया,
प्रकृति को माधुर्य दे वह ललित में नाचा किया;
थिरकता मधु नाद में वह नीति को साधा किया,
चेतनों को चेतना दे चित्त को चेतन किया।

संस्कृति की सूक्ष्म धारा को फुरा कर चल दिया,
विकृति की प्राचीर को वह चीर कर चिर कर गया;
सूक्ष्म मानव हृदय को उसने सजाया सँजोया,
गीति रच, रस प्रीति भर, उर मीति भर, वह चल दिया।

विश्व उर आनन्द धारा में बहा ही रह गया,
क्रन्दनों के वेग को वह सहज में ही सह गया;
द्रश्य बदले, द्रूम हैं महके, बादलों को भा गया,
दृग द्रवित कर, हृद स्रवित कर, उर सभी के छा गया।

स्रोत 'मधु' माधुर्य के वह सब खिला कर चल दिया,
दीप नव सौन्दर्य के वह जग खिला कर चल दिया;
मैं अचेतन चेतना के गीत मधु गाया किया,
वह मुरलिया तान पर सबको नचाकर चल दिया।

2. सूक्ष्म प्रेम की अनुभूतियां

* 132/ 08.08.08

तुम्हारे सूक्ष्म प्रेम की अनुभूतियों को,
मैं आनन्द उमङ्ग कहूँ या आनन्द तरङ्ग कहूँ!
आनन्द अनुभूति कहूँ या अनुभूति आनन्द कहूँ,
सृष्टि प्रबन्ध के सुर कहूँ या आध्यात्मिक प्रबन्ध कहूँ!

जो भी कहूँ वे तुम्हारी ही कृपा की कला हैं,
तुम्हारे लिये बनाई पुष्प माला हैं;
उनकी सुगन्ध सौन्दर्य तुम्हारा है,
उनको धागे में पिरोने का आनन्द मेरा है.

तुम उनके सहस्रार के हर दल पर,
अपने पद कमल रखो;
उनका हृदय कमल अधरों से स्पर्ष करो,
अपने हृदय पटल पर रख उसे आनन्दित करो.

उनके रोम रोम में रम जाओ, तुम जन जन को मृदु सिहराओ;
हर तन मन में भव भर जाओ, हर 'मधु' धड़कन में गा जाओ.

3. आनन्द रस * 286/12.04.09

आनन्द रस फुहरत गगन, त्रिभुवन मगन मानव मगन;
आनन्द में थिरकित पवन, जीवन सुरभि आनन्द घन।

जन मन मगन सुरभित सुमन, नाचत गगन आनन्द में;
मधु चाँद है सुर छन्द में, थिरकित धरा मधु नाद में।
आकाश नीलाञ्जन लिये, नव मेघ थिरकित हो चले;
आनन्द सागर में मगन, ध्रुव सहित तारे बह चले।

आनन्द रस में सरसती, उल्का अलोकित हो उठी;
तारे सभी थिरकित हुए, पृथ्वी उमड़ती प्रेम में।
सुर सूर्य में बहने लगे, ग्रह मगन मन रहने लगे;
गुरु कृपा बरसाते मगन, प्रभु भक्ति में 'मधु' है मगन।

4. आनन्द घन * 328/30.05.09

आनन्द घन छाया हुआ, आकाश मन भाया हुआ;
आल्हाद इठलाया हुआ, है अरुण नभ आया हुआ।

हैं विहरती चिड़ियाँ बिखर, है मगन मन मानव प्रखर;
अरमान में उछला पवन, गारहा है ग़ज़लें गगन।
सुर मधुर हैं कुछ बज उठे, शाश्वत हिया कुछ कह उठे;
सह राग में कुछ गा उठे, अनुराग रंजित कुछ हुए।

आनन्द मधु मोहित धरा, 'मधु' पुष्प की माधुर्यता;
सार्थक प्रकृति की पुण्यता, धारक ध्वनि की प्रणवता।
है अधर अकुलाया हुआ, है मधुर मन गाया हुआ;
है शोभिता संशोधिता, आराधना की द्योतना।

5. सुर में लहर * 330/30.5.09. (हिन्दी / ब्रज)

सुर में लहर, मन में कहर, 'मधु' चातकी चाकति मधुर;
उर ध्यान धरि, कर करम करि, बुधि बृहत करि, हिय हरष भरि।

मन पुलक भरि, प्रकृति परखि, प्राणीनता की छवि निरखि;
मधु व्योम में सुरभि लखति, शाश्वत चलन में रत रहति।
धन धान्य पूरित धरा पर, अद्भुत अनोखी छवि निरखि;
गाती रही मृदु तान पर, फुरकित अलौकिक मधु लहर।

मन उल्लसित तन प्रफुल्लित, उद्वेग रहित प्रकृति निरखि;
शालीनता की ज्योति लखि, पावन पपीहा को परखि।
उर सुरभि को धारति रहति, सुर सुरभि की शोभा लखति;
पल में पुलकि, पल में बिखरि, गावति रहति 'मधु' अधर पर।

6. प्रत्याशित प्रमुदित * 191/26.11.08

प्रत्याशित प्रमुदित जीवन धुन, अभिनव अनुभव आनन्द चुभन;
मधुमय प्राङ्गण के प्रमुदित मन, जीवन आभा के दीप मगन।
गाओ सुमधुर नाचो सुन्दर, जीवन धारा त्रिभुवन भास्वर;
मन मन्दिर में ध्याओ मोहन, आओ त्रिभुवन राधा चितवन।

राधा के रोम रोम में रस, बरसाने के कानन में बस;
गोपी मन के दधि में तुम रस, जीवन के शाश्वत गोपन रस।
गोपी के रास भरे मन में, गोपों के आल्हादित तन में;
राधा की नटखट चितवन में, श्यामा के मधुवन से मन में।

मानव मन की अरुणाई में, पक्षी की मोहक चितवन में;
माता के मधुर विलोचन में, भक्ति की मोहन थिरकन में।
'मधु' मन शोभन जीवन उपवन, मोहन मुरली की मनहर धुन;
श्यामल घन की मोहन गर्जन, प्रभु व्यापकता की प्रणवित धुन।

7. प्राङ्गण प्रचुर * 192/26.11.08

प्राङ्गण प्रचुर प्राणी प्रखर, प्रकृति प्रमुत्थित प्रभाकर;
प्राणीनता प्राचीनता प्रमुदित प्रफुल्लित मनुज स्वर.
प्राचीर चीर बढ़ो मगन, धरती खड़े छू लो गगन;
पृथ्वी तरङ्गित 'मधु' सुमन, आकाश गङ्गा मय गगन.

आनन्द की सुर तान में, सृष्टि रचित सोपान में,
सायुज्य के शुभ चलन में, प्रति विम्ब के प्रतिविम्ब में;
आभास है, मृदु आश है, मन में भरा विश्वास है,
निश्चय भरा निःश्वास है, निश्छल हृदय आकाश है.

तल्लीनता प्रतिबद्धता, प्राणीनता संशोधिता,
शोभित हृदय की सरलता, सिंचित हृदय की प्रखरता;
चंचल हृदय की विकलता, चाणक्य मन की चतुरता,
देदीप्य मन की धवलता, आनन्द रस की नवलता.

8. पुलकित प्रफुल्लित * 193/26.11.08

पुलकित प्रफुल्लित सुभग तन, आनन्द लसित प्रभा रतन;
जीवन प्रमोदित लसित मन, सुरभित सुमन आनन्द घन.

मम मन प्रणव आनन्द मय, जीवन सुरभि शुभ छन्द मय;
प्रारब्ध प्रेरित प्राण मय, संस्कार सेवित 'मधु' मय.
मलयज पवन सारङ्ग सुर, सारङ्ग अङ्ग सुधा प्रचुर;
अनुभूति आनन्दम मधुर, तत्पर तरल तन तरुण चिर.

आनन्द शोभित स्वयं तुम, आनन्द राशि धरा वरम;
सोहं वराभय स्वयं तुम, रस सघन हृद शिव सरिस तुम.
तुम धर्म प्रेरित कर्म रत, तुम गरल पान किये फिरत;
आधार भूत धरा धरत, सोहं बने सृष्टि धरत.

9. सोहन सुभग सुन्दर सुमन * 195/26.11.08

सोहन सुभग सुन्दर सुमन, सुमधुर सरल चैतन्य मन;
आनन्द घन मन्दित नयन, चेतन चुभन जीवन तरन.

मन उल्लसित, तन प्रफुल्लित, धाये धरा पुलकित पवन;
आनन्द में लिपटा गगन, लेता स्वपन मूँदे नयन.
आनन्द थिरकित बृह्म मन, शंका तिरोहित बृहत मन;
आशा तरङ्गित मनुज मन, आनन्द उत्प्रेरित सुजन.

शुभ कर्म रत योगी विकल, कल कल करत धारा विकल;
विश्वास अर्पित मन अटल, संताप रहित सुहास पल.
गावत जगत, नाचत निखिल, खिलती सुहानी धूप खिल;
झिलमिलाती चाँदनी बाजे विगुल,
नाचती 'मधु' यामिनी होकर मृदुल.

10. कितनी सदियाँ * 308/20.05.09

कितनी सदियाँ बीत चली हैं, तुम आए ना मैं पहुँचा हूँ;
तारे कितने चमक चले हैं; धरती कितनीं धर थायीं हैं.

कितने नभ मुझको देखे हैं, कितने जल मुझको सींचे हैं;
चिड़ियाँ कितनी चहक गयीं हैं, गर्जन सिंह किये कितने हैं.
मानवता कितनी बिखरी है, दानवता कितनी निखरी है;
कितने पाषाणों की काया, प्रतिसंचर में पुष्प बनी है.

मेरे उर में तुम ना आये, सुर ना पाये, सुधि ना पायी;
प्राणों की इस ऊह पोह में, ऋतु ना भायी, गति ना पायी.
प्रेम पयोनिधि विकल हुए हैं, सुर सुरभित हो बिखर रहे हैं;
काया की माया में मोहन, 'मधु' मन राधा निरख रहे हैं.

11. सरसता सा रहा * 312/20.05.09

सरसता सा रहा मैं सजन, बरसता सा रहा 'मधु' गगन;
तरसता सा रहा ये चमन, चाहता सा रहा ये सुमन।

जीव जाग्रत नहीं हो रहा, तन्द्रा उर से निकल ना रही;
भीति उर में है छायी हुयी, मीति मन में नहीं आ रही।
गा भी दो सुर नया सा सजन, रच भी दो कुछ नया सा भुवन;
रङ्ग दो ये रंगीला सा मन, प्रीति पृथ्वी पै जाये बिखर।

नाचता सा रहा उम्र भर, काँपता सा रहा स्वप्न भर;
दिन निकलता रहा बेखबर, रात रोती रही बेअसर।
सुरभि भरदो सुमन में सजन, साँझ गा जाये मीठी गज़ल;
पवन नाचे दे कर तल की ध्वनि, प्रात पाजाये प्राणों में धुन।

12. धरा धूलि की भूषित मणि * 163/23.09.08

तुम धरा धूलि की भूषित मणि, आभूषित जीवन की चिरध्वनि;
सागर तल की 'मधु' हीर कणी, जीवन की नन्दित वैतरिणी।

नभ उर की एक किरण सहमी, वायु से विचरित बूँद नयी;
आनन्दित गङ्ग की ठिठुरी, सिमटी सिसकी शिशित लहरी।
पुष्पित पुलकित सुरभित वृष्टि, आनन्दित गायित सुर प्रमुदित;
रागों की एक लहर थिरकित, जीवन का एक स्वपन सुरभित।

मैं ना जानूँ, मैं ना मानूँ, जीवन की धुन सुनना जानूँ;
जीवन की राग भरी बातें, कहता सुनता गाता जाऊँ।
तुम आजाओ, 'मधु' गाजाओ, जीवन के स्रोत बहा जाओ;
आनन्द धरा पर दे जाओ, आनन्द सुधा लेते जाओ।

13. मधु तुम आजाओ तो! * 28/03.04.08

'मधु' तुम आजाओ तो, रंग भरें जीवन में.
राग भरें, छंद भरें, गीत भरें त्रिभुवन में;
रूप भरें, रस भरदें, गँध भरें हर मन में.

तृषा क्षुधा मिट जावे, जगमग जग हो जावे;
स्वस्थियत तन हो जावें, स्व-स्थित मन हो जावें.
कर्म करें ध्यान धरें, भक्ति भरें जीवन में;
आशा अभिलाशा की पूर्ति करें जग जन में.

भाषा भावों से भरें, हर जीवन हृद की कह पाये;
हर मन कुछ सुन पाये, हर हृद हद सह पाये.
कुँठा को काट सकें, कटुता को बाँट सकें;
कम्पित मन प्राण न हों, झँकृत आनन्दित हों.
सृष्टा का प्रेम पगे, भूमा के कण कण में.

हर्षित पृथ्वी का हर कण हो, प्रति पुष्प प्रफुल्लित हो जावे;
विहँसे विचरें जग में जन्तु, हर तन्तु तरङ्गित हो जावे.
तुम आजाओ, अब आजाओ, भव भर जाओ तुम भव भर में;
विचरो विहरो भूमा मन में, अणु के मन में, जग जीवन में.

14. पुरुष के पुरुषार्थ * 29/04.04.08

पुरुष के पुरुषार्थ तुम, मैं प्रकृति की कृतबद्धता;
मेघ मन्द्रित मधुर तुम, मैं मयूरी की मधुरता.

चंचल चपल मैं चतुरता, तुम श्याम सुन्दर सघनता;
मैं कर्म प्रेरित रत विरत, तुम धर्म प्रेरित मन विरत.

तुम प्रकृति को प्राकृत करत, मैं प्रकृति की गति में प्रवृत;
प्रकृति मुझे पर–कृति लगे, स्वकृति सरिस तुम में पगे.

चिन्तित सभय विचलित व्यथित, मैं विचरती इस विश्व में;
विषपान कर तुम विकट विहँसे, विहरते बृह्माण्ड में.

तुम धरा की धूल धरते विचरते, मैं धरा के फूल 'मधु' चुनते बिखरती.
फूल मेरे धूल अपनी में मिलालो, प्रकृति को निज अँक ले प्रभु तुम सुला लो.

15. 'मधु' गान तुम गाओ * 53/08.05.08

'मधु' गान तुम गाओ सुहृद, मन को हृदय में ले चलो;
तुम राग एक गाओ गहन, आनन्द में अब ले चलो.

मन लिये आकाश में, तुम दूर बह कर चल पड़ो;
मेरे हृदय के राग को, आकाश गङ्गा बनादो.
तुम चलो, आनन्द की लय में बहो;
ले चलो, प्रिय के निकट, तुम ले चलो.

विश्व सरिता में, मुझे तुम बहालो; मधुर मधुकर कर नचालो.
सुहृद मेरे हृदय को, तुम देख लो, मधुर मुरली तान पर, तुम नचालो.
गीत तुम गालो, मुझे माध्यम बनालो; सुरसरी बन मधुरता में डुबालो.
मेरे मन को तरङ्जित कर ले चलो; गीत में भर कर मुझे तुम ले चलो.

16. मयूरी को मेघ में * 30/04.04.08

मयूरी को मेघ में प्रभु तुम नचालो;
प्रकृति को थिरकित करो,
नव विश्व ढालो.

मधुर भाषाएं बहें हर कण्ठ में;
कण्ठ आनन्दित रहें वैकुण्ठ में.
सरस सुरभित प्रफुल्लित हर पुष्प हो;
चित्त निर्मल, मन अभय, स्वच्छन्द हो.
सुधा वसुधा पर बहा दो.

नाच जाएं मन, मगन मानव रहे,
सृष्टि की शोभा, अक्षुण्ण अनुपम रहे;
थिरक जाएं जीव, जीवन की छटा में,
अमिय जाये वरस, सावन की घटा में.
शिव जटा से सुरसरी को फिर बहा दो.

प्रदूषण मन का हरो, तन का हरो,
विभूषित जल को करो, वन को करो;
वायु को विचरित करो, गद् गद् गगन में,
मुक्त धाराएं बहें, जड़ जीव जग में.
कोकिला के राग से किसलय खिलादो.

भाव जड़ता को जगत से हटालो,
मज़हबों को हवाओं से बचालो;
विश्व को व्यापक बना व्यवहार करलो,
संपदा समुचित 'मधु' को दिलादो.
विश्व सरिता बन सभी को प्रभु बहालो.

17. विश्व विश्वास से खिला रहता * 586/02.11.09

विश्व विश्वास से खिला रहता, खुला खिला हिया 'वही' देता;
विविधता विश्व में भरे रहता, स्व स्वयं बिखर विश्व बन जाता.

विश्व की विचरती विधाओं में, प्राण की खुल रही गुफाओं में;
उफनती मचलती घटाओं में, सिहरती सौम्य सी अदाओं में.
रचियता विश्व का बसा रहता, नियंत्रण सभी कुछ वही करता:
चाँद तारों को घुमाता रहता, अणु जीवत को वही फुर करता.

चेतना चिर चहकते जीवन में, चरैवति सिखाती सहज पन में;
प्रकृति के पनपते प्रयोगों में, विकृति के झटकते झरोखों में.
विश्व प्रति क्षण क्षरित उदित होता, विलक्षण गति लिये त्वरित होता;
'मधु' दृष्ट बने सदा रहता, विश्व त्राता सदा हृदय रखता.

18. कपोतों पर कृपा बरस जाती * 575/22.10.09

कपोतों पर कृपा बरस जाती, चाँदनी में घटा है खिल जाती;
त्रसित तन पर बहार आजाती, रसित मन भक्ति लहर छाजाती.

कल्पना से घिरे कपोलों पर, करूण काया खिले नवेलों पर;
कृष्ण की काञ्चनी कमल काया, कष्ट कर दूर तरती मन माया.
काननों की कठोर कटु गाथा, कह नहीं पाता काग कष्ट कथा;
हिरणि के सहमते से नयनों में, भरी कितनी कथा है काजल में.

क्रन्दनों का कसाब कड़वा है, चन्दनों का रखाब तीखा है;
बन्धनों का बहाव सिकुड़ा है, प्रभु स्पन्दनों से तरना है.
स्वाति की बूँद कभी गिर जाती, सीप मोती बने है खिल जाती;
कपोलों पर बहार आजाती, 'मधु' कानन में कलियाँ खिल जातीं.

19. अनन्त की अँगड़ाई * 21/28.03.08

तुम हो अनन्त की अँगड़ाई;
मैं हूँ 'मधु' जग की गहराई.

देश काल पात्र, तुम्हारे आयाम हैं;
सत रज तम, तुम्हारी प्रकृति के निःश्वास हैं.
महत अहम् चित्त, तुम्हारी प्रबन्ध शैली की लहरें हैं;
पञ्च तत्व तुम्हारी सम्पदा हैं,
प्रकृति जनित जीव, तुम्हारी प्रजा हैं.

जीव को, देश काल पात्रों से विलग कर,
विलय लेते हो, स्वयं में जब कभी;
सृष्टि कर देते हो, जीव के शून्य में, स्वयं की;
जगत सज उठता है, पञ्च तत्व की चमक से.

सृजन करते हो, अपनी हर विधा में, हर अदा में;
विचित्र जीव रच लेते हो, पञ्च तत्व की हर परत में.
कर लेते हो विरचित वन जन्तु जन सुजन स्वयं में;
सब विचरित, विकासशील रहते हैं, जन विजन में.

तुम सञ्चर रच, प्रतिसञ्चर पैदा करते हो,
सुजन को स्वयम् में समेट, सृजन करा देते हो.
सृजन के हर पल, हर पात्र व देश में सृजित करते हो;
नव सृष्टि, नव भाव, नव राग, नव लहर, नयी गहराई.

***

19 H. मधु छन्द * 550 D/08.10.09

स्वयं प्रभु हृदय आ ही जावेंगे, मन ही मन भाव गुदगुदायेंगे;
उर में व्यापक विहाग फूटेंगे, सुर में स्वायत्त राग सुलगेंगे.

20. प्रभु तुम्हारे प्रकाश में * 42/22.04.08

प्रभु तुम्हारे प्रकाश में, कितने उजाले आये;
तुम्हारी नीरव निशा में, कितने तारे जगमगाये.
कौने में बैठा मेरा मन, देख नहीं पाया,
समझ नहीं पाया.

कितनी चिंगारीं, बुझते बुझते जलीं;
कितनी आत्माएं, चिताओं के ढेर से उठीं.
कितने पतंगे प्रकाश के प्रेम में तरे;
कितने जीव दूसरों को जीवित रखने में उठे.

अपनी प्रकृति में, तुम कितने जीव रचते हो;
उनकी भूख प्यास का ध्यान रखते हो.
एक एक कोशिका को रक्त रस देते हो;
फिर कभी, एक का जीवन, दूसरे को ले लेने देते हो!

कभी कभी मैं सोचता हूँ! तुम अपना यह खेल,
किसी और तरह, क्यों नहीं कर लेते!
क्यों इतनी अनुपम निरीह आत्माओं को नचाते हो;
क्यों हर प्राण को बार बार, मिटने सिमटने का कष्ट देते हो.

शायद तुम हर आत्मा की, उसकी हर जीवन लीला की,
अनुभूति का प्राण रस परखते हो;
उस प्राण रस को सृष्टि में फिर बो देते हो.

शरीर यंत्र में, मन मन्त्र का 'मधु' बीज बो,
आत्म तन्त्र की फसल उगाते हो.
फिर कभी, दग्ध बीज हो जाने पर,
उर में रख लेते हो.

21. अनन्त का राही * 11/27.03.08

प्रभु मैं अनन्त का राही हूँ,
तुम मेरे साक्षी हो, मेरे हम सफ़र हो.

कितनी व्यथायें विहरती हैं विश्व में,
बिखरते हैं पुष्प कितने तुम्हारे शिखर में.
कितनी कलियों को तुम करुणा देते हो,
कितने काँटों को तुम हटवा देते हो.

तुम चलते रहते हो, चलाते रहते हो;
मुस्कराते हो, हँसाते हो, प्रेरणा देते हो.
कभी रुला देते हो, कभी सुला लेते हो;
प्यार में कँपा देते हो, क्रोध में हँसा लेते हो.

तुम्हारी लीला कभी समझ आती है,
कभी समझी हुई होकर भी
बेग़ानी हो जाती है.
कभी तुम चिर दयालु लगते हो,
कभी दया बिना विरही बेराही लगते हो.

तुम जीवों को कभी स्वच्छंद विचरण करने देते हो;
कभी उनकी एक एक इन्द्रिय को जकड़ देते हो,
मन प्राण को भटकने देते हो.

कभी उनका सब कुछ समेट अपने हृदय में रख,
उनसे भिक्षा मगवाकर प्रसाद माग लेते हो;
तो कभी उनके गुरु चक्र पर बैठ,
'मधु' कृपा बिखेर देते हो,
मालिक बना देते हो.

22. निर्गुण सगुण सत्ता * 56/13.05.08

निर्गुण सत्ता सगुण हो सृष्टि रचती है,
प्रकृति उसकी प्रबंध शक्ति बन प्रकट होती है;
सृष्टि में त्रिगुणात्मक संतुलन होता है,
सत रज तम, गुणों में, संतुलन साम्य रहता है।

सत रज तम का संतुलन असाम्य होने पर,
प्रतिसंचर में प्रबंध सुधारने, प्रकृति क्रियाशील होती है;
सगुण सत्ता, महत भाव धारण कर लेती है,
सृष्ट संस्था और विकसित होने पर, महत अहम् प्रकट करता है।

अवश्यकता होने पर, अहम चित्त का अविर्भाव करता है,
सृष्टि को सगुण, महत, अहम, चित्त चलाते हैं;
प्रकृति प्रबंध कला में परिमार्जित होती जाती है,
सगुण द्वैत और फिर अनन्त होता जाता है।

विकसित सृष्टि में, सगुण की प्रकृति का नियन्त्रण बढ़ता है;
सगुण स्वयं भी प्रबंध के अनन्त पद विभागों में प्रकट होता है।
सगुण की सृष्टि का विस्तार, प्रतिसंचर को 'मधु' गति देता है;
उसकी प्रकृति की प्रबंध शैली, सृष्टि को प्रगति देती है।

***

22 H. मधु छन्द * 551 CE/08.10.09

प्रलय लय विचरती सदा जिसमें, ललित ताण्डव सुहाते हैं जिसमें;
ऋद्धियां सिद्धियां बसें उर में, सृष्टि संवित सदा रहे जिसमें।

सृष्टि की सुहानी विधाएं हैं, भक्त भगवान की ऋचाएं हैं;
दृष्टि की अदद सी अदाएं हैं, बहारें राह की कृपाएं हैं।

23. अनन्त रचियता * 14/27.03.08

तुम अनन्त रचियता हो देश काल पात्र के;
चित्त के, महत के, त्रिगुणात्मक प्रकृति के, सगुण के।

पञ्चभूत भूषित है तुम्हारी ही पृथ्वी
जल अग्नि वायु एवं आकाश में
तुम्हारा ही चित्त व्याकुल हो पृथ्वी के क्लेश से;
रच लेता है वन जन्तु जन,
सुजन योगी अपनी ही सृष्टि में।

योगी योग करता है, तुम्हारे ही सगुण से,
तुम्हारा सगुण योग करता है सृष्टि के योगरस से;
आल्हादित स्पन्दित हो मिल जाता है निर्गुण से।
निर्गुण फिर कभी भी सगुण हो उठता है;
हो उठती है नव सृष्टि नव प्रकृति की उसी से।

सृष्टि विहँसित, रसित हो, रचती है नव सृष्टि,
सृष्टि नव सृष्टि, अन्तर्सृष्टि, वाह्यसृष्टि,
रचती है हमारी सृष्टि पात्रों को देश काल में;
देश काल पात्र नाच उठते हैं तुम्हारी इस क्रीड़ा से।
विस्मृत प्रकृति विहँस उठती है,
त्रिगुण गुणायमन हो उठते हैं।

निर्गुण की गहराई गुण रच लेती है;
हर देश काल में प्रति पात्र से प्रयास करा लेती है।
गुण विचरित हो, विकसित हो;
निर्गुण के गुण को समझ लेते हैं।
देश काल पात्र, सृष्टि को आनन्द से भर देते हैं।
अपनी इस लीला का आनन्द रस तुम
'मधु' मन में बैठे ले लेते हो।

24. सगुण * 57/13.05.08

सगुण का महत अहम बना, अहम चित्त बना,
हर चित्त ने अपना आकाश रचा;
आकाश में वायु विचरी, वायु अग्नि बनी, अग्नि जल बनी,
जल पृथ्वी बना, पञ्च तत्व मय जगत बना.

पृथ्वी के कण जब अतिशय संघर्ष रत हुए,
तब उसने, किसी पृथ्वी कण के अन्दर, चित्त को जगाया;
वनस्पति प्रकट हुई, विकसित हुई, संघर्ष रत हुई,
वनस्पति के संघर्ष से सृजन हुआ जन्तु का.

जन्तु विकसित, संघर्ष रत हो, मानव बन उठा,
मानव संघर्ष करता करता, बुद्धि जीवी बना;
बुद्धि जीवी मानव संघर्ष से आध्यात्मिक बना,
सगुण, निर्गुण, सृष्टि चक्र व प्रकृति को जाना.

आध्यात्मिक मानव अन्तत: मिलाया मन को सगुण में,
समाधिष्ठ हो समर्पित हुआ, सगुण निर्गुण में;
सगुण ने अपने इस नये समर्पित मानव को,
सगुणित किया सृष्टि के संचालन में.

फिर रची सृष्टि सगुण, महत, अहम चित्त की,
पञ्च तत्त्व, वन, जन्तु, जन, सुजन की;
सृष्टि के चक्र पर चक्र चले, सत्ताएं सगुण निर्गुण हुईं,
'मधु' आनन्द धाराएं अनेक बहीं, सम्भूति कुछेक हुईं.

***

24 H. मधु छन्द * 476 E/07:08.09

सब जीव तुमरे यन्त्र हैं, सब प्राण तुमरे मन्त्र हैं;
सब आत्माएं तन्त्र हैं, 'मधु' मर्म सब तुम में बसें.

25. तुम कब क्या करोगे * 13/27.03.08

तुम कब क्या करोगे, किसको क्यों करोगे;
देश काल पात्र की सीमा में बँधा मेरा मन,
समझ नहीं पाता, सह नहीं पाता।

देख नहीं पाता मैं देश व पात्रों का काल,
काल व पात्रों का देश, देश व काल के पात्र;
तुम झाँक लेते हो देश काल पात्र को, झकझोर झंकार देते हो उनको।
सृष्टि कर देते हो कभी किसी 'मधु' काल में, देश की पात्र की,
देश में देश की, पात्र में पात्र की, काल में काल की;
अथवा लय कर लेते हो सबको स्वयं में।

26. योग में प्रतिष्ठित होने पर * 61/13.05.08

योग में प्रतिष्ठित होने पर, तन्त्र ज्ञान का सुयोग पाने का भाव आता है;
योग के त्वरित प्रयोग का अभ्यास, सृष्टा की कृपा, तन्त्रोन्मुख करा देती है।
तन्त्र में स्थित होने पर, सृष्टि में महा प्रबन्ध की क्षमता आजाती है;
निरन्तर अभ्यास व भक्ति से, सृष्टि की सेवा में और आनन्द आजाता है।

योग तन्त्र सिद्ध होने पर, भक्ति और सुदृढ़ होती है,
सृष्टा में आस्था और विश्वास और बढ़ता है;
ज्ञान व कर्म समर्पित सम्पर्कित योग से रहता है,
भक्ति तन्त्र से तरङ्गित हो, केवला बनी रहती है।

भक्ति ज्ञान कर्म योग तन्त्र, सुस्थिर होने पर,
सृष्टा कृपा कर सकते हैं, स्वयं में लय कर सकते हैं;
अपनी सृष्टि का और उत्तरदायित्व उसे दे सकते हैं,
उसके सभी संस्कारों का भार ले सकते हैं।

फिर कभी समय आने पर, मानव को दग्ध बीज कर सकते हैं;
और कभी, सृष्टि चक्र के नियन्त्रण का 'मधु' कार्य दे सकते हैं!

27. पारखी * 12/27.03.08

तुम कितने पारखी हो, परीक्षक हो,
परिद्रष्टा प्रबंधक प्रायोजक हो; प्राण मय प्रतिष्ठित प्रयोगमय हो।

योग से रचते हो संयोग वियोग, प्रकृति को प्रयोग कर कराते हो संयोग।
स्वयं तुम अदृष्टा असृष्टा बन, सृष्टि के दृश्यों को द्युति देते हो;
कभी सृष्टि को निज अङ्क में सुला लेते हो,
कभी निज हृदय में सृष्टि को बिठा, स्फुरित कर देते हो।

तुम अन्तर्मन में हँस कभी,
सृष्टि के 'मधु' जीवों को खुशी से आलोड़ित कर देते हो।
कभी अपनी पैनी दृष्टि से पार जाकर,
प्रजा की प्रज्ञा को प्रस्फुटित कर देते हो।

28. समय * 68/21.05.08

समय क्या सृष्टि का आपेक्षिक आयाम है!
समय क्या देश पात्र का सहोदर है!

समय क्या सम्भावना की पथ तरङ्ग है! समय क्या अनादि अनन्त की रेखा है!
समय क्या सृष्टि की लय है! समय का उद्गम क्या सगुण से है!

मानव क्या सगुण में समर्पित हो काल को भेद सकता है!
मानव क्या देश के काल को झाँक सकता है!
क्या वह पात्रों के भूत भविष्य को देख सकता है!

काल का नियन्ता क्या सगुण है! काल का द्रष्टा क्या ब्राह्मी मन है!
क्या 'मधु' मानव मन को ब्राह्मी मन बना;
देश काल पात्र में स्वच्छन्द विचर सकता है!

29. देश काल पात्र *69/21.05.08

देश काल पात्र की स्वर लहरियां,
सृष्टा से तरङ्गित हैं;
अनन्त पात्र, अनन्त देशों में,
अनन्त काल में, लीलायित हैं;
छन्दित स्पन्दित हैं, थिरकित आनन्दित हैं.

पृथ्वी की परिक्रमा करते उपग्रह का पथ,
शून्य से सीधी रेखा जान पड़ता है;
सृष्टि का समय भी वैसे ही,
आदि अनन्त के बीच आयोजित है.

ब्राह्मी मन काल चक्र की गति को भाँप सकता है,
माप सकता है, छलाँग सकता है;
झाँक सकता है, झकझोर सकता है,
त्वरित कर सकता है, झंकृत कर सकता है.

ब्राह्मी मन 'मधु' जीवात्मा को सुनियोजित करता है,
देश को व्यापक व्यवस्थित करता है;
काल की आपेक्षिक गति को संयोजित करता है,
सृष्टि प्रबन्ध को प्रगतिशील बनाता है.

***

29 H. मधु छन्द * 560 CD/15.10.09

शून्य के जगत में तुम्हीं बसते, पुण्य के प्राण में तुम्हीं बसते;
सृष्टि के उदर को तुम्हीं रसते, वृष्टि की बूंद को तुम्हीं चखते.

भ्रूण की प्रगति तुम्हीं हो लखते, जीव की गति तुम्हीं बढ़ा देते;
प्राण की ऊह पोह तुम रचते, त्राण की रीति तुम बता देते.

30. गतिशील ब्राह्मी मन * 70/23.05.08

गतिशील ब्राह्मी मन की सूक्ष्म क्रिया,
ब्रह्माण्ड को आनन्दित करती है।

चलती गाड़ी में, बच्चे की फेंकी गेंद,
जैसे यात्रियों को आनन्द देती है;
राह में चलते यात्री को वही गेंद,
गाड़ी की खिड़की से निकल,
आहत या आनन्दित कर सकती है।

पृथ्वी की कक्षा से निकल यही गेंद,
शून्य स्थित यान को नष्ट कर सकती है।
अथवा उसे दूसरी कक्षा में स्थापित कर सकती है।

चलती गाड़ी में फेंकी गेंद की सूक्ष्म गति,
बाहर निकल गाड़ी की गति से तेज लगती है।
वही गेंद शून्य में जा, पृथ्वी की गति से अधिक तेज लगती है।

गतिशील ब्राह्मी मन की सूक्ष्म 'मधु' क्रिया भी वैसे ही,
पञ्चभूत जीव जगत को झँकृत स्पन्दित करती है।
नियन्त्रित, तरङ्गित करती है, थिरकित आनन्दित करती है।

***

30 H. मधु छन्द * 574 BC/22.10.09

तीव्र गति से कहीं पहुँच जाता, प्रकृति की मधुर शोभा लख आता;
सभी जीवों से मैं हूँ मिल आता, देश कालों में मैं नहीं थमता।

कभी ज्योति कभी कभी तारे, नजारे दिखाते बहुत प्यारे;
कभी मैं स्रोत में सिहर जाता, स्वप्न में बहता जग नदी तरता।

31. सृष्टि प्रबन्ध क्षमता * 76/28.05.08

अद्भुत है, तुम्हारी सृष्टि की प्रबन्ध क्षमता!
विचित्र है, तुम्हारे नियन्त्रण की कौशलता!

निर्गुण से सगुण हो, सृष्टि रच, तुम्हारा अनन्त होना;
महत में अहम, चित्त, पञ्च तत्व रच लेना।
पृथ्वी से एक कोशी और फिर, अनन्त कोशी जीव गढ़ लेना;
मानव के विकराल मन को भी, स्वयं में मिला लेना।

प्रति जीव को प्रतिसंचर में, प्रगति की ओर प्रेरित करना;
स्वयम् हर देश काल में, पात्रों को प्रोत्साहित करना।
हर जीव के मन की बात सुन लेना; हर 'मधु' हृदय को अपना निर्देशन देना।
हर जीव की मृत्यु का मर्म समझना; हर जीव को उत्तरोत्तर जन्म देना।

32. सृष्टि प्रबन्ध प्रशिक्षण * 77/28.05.08

कितना रहस्यमय है तुम्हारा हर प्राण को, सृष्टि प्रबन्ध में प्रशिक्षित करना।

युगों युगों मानव को ज्ञान, विज्ञान, भाषा, कला, धर्म, अध्यात्म,
जीवन शैली, समाज व्यवस्था व राज तन्त्र सिखाना;
संचार, यात्रा, ग्रह यात्रा, बृहाण्ड प्रबन्ध में प्रशिक्षित प्रतिष्ठित करना,
मानव मन की जड़ चेतन शक्तियों को विकसित नियन्त्रित करना।

व्यक्ति व समाज को शूद्र, क्षत्रिय, वैश्य व विप्र समाज चक्रों में,
उत्तरोत्तर प्रवीण व प्रतिष्ठित कराना;
विज्ञान को अध्यात्म में ले जाना, अध्यात्म को विज्ञानमय करना।

प्रति 'मधु' जीव को, सृष्टि विकास के लिये,
पूर्ण विकसित प्रफुल्लित होने का सुयोग संयोग देना;
सृष्टि विकास में उन्मुख विमुख होने पर उसे स्वयं में समेट लेना।

33. गुरुत्व का आकर्षण * 86/05.06.08

गुरुत्व का आकर्षण, गुरुत्वाकर्षण स्वाभाविक है,
गुरुत्व से महत्व, गति अवस्थिति परियोजित है;
गुरुत्वाकर्षण से ही सृष्टि गतिशील है,
गुरुत्वाकर्षण से ही जगत प्रगतिशील है.

पृथ्वी की गुरुत्वाकर्षण शक्ति बाँधती है,
पञ्चभूत वन जन्तु जन सुजन;
गति शक्ति बाधित है गुरुत्वाकर्षण से,
नियन्त्रित हैं गतिशील जीव जन सुजन.

मात्राओं का गुणत्व, परस्पर दूरत्व,
अनुपालित करते हैं आकर्षण का गुरुत्व;
अंधकार से प्रकाश में चलता प्रति पथिक,
जूझता है जड़ जागतिक सात्विक आकर्षण से प्रति पल.

मानव बुद्धि से परिचालित शून्य यान,
उचित गति व निकास कोण से ही धरा से परे जाते हैं;
ध्येय पूरा कर शून्य यान में लौट आते हैं,
'मधु' गुरुत्वाकर्षण को पार कर आते जाते हैं.

***

33 H. मधु छन्द * 430 AB/17.07.09

सौन्दर्य के शुभ शोध में, आनन्द के 'मधु' बोध में;
सब चल रहे बृह्माण्ड में, प्रति पिंड है मधु ध्यान में.

धाये धरा, ध्याये गगन, गाये पवन, नाचे अगिन;
जल है मगन, पुलकित सुमन,
सुरभित चमन, जीवन तरन.

34. गुरु शिष्य गुरुत्व * 87/05.06.08

गुरुत्व का आकर्षण गौरव पूर्ण है;
गुरुत्व से ही, महत्व गति स्थिति परिचालित है.

गुरु का गुरुत्व व महत्व प्रेरित करता है,
शिष्य का समर्पण, गुरु की ओर गमन;
गुरु को अर्पण, गुरु के प्रति भक्ति,
शिष्य को दिला देती है
गुरु कृपा व गुरु नमन.

गुरु शिष्य अपनी आत्माओं की
मात्रा स्थिति अवस्था से
परस्पर आकर्षित करते हैं;
बृह्माण्ड को भावाकर्षित करते हैं,
जगत को भी वे भक्ति से
तरङ्गित थिरकित करते हैं.

शिष्य का ध्येय गुरु है,
शिष्य का गुरुत्व गरिमा मय होता हुआ,
बन उठता है महत्व;
गुरु का गुरुत्व,
सूक्ष्म गहन करुण व कृपा मय हुए,
हो उठता है सहजतम ममत्व.

गुरुत्वाकर्षण सृष्टि का 'मधु' सत्य है,
गुरुत्वाकर्षण सृष्टि का महत्व है;
गुरुत्वाकर्षण होते हुए ही गुरु गतिशील है,
गुरुत्वाकर्षण होते हुए ही
शिष्य प्रगतिशील है.

35. गुरुत्वाकर्षण * 88/06.06.08

गुरुत्व का आकर्षण है,
गुरुत्वाकर्षण.

ऊपर फेंकी गेंद का,
पृथ्वी की गोद में पुनः लौट आना;
खेलने गये शिशु का घर बापस आ,
माँ की गोद में लेट जाना.

तीव्र प्रकाश में पतंगों का
प्रकाश स्रोत के साथ क्रीड़ा करना;
चकोरी का निरन्तर चाँद को निहारना,
सूर्यमुखी का सूर्योन्मुख होना.

युवा संतति का जागतिक सम्मोहन उपरान्त,
पुनः पारिवारीय आस्था में लौट आना;
शिष्य का गुरु से विकर्षित होना,
ज्ञान होने पर पुनः
गुरु के आकर्षण में आजाना.

सात्विकता में पृथ्वी शयन,
शिष्य का साष्टाङ्ग प्रणाम;
शैशव में माँ का दुग्ध पान,
जीवन समझने के बाद,
वृद्ध का शिशुपन.

तिमिर से प्रकाशोन्मुख कराना,
जड़ से सूक्ष्मतर भाव में लिये चलना;
गुरु का कृपा भरा 'मधु' विलोचन,
सगुण का है सृष्टि चक्र आयोजन.

36. अणु जीवत का प्रेम * 89/06.06.08

सृष्टि के प्रति अणु जीवत का, परस्पर प्रेम गुरुत्वाकर्षण है;
गुरुत्व की मात्राएं, परस्पर दूरी, स्थिति अवस्थाएं,
गुरुत्वाकर्षण बल का मापदंड हैं।

प्रति अणुजीवत में विद्यमान प्राण,
आकर्षित करते है सभी प्राणों को;
प्रेरणा प्रोत्साहन, चेतना देते हैं,
उनके चैतन्य के साहचर्य को।

सृष्टि में स्वयं गुणित सगुण,
निहारता परखता है, निज सृष्टि को;
आनन्द लेता देता है, सृष्टि में फैले,
अपने ही अङ्गों से, निज अङ्गों को।

उद्गारित उत्प्रेरित करते हुए, सगुण आकर्षित करता है,
निज शरीर मन प्राण में सभी प्राणों को;
आकर्षित करते हैं सभी प्राण भी,
निज भौतिक मानसिक आत्मिक भाव से सगुण को।

धा उठते हैं पञ्चभूत, वन जीव सुजन,
भाँप गुरुत्व के इङ्गित उद्गार को;
थिरकते हुए अपनी कक्षा व चक्र में,
अथवा तोड़ते बदलते हुए सीमाओं को।

पात्रों का भौतिक मानसिक आध्यात्मिक परिमाप,
परस्पर भौतिक मानसिक आध्यात्मिक दूरियां;
सृष्टि का भार बल, मन आत्म साम्य, स्थिति, गति,
'मधु' मान्यतायें नियन्त्रित करता है।

37. अनन्त का छन्द * 117/27.06.08

मेरा प्रति पल अनन्त का छन्द है, मेरा अस्तित्व अनन्त का आनन्द है;
मेरा प्रति अँश अनन्त का आश्रय है, मेरा व्यक्तित्व अनन्त का काव्य है.

सर्व व्याप्त का मैं अभिन्न अस्तित्व हूँ, सर्व शक्तिशाली का मैं सतत स्वरूप हूँ;
सर्वांतर्यामी की अभिन्न सत्ता हूँ, अनादि के अनन्त रिश्तों की सतत कड़ी हूँ.

देश काल की निरन्तरता की आत्मा साक्षी है,
आत्मा दृष्टा व दृश्य के रिश्तों की दूरियां देश से मापती है;
आत्मा अनुभवों का अन्तर समय से मापती है.
पर समय भी विचार मात्र है,
उसकी अनुभूति आत्मा के आनन्द से प्रकट या प्रतीत होती है.
'ब्रह्म सत्य है, जगत आपेक्षिक सत्य है', 'यथा पिण्डे तथा ब्रह्माण्डे' सत्य है;
जो जीव मन में है, वही ब्रह्म मन में है.
जो पल मेरा है, वह उसके अनादि में है, जो 'मधु' आत्मा मेरी है उसी की है.

38. मन में बसे बृज राज * 52/08.05.08

मन में बसे बृज राज तुम, 'मधु' हृदय में छाये रहो;
तुम पवन बन बहते रहो, अज्ञान को दहते रहो.

तुम महत हो, मधु ज्ञान हो, आनन्द की सुर तान हो;
तुम रंग हो, मधु रूप हो, आनन्द के प्रतिरूप हो.
आशा भरा विज्ञान हो, तुम आध्यात्मिक ज्ञान हो;
आनन्द की उत्प्रेरणा, तुम साधना की ज्योति हो.

तुम महत के अनुराग हो, तुम ज्ञान के सौभाग्य हो;
भाव के आधीष तुम हो, मधुरता की तान हो.
पुष्पों की सुरभि तुम हो, ज्ञान के आनन्द हो;
विज्ञान के तुम ज्ञान हो, तुम ज्ञान के विज्ञान हो.

39. आनन्द की अनुभूति * 123/28.06.08

क्या मैं आनन्द की अनुभूति नहीं! क्या मैं आनन्द का प्रतिरूप नहीं!
क्या मेरे पल सृष्टि में समाहित नहीं! क्या मेरा स्थान ब्रह्माण्ड में नहीं!

क्या ध्रुव तारे से मैं आकर्षित नहीं! क्या ब्रह्माण्ड में मैं आनन्दित नहीं!
क्या मेरे चक्र, गुरु स्पर्ष से आनन्दित नहीं?
क्या मेरी कुण्डलिनी, प्रभु प्रेम में अल्हादित नहीं!
क्या मेरे सहस्रार पर, गुरु का वराभय नहीं?
क्या मेरे ऊपर, प्रभु की कृपा नहीं!

मुझे तुम प्रकाश से भर देते हो, स्वयमेव मुझे आकर्षित कर लेते हो;
'मधु' मन को स्वयं में समेट, समाधिष्ट कर देते हो.
मेरे मन प्राण को भावाप्लुत कर, क्या तुमने मुझे आनन्दित किया नहीं?
क्या यह तुम्हारी अपार अहैतुकी कृपा नहीं!

40. सृष्टि उसकी है * 8/19.03.08

सृष्टि उसकी है, मेरी है, तेरी है, सबकी है,
सब में है, सब सृष्टि में हैं.

साँस लेते हैं, वही जो दूसरे देते हैं,
साँस देते हैं, वही दूसरे ले लेते हैं;
अपने अंदर का प्रदूषण फेंक देते हैं बाहर,
उठा लेता है हर दूसरा जीव, जीवन समझ कर.

साँसों की यही क्रीड़ा रचती है सृष्टि योग,
पञ्च तत्वों का यही संयोग, करता है प्रयोग;
संयोग से ही 'मधु' सुयोग होता है,
जीव का ब्रह्म से योग ही सृष्टि का सुयोग है.

41. अनन्त सत्ता के अङ्ग * 116/26.06.08

क्या हम अनन्त सत्ता के अभिन्न अङ्ग नहीं!
क्या हमारा शरीर, ब्रह्माण्ड में समायोजित नहीं!

क्या हमारा मन, ब्रह्म से सम्पर्कित नहीं!
क्या हमारा शरीर मन से संयुज्य नहीं!

क्या हमारे शरीर के अङ्ग व रक्षा प्रणाली एक नहीं!
क्या हमारे हृदय व अङ्ग प्रत्यङ्ग मस्तिष्क से संयुक्त नहीं!

क्या हमारा चित्त हर पल थिरकित नहीं!
क्या वह ब्रह्माण्ड की बदलती स्थितियों से प्रभावित नहीं!

क्या वह सागर की बूँदों जैसा तरङ्गित नहीं!
क्या ब्रह्माण्ड हर पल हमारे चित्त को संभालता नहीं!

हमारे शरीर का प्रति अँश, सृष्टि का इतिहास है;
हमारे शरी का प्रति अङ्ग, प्रति पल परिवर्तित है.

हमारे शरीर की कोशिकायें, आत्म रक्षा में प्रवीण हैं;
हमारी श्वाँस द्वारा ब्रह्माण्ड हर पल, आता जाता है.

हमारा मन ब्रह्माण्ड की हर गति में संतुलन रखता है;
हमारा मन ब्रह्माण्ड की हर स्थिति से साम्य बनाता है.

क्या हमारा शरीर मन का ही स्वरूप नहीं!
क्या हमारा 'मधु' मन, बृह्म की ही सत्ता नहीं!

42. अद्वैत द्वैत अद्वैत * 129/11.07.08

प्रभु क्या तुम द्वैत हो! क्या तुम अद्वैत हो!
या फिर 'अद्वैत द्वैत अद्वैत' हो!
क्या तुम अद्वैत से सगुण हो, द्वैत हुए, अनन्त हुए!
तुम्हारी अनन्त सत्ता के अँश; तुम में मिल, क्या फिर अद्वैत हुए!

मानव का 'अहम् ब्रह्मास्मि' अनुभव करना, अपने अस्तित्व को है, समझ लेना;
स्वाभाविक है तुमसे मिलने पर, अहङ्कार का आकर तुममें विलीन होना।
तत्वतः चराचर सत्ता को तुम्हारी समझ लेना;
'अहम् ब्रह्मास्मि' से परे, 'सर्वङ्खम् ब्रह्म मयङ्ख् जगत', अनुभूत करना।

जैसे पिता बनकर ही, पिता कुछ समझ आते हैं;
वैसे ही 'अहम् ब्रह्मास्मि' अनुभूत कर, जीव तुम को कुछ समझ पाते हैं।
किन्तु जैसे पिता बनते ही, अधिकार व कर्त्तव्य बढ़ जाते हैं;
तुम्हारा 'मधु' स्वरूप अनुभूत करते ही,
मानव के अधिकार व कर्त्तव्य बढ़ जाते हैं।

43. अनुभुतियां व ज्ञान * 130/11.07.08

अनुभुतियां व ज्ञान, विकासशील की अवस्था है;
अनभिज्ञता व अज्ञान, विकासोन्मुख की, स्वाभाविक अवस्था है।
अज्ञान, ज्ञान से संघर्ष करता है, ज्ञान, अज्ञान से स्नेह करता है;
अज्ञान, अहङ्कार विकार बढ़ाता है, ज्ञान, भक्ति व कृपा लाता है।

बिना पिता बने, हम अपने पिता को नहीं समझ पाते;
पिता बनने पर, हमारे पुत्र पुत्री, हमें समझ नहीं पाते।
यह आपेक्षिक ज्ञान अज्ञान, सृष्टि प्रबन्ध में स्वाभाविक है;
बिना अज्ञान, 'मधु' ज्ञान नहीं हो पाता है,
बिना ज्ञान के अज्ञान समझ नहीं आता है।

44. सर्वव्याप्त पूर्ण सत्ता * 115/26.06.08

परमात्मा सर्वव्याप्त सम्पूर्ण सत्ता है;
वही एक मात्र सृष्टा भोक्ता परित्रप्ता है।

स्वयं को निहारने के लिये सृष्टा, जब कभी, बन जाते हैं आत्म दृष्टा;
गढ़ लेते हैं निहारने की विधि, रच लेते हैं मन बुद्धि।
शरीर व जगत बन जाते हैं दृश्य; प्रकट होते हैं, दृष्टा दृष्य व दृश्य।
दृष्टा व दृश्य परस्पर सम्बंध रचते हैं; यही सम्बंध देश बन प्रकट होते हैं।
रिश्तों में गति आने से घटनाएं घटती हैं; घटनाएं काल की द्योतक हैं।

देश काल पात्र, अनन्त आत्म सत्ता के स्थिति जन्य आयाम हैं।
पात्र हो जाते हैं कैदी बुद्धि के; सीमित देश काल में रम जाते हैं।
बुद्धि से मुक्ति ही, जगत से मुक्त होने की 'मधु' युक्ति है।
वास्तविकता के प्रतिविम्ब के बजाय; वास्तविकता देखना ही मुक्ति है।

45. जीव जानता है * 131/11.07.08

जीव जानता है मन ही मन, कि वह ब्रह्म का अँश है;
सतत संघर्ष उत्तरोत्तर उत्थान, ब्रह्म से उसका मिलने का प्रयास है।

पहले वह एकाकी अनुभव कर, उससे सम्पर्कित नहीं हो पाता;
फिर 'अहं ब्रह्मास्मि' अनुभव कर, वह औरों से नहीं कह पाता।
सृष्टि में सभी तो उसीके अँश हैं, 'वयं ब्रह्म' सबका स्वरूप है;
उसे जान लेने पर लज्जा भय क्यों, सभी तो हमारी भाँति, उसके अपने हैं।

वे सृष्टि परिवार को, स्नेह निर्देश आशीष देते हैं;
सृष्टि में हमारी उपलब्धियों को, यथोचित सभी को उपलब्ध कराते हैं।
हम स्वयं को सृष्ट जीवों को समझें, यथोचित कर्म ज्ञान भक्ति करें;
योग तन्त्र ध्यान में 'मधु' सुदृढ़ हों, सृष्टा को समझें, सृष्टि की सेवा करें।

46. अंतरङ्ग तरङ्ग *135/11.08.08

प्रभु! तुम्हारी अन्तरङ्ग तरङ्ग पा,
तुम्हारे कुछ भक्त क्यों सहज नहीं रह पाते?

क्यों भाव जड़ता में स्वयं को जकड़,
चिर चेतन जगत को जड़ समझ बैठते हैं.

तुम्हारे सृष्टि प्रबन्ध की स्वल्प अनुभूति,
क्यों उन्हें अन्य मनस्क कर देती है?

क्यों वे तुम्हारी बृहत्तर सत्ता की गूढ़ लीला को
गहराई से देख नहीं पाते हैं!

क्यों वे सात्विक अहङ्कार में उलझ जाते हैं?
क्यों वे सृष्टि के तारक बन जाना चाहते हैं!

क्यों वे तुम्हें भूल, तुम्हारी सिद्धियों को पकड़ने का प्रयास करते हैं?
क्यों वे तुम्हारी सृष्टि को, अपनी पैत्रिक सम्पत्ति समझ लेते हैं!

शायद तुम भी सबका अधिकतम उपयोग करते रहते हो;
अपनी लीला में अन्त तक सबको शामिल रखते हो!

तुम किसी की भी जीवन लीला कभी भी रोक सकते हो;
तत्क्षण दूसरी लीला उससे प्रारम्भ करा सकते हो.

राजा को तुम भिखारी बना सकते हो;
भिखारी को राजा का 'मधु' उत्तरदायित्व दे सकते हो.

आस्थावान की आस्था कम कर सकते हो;
कम आस्थावान पूर्ण आस्था पा सकते हैं.

47. महत बृहत * 50/08.05.08

कितने महत तुम हो बृहत! कितने मधुर तुम हो महत!
कितने सुहृद तुम हो महत! कितने सहृद तुम हो सुहृद!

तुम विश्व की महिमा बने, ब्रह्माण्ड में छाये हुये;
तुम विहरते ब्रह्माण्ड में, आकाश गङ्गा बन गये!

तुम रमणते रचना भरे, आकाश में, ऊषा लिये;
घन बादलों से वरष कर, तुम धरा को सींचा किये.

तुम विहरते रहते सदा, इस विश्व में, ब्रह्माण्ड में;
तुम आदि के आनन्द में, आनन्द के इस छन्द में.

तुम जगत की आशा बने, तुम विश्व की भाषा बने;
तुम आ सको तो आही जाओ हे मधुर!
गान 'मधु' मुझ को सुनाओ हे महत!

48. मधुर महत *51/08.05.08

कितने मधुर तुम हो महत, कितने सहज तुम हो महत!
तुम मधुर मन की आश में, तुम हास में, परिहास में.
तुम मयूरी के नाच में, तुम चकोरी की चाह में;
तुम ख्वाब हो, आनन्द हो, मधु छन्द हो, 'मधु' राग हो.

तुम ज्ञान की गङ्गा बहाये, शिव जटा से बह चले;
तुम कन्हैया का रास रच, कालिया मर्दन कर चले.
तुम मधुर बन कर चल उठे, आनन्द के रंग में रंगे;
हर हृदय में तुम बस गये, आनन्द की गङ्गा बने!

49. सगुण सत्ता का आयोजन * 58/13.05.08

सृष्टि सगुण सत्ता का आयोजन है; सृष्टि चक्र उसकी संस्था है।
देश काल पात्रों का आयोजन उसकी प्रबन्ध ब्यवस्था का वर्गीकरण है।

प्रकृति उसके प्रबन्ध का क्रिया भाव है;
ज्ञान कर्म भक्ति, उसके पात्रों के मापदंड हैं।
कर्म की गतिशीलता का माप काल है;
पञ्च तत्त्वों के संघर्ष से प्रकटे जीव पात्र हैं।

देश की देह में व्याप्त सगुण का चित्त;
पात्रों के चित्त अहम् महत से, प्रबन्ध करा लेता है।
देश काल पात्र, सृष्टि के आयाम हैं;
ज्ञान कर्म भक्ति, पात्रों के मापदंड हैं।

सगुण सृष्टि में उत्तरोत्तर बृद्धि गुणवत्ता लाता है;
संस्थागत उद्देश्यों को, 'मधु' पात्रों द्वारा, क्रियान्वित कराता है।

50. अभिनव अभिनय * 235/06.02.09

क्या क्या अभिनव अभिनय करते, चित्तों को तुम मुखरित करते;
गगनों को तुम गरिमा देते, वायु को तुम विचला देते।
जीवों को जाग्रत तुम करते, मानव मन को भाषा देते;
चेतन को अवचेतन करते, अवचेतन को भास्वर करते।

आध्यत्मिकता को लय देते, बुद्धि को मुक्त करा देते;
आत्मा को बीज बना लेते, सृष्टि में तुम बिखरा देते।
सृष्टि चक्रों की माया में, मधु मन की कोमल काया में;
तुम बीज बने चलते रहते, प्रकृति को 'मधु' प्रमुदित करते।

51. कितने ब्यथित तुम हो पथिक * 49/06.05.08

कितने ब्यथित तुम हो पथिक!
कितनी उषा आयीं गयीं, कितनी निशा धायीं रहीं;
आनन्द तुम पाये नहीं, चलते रहे, चलते रहे!

आनन्द की इस गेह में,
अरमान की इस देह में, नीरव ब्यथा की गांठ में;
तुम क्या सकोगे बाँध सुर, प्रभु के हृदय आकाश में!

कितनी धरा पर तुम चले, कितने जलों में तुम बहे;
कितनी ज्वालाएं तुम सहे, कितने वायु के वेग सहे.
कितने नभ आये और गये, कितने नभ तुमको देखे हैं!
चुपके से तुमको देखे हैं!

प्रभु ध्यान में अर्पित करो, निज ज्ञान को,
निज कर्म को, निज शक्ति को, निज भक्ति को!
तुम आसको तो आभी जाओ, प्रभु के निकट!
आनन्द के इस ज्वार में!

मेरे हृदय के गीत सुनलो, हे पथिक!
सबके हृदय के गीत, तुम गाओ पथिक.
तुमरी ब्यथा उसकी ब्यथा, देदो उसे, देदो उसे!
चरणों में सर नबा ही दो, हे 'मधु' पथिक!

***

51 H. मधु छन्द * 442 BC/24.07.09

लौह सी गूढ़ सी, मूढ़ सी म्लान सी, भ्रान्त सी भटकती, सिसकती बिखरती;
भित्तियाँ मनों की, क्रतियाँ जनों की, वृत्तियाँ बदन की, सुरतियाँ मनों की.

याद आती रहीं, मन भ्रमाती रहीं, भ्रमर की भाँति भव को भगाती रहीं;
भाव आये नहीं, भक्ति जागी नहीं, कृपा याची नहीं, ज्ञान आया नहीं.

52. ज्ञान कर्म भक्ति का माप * 60/13.05.08

सृष्टा जीवों के ज्ञान कर्म भक्ति को माप कर, भाँप कर, निर्णय लेते हैं.
उत्तम होने पर, कृपा कर, पदोन्नति दे देते हैं;
जीव को पञ्च भूत का, दूसरे जीवों का, नियन्त्रण दे देते हैं.

सृष्टि का प्रबन्धन मिलने से पूर्व, योग का ज्ञान व अनुभव आवश्यक है;
योग सृष्टि की संस्था का, सृष्टा का, प्रकृति, पञ्चभूत, देश, काल, पात्रों का,
सम्यक प्रबन्ध ज्ञान व प्रबन्ध अभ्यास है.
संयोग द्वारा योग होने पर, जीव को पद सिद्धि मोह न हो;
सृष्टा के निर्देशन में, मात्र सृष्टि सेवा ही करणीय हो!

सृष्टि प्रबन्ध के योग में प्रवृत हो जीव, भक्ति ज्ञान कर्म और सुदृढ़ करता है;
सृष्टि विभाग अनुसार, सृष्टा के 'मधु' नियन्त्रण में,
देश और पात्रों का, उस काल में, प्रबन्ध करता है.

53. अवतरण से पूर्व आकाश वाणी करा * 78/13.05.08

हे कृष्ण! अवतरण से पूर्व आकाश वाणी करा, जगत को पूर्व सूचित करना;
क्या था, अपने ऊपर, आपत्तियों को आमन्त्रित करना?
या था, अपनी सृष्टि में, आने का काम आसान करना!

पूर्व सूचना दे, शोषक शासक की, भय वृत्ति को प्रज्ज्वलित करना;
और फिर, उसकी क्रोधाग्नि को जगा, कर्म में उसे प्रेरित करना.
जगत को उसके कर्म दिखा, उसकी बास्तविकता का भान कराना.

स्वयं पर, निज जनों पर, शोषक का आक्रमण झेलना, सहना,
शोषक को असफल करा, उस पर 'मधु' नियंत्रण करना;
आसुरी शक्ति को शमित कर, सात्विकता को प्रोत्साहित करना,
धीरे धीरे शोषण को समाप्त या समर्पित कराना.

54. तुम्हारा आना, जाना और रहना * 78A/30.05.08

विचित्र होता है प्रभु! तुम्हारा आना, जाना और रहना;
अति सूक्ष्म होता है तुम्हारा कहना, सुनना, और करना।

विशेष होता है तुम्हारा आकर्षण,
विकर्षण, मिलन और विलयन;
यही तो है तुम्हारी प्रबन्ध लीला का अनोखापन।

तुम्हारी जगत क्रीड़ा का अजीव होना;
जीव को ओत प्रोत हो विकशित नियन्त्रित करना।

अति त्वरित द्रुत तुम्हारा 'मधु' सृष्टि संचालन करना;
सतत पल्लवित सुप्रबन्धित तुम्हारी सत्ता का जाग्रत रहना।

55. संस्कारों से उऋणता * 79/30.05.08

जीवन के संस्कारों से ऋणी जीव,
क्या कभी बिना प्रभु कृपा, उऋण हो सकता है!
जन्म के अधिकारों से प्राप्त संपदाएं,
क्या प्रभु की नहीं, क्या वंशजों को देय नहीं है!

हमारे मन, प्राण, देह, श्वाँस, सभी तो उसके हैं;
माँ बाप, परिवार, गाँव, देश, दुनियां भी तो उसी की देन है।
हमारा पालन पोषण, शिक्षण, कार्य, सभी तो उसी के समाज का है।

प्रभु प्रदत्त प्रेम, सम्बंध, देश काल पात्र की 'मधु' स्थिति अवस्थाएं;
सृष्टि में हमसे कार्य लेने के लिये, दिये उसके आयोजन अवयव हैं।

56. मानव आत्मा की अवस्था * 71/23.05.08

मानव आत्मा की अवस्था, उसकी देश काल स्थिति,
अन्य पात्रों की देश काल आत्म स्थिति,
सृष्टि चक्र में मानव की अवस्था स्थिति;
विभिन्न देशों में, विभिन्न समय में,
विभिन्न पात्रों से कर्म करा लेती है.

आत्मा की सुदृढ़ अवस्था में, अनुकूल देश पात्र में,
सृष्टि चक्र की उन्नत प्रबन्ध अवस्था में,
'मधु' मानव, देश काल पात्र को नियन्त्रित कर सकता है.
काल को झाँक सर्वव्याप्त हो सकता है,
अन्तर्यामित्व व सिद्धि पा सकता है

57. सृष्टि में प्राप्त प्राणी * 80/30.05.08

सृष्टि में प्राप्त प्राणी, पद, अर्थ, पदार्थ,
पहले सब प्रभु का है, फिर हमारा है;
हम स्वयं अपने नहीं, उसके हैं,
हमारे श्वाँस विश्वास उसके हैं.

जो दें उसमें समर्पित हो दें, जो लें उसी से समर्पित हो लें;
लेकर देने का प्रयास करें, देकर उसमें समर्पित हो कर मागें.
न दे या ले सकें तो स्वयं को उसी में समर्पित करें.

हम 'मधु' सृजन की कड़ी बनें, कड़ुवाहट न बनें,
धरोहर को जकड़ें नहीं, प्रायोजित संचालित करें;
समय बदलता है, धन आता है, जाता है,
वक्त अच्छा बुरा, आता है जाता है,
व्यवहार याद रह जाता है.

58. हे विश्व प्रबन्धक * 133/08.08.08

हे विश्व प्रबन्धक!
क्या तुम्हारी प्रजा के तन्त्र अभी,
तुम्हारे प्रज्ञा तन्त्र से तरङ्गित नहीं हो पाये!
क्या तुम्हारे 'मधु' मानव अभी अष्ट पाशों से मुक्त नहीं हो पाये!
क्या वे तुम्हारी प्रबन्ध कला को
अभी समझ नहीं पाये!

क्या आदर्श सींचित तुमारे मानव,
अभी मर्यादा में नहीं बंध पाये!
क्या वे प्रबंध विज्ञान में प्रवीण नहीं हो पाये!
क्या वे भक्ति कर्म ज्ञान में प्रतिष्ठित नहीं हो पाये!

कुछ समय पूर्व प्रजा द्वारा चुने योग्य व्यक्ति भी,
पद पर पहुँच पथभ्रष्ट क्यों हो जाते हैं?
आदर्श की प्रतिज्ञा करने बाले कुछ समय में,
श्रेय को भूल प्रेय को क्यों पकड़ लेते हैं?

तुम्हारे प्रजा तन्त्र अभी प्रकृति में क्यों उलझे हैं?
तुम्हारे राजतन्त्र, राजसिक व तामसिक क्यों हैं?
पद पर पहुँच सात्विकता क्यों बहक जाती है?
तामसिकता, सात्विकता को क्यों भटका देती है?

धूल धूसरित जर्जरित मानवता के साथ,
अब तुम और प्रयोग मत करो;
भ्रष्ट कपटाचारी प्रबन्धकों से धरा को मुक्त करो.
सात्विक मानवों को सम्वल दो, सक्षम करो,
धरा को उर में धरो, झँकृत करो, तन्नित करो.

59. तुम्हारी अनन्त सत्ता * 122/28.06.08

मैं तुम्हारी अनन्त सत्ता हूँ, अनन्त हमारा साम्राज्य है;
आदि से हम अनन्त हैं, अनन्त के हम आदि हैं।

हम अनन्त के राही हैं, बृह्माण्ड के विशिष्ट व्यक्ति हैं;
अनन्त की हम शक्ति हैं, बृह्म के व्यक्त 'मधु' रूप हैं।

तुम मेरे हो, मैं तुम्हारा हूँ, सब अपने हैं, अपने ही स्वरूप हैं;
हम अनन्त हैं, सगुण निर्गुण हैं, पञ्चभूत वन जन्तु जन, सुजन हैं।

60. ज्ञान होते हुए भी * 59/08.08.08

ज्ञान होते हुए भी, कर्म करते हुए भी, भक्ति प्रमुख है;
भक्ति और ज्ञान होते हुए भी, कर्म आवश्यक है।

जीव का सृष्टा की ओर, चलने का प्रयास भक्ति है;
सृष्टा का जीव की ओर, चलने का प्रयास कृपा है।

बिना भक्ति के, ज्ञान व कर्म का फलित होना आवश्यक नहीं;
भक्ति होने पर भी, कृपा पा जाना आवश्यक नहीं।

कृपा कर पाना, न कर पाना, सृष्टा की परिस्थिति पर निर्भर है;
बिना भक्ति के भी वे 'मधु' पर कृपा कर सकते हैं।
भक्ति होने पर भी कृपा करने में, देर लगा सकते हैं।

***

60 H. मधु छन्द * 397 D/03.07.09

मन मिला रूह में, रूह गुरु रूह में, गुरू की रूह में मन मेरा खिल गया;
तन बदन खिल गया, मन बृहत हो गया, जगत मन में बसा, भेद जग का मिटा।

61. मेरे शरीर का क्षितिज * 121/28.06.08

क्या मेरे शरीर का क्षितिज
ब्रह्माण्ड के क्षितिज से नहीं मिलता!
क्या मेरा मन ब्राह्मी मन से संयुक्त नहीं!
क्या मेरी आत्मा, परमात्मा में व्याप्त नहीं!

क्या सूर्य मुझे धूप स्नान नहीं कराता;
क्या जल मुझे प्लावित नहीं करता?
क्या वायु मुझे पुलकित नहीं करती;
क्या आकाश मुझे आल्हादित नहीं करता!
मेरा मन क्या, तुम्हारे मन में नहीं समा जाता!

मेरा मन क्या, तुम्हारे मन के क्षितिज के परे नहीं चला जाता!
मेरा मन क्या, ब्रह्माण्ड के परे नहीं चला जाता!
क्या मेरा मन, तुम्हारी ब्यथा को अनुभव नहीं करता!
क्या मेरा 'मधु' मन, तुम्हारे आनन्द की अभिव्यक्ति नहीं करता!

62. कितने सुर मैंने गाये हैं * 225/01.02.09

कितने सुर मैंने गाये हैं, कितने उर मैंने देखे हैं;
कितनी बाधाएं बेधी हैं, कितनी ब्याधाएं बाँटी हैं।

आतुर विचलित तुम क्यों होते, अर्पित आनन्दित ना होते;
मानवता को मधु धुन देते, क्यों प्राण सुधा तुम ना रसते।

जीवन में जब उलझे बिखरे, मधु दृष्टि किये चलते सँवरे;
प्रभु के जब निकट चले आये, जीवन धारा को तर आये।

तुम क्यों ना सूक्ष्म दृष्टि धारो, आध्यात्मिकता मन में धारो;
इस भूमा को हृदि में ढालो, मानवता को तुम 'मधु' ढालो।

अध्याय 2
आध्यात्मिक प्रबन्ध विज्ञान व शोध

63. ध्यान औ' यान
* मधु गीति सं. ५२१/ रचना दि. २१.०९.०९

ध्यान से यान सभी उड़ जाते, यान से वद्ध प्राण उठ जाते;
ध्यान में यान सभी उतराते, यान में वद्ध प्राण आजाते।

धरा से यान ध्यान से जाता, चलता रुकता प्रकाश चमकाता;
सिद्ध आसन में यात्री फुर होता, उड़ते फुरते है ध्यान कर लेता।

शून्य तक समर्पित सभी होते, छटाएं बादलों की लख लेते;
धरा को झाँककर हैं तक लेते, यान की सिद्धियों को चख लेते।

यान में घूम फिर हैं कुछ पाते, खिड़कियों से क्षितिज को लख लेते;
सूर्य की स्वर्ण प्रभा लख पाते, चन्द्र तात्रों को देख हरषाते।

ध्यान के यान में 'वही' होता, चित्त चलता आत्म साक्षी होता;
सृष्टि को शून्य से परख पाते, ध्यान 'मधु' चख के प्राण तर जाते।

64. सृष्टि औ' दृष्टि * ५२०/२१.०९.०९

सृष्टि है निकट से न लख पाती, दृष्टि है दृश्य पर न टिक पाती;
धरा से उठके अधिक लख पाता, व्योम से दृश्य अधिक दिख जाता।

धरा पर यान बृहत है लखता, व्योम में यान लघु है लगता;
धरा से दृश्य लघु है लखता, व्योम से दृश्य बृहत है दिखता।

शून्य से धरा सभी दिख जाती, सृष्टि लघु रूप लिये लख जाती;
देश पात्रों की सभी सीमाएं, काल को भेद निकट दिख जाती।

ध्यान के शून्य में स्वयं जाकर, जीव सब देश भेद पाते हैं;
पात्र को उर में समा पाते हैं, काल को स्वयं देख पाते हैं।

सृष्टि शोभा सुहानी तब लखती, दृष्टि सुमधुर सदा जगत तकती;
धरा सुन्दर सुयोग्य शुभ लगती, व्योम में व्याप्त सृष्टि 'मधु' लखती।

65. शाश्वत सुन्दर * 138/14.08.08

तुम शाश्वत सुन्दर अभिनव हो, जीवन के राग सुना जाओ;
हे आनन्दित प्रभु के प्राणी, प्राणों के गीत सुना जाओ।

तुम मधुमय रुप लिये आओ, भावों में भरकर गा जाओ;
जीवन का स्रोत दिखा जाओ, स्रोतों को जीवन दे जाओ।

'मधु' माखे सारंग के साक्षी, स्वप्नों से दूर नहीं जाओ;
मोहन विज्ञान भरी ममता, मानव को आज दिखा जाओ।

भूमि की भाषा भावों में, आनन्द उमंगें भर जाओ;
भूमा की अनहद वाणी में, आनन्द सुधा रस सरसाओ।

66. प्रिय आत्मन्! * 1/1983

प्रिय आत्मन् उठो जागो! उठो जागो, प्रिय आत्मन्!
उठो जागो प्रिय आत्मन्! उठो जागो, प्रिय आत्मन्!

सोये थे हम दोनों, उसकी ही गोदी में,
और खोगये थे हम, स्वप्न की उस सृष्टि में.
कितनी वास्तविक लगती थी, वह अवास्तविक स्वज सृष्टि;
मिथ्या संकल्प जनित थे, जिसके दृष्टा व द्रश्य.

उस स्वप्न में भी हम मिले थे एक बार,
प्यार किया था, घर बसाये थे, बनाये थे, बिगाड़े थे;
और प्रारब्ध वश, परस्पर प्रहार भी किये थे.
एक बार, तुम्हारे प्रतारण की पीड़ा वश, जब मैं कराहा;
उसने मुझे प्यार किया और थपथपाया, पर फिर मैं सो न सका.

उठने पर देखता हूँ, कि तुम अभी सोये हो,
विस्मृत हो भयमय हो, खोये हो मोहे हो;
मैं थपथपाता हूँ, तुम्हें उठाने के लिये,
पर तुम डरते हो, मेरे प्रेम भरे स्पर्ष से.

और सोचते हो कि कहीं, तुम्हारे उस स्वप्न के
प्रतारण का प्रतिकार तो नहीं कर रहा मैं!
पर तुम नहीं जानते कि, क्या कोई जगने पर, व्यथित करेगा उसको,
जिसने व्यथित किया हो उसको स्वप्न में!

स्वप्न का वह प्रेम या प्रतारण, मात्र एक सुखद अनुभुति है;
इस जाग्रत जीवन का, हर कौना जाग्रत है,
सुरभित स्पन्दित है, थिरकित आनन्दित है.

इसीलिये कहता हूँ और थपथपाता हूँ, आँखें खोलो 'मधु' आत्मन्!
उठो जागो प्रिय आत्मन्! प्रिय आत्मन, प्रिय आत्मन्!

67. दीप अवलि अवनि पै शोभित है * 566/16.10.09

दीप अवलि अवनि पै शोभित है, तारे अगणित गगन में हर्षित हैं;
हृदय में प्राण शिखा प्रज्ज्वलित है, देह में ज्योति लहर थिरकित है।

प्रभु आकर जलाओ सब दीपक, साधना ज्योति दे करो चेतन;
दिवाली दिव्य आभा की आली, खुशाली सब मनों की दीवाली।
घरों में दीप जगमगाते हैं, हृदय में ज्योति सब जगाते हैं;
विश्व जन मन फुरक भी जाते हैं, विश्व आत्मा चहक ही जाती है।

शान्ति आनन्द दीप देते हैं, उर्जा उत्कण्ठा उर्मि देते हैं;
उल्लसित परागित सुमन होते, प्रफुल्लित पल्लवित चमन होते।
दीप माला प्रभु को अर्पित है, दीप अवलि भुवन की प्रीति है;
जीव ज्योति सृष्टि की श्रीति है, 'मधु' द्योति जगत की ज्योति है।

68. मैं दीप जलाता हूँ उर में * 567/16.10.09

मैं दीप जलाता हूँ उर में, मैं राग जगाता हूँ सुर में;
तुम शाश्वत दीप जला दो ना, तुम निर्झर सुर में गा दो ना।

मेरी दीवाली तुम में है, मेरी होली तुम संग ही है;
मेरी रँग रोली तव मन है, मेरी राखी तव हृद में है।
तुम अभिनव नट नागर प्रभु हो, तुम नित्य सनातन चेतन हो;
तुम ओजस्वी आनन्द स्रोत, तुम तेजस्वी त्रैलोक्य प्रवृत्।

मैं तुमरा ही तो उर दीपक, तुम ही तो मेरे सुर प्रेरक;
तव संस्कारों की मैं द्योति, तुम मम जीवन की चिर ज्योति।
तुमरे ही दीपक सब उर हैं, तुमरे ही सुर सबके उर हैं;
मैं गा देता तुमरे सुर में, सब सुन लेते 'मधु' से उर में।

69. प्रभु के सृजन में * 6/19.03.08

प्रभु के सृजन में जीव का सृजन,
कितना मधुमय है, कितना अनुपम है!
क्या जीव की योजनाएं, उसकी परिकल्पना में समायोजित नहीं?
क्या जीव का प्रयास, उसके भूमा प्रयास का अंश नहीं?

क्यों कुछ जीव चाहते है तोड़ना
मर्यादाएं उसकी सृष्टि और पात्रों की?
क्यों नहीं सेवा करते वे, उस के दिये समय में,
उस की सृष्टि की, उस के पात्रों की?

क्यों रचना चाहते है वे अपनी भ्रम भित्तियां,
उसके अगाध अनन्त ब्राह्मी शून्य में?
बिखर जाती हैं जो, उसकी हवा के झोंकों से,
समुद्र तट की रेत की लहरों जैसे।

उसी के पञ्च तत्वों से, उसी के पात्रों द्वारा दीवार बनबा कर,
अवरुद्ध करते हैं, पञ्च तत्वों व पात्रों का, आवागमन अवरोहण आरोहण;
उसी के बृह्माण्ड में अण्ड बना कर,
पिण्डों का आकार छोटा करने का करते हैं प्रयास।

आत्माओं को आत्माओं से अलग करने का
प्रयास करते हैं, त्रास पाते हैं;
उसकी प्रकृति का अपनी रचना पर आघात झेलते हैं,
मन को व्यथा देते हैं, सब को व्यथित करते हैं।

फिर भी प्रभु सृष्टि का प्रबंध,
अभियंत्रण व विकाश, सुव्यवस्थित चलाये रखते हैं;
सब जीवों को, सृष्टि में सब समय ओत प्रोत रहते हुए,
पुलकित प्रफुल्लित रखने का 'मधु' प्रयास करते हैं।

70. रझ कितने भरे हो ∗ 509/10.09.09

रझ कितने भरे हो जीवन में, भर रहे 'मधु' तरझ   हर मन में;
श्वास प्रश्वास में बसे चलते, राह अनजान पर लिये चलते.

तुम्हारी सम्पदा सुहानी है, तुम्हारी आपदा अनौखी है;
तुम्हारी व्याप्तता निराली है, तुम्हारी आप्तता रुहानी है.
आहटें कितनी किये जाते हो, राहतें कितनी दिये जाते हो;
चाहतें कितनी भरे जाते हो, मिन्नतें कितनी तुम कराते हो.

रझ हर है तरझ अपनी में, तरझें रझ अपने अपने में;
उमंगें रोज तुम भरे जाते, संग सबके सदा हो तुम रहते.
चाहते रहते सद हर उर में, गबाते रहते सदा निज सुर में;
सृष्टि की छटा 'मधु' सुहानी में, ढालते रहते गज़ल हर उर में.

71. मन के रहस्य ∗ 26/02.04.08

मन के रहस्य, निराले हैं; जाने अनजाने हैं, चाहे अनचाहे हैं.
हर जाने अनजाने की आँखों में आँखें डाल खोजते हैं,
हम अपने "उस" को उनमें, या उनको अपने मन की गहराई में.

लगते हैं सब मिले हुए से, कभी न कभी, कहीं न कहीं;
रिश्ते निकाल लेते हैं, प्रेम पाल लेते हैं, व्यथा बाँट लेते हैं.
सम्बंध बना लेते हैं, कुछ कर बैठते हैं,
और कभी कभी, चाहे अनचाहे, लड़ झगड़ भी लेते हैं.

परदेश या स्वदेश से आने पर, कुछ रात हमें नींद नहीं आती है;
जैट लैग से 'मधु' प्रभावित प्रतीत हम होते हैं.
पर क्या यह, परदेश के परिजनों की भावनाओं की प्रतिक्रिया नहीं है!
उनके दिनों में वे हमें याद करते हैं, हमारी रातों की नींद उड़ जाती है.

72. जीवों में बृह्म
* 7/19.03.08

जीव तुम क्यों सहज नहीं हो पाते,
क्यों नहीं खोजाते उनके मन में;
उन्हीं के मन में तो तुम हो सृष्टि में,
क्यों नहीं खेल लेते तुम उसी सृष्टि में.

तुम घर, योजनाएं एवं मीत बनाओगे,
अहं सिंचित हुए, सृष्टिमय न हुए तो वे विखर जावेंगे;
एक रसता बनी रहेगी, हम कुछ न कर पावेंगे,
कुछ न कह पावेंगे.

हमारा हर योजन उनकी परियोजना है,
हमारा मन प्राण शरीर उनकी परियोजना है;
उनकी योजनानुसार वे न हुए, तो वे हमारी योजना बदल देंगे,
उनकी सृष्टि, उनके पञ्चभूत, उन्हीं की प्रकृति से क्रीड़ा करा देंगे.

क्यों न हम उनको सहयोग करें,
क्यों न योग करें, उनसे जुड़ें;
क्यों न तन्त्र से तरें और तारें,
क्यों न ध्यान में उन्हें धरें और धारें.
अपनी परियोजना में उन्हें वरें,
उनकी और अपनी योजना को परियोजित करें.

क्यों न समाधि में उन्हें वरें,
क्यों न जीवन को समाधित करें;
क्यों न मृत्यु को चिर जीवित करें, क्यों न शरीर को श्री करें.
क्यों न उनकी परिकल्पना को हम अपनी बनालें,
क्यों न 'मधु' जीवों में बृह्म देखें.

73. प्रेम में जीव
* 27/02.04.08

प्रेम में जीव परवश हो जाते हैं,
देश काल पात्र की सीमाएं लाँघ जाते हैं;
सृजन हो जाता है 'मधु' जीव का,
सृष्टि एक पीढी आगे बढ जाती है।

प्रेमी जीव माँ बाप बन, नये अजनवी को,
निज से ज्यादा प्रेम करने लगते हैं;
यह आने बाला हर नया जीव, हमारा पूर्बज हो सकता है।
हमारी उँगली पकड बड़ा हो सकता है;
फिर कभी वह हमारे पितामह जैसा ब्यवहार कर सकता है।

जो दर्द, जो दवा, हमने उसे दी; उसकी प्रतिक्रिया वह कर सकता है;
अपना बन कर दर्द दे सकता है, पराया आकर दवा दे सकता है।

उसके कुछ संस्कार सुसंस्कृत हो सकते हैं,
कुछ और अच्छे या बुरे हो सकते हैं।
कुछ संस्कार आ सकते हैं, उसके जीवन के बीच के पड़ावों के;
कुछ नये संस्कार आ सकते हैं, इसी जीवन के और संयोगों के।

अनन्त जीवनों में जो जीव सम्पर्कित हुए,
जो जीव पाये, जो आये, जो गये, जो आयेंगे;
सब हमारे मन को तरङ्गित करते हैं,
हमारे भाव स्वभाव ढालते संवारते हैं।

इसीलिये विश्व कभी अपना लगता है,
और कभी वह बेग़ाना पराया लगता है;
सब अपने हैं, सब सपने हैं, सब मन में हैं, सब जाने हैं।
सब आने हैं, सब जाने हैं, सब जाने, अनजाने हैं।

74. सम्भावना
*20/28.03.08

सम्भावना सम भावना की सृष्टि है;
सम्भावना सद् भावना की वृष्टि है.

साधना के समन्वय से, सम भाव सम्भव है,
तप की तन्मयता से, सद्भाव का उद्भव है;
साधना साधती है, मन को तन में, प्राण में,
तप निखारता है, तन को, मन को, प्राण को.

सधे मन में, तपे तन में, आत्मा विचरती है, जगत जन में,
सब सम, सब सत, सब सम्भव हो उठता है सृष्ट जगत में;
सृष्टि हो जाती है, अन्तर्वाह्य जगत में.

सम समन्वित होता है सहज से, शून्य व अनन्त के मिलन से;
आत्मा के सब में समा जाने से, जीव के बृह्म से, मिल जाने से.

और तब सभी सम, सभी सत, कर देते हैं नव सृष्टि,
सम्भावना की, सफलता की, 'मधु' सृजन की.
सम्भावना सम भावना की वृष्टि है.

***

74 H. मधु छन्द * 398 BD/03.07.09

तुम मुझे देखते, मैं तुम्हें देखता, दर्द को झेलता, प्रेम को पालता;
जब कभी चोट गहरी लगी थी मुझे, दर्द तुमको हुआ था लगा था मुझे.

वक्त की बाट में जाँचते तुम मुझे, पकाते तुम मुझे, परखते तुम मुझे;
जब अहमियत जो थी तुम में मिल जाती, तुम निकट आके मुझसे चस्प जाते.

75. ममता * 45/24.04.08

ममता जीवों में, प्रेम की वृत्ति है.
पर वह, देश काल पात्र के मोह से, बंधी हो सकती है.

माँ अपने शिशु की ममता में,
उसके लिये सब कुछ बलिदान कर सकती है;
पर वही माँ, दूसरे शिशु, जीव या जन्तु के प्रति,
भाव रहित, निर्मम व निर्दय हो सकती है.

व्यक्ति स्वदेश के अतिशय मोह में,
स्वदेश की गुणहीन वस्तुओं की प्रशंसा कर सकते हैं;
पर वे, स्वदेश के सभी लोगों से भी सब समय,
सभी स्थानों पर प्रेम नहीं कर पाते हैं.

मानव तीव्र अथक प्रयास से, साधना से,
ममता वृत्ति को मोह से, मुक्त कर सकता है;
देश काल पात्र की सीमा से परे जा सकता है,
ममता को मधुर बना, महा मानव बन सकता है.

महा मानव बन, हर देश काल पात्र से प्रेम कर सकता है,
ममता को 'मधु' मानव भूमा भाव में भूषित कर सकता है.

***

75 H. मधु छन्द * 538 BC/05.10.09

हे मधुर स्पर्ष करके तुम कहाँ हो चल दिये;
मन मेरा आनन्द में लेकर कहाँ तुम चल दिये.

हे प्रभु आनन्द की सुर धार में तुम बस गये;
क्या गये हो गीत देकर, मीत बन कर रह गये.

76. तुम कब क्या कराते हो * 72/28.05.08

तुम कब क्या क्यों और कैसे कराते हो,
मैं समझ नहीं पाता;
तुम्हारे न्याय धर्म की कर्म लीला,
मैं पूर्णत: आत्मसात नहीं कर पाता।

रेल्वे फाटक के एक ओर ढकेल पर या किसी दुकान पर,
मासूम बेखबर पक्षी लिये वांये कर, लौह यन्त्र लिये दांये कर;
ग्राहक से पसन्द कराते, दाम करते,
व्यस्त विक्रेता को लेते हो तुम देख,
मासूम पक्षी की मन व्यथा, लेते हो तुम भाँप।

शायद उसे भान नहीं, ज्ञान नहीं कि,
अगले पल वह नहीं रहेगा जगत में!
विक्रेता व्यस्त है, अभ्यस्त है, पक्षी से आँख मिलाने में असमर्थ है;
ग्राहक शायद पक्षी के शरीर का सौंदर्य और गुणवत्ता परखता है,
पक्षी की आत्म एषणा, मन वेदना,
मृत्यु की तड़पन, उसके लिये गौण है।

विक्रेता पक्षी के शरीर को
लिफाफे में बंद कर ग्राहक को दे देता है,
उसके पँख पँजे रक्त अवशेष रह जाते हैं,
जीवित प्राण पल में निष्प्राण हो जाते हैं;
परम पुरुष व प्रकृति के सृष्ट प्राण,
सेवित शरीर मन लुप्त हो जाते हैं।

देख लेते हो तुम बन कर 'मधु' दृष्टा,
मानव की यह निरीह निर्दय अकरुण क्रिया;
शायद उसी से हो क्षुब्ध, कहीं तुम देते हो धरा पर कुछ करा!

77. न्याय की चैतन्यता * 73/28.05.08

प्रभु, तुम्हारे न्याय की चैतन्यता,
कुछ समझ पाता हूँ, कुछ समझ नहीं पाता!

शहर को आते वाहनों में बन्द,
वेवश निरीह पशु पक्षियों के परिवारों का सन्नाटा;
उनकी जीवित आँखों में, स्पष्ट दीखता उनकी मृत्यु का साया,
जगत के प्रति उनकी हताशा, मानव के प्रति निराशा।
अज्ञात भविष्य का भय, पूर्व में आये अग्रजों का विछुड़ना;
न जान पाना कि उनका क्या हस्र हुआ,
कुल मिला कर देता है उन्हें तिलमिला।

पीछे चलते वाहन में बैठे तुम, उनका दर्द समझ लेते हो,
उनकी आँखों में, मृत्यु का भय पढ़ लेते हो।
पर तुम भी प्रतक्ष में उस पल, कुछ कर नहीं पाते, कुछ कह नहीं पाते हो।
तुम उनके 'मधु' मन की व्यथा, शायद सृष्टि प्रबन्धक को देते हो बता;
और उससे कुछ न्याय, यथा शीघ्र देते हो करा!

78. बृहाण्ड की प्रबन्ध क्षमता * 74/28.05.08

अनुपम है तुम्हारी बृहाण्ड की प्रबन्ध क्षमता;
विचित्र है तुम्हारे 'मधु' प्रशासन की कौशलता।

तुम्हारे जगत के दिग्गज प्रबन्धक भी, मूक, विमुख हो जाते हैं जब कभी;
पृथ्वी की प्रजा की मूल आवश्यकताओं के प्रति भी।
प्रजा का प्रदर्शन निर्वासन आह्वान, प्रताड़ित प्रजा का निवेदन;
नहीं सुनपाता उनका पदार्थ व स्वार्थ लिप्त मन।

तब तुम्हारी प्रबन्ध प्रवीण प्रकृति, शायद, पृथ्वी हिला, वायु बहा, वर्षा करा;
उनकी आत्माएं जगा, तन्द्रा देती है हटा, अनचाहा देती है घटा।

79. नेत्रों की निहारिकाओं में * 92/14.06.08

शहर की सरकती सड़क पर, हर व्यक्ति स्वयं में कुछ सिकुड़ा है;
निज मन में कहीं व्यस्त है, भरी भीड़ में कुछ अकेला है।
बस में विचरता हर व्यक्ति, स्वयं में अजनवी एकाकी है;
आँख बन्द किये ध्यान में है या कान में फोन लगा, कुछ सुनने में लगा है।

स्वयं में हर व्यक्ति अनौखा है, ब्यक्त है, व्यस्त है, सिद्ध है, प्रसिद्ध है;
फिर भी अनजानों की भीड़ में, अपने में गया सिमट है।
मन संस्कारों से ग्रसित है, विचारों से आप्लुत है;
आत्मा किसी की चाहत में रसित है, निकट बैठी आत्मा से विलग है।

क्यों न स्वयं में खोई सृष्टि को निरखें, मन ही मन, आँखों ही आँखों में देखें;
कुछ कहें, कुछ सुनें, रस उड़ेलें, मुक्त हो, आनन्द दें, आनन्द लें।
क्यों न हम 'मधु' चेतन हों, अनजानों को निहारें युक्त हों;
हमें निहारती नेत्रों की निहारिकाओं में, सृष्टा को देखें जाग्रत हों।

80. तुम्हारा प्रत्येक प्राणी * 134/11.08.08

प्रभु तुम्हारा प्रत्येक प्राणी क्या रहस्यमय नहीं!
उसका रूप स्वरूप, भाव भाषा क्या अनुपम नहीं!
पृथ्वी के मानव भी क्या अन्य ग्रहों जैसे विलक्षण नहीं?
पृथ्वी के सब तत्व, क्या बृह्माण्ड के अंश नहीं!
मानव मन का सदैव सतत परतों में चलायमान रहना,
क्या विचित्र नहीं, क्या आश्चर्य नहीं?

कौन है जो नित्य नव रूपों में हमें ढालता सजाता है?
विचार तरङ्गों को हर पल, उद्वेलित उत्प्रेरित करता है।
अगणित निहारिकाओं का प्रति परमाणु
क्या हमारे साथ 'मधु' रास रचाता नहीं?
सारी चराचर 'मधु' सत्ता क्या हमें हर पल हँसाती नचाती चलती नहीं!

81. प्रजातन्त्र * 75/28.05.08

धर्म निरपेक्ष एवं मजहवी तरज़ में चलते
तुम्हारे प्रजातन्त्र के कुछ लोक;
प्रजा की सहज आस्था व अटूट विश्वास वश
हो जाते हैं निर्भीक.

संकुचित देश काल पात्रों की परिधि में
सीमित स्वार्थी जन बन बैठते हैं शासक;
यथाशीघ्र नग्न करते हो तुम उनका
छद्म चरित्र नैतिकता मानसिकता व अविवेक.

शासकों का व्यक्तियों, परिवारों, जाति,
समाज व मज़हवों के लिये सतही प्रेम प्रचार;
अन्दर से स्वार्थ, धन गवन, शोषण,
चरित्र हीनता, भ्रष्टाचार व अत्याचार का विचार.

विश्व की प्राण वायु को देश, प्रदेश,
जिलों, पंचायतों, गाँवों की गुफाओं में उलझाने का विचार;
देश काल पात्र प्रेमी आध्यात्मिक मानव आत्मा को कुंठित कर,
कुशासन करने का कुविचार.

जड़ भोग, पद सत्ता मोह, भाव जड़ता का सम्मोहन,
स्वार्थ केन्द्रित शक्तियों का संवेग प्रलोभन;
अच्छे शासकों को भी कर देता है पथ च्युत,
सद् प्रबन्धकों को करते हो तब तुम जाग्रत उत्प्रेरित.

अपनी प्रकृति से सब की 'मधु' प्रज्ञा को प्रेरित कर,
शासक का मन भ्रमित कर, करा डालते हो चुनाव;
बदल डालते हो तब तुम शासन व्यवस्था प्रबन्ध,
तरङ्गित करते हो जगत के समाज चक्रों का सुप्रबन्ध.

82. सम्मिलित निर्णय * 152/04.09.08

समाज में सम्मिलित निर्णय की महत्ता, गुरुत्तम व महत्तम है;
व्यक्तिगत निर्णय को समाज से, अनुमोदित करा लेना अत्युत्तम है.

वैयक्तिक निर्णय हमारे मन शरीर आत्मा की,
अवस्थिति का प्रतिफलन है;
सामाजिक आशीर्वाद हमारे आत्मीय निर्णय को,
परिपक्व, अनुमोदित व तरङ्गित करता है.

परस्पर विनिमय से किया व्यक्ति व समाज का निर्णय,
सन्तुलन, सुव्यवस्था व सुयोग देता है;
जीवन में किये सम्मिलित निर्णय कर्म,
आनन्द तरङ्ग, साफल्य और साधना लाते हैं.

निर्णय जितने सहज आत्मीय सम्मति से हों,
सामजिक सफलता और आत्मोन्नति उतने ही त्वरित होते हैं;
पारिवारिक व सामाजिक निर्णय सदैव,
परस्पर उपकारी, प्रभावकारी और आनन्द देय होते हैं.

आत्माएं उन्नत हों, श्रेय को समझें, महत की महत्ता जानें,
इष्ट को पहचानें, आशीर्वाद का महत्व जानें, मिलित निर्णय करें;
भक्ति व कृपा करें एवं 'मधु' सृष्टि को आनन्द से भरें.

***

82 H. मधु छन्द * 415 E/11.07.09

मधुर सी मार्मिक मनोहर मुस्कारहट तुम दिये,
विश्व को विश्वास देकर धर्म नव तुम गढ़ लिये.

आश में बाँधा निखिल को, खिलखिलाहट से भरा,
उर मिलाकर उरों से, सुर में भरा एक सुर नया.

83. ताण्डव जग में * 141/15.08.08

मानवता शोषित विचलित है, आतङ्कित शंकित भयमय है;
ताण्डव जग में प्रभु कम करदो, आनन्दित जन गण मन करदो.

मानव मन विहँसित थिरकित हो, भोजन शिक्षा सब को घर हो;
औषधि वस्त्रों की कमी न हो, मन प्राणों में सात्विकता हो.
सब धर्मों में हो मधु प्रीति, शुभ नीति सीखे राजनीति;
व्यापारी व्यापक धर्म सहित, सेवा भावी हों कर्म प्रवृत.

सत कर्मों में मानव हों रत, क्रय शक्ति सभी पायें अविरत;
हों दूर मूल्य वृद्धि रिश्वत, शासन शासक हों अनुशासित.
जाग्रत प्रभु सब जन को कर दो, मन्त्रित अभिमन्त्रित मन कर दो;
तन्त्रित झँकृत जग को कर दो, आनन्दित 'मधु' पृथ्वी कर दो.

84. भारत भुवन को उर रखो * 411/10.07.09

भारत* भुवन को उर रखो, सुरसरी बन भव को तरो;
सुषमा भरो संस्कृति भरो, भारत बने भूमा वरो.

सुर ताल में गाओ सभी, नव राग में नाचो सभी;
हासो सभी, रस दो सभी, सुख दो सभी, सुर दो सभी.
रस दो धरा, क्षुध दो मिटा, मन क्षुब्ध को सुध दो पिला;
सुध में रखो सब दनुजता, सुधि में रखो सब मनुजता.

गीता सुगीता भव करो, भावों को आध्यात्मिक करो;
मन को बृहत करते चलो, सबको सहित ले कर चलो.
'मधु' राग में गाते चलो, जन गण मनों को ले चलो;
वसुधा कुटुम्ब बना चलो, भूमा को भारत कर चलो.

-----

*भारत= भरण पोषण कर्त्ता, अर्जुन, भारत देश, भरत वंशी

85. हे वायुयान * 146/25.08.08

हे वायुयान अपने लघु पहियों पर, सरपट दौड़ते वायुपट्टी पर;
यकायक उठ कर तुम वायु में हो जाते फुर,
पृथ्वी से आकाश की ओर रुख कर.

कितने यात्रियों की आशाओं के सुर, शंकित कम्पित होते हुए होजाते हैं फुर;
कितने दर्शकों की आशाएं हो उठती हैं प्रज्ज्वलित,
कितने हृदय आने की सुन हो जाते हैं तरङ्गित.

हर घड़ी उड़ते विमानों को देख कर, 'मधु' मन के अरमान हो उठते हैं फुर;
पृथ्वी से आकाश को धाते हुए निरन्तर,
जीवन को झकझोरते संकल्प आते हैं नज़र.

86. जीवन के हवाई अड्डे पर * 147/25.08.08

विदा करने आये स्वजनों को देख,
हवाई अड्डे पर विदाई ले रहे यात्रियों को देख;
स्वागत करने आये स्वजनों के मनों को देख,
स्वागत पा रहे परिजनों को देख;
मेरा मन अनायास उनकी आत्माओं की
पीड़ा, हर्ष, विषाद, आनन्द से आता है भर.

पर 'मधु' को तो जीवन के इस हवाई अड्डे पर,
सदैव ही विमानों व यात्रियों का देखना है आवागमन;
देखते हुए उन्हें साक्षीवत, रखना है उनकी सुविधा व सुरक्षा का खयाल.

उनकी आशा निराशा मुस्काराहट में देखना है अनन्त,
स्नेहभरी मुस्कराहट देनी है, रहते हुए कर्मरत;
करनी है 'मधु' सेवा समर्पण यथोचित,
जिम्मेदारी दे पारी के उपरान्त, जाना है चले अपने घर.

87. नाशपाती के बीज में
* 148/31.08.08

नाशपाती के मधुर फल में तुम्हारा,
उसके बीज को इतना सहेज कर रखना;
उसके विशाल बृक्ष के नीचे मूल बीज को,
भूमि में इतना गहरा दबा कर रखना।

भूमिगत बीज को अनुकूल जलवायु दे,
अँकुरित कर धीरे धीरे पौधा बना देना।
बीज को धरा धूल में मिला, समाप्त प्राय: कर देना;
सर्दी गर्मी हिम वर्षा सहते हुए, पौधे का बृक्ष बन जाना।

वसन्त में विशाल बृक्ष का पल्लवित पुष्पित हो जाना,
कितने जन जीवन को छाया व सुगन्ध से त्रप्त कर देना;
अगणित फल खिला मानव पशु पक्षियों को सात्विक कर देना,
इतने सुख दुख देखते हुए भी, एक रस आनन्दित रहना।

हेमन्त की आहट में, बृक्ष का पत्र विहीन हो जाना,
हिम वर्षा सहर्ष सह, वसन्त की राह तकना;
अनुकूल समय आने पर पुन: पल्लवित हो जाना,
श्वेत पुष्पों का खिल उठना, फलों का अवतरित हो जाना।

रहस्यमय है प्रभु, तुम्हारे बीज का जीना,
भूमिगत हो समय आने पर, बृक्ष बन जाना;
सृष्टि को यथसम्भव 'मधु' फल खिलाते जाना,
फल में अन्तर्निहित बीज का सृष्टि में बिखर जाना।

88. बीज का इतिहास * 149/31.08.08

कितना हृदय स्पर्षी है बीज का इतिहास,
कितना मर्म भेदी है, उसका भविष्य;
बीज का फल के अन्दर प्रकट होने का रहस्य,
अनेक फलों में अनेक हो करना सतत विकास.

क्या बृक्ष शाखायें पत्र व फल, मूल बीज को पहचाने?
क्या आश्रय आनन्द लेने वाले, बीज की गरिमा महिमा लघिमा जाने?
फल भी क्या स्वयं में छिपे, बीज का भविष्य जाने?
पुष्प भी क्या, भूमि में छिपे बीज का इतिहास जाने?

एक बीज का प्रति पल और उन्नत अनन्त होते जाना,
साथ में सृष्टि करते हुए, सृष्टि सेवा करते जाना;
स्वयं अपरिचित अदृष्टय रह, अनन्त उत्पादन करते जाना,
सृष्टा बन सृष्टि में है, 'मधु' मय लीला करते जाना.

89. आशीर्वाद * 151/04.09.08

आशीर्वाद आनन्द का प्रसाद है, आशीर्वाद विश्वास का निःश्वास है;
आशीष शीष का अभिमन्त्रण है, आशीष आशा को आमन्त्रण है.

आनन्द का मधु वाद दे महत आत्मा, हमारा पथ प्रशस्त करती है;
अपनी आत्मा के संवेग से हमारी गति त्वरित कर, तरंगित करती है.

प्रभु हमें आशीर्वाद ले दे पाने में सक्षम करें, धरा पर भरपूर भक्ति भाव बहें;
कृपा धारा धरा पर अविरत बहे, गुरुत्वपूर्ण कृपा भाव बरसते रहें.

महत भाव पाकर ही, आशीर्वाद लेने का भाव समझ आता है;
बृहत भाव अनन्त हो कर ही, 'मधु' आशीर्वाद दे पाता है.

90. महा विष्फोट व बृह्म कण
* 155/10.09.08

'महा विष्फोट' का प्रयोग कर वैज्ञानिक,
'बृह्म कण' को जानना चाहते हैं;
पर क्या बृह्म उन्हें, सब कुछ जनाने को
स्वयं युगों से तत्पर नहीं है?

दो वर्ष त्वरक* में रख,
एक खरब डिग्री सेन्टीग्रेड तक गर्म कर,
पदार्थ के आधारभूत अविभाज्य कण को
'कण भौतिक शास्त्री' समझना चाहते हैं;
पर क्या मानव आठ अरब डॉलर का यह प्रयोग कर,
पदार्थ व परमात्म सत्ता के रहस्यों को
ढंग से जान सकता है?

क्या किसी सत्ता का अस्तित्व,
बिना सृष्टा के पल भर भी रह सकता है?
क्या सृष्टि का हर जीव, हर पल, हर विधा में,
सृष्टा, ब्रह्म कण, विश्व व्यवस्था का
इज़हार नहीं कर रहा होता है?

सृष्टि का रहस्य क्या, पदार्थ को
बिना विष्फोटित किये नहीं जाना जा सकता है?
क्या सृष्टि के प्राणी, मानसाध्यात्मिक विज्ञान द्वारा,
यह रहस्य जानते हुए, हर पल प्रयोग नहीं कर रहे हैं.
क्या सृष्टि प्रबन्ध की 'मधु' व्यवस्था,
वे नहीं कर रहे हैं!

- - - -

* त्वरक = ऐक्सीलेरेटर

91. सृष्टा शक्ति
* 156/10.09.08

पदार्थ के ऊपर महा विष्फोट कर वैज्ञानिक,
उसमें अविभाज्य 'सृष्टा शक्ति' को खोजना चाहते हैं।
पर क्या यह 'उसकी' वही चित्त शक्ति नहीं,
जो हर जीव में प्रष्फुटित अन्तर्निहित है!

मधु चित शक्ति का स्रोत ब्राह्मी मन है,
ब्राह्मी मन के शून्य में अँधकूप* हो सकता है;
ब्राह्मी मन का स्फुरण महा विष्फोट करा सकता है,
ब्राह्मी मन का संकल्प सृष्टि को लय विलय कर सकता है।

पदार्थ के महा विष्फोट से सृष्टि समाप्त नहीं हो सकती है;
मानवीय योग प्रयोग चित्त, हर क्षण, हर स्थान पर,
ब्राह्मी मन के सन्तुलित नियन्त्रण में रहते हैं।
देश काल पात्र के क्षुद्र छिद्र, आयाम व शून्य,
सब उसके प्रयोग हैं।

मानव के पदार्थ के साथ किये प्रयोग,
उसके जागतिक मानसाध्यात्मिक ज्ञान व सुविधा में उपयोगी हैं;
मानव मन की सामर्थ्य सीमित किन्तु प्रगतिशील है,
ज्ञान विज्ञान का हर 'मधु' प्रयोग उसे
सृष्टा के और निकट ले जाता है।

-----

* अँधकूप = ब्लैक होल

92. सृष्टि के रहस्य * 157/10.09.08

बृह्माण्ड कारण व प्रभाव के
प्रतिफलन की सत्ता स्थिति है;
उसमें किसी भी अवयव द्वारा सिद्धान्तत:
हम पूर्ण को पहचान सकते हैं.

बृक्ष को जैसे मूल बीज, मूल, तना, शाखाओं,
पत्र पुष्प व नव बीजों से पहचान सकते हैं;
फिर भी बीज द्वारा उसे पहचानना, उगाना,
विकसित करना आसान हो सकता है.

सृष्टि के पुरातन व नवीन मानव बीज द्वारा,
सृष्टा व सृष्टि को समझना वैसे ही आसान है;
पदार्थ पञ्च भूत के प्रयोगों से उसे समझना,
समय अर्थ प्रयास में महँगा पड़ सकता है.

मानव के कर्म गति प्रभाव को समझने का प्रयास,
जैसे उसका मन संकल्प आत्मा समझने में उतने सहायक नहीं;
पदार्थ की गति स्थिति गुण स्वभाव समझने का प्रयास,
वैसे ही सृष्टि सृष्टा को समझने में उतने सहायक नहीं.

मानव चित्त का सृष्टा के चित्त में
विलय कर देना, आसान उपाय है;
सृष्टा के मन प्राण में पैठ, सृष्टि व सृष्टा के
'मधु' रहस्य समझ लेना, सरल कुञ्जी है.

***

92 H.   मधु छन्द * 551 E/08.10.09

सृष्टि की सुहानी विधाएं हैं, जीव औ' बृह्म की ऋचाएं हैं;
दृष्टि की अदद सी अदाएं हैं, बहारें राह की कृपायें हैं.

93. बृह्म कण – सृष्टि प्रबन्ध
* 158/10.09.08

वैज्ञानिकों द्वारा १५ अरब वर्ष पूर्व सृष्ट,
'सृष्टि कण' को आज, पहचानने का प्रयोग कर पाना;
पदार्थ कण की गति त्वरित कर,
'बृह्म कण' को पहचानने का प्रयोग करना,
क्या नहीं है, "कण भौतिकी" का इतना पीछे चलना?

इतने युगों में विज्ञान का इतना ही प्रयास कर पाना,
'जीवाणु' व 'बृह्माणु' को 'पदार्थ कण' द्वारा समझने का प्रयास करना;
पञ्च तत्वों व बृाह्मी मन की व्यापकता को न समझ पाना,
बृह्म, बृाह्मी योजना, सृष्टि को, विज्ञान द्वारा न समझ पाना।

क्या सृष्टि में ऐसे प्रचुर प्रबन्धक नहीं,
जो उसे हजारों वर्षों से समझे हुए हैं?
सृष्टा के हर कण, हर मन, हर उर लहर को समझते हैं;
सृष्टा की योजनाओं को बखूबी क्रियान्वित कराते रहते हैं।

सृष्टि क्या चल सकती है,
सृष्टा, प्रबन्धकों व संस्था के जाग्रत झँकृत विनिमय के बिना!
प्रकट विकसित या क्षीण हो सकता है
'महा विष्फोट' या 'काला छिद्र' क्या!
सृष्टि प्रबन्धकों के 'मधु' संज्ञान बिना!

***

93 H. मधु छन्द * 419 D/12.07.09

सृष्टि में इष्ट लखि, दृष्टि में ब्रह्म वरि,
बृहत की गति परखि, गति में विरति लखि।
विरस में रस बहा, रूप ऋतु में मिला,
ऋतु के रस में बहा, प्रज्ञा रस जा चखा।

94. आपत्तिकाल का फोन
* 185/13.11.08

आपत्तिकाल का फोन प्रायः हम प्रयोग नहीं करते,
पर सर्वोच्च सत्ता चाहती है कि हम उसे याद रखें;
आवश्यकता पड़ने पर अवश्यमेव प्रयोग करें.

परीक्षण करने के लिये, जीवन द्वार पर स्वयं वे,
अपना वाहन कभी तेजी से दौड़ाकर ले जा सकते हैं;
और हमसे फोन करने की अपेक्षा कर सकते हैं.

फोन न करने पर वे हमें दंडित कर सकते हैं,
पुनः प्रशिक्षण के लिये भेज सकते हैं;
दैनिक कार्य प्रणाली से कुछ दिन के लिये दूर कर सकते हैं.

प्रभु से हम प्रतिदिन अच्छा कार्य करते हुए, बात नहीं करते,
उन्हें फोन करने या पुकारने की आवश्यकता नहीं समझते;
प्रबन्ध व्यवस्था सब की कर्मठता से चलती रहती है.

पर कभी वे स्वयं परीक्षण करने, वार्तालाप करने आसकते हैं,
निरन्तर उनके आने व अन्तर्मन में चाहने की प्रतीक्षा करते रहें;
ध्यान द्वार पर सदैव सजग रहते हुए, प्रभु से 'मधु' संपर्कित रहें.

***

94 H. मधु छन्द * 418 B/12.07.09

ना है कोयल कहे, ना कुहक कोई भरे,
कूँजता फिरता वह, गूँज सबमें भरे;
गुज़रते गुँजरित स्वर उसी से भरे,
गूँज उसकी लिये, गुज़रता विश्व रे.

95. तुम्हारे जीवों की हृदय हीनता
* 201/19.12.08

प्रभु! तुम्हारे जीवों की हृदय हीनता,
उससे आहत तुम्हारे हृदय की विह्वलता;
उनकी भाव हीनता से आहत तुम्हारी विकलता,
अनुभूत करती है 'मधु' हृदय की नीरवता।

जीवों को आहत करती उनकी उद्दंडता,
व्यथित करती है मानवीय चेतनता;
अहंकार अज्ञान अनाचार में डूबी उनकी जड़ता,
आतंकित करती है जागतिक सात्विकता।

अनवरत उत्पीड़न से उन्मीलित तुम्हारी बृहत्ता,
सह नहीं पाती जब उनकी दानवता।
तुम्हारा आग्रह उद्धार नहीं बदल पाता, जब उनकी भाव जड़ता;
करनी पड़ जाती है प्रयोग तब, तुम्हें आध्यात्मिक प्रबन्ध क्षमता।

तुम्हारी सेवा कर्मलीनता, दयालुता भाव सहजता;
नहीं जान पाती जब, हर जीव की मानसिकता।
तुम्हारे ताण्डव की थाप, दावानल की दाहनता;
मिटा देती है तब उनकी मलिनता दानवता।

***

95 H. मधु छन्द * 431 C/17.07.09

तुम स्वयं मम मन महिं प्रवसि,
होकर प्रकट भरदो सुरभि;
रस दो सुधा, भर दो भगति,
अनुरक्ति दो, दे दो सुगति।

96. तुम्हारे ताण्डव का स्पन्दन * 203/19.12.08

प्रभु! तुम्हारे ताण्डव का स्पन्दन, भर देता है सृष्ट जगत में सिहरन;
विनष्ट करता है सृष्टि की शिथिलता उत्पीड़न, तरङ्गित हो उठती है हर धड़कन।

अहंकार विकार में ग्रसित मानव मन, डूब जाता है जब कभी तन्द्रा में चेतन;
आहत करता है जब सुजन मन, व्याहत करता है जब वह प्रभु प्रयोजन।

उत्तिष्ठ हो उठते हैं, तब सात्विक प्राण मन,
समर्पित हो कर उठते हैं, गान साधना ध्यान;
हो उठता है, ललित कौशिकी ताण्डव गहन,
विराजित प्रकट होते हैं, प्रभु सुजन मन।

सृष्टि की शालीनता के लिये करते हैं प्रभु! प्रबन्ध मन्थन,
व्यापक उथल पुथल परिवर्तन करते हैं वे उस क्षण;
विनाश करते हैं वे सृष्टि की अन्ध तमिस्रा गहन,
आलोकित आलोड़ित करते हैं प्रभु 'मधु' मन।

97. सृष्टा से सम्पर्कित रहना * 186/13.11.08

सर्वोच्च सत्ता का प्रबन्ध व्यवस्था का, अनायास परीक्षण करना अजीव बात है;
पर 'मधु' जीव को अजीव दौर से गुजार कर,
जीवों की चैतन्यता परखना भी उसकी आवश्यकता है।

सब जाग्रत चेतन जागरूक रहें, अपना कर्म समुचित सचेत करें,
सर्वोच्च सत्ता की स्वयं सुरक्षा भंग करने की अवस्था में भी;
उसकी अपेक्षा है कि हम उसे रोकें, टोकें, फोन कर शिकायत करें।

मात्र काम करना, यथोचित सृष्टि सेवा करना पर्याप्त नहीं है,
उससे उसीकी, उसके जीवों की, तत्काल शिकायत करना, उसकी अपेक्षा है;
सृष्टा से सदैव सम्पर्कित रहना, सृष्टि की आवश्यकता है।

98. तुम्हारी व्यापकता

* 202/19.12.08

प्रभु! तुम्हारी व्यापकता, बृहतता, विशाल हृदयता;
विश्व मानव अहसास नहीं कर पाता.
तुम्हारी मधुरता मोहकता विनय शीलता;
जड़ जीव का क्रूर मन अनुभूत नहीं कर पाता.

अहो रात्रि तरङ्गित तुम्हारी स्नेह भरी शीलता;
मानव मन की अनवरत अनन्त अनुचितता.
मन कर्म भाव से भरी तुम्हारी महत्ता;
संकुचित सतही उनकी स्वार्थ लिप्तता.

तुम्हारा सतत प्रेम, सहज संवेदन शीलता;
तुम्हारी विश्व दृष्टि में त्रुटि निरखती उनकी मानसिकता.
आहत करती है 'मधु' हृदय की नीरवता;
तुम्हारे अनन्त कर्मों में धूल झाँकती उनकी बौद्धिकता.

अनचाहे करनी पड़ती है तुम्हें उपयोगिता,
अपने अधिकार व आवश्यकता की प्रयोग शीलता;
ओत प्रोत हो तरङ्गित करते हो विश्व प्रबन्ध शीलता,
लय विलय कर उठते हो सृष्टि संचालनता.

99. मेरी व्यथा * 23/02.04.08

मेरी व्यथा, मेरी कथा, मेरी विधा;
मेरी द्विधा, मेरी क्षुधा, मेरी सुधा.

उर की अरुणिमा तुम, अँखियों के अश्रु तुम;
आहत के अनाहत तुम, अनाहत के स्वर स्वयं.
'मधु' तुम गा दो गायन, व्यथा करे पलायन;
सुर गूँजे शाश्वत का, अनाहत हो आज्ञा का.

मैं सोजाता हूँ, तुमरी ही गोदी में;
खोजाता मन मेरा, तुमरी मन सृष्टि में.
तुम आजाते हो, सर थपथपाते हो;
सहस्रार खिल जाता है, विशुद्ध सुधा लाता है.

मन खिल जाता है, मैं उठ जाता हूँ;
व्यथा बिखर जाती है, आनन्द आजाता है.
क्षुधा मेरी क्षुद्र हुई, बनी द्विधा सुविधा;
कथा मेरी कविता बनी, विधा बनी विद्या.

100. सुरभि * 322 AE/28.05.09

प्रेम में पुलकती, मधुर सी सिहरती,
सहसा सुरभि बिखरती रही सरसती;
प्रेय सी श्रेय सी, सौम्य सी शान्त सी,
नीर सी क्षीर सी, धीर सी वीर सी.

उदित आत्मा की प्रखरित सरसती सुरभि,
नव्य मानव की परिचय भरी सी सुरभि;
ब्रह्म की चेतना से उभरती सुरभि,
प्रकृति की प्रेरणा की 'मधु' सी सुरभि.

101. तरलता तरुणता * 320/28.05.09

तरलता तरुणता तीक्ष्णता तीव्रता, ताल पर नाचता ताकता भाँपता;
जीव का मन मगन प्रकृति को झाँकता, मापता जाँचता थिरकता काँपता।

सौम्यता शोधिता संतुलन साम्यता, धीरता गहनता शोभिता मधुरता;
सुरभि ढाले चले प्रकृति प्राणीनता, प्रचुरता प्रखरता प्राण उद्वेलिता।
नाचता कूदता बहकता फुदकता, चलता रहता मनुज माधुरी ढालता;
विहरता विहँसता, व्योम में झाँकता, धरणि पर उछलता, प्रेम में पुलकता।

शिखर पर नाचता, हिम सरिस सिहरता, बरसता बिखरता तरसता तड़पता;
लसित मन, त्रसित तन, तान पर नाचता, नयन मूँदे नवेली प्रकृति देखता।
शान्त मन प्रेयसी प्रकृति की सौम्यता, परख पाता 'मधु' मन, मनन गहनता;
मनुजता चहकती निरख चैतन्यता, महा मानव ढले सृष्टि माधुर्यता।

102. सृष्टि बीज * 150/31.08.08

प्रभु तुम्हारा बीज वत, भूमा मन भूमि में रहना,
सृष्टि को प्रस्फुटित पुष्पित, फलित व विकसित कर देना;
स्वयं सृष्टि में छिपे रहना, सृष्टि को गुण धर्म देते जाना,
उचित समय आने पर, सबको पल्लवित प्रफुल्लित कर देना।

अनन्त फलों में अनन्त बीजों की सृष्टि कर देना,
फलों को सृष्ट जीवों को खिलाते जाना;
बीजों को जीवों पञ्चभूतों द्वारा सृष्टि में बिखरवा देना,
उचित वातावरण में बीजों को अँकुरित कर बृक्ष बना देना।

तुम्हारी 'मधु' सृष्टि का सतत विकसित रहना,
रहस्यमय है तुम्हारा सृष्टि संचालन करना;
अधिकाँश जीवों को जीवन लीला का रस लेने में रत रखना,
कुछ जीवों को अपनी कारण सत्ता का स्वरूप जनाने का प्रयास करा देना।

अध्याय 3 – भक्ति व कृपा

103. ले चलो मुझको प्रिये
* 118/ 27.06.08

ले चलो मुझको प्रिये, तुम ले चलो!
मुझे रख अपने हृदय में, ले चलो.

गा सको तो, गान तुम गाते चलो, गुञ्जरित हृद को किये, चलते चलो;
प्रेम को पैदा किये, कुछ कर चलो, विश्व को नाटक समझ, देखे चलो.

मधुर के आनन्द में, बहते चलो,
मधुर सरिता में बहाकर, ले चलो;
विश्व को सुमधुर बना निज में डुबालो,
ले चलो मुझको निकट निज में डुबालो.

हे हरि, मुझको बहाकर ले चलो, पल मेरे अब निज पलों में मिलालो;
पलक अपनी पर, बिठाकर ले चलो, मन मेरा 'मधु' मन बनाकर ले चलो.

104. आनन्द की सुर तान ढ़ालो
* 119/27.06.08

हे प्रभु! आनन्द की सुर तान ढ़ालो!
हे प्रभु! मुझको बहालो!

बुद्धि को व्यापक बना तव मन बनालो, मुझे तुम वँशी बनाकर गुन गुनालो;
निकट मेरे आ तुम्हीं कविता रचा लो, मधुर मेरे राग में तुम खूब गालो.

विश्व में सबसे मिलाकर निज बनालो, विश्व में सबको तुम्हीं मेरा बनादो;
स्वयं की सेवा प्रभु मुझसे करालो; हृद बनाकर ध्यान में 'मधु' को लगालो.

105. आनन्द उमङ्गों में भरकर * 127/10.07.08

आनन्द उमङ्गों में भरकर, तुमरा मैं गीत सुना जाऊँ;
मैं तारक बृह्म लिये मन में, तरता जाऊँ, गाता जाऊँ.

वरता जाऊँ तव चरणों को, तव मन की मैं करता जाऊँ;
तव कर्मों में भव भर जाऊँ, आनन्दित हो, गाता जाऊँ.

तुम शाश्वत सुन्दर अभिनव हो, तुम में गाऊँ, तुम को पाऊँ;
आनन्द पयोनिधि पा जाऊँ, मैं अभिनव 'मधु' घन हो जाऊँ.

तुम नीरव ज्ञान पयोधि हो, भक्ति में योगी हो जाऊँ;
झँक्रत तन्त्रित, तुम कर्म प्रवृत, यन्त्रित अनुरागी हो जाऊँ.

106. राग कितने फुर चले हैं * 651/09.12.09

राग कितने फुर चले हैं आज मन, तान कितनी आगयी हैं धीर मन;
शून्य की मधु रागिनी में विकल तन, थिरकता सा रह गया है प्राण मन.

सौम्यता की सरहदों में क्षीर मन, तुष्टता की तीव्र धारा में थिरन;
तेज की मधु रोशनी में है तरन, त्राण की नव द्योतना में है फुरन.

गान कितने गा रही है ये धरा, पवन कितने लख रहा है मन मेरा;
गगन की अद्भुत छटा मन मोहती, सलिल की सौन्दर्यता सुधि खोजती.

जोहता है बाट मेरा हृद सदा, सद्य के सङ्गीत को देता धरा;
धरणि के प्रति अणु को देता सुधा, क्षुधा की क्षुध आकृति करता विदा.

विदाई के 'मधु' मिलन में मथित मन, जुदाई की खुदाई में लसित मन;
राग तानों की बुनाई में मगन, सृष्टि की सुर तान पर रच रहा धुन.

107. किसलय की लय में मैं गाऊँ * 126/10.07.08

किसलय की लय में मैं गाऊँ, किसके लिये गाता जाऊँ?
किसकी शाला में 'मधु' पाऊँ? किसके किसलय पर लय पाऊँ?

किसके मन में, मैं मुसकाऊँ, किसके हृद में, सुनता जाऊँ?
किसके अधरों से कह जाऊँ, किसके तन में मैं, भव जाऊँ?
मेरा मन उसका ही तन है, मेरा तन उसका ही मन है;
मेरा हृद उसकी ही लय है, मेरी लय उसकी ही धुन है.

मैं क्या गाऊँ, क्या ना गाऊँ, केवल उसकी सुनता जाऊँ;
केवल उसकी करता जाऊँ, उसके बल मैं जीता जाऊँ.

108. मैं अकेली गोप बाला * 2/19.03.08 (ब्रज)

मैं अकेली गोप बाला, बसति जमुना तीर.
उठ्यौ जोवन ज्वार मो पर, हिय उठी एक पीर;
मिलन हो पिय संग, ऐसी हियहि उठी हिलोर.
सरस शीतल बहति पवन, सुभग सुन्दर यमुना जल;
नाचत मयूर कदम्ब तल, उदित सूरज नभ विशाल.

यमुना तट बट निकट सखी लखि, जल बिच न्हाबन चली गोप मन;
आनन्दित थिरकित आल्हादित, अङ्ग सुयोग भयौ जल संग जब.
मन की पीर, जगत की पीड़ा, जमुना जल पल में हरि लीन्हा;
दैहिक दैविक भौतिक पीड़ा, गोप वालिका कछु नहिं चीन्हा.

मन पुलकित, आत्मा आनन्दित, गोपी जल समाधि आप्लावित;
मन हल्का, तन सुभग प्रफुल्लित, रोम रोम सिहरत अल्हादित.
केका कोयल कलरव करत, गोप वालिका मन सिहरावत;
मन शरीर सब भयौ 'मधु' मय, सौम्य शांत सुरभित ज्यों हरि मय.

109. हरि मेरौ हरि लियो तुम चीर * 3/19.03.08 (ब्रज)

हरि मेरौ हरि लियो तुम चीर!
मैं अकेली गोप बाला, बसति यमुना तीर.

जल समाधि गोपी जब डूबी, पुलकित मन सत्संगति भोगी;
रक्षा करत चीर की हिय हरि, हिय माँह बैठि वस्त्र लिये हारी!
कृष्ण उठाये चीर तीर तों, बैठेउ उच्च कदम्ब शाख पर;
ध्यान गयौ गोपी वस्त्रन पर जब,
लखे वस्त्र संग श्याम मनोहर.

चीर हर्यौ अथवा हिय हार्यौ, हिय चिर हार्यौ, चीर हरायो;
उर माँह वह, बाहर वह बैठा, जीव संग खेलहि अति नीका.
जिमि भक्तीमय भक्त समर्पित, सत्संगति जल बिच अवरोहित;
कष्ट विलय आपन संतन बिच, संत रहहिं आनन्दित पुलकित.

लाज भय नग्नता का भाव किससे, क्रीड़ा करे करबाये जो हमीं से!
चीर उसके, तन उसी के, मन उस के, लाज भय उसी के!
अंदर वह, बाहर वह, चीर देने से पहले वह,
'मधु' चीर लेने के बाद भी वह!

110. नाच जाऊँ मैं * 120/27.06.08

नाच जाऊँ मैं तुम्हारे हृदय में,
वरस जाऊँ मैं तुम्हारे ध्यान में.

मन मिले आनन्द में तव हृदय में, गगन मिल जाये तुम्हारे रङ्ग में;
मगन मैं नाचूँ तुम्हारे छन्द में, गगन जाये डूब तुमरे चित्त में.

मन जाये मिल तुमरे ध्यान में, विश्व जाये मिल तुमरे वेश में;
पल जायें मिल तुमरे हृदय में, 'मधु' जाये मिल तुमरे चरण में.

111. धीरे धीरे गोपी चली * 4/19.03.08 (ब्रज)

धीरे धीरे गोपी चली, बिलग हो सत्संगति के जल से;
सलाज सभय छिपाये अपने अंगों को, अपने करों से।

छोड़ि सब भवितव्यता, निज नग्नता की लाज;
चल पड़ी उस ओर गोपी, जिस दिक लखे नन्दकुमार।
जल छूटा, मन तट से जुटा, तन मन में मिटा;
किन्तु कृष्ण देखे मात्र उसके मन में, उसकी भक्ति द्रवित आँखों में।

गोपी विश्वास बढा, तप निखरा, समर्पण बढा;
भक्ति अनन्त में मिली, मन आनन्दित हुआ, अर्पण बढा।
नेत्र आत्मा बने, नेत्रों ने आत्म दान दिया; कृष्ण चल दिये, वस्त्र मिल गये।
रास रस गये, बिरस वस्त्र हुए, आनन्द थिरका;
'मधु' आत्मा परम हुई, गोपी राधा हुई।

112. क्यों न चुरायें चीर मेरा * 5/19.03.08 (ब्रज)

क्यों न चुरायें चीर मेरा कृष्ण हर पल, शरीर क्यों न हो जाये शाश्वत!
क्यों मैं चीरों की चिन्ता करूँ, क्यों न उन्हें चीर दूँ हर पल!

हर पल जमुना की सत्संगति से निकल,
क्यों न उनकी गोद में बिसरूँ, बिखरूँ;
वे मुझे देखें, वराभय दें, मैं उनके चरणों में सर रख सो जाऊँ!

क्यों न उन्हें अपने गुरुचक्र पर सहस्र पद्म दलों पर बिठाऊँ;
और मैं उनके शाश्वत चरणों में लेट जाऊँ!
वे मेरे शरीर मन आत्मा को सहलाएं, और मैं उनके अनाहत में मिल जाऊँ!

क्यों न मैं उनको स्नेह दूँ, उनके चक्रों को सहलाऊँ!
क्या वे थक नहीं गये देते देते, क्यों न उन्हें, उन्हीं की 'मधु' आत्म सृष्टि दे दूँ!

113. मेरा अस्तित्व अनन्त है * 17/28.03.08

मेरा अस्तित्व अनन्त है, मैं अनन्त का राही हूँ.

कभी मैं अनन्त का आदि खोजता हूँ, कभी मैं आदि का अन्त खोजता हूँ;
कभी अस्तित्व पाजाता हूँ, कभी अस्तित्व खोदेता हूँ.

कभी तुम मुझे मिल जाते हो मध्य में, कभी तरसाते हो अन्त तक;
कभी समझ आते हो, कभी समझा जाते हो.

मेरा अस्तित्व तुम्हीं में है, तुम मिलो तो मैं मिलूँ;
तुम गले लगाओ तो मैं लगूँ, तुम नजर आओ तो मैं चरण पड़ूँ.

तुम मेरे निकट रहो, निकटता रखो, कटुता मत रखो, कृपणता मत करो;
तुम ब्यस्त हो सृष्टि के नियन्त्रण में, साथ फिर भी रहो मेरे हर पल में.

तुम्हारे सानिध्य में, तुम्हारे अस्तित्व में,
पा जाऊँगा मैं राह, अपना 'मधु' अस्तित्व.

114. प्रभु तुम्हारे आलोक में! * 159/14.09.08

प्रभु तुम्हारे आलोक में, कितनी आभाएं उभरीं!
प्रभु तुम्हारे माधुर्य में, कितनी 'मधु'गीति उतरीं!

कितनी विधाएं विद्या बन गयीं, कितनी प्रतिभाएं प्रतिभूत हुयीं?
कितने सुख दुख आनन्द धारा बन बहे, कितनी पीड़ा वीणा बन गयीं?
विश्व की व्यापकता उर में आगयी; जीवन की सार्थकता अन्तर्मन रंग गयी.
गुरु की कृपा कितना रंग लायी! धरा की धूलि कितनी मन भायी!

कितने दानव, मानव बन गये! कितने मानव, मन से तर गये!
कितनी प्रतिक्रियाएं, प्रेरणा बन गयीं! कितनी द्योतनाएं चेतना बन गयीं!

115. भाव के भँवर में भावना * 18/28.03.08

भाव के भँवर में भावना भावुक है, भँवरा भावात्मक है, पृथ्वी आनन्दित है;
'मधु' तुम आजाओ तो भाव भरें भाषा में,
गायें कुछ गीत यहाँ, पायें कुछ मीत यहाँ.

तारे आजायेंगे चाँद साथ लाएंगे, खञ्जन मन रञ्जन कर गुँजन भर जाएंगे;
तुम खोजाना मत अपने ही रागों में! राग मिला देना तुम, सब के ही रागों में.
पञ्चम स्वर फूटेगा, पपीहरा बोलेगा, चाँद मुस्करा देगा, चकोरी गा देगी;
चल देगा भावुक जल, हिम से विस्रवित हो कर,
सूरज सुर दे देगा, वायु से संयत हो कर.

नभ सर पर होगा, सरपट मन डोलेगा;
आज्ञा से भाव बिखर, मन मन में बोलेंगे.
तब तुम भी सुन लेना और उसे गा देना,
पृथ्वी खिल जाएगी, चाँद शरम जाएगा.
भाव भाँप जाएंगे, भावन के आने को,
मन भावन भगवन बन, विहँस बिखर जाएंगे.

116. जीवन के सूत्रधार * 140/14.08.08

जीवन के सूत्रधार, मुझको देदो आधार;
देकर आनन्द ज्वार, 'मधु' का करदो उद्धार.
जीवन सरिता भरकर, सागर मय हो जाकर;
मेरा अभिनव उद्गार, ले चलो सागर पार.

जीवन के स्रोतधार, जीवन को देदो धार;
खोल दो आनन्द द्वार, झरा दो मुक्ति हार.
हरलो धरिणी का भार, भाव भरो, हरलो रार;
त्रिभुवन के कर्णधार, करदो सब का उद्धार.

117. पूर्ण की यात्रा * 25/02.04.08

पूर्ण की पूर्ण से पूर्ण तक की यात्रा; पूर्ण है, परिपूर्ण है, पूर्ण थी, पूर्ण होगी।
मेरा हर पल, हर श्वाँस, पूर्ण का पर्व है; मेरा हर पग पूर्ण का छन्द है।
मेरी जीवन यात्रा, पूर्ण की परियोजना है;
मेरी हर रुकाबट, पूर्ण में पड़ाब है।

मेरी योजनाएं उसी के आयोजन हैं;
मेरी शक्ति, मेरा संकल्प, उसी का प्राणायाम है।
मेरे दुख, मेरे दर्द, पूर्ण के उपचार हैं;
मेरी उपलब्धियां, मेरी सफलताएं, उसी की कृपा का प्रसाद हैं।

मेरी अपूर्ण कथा, मेरी अपूर्ण ब्यथा; पूर्ण की ही इच्छा–स्थिति है।
भविष्य की धरोहर है, मेरी साज सज्जा; पूर्ण की कल्पना है, मेरी हर इच्छा।

मैं भयभीत, चिन्तित, ब्यथित क्यों हूँ; पल पल बदलती नियति की स्थितियों में।
'मधु' गीत हूँ उसका, साज हूँ उसका;
सुनता हूँ गीत उसके, वीणा पर उसकी ही।

118. प्रभु के मैं राग सुनाता हूँ * 55/08.05.08

प्रभु के मैं राग सुनाता हूँ, आनन्द में डूबा जाता हूँ!

तुम आजाओ, मेरे हृदि में, मन में सुर में, मधु गायन में;
तुम नाचो मेरे आँगन में, आनन्दित हो सुर भावन में।
मेरे मन को तुम लेजाओ, आनन्द धरा पर ले जाओ;
तुम आजाओ, अब आजाओ! मुझको धारा में ले जाओ।

आनन्दित गङ्गा में लेजा कर, डुबकी तुम मुझको लगबाओ;
मृदु आनन्दित कर ले आओ, रस भर जाओ, 'मधु' दे जाओ।

119. भाव समुद्रों में बहकर * 37/08.04.08

भाव समुद्रों में बहकर, 'मधु' तुम गाओ नव गीति;
धरा प्रफुल्लित हो जाये, गाओ ऐसी मधु गीति.
नभ गा उठे, तरंगित हो, मीठी मीठी अनुभूति.

तुम आजाओ वायु में बह, अग्नि में जल, जल में मिलकर,
कुछ गा जाओ मृदु संस्मरण;
धरा मुस्कराकर धाये, जन दे जन जन में नव प्रीति.
राह बने आनन्दित छन्दित, फूटे नव अनुभूति.

नभ से आकर हृदि में छाकर, आनन्दित हो अभिनव बनकर;
तन यन्त्रित कर, मन मन्त्रित कर, तुम मधुर मधुप गुँजन बनकर.
गा कर, पा कर, हृदि सरसा कर.

तुम मधु मय हो, मधु कर मधु हो, नभ में तुम हो, हृदि में भी हो;
मुझ में तुम हो, सब ही में हो, तुम हो तो में हूँ, सब जग है.
तन है, मन है, जन जीवन है.
आओ हम सब नाचें गायें, मधु क्षरा 'मधु गीति'.

120. तुम प्रभु का मधु गान हो * 128/10.07.08

तुम प्रभु का मधु गान हो, आनन्द की सुर तान हो;
मेरे हृदय का ज्वार हो, मेरा तुम्ही उद्गार हो.
तुम सृष्टि के आनन्द हो, तुम अधर में छाये रहो;
तुम विश्व के विकसित मनुज, आनन्द का तुम राग हो.

अब आ भी जाओ विश्व में, तुम मानवों के मर्म में;
प्रेम तुम देते रहे हो सृष्टि में, विश्व में आओ, तुम्ही आनन्द हो.
सभी के मन में बहा अमृत तुम्हीं, ज्ञान दो, अभिध्यान दो, सुर तान दो;
मधुर बन कर गान मेरे सुनादो, 'मधु' बना, आनन्द की सुर तान दो.

121. गोकुल की कुलबाला
* 46/01.05.08

मैं हूँ गोकुल* की कुल–बाला, तुम हो मधुपुर# के नंदलाला;
मैं कुल कुण्डलिनी की राधा, तुम सहस्रार के परम शिवा।

तुमरी मुरलीध्वनि में माखी, मैं मधु की प्यासी मधुमाखी;
कितनी मधुमाखी मधु चाखीं? कितनी मधुमाखी मधु राखीं?
कितनी क्रीड़ा मधु लीला में? कितना मोहन मधु नगरी में?
घन आकर्षण मधुमय मधु में, सुप्रबन्ध सुरक्षा सब मधु में।

मैं मूलाधार की 'मधु' वाला, तुम गुरुचक्र# की मधुशाला;
अभिनव बाला मैं नव ज्वाला, नव मधु ढाला, तुम नभ ज्वाला।

- - - - - - - - - - -

* गोकुल = मथुरा ने निकट कृष्ण की शैशव स्थली = मूलाधार चक्र
\# मधुपुर = मथुरा = गुरु चक्र (सहस्रार का जीवोन्मुख स्वरूप)

122. प्रभु की निर्मित यह मधु काया
* 47/01.05.08

प्रभु की निर्मित यह 'मधु' काया, कितने जन्मों की मधु माया;
कुल कुण्डलिनी की लघु काया, कितने कल्पों की प्रतिछाया।

मूलाधार की गोपी की प्रणय कथा, मोहन मुरली की प्रणव कथा;
गोपी के कृष्ण से मिलने तक की कथा,
सहस्रार के परम शिवा की मर्म कथा।

मूलाधार से सहस्रार की यात्रा, जीव से ब्रह्म की यह यात्रा;
कितनी छोटी है, पर क्यों इतनी लम्बी लगती है, समय लेती है।
सम्भवतः प्रभु अपने हर प्राण को, मिलने सँवरने सजने देते हैं;
आनन्द देते हैं, आनन्द लेते हैं।

123. मैं क्या गाऊँ अब तुम गाओ
* 54/08.05.08

मैं क्या गाऊँ, अब तुम गाओ!

सविता बन कर तुम आजाओ, आनन्द बने तुम छा जाओ;
मेरे हृदि में आकर गाओ, मुरली की तान सुना जाओ।

मैं आनन्दित हो जाता हूँ, जब तुमरी टेर सुनाता हूँ;
रस रागों से भर जाता हूँ, आल्हादित मैं हो जाता हूँ।

तुम आजाओ अब आजाओ, नटवर नागर तुम आजाओ;
भव सागर में तुम आजाओ, मेरे मन को अब ले जाओ।

अपने चरणों को दब बाओ, मेरे सर को तुम सहलाओ;
मैं आनन्दित सुनता जाऊँ, 'मधु' गीति तुम्हीं गाते जाओ।

124. तुम जीवन हो जीवन सुर हो
* 137/14.08.08

तुम जीवन हो जीवन सुर हो, अभिनव मधुमय मानव स्वर हो!

आनन्द महुल 'मधु' में बहकर, 'मधु गीति' तुम्हीं गाते जाओ;
देते जाओ आनन्द मधुर, अनुभूति कुछ कहते जाओ।

मैं आता हूँ, गा जाता हूँ, तुम सुनकर ही मत रह जाओ;
आनन्द अनन्त लिये मन में, उत्सुक अनुरागी हो जाओ।

अब राग धरा के तुम गाओ, अरमान हृदय के दिखलाओ;
सबके उर के गाने गाओ; सबके हृद में जाकर गाओ।

125. पुष्पों के दल दल पर
* 160/23.09.08

पुष्पों के दल दल पर, मधु माखी धाती है;
परागित कण कण लेकर, प्रगटित मधु करती है.

सहमित सुरभित सिहरत, पुष्पों के झुँड मधुर;
मधुकर की धुन मनहर, धरिणी की गन्ध मधुर.

बिखराता दिन राति, प्रभा कुसुम बहु भाँति;
मेरा मन हो विहँसित, खिल जाता नव भाँति.

तुम भी 'मधु' हो प्रमुदित, प्रष्फुट मन, तन थिरकित;
प्राणों से आनन्दित, झँकृत पुलकित मन्द्रित.

126. मैं राग धरा के क्या गाऊँ
* 139/14.08.08

मैं राग धरा के क्या गाऊँ! तुमरे सुर में उलझा जाऊँ!
तुमरे रंग में रँगता जाऊँ! जीवन की कम सुनता जाऊँ!

मैं क्या देखूँगा सुनलूँगा, क्या तुम से कुछ कह पाऊँगा;
मुझसे तुम क्या ले पाओगे, तुमको मैं क्या दे पाऊँगा.

सुमधुर शोभन है तुमरा सुर, मोहन अभिनव मधु से मधुकर;
तुम सुनलो मेरे उर के सुर, उर में सुर ले, दे दो नव स्वर.

मैं आनन्दित सुरभित सुर हूँ, अनुभूति से मोहित 'मधु' हूँ;
ऋद्धि सिद्धि की माया से, थिरकित अभिमोहित मोदित हूँ.

127. मेरा मोहन मन मधु माखा * 161/23.09.08

मेरा मोहन मन मधु माखा, मधुमाखी से है ये चाखा;
काँटों ने है इसको राखा, पुष्पों का है ये मधु माखा।

मधु प्रीति माखी मधु विद्या, भर देती मन में मधुर विधा;
प्रभु कृपा ने 'मधु' को साधा, भक्ति ने मन को है बांधा।

धारणा की ध्येयित धारा, प्राणायाम प्रयोजित धरा;
समाधि सम्बोधि क्षरा, यम नियमों से धारित धरा।

प्रत्याहार प्रलोभन हारा, योगासन मुद्रा मधु द्वारा;
ध्यान ध्येय में अर्पित हारा, मिलित साधना का सुर न्यारा।

उपवासों की देह माधुरी, मन आत्मा की प्रीति निखारी;
कीर्तन का रस बरसे प्यारा, आनन्दित बहती प्रभु धारा।

128. मैं मधुमाखी बन कर जाता * 164/23.09.08

मैं मधुमाखी बन कर जाता, पुष्पों से मधु कण ले आता;
मधु ग्रह में मधु को रख आता, मधु स्वामी को अर्पित करता।

प्रति दिन धाता, आता जाता, मधु को अर्जित करता रहता;
एक दिन कोई ऐसा आजाता, मधु माखे मधु को लेजाता।

मैं फिर मधु ग्रह से उड़ जाता, आनन्दित मधु अर्जित करता;
मधु चोरी की आशा करता, 'स्वामी के स्वामी' को लखता!

मेरा माखी मन मख जाता, रखने का भाव बिखर जाता;
मधु जीवन मधु माखा करता, मधु 'मधु' को दे मधुमय करता।

अध्याय 4– करुणानुभूति

129. कंकड़ के कण कण की
* 153/ 05.09.08

कंकड़ के कण कण की कथा कुछ करुण है,
पर 'मधु' रस में डूबी वह आनन्दित सगुण है;
हृदय क्रन्दन से किञ्चित विचलित है,
पर मर्म में वह थिरकित विहँसित है.

उसके बहुरँगी बहुरूपी विरल स्वरूप में,
कितना सौन्दर्य लसित इतिहास छिपा है;
उसके अरमानों की अट्टालिकाओं में,
कितनी विधायें बहारें व्यवस्थायें बिखरीं हैं.

कितनी उल्कायें, आकाश से आकर, उससे मिलीं हैं,
कितने सागरों की मणि, धूल कण बनी हैं;
कितनी पर्वत शिखायें, हिम में ठिठुरीं हैं,
हिम नद सँग नन्दित हो, धरा पर बिखरीं हैं.

पावन पर्वत शिलायें भी मानव से पुजती हैं,
धाराओं में बहे पत्थर भी सुन्दर हो सिहरते हैं;
कितनी शिला कंकड़ धूल, ग्रह उपग्रहों से ला हम देखे हैं,
हमारे कितने शून्य यान अन्य ग्रहों पर जा धूल कण बने हैं.

130. सड़क के कंकड़ का उर कण

मधु गीति सं. 154,   रचना दि. 05.09.08

सड़क के कंकड़ का उर कण,
आज कुछ विरहित विधुर अनमना है;
अपने अतीत के आनन्द सौन्दर्य की याद में,
विचलित व्यथित उन्मना है।

अनन्त रँग रूपों से भरी उसकी काया है,
धूल धूसरित धरा उसकी धाया है;
आकाश जल वायु धूप का साया है,
श्वेत हिम की उसके ऊपर छाया है।

कंकड़ की कड़क से ही, धरा की धड़कन है,
कंकड़ की अकड़ से ही उसकी जकड़न है;
कंकड़ की पकड़ ही उसे बाँधे रखती है,
कंकड़ की सहनशीलता से ही
औरों की सड़क है।

कंकड़ का घनत्व
उसके अन्तरङ्ग आकर्षण से है,
उसकी मन भूमि पञ्च तत्वों से प्लावित है;
उसका छिद्र युक्त भाव भारत्व,
क्या कुछ नहीं सोख सह लेता है।

अपने हृदय के वीरान में भी वह,
जीवाणुओं की 'मधु' बस्ती बसा लेता है;
अपने सर पर मानव वाहन चलने दे,
मानवों को मंजिल पर पहुँचा देता है।

131. मेरे मन की ये श्यामलिमा * 176/13.11.08

मेरे मन की ये श्यामलिमा, मेरे तन की यह काजलिमा!
तुमने ही तो ढलवा दी है, तुमने ही तो रंगवा दी है.

क्यों मानव मन को रचते हो, क्यों निज कर्मों में रंगते हो?
क्यों सेवा में लगवाते हो, क्यों मन को भटका देते हो?

सब सृष्टि की आतुरताएं, सब दृष्टि की कातरताएं;
तुमने दी हैं चेतनताएं, तुमने ली हैं श्यामलिमाएं.

क्यों चिर दयालु तुम हो जाते, क्यों कुछ कठोर प्रभु हो जाते!
क्यों तुम 'मधु' से करवा लेते, क्यों तुम मुझ से बिखरा देते!

मेरा उर गोरा श्यामल है, संस्कारों की गोधूलि है;
प्रारब्धों की प्राकृतता है, तुमरी प्रकृति की भाषा है.

132. चल चल मेरे मन मधुवन में * 182/13.11.08

चल चल मेरे मन मधुवन में, एकाकी प्रचलित प्रति पल में;
आनन्दित यमुना की धुन में, शाखा मृग की मृदु कुँजन में.

मधु माखी के मधु व्यञ्जन में, आँखों के प्यारे खञ्जन में;
तारों की प्रणव भरी ध्वनि में, मन के 'मधु' थिरकित गुँजन में.

सोहं की ध्वनि में मैं गाऊँ, जीवन आभा को दमकाऊँ;
प्रीतम के सुख में रम जाऊँ, धरती की ध्वनि में बह जाऊँ.

अभिनव मधुमय शाश्वत सुन्दर, चेतनता की भरपूर लहर;
जीवन की अभिनव प्रति ध्वनि में, पावनता की प्रति प्रतिध्वनि में.

133. हे हरि तुमने क्या कर डाला
* मधु गीति सं. 175/ रचना दि. 13.11.08

हे हरि! तुमने क्या कर डाला, मेरा मन क्यों यों रंग डाला?
कितनी देदी मुझको ज्वाला, मेरा मन कैसा कर डाला?

हे प्रियतम, कितने दुख देते, मन अपना मम तन को देते;
सीमाओं में सिकुड़ा देते, कुँठाओं में जकड़ा देते।
जब चाहे तुम चलबा देते, जब चाहे तब ठहरा देते;
कब जाने क्या कहला देते, कैसे तुम कुछ करबा देते।

क्यों मैं चिन्ता भय को पालूँ, जो हो पाता, वह कर डालूँ;
जो रह जाता, तुम पर डालूँ, मन तुममें अर्पित कर डालूँ।
तुम ही तो मम मन के प्रेरक, प्रियतम तुम हो जग के सेवक;
सेवक के तुम एकक धारक, 'मधु' आत्मा के तुम प्रति पालक।

134. तुम मेरी मधुरता की मुस्कान हो
* मधु गीति सं. 179, रचना दि. 13.11.08

तुम मेरी मधुरता की मुस्कान हो, क्या तुम मुझे पहचान पा रहे हो?
तुम मेरी व्यापकता की बौछार हो, क्या तुम मुझे परख पा रहे हो?

तुम विश्व की बाधाओं की व्यापकता हो, अनन्त आभा की तुम शोभा हो;
तुम अखिलता की खिलखिलाहट हो, अपरूप का तुम अभिनव स्वरूप हो।
तुम क्यों अशान्त दिग्भ्रान्त हो, तुम क्यों द्विविधा में भयाक्रान्त हो;
तुम उज्ज्वल आशा के निःश्वास हो,
ब्रह्माण्ड की अरुणिमा के तुम प्रतीक हो।

तुम पावन पावक की पहेली हो, जीवन यामिनी की तुम सहेली हो;
'मधु' जीवन के तुम प्रदीप हो, सौष्ठव सरिता के मधु भँवर हो।

135. जगत की जननी नीरवता * 178/13.11.08

जगत की जननी नीरवता, मानव मन की मोदक माधुर्यता;
चेतक की चेतन चतुरता, पावन की प्रेरक प्राणीनता।

प्रभु के प्रेरणा स्रोत को निकट लाओ, विकट वन में नज़र आओ;
प्रकट तन में सिहर जाओ, निकट मन में भव जाओ।

मैं तुम्हारी कृपा को समझ नहीं पाता, तुम्हारी निकटता को देख नहीं पाता;
तुम्हारी चाहत को पहचान नहीं पाता, तुम्हारी राहत को परख नहीं पाता।

तुम अनन्त मर्यादाओं की पहेली हो, विश्व की व्यापकता की तुम सहेली हो;
अनन्त भोगों की तुम भयानकता हो, अनेक रागों की तुम सुरभि हो।

तुम हो सृष्टि के स्नेह प्रेरक ललित नृत्य,
तुम्ही हो सर्व बाधाओं को बेधते ताण्डव;
जीवन की तुम व्यापक धारा, हो 'मधु' आनन्दित प्रखर प्रभा।

136. मम माधुरी की मुखरता * 180/13.11.08

मम माधुरी की मुखरता, तुम प्रकृति की प्राचुर्यता;
मम मनुजता की मधुरिमा, तुम शान्त सुस्मित सघनता।

मन मयूरी की लाज तुम, मधु प्रकृति के सोपान तुम;
मम भाग्य के मधु यान तुम, मेरे हृदय के ध्यान तुम।
में क्या पुकारूँ, क्या कहूँ! तुम को कहाँ कैसे लखूँ!
निज हृदय में कैसे रखूँ! सब सहज मैं कैसे करूँ!

तुम एक रस 'मधु' प्रान्त हो, मैं विरल विरही क्लान्त हूँ;
लखि प्रकृति की प्राचीनता, अभिनव मधुर मैं शान्त हूँ।

137. हे मधु पक्षी तुम क्या देखते हो! * 183/13.11.08

हे 'मधु' पक्षी! तुम क्या देखते हो? क्या परखते हो, क्या सूँघते हो?
क्या सुनते हो, क्या चाहते हो? क्यों आते हो, क्यों चले जाते हो?

तुम कुछ खोजते हो, कुछ सोचते हो; कुछ बोलते हो, कुछ चहकते हो।
कुछ फुदकते हो, कुछ सहमते हो, कुछ शरमाते हो, फिर उड़ जाते हो।

मानव से तुम्हारा रिश्ता पुराना है, तिनकों में तुम्हारा खजाना है;
तनिक देर में तुम्हें उड़ जाना है, हवा के झोंकों संग तुम्हें चल देना है।

तुम्हारा मन प्राण मधु उत्साह भरा है, महाद्वीपों की यात्रा का शौर्य भरा है;
जीवन की माधुरी का रस तुमने पिया है,
सृष्टि की शोभा का रस तुमने चखा है।

138. थिरकित पुलकित सहमित मोहित * 184/13.11.08

थिरकित पुलकित सहमित मोहित, मम मन आशङ्का से पीड़ित;
उर की व्यवधान भरी वीथी, मन की अरमान भरी गीती।

आशा पूरित जीवन चेष्टा, भाषा भावित भूषित निष्ठा;
मानवता की प्रकटित चेष्टा, जीवन की मधुर प्रीति निष्ठा।

देदीप्यमान दीप्तित दृष्टा, दावानल की दाहित चेष्टा;
देदूँ मैं निज मन की इच्छा, उनकी इच्छा मेरी निष्ठा।

अर्पण के पुण्य समर्पण में, तर्पण के तप मोहित मन में;
मैं क्यों सोचूँ, क्यों चिन्तित हूँ! न्यौछावर निर्भर उन पर हूँ!

वे क्या चाहें, मैं क्या जानूँ, क्या कर डालेंगे क्या जानूँ;
सब कुछ उनको मैं दे जाऊँ, 'मधु' प्रेम पयोधि ले जाऊँ।

139. मेरे मन की शून्यता * 162/23.09.08

मेरे मन की शून्यता, कहाँ से आयी, कैसे आयी!
मेरे मन की धैर्यता, कोंन लाया, कैसे आयी!

क्या पाया मैंने, क्या खोया? क्या चाहा मैंने, क्या बोया?
क्यों मोहा मैं हूँ, क्यों रोया? क्यों जागा मैं हूँ, क्यों सोया?
कैसे मेरी प्रकृति उपजी? कैसे पीड़ा मन में उपजी?
क्यों विकृति मेरी थी बिगड़ी? कैसे चाहत मेरी उजड़ी?

तुम क्यों आते हो, गाते हो? क्यों वरवश तुम चल देते हो?
मन वीणा को सुर देते हो, थिरकित पुलकित कर देते हो.
मानव मन के विहँसित साथी, शोभित सज्जा के परिलक्षी!
क्षोभित मन के हे परिदृष्टी, आनन्दित 'मधु' मन के साक्षी!

140. मेरे क्षितिज की गहराइयों में * 226/03.02.09

मेरे क्षितिज की गहराइयों में तुम न झाँको,
मेरे हृदय सागर की लहरों में खोजाओ;
मेरे मन की गहराइयों में सिमट जाओ,
मेरे आनन्द सागर की लहरों में बिखर जाओ.

मेरे उपहास के अट्टहास में तुम न खोओ,
मेरे हृदय की स्रोत गझ में मुझे पाओ;
मेरे मन की नीरवता में मुझे देखो,
मेरे आनन्द की सरिता में तुम खो जाओ.

मेरे उर के उदधि की आभा को तुम निहारो,
मेरे सौन्दर्य की शोभा में दमक जाओ;
मेरे सुरों के सङ्गीत में बिखर जाओ,
मेरे आनन्द की 'मधु' गुफा में सिहर जाओ.

141. मैं मानवता को क्या सुख दूँ * 236/06.02.09

मैं मानवता को क्या सुख दूँ, मैं दानवता को क्या दुख दूँ!
दुख सुख की लहरों में   बहलूँ, आनन्द सुधा हृदि में भरलूँ।

मैं क्यों थिरकित जग को कर दूँ, पुलकित प्रमुदित भव को कर दूँ!
मैं क्यों जागूँ, क्यों सो जाऊँ, मैं क्यों आऊँ, मैं क्यों जाऊँ!

तुम सबके कारण धारण हो, तुम सबके प्रेरक द्योतक हो;
मैं क्यों क्रोधित हूँ विकरित हूँ, मैं क्यों प्रेरित आल्हादित हूँ!

मैं क्यों गीतों से भर जाता, मैं क्यों शोकों को सह जाता!
मैं क्यों अग्नि को उर लेता, मैं क्यों आनन्द सुधा देता!

मैं क्यों आता, मैं क्यों गाता, मैं क्यों मधुकर बन उड़ जाता!
मैं क्यों पानी की धार बना, अग्नि ज्वाला को सह लेता!

मैं क्यों पवनों को उर देदूँ, क्यों गगनों को मैं फैलादूँ;
मैं क्यों ऐसी सृष्टि रचदूँ, 'मधु' चित्तों को क्यों बिखरादूँ!

142. क्या तुम मुझसे गब बाओगे * 238/06.02.09

क्या तुम मुझसे गब बाओगे, क्या तुम 'मधु' को अपनाओगे!
कालिखता मेरी पोंछोगे, पावनता क्या अपनी दोगे!
मैं क्या करता जाता आता, गाता जाता मैं मतियाता;
मानव मन की सुध बुध खोता, तुमरे हृदि की धुन में रहता।

घन घन घन घन घनघोर घटा, तुमरे उर की मोहन त्रिजटा;
मैं लटपटात मन में सिहात, तन सुलझ जात, लट उलझ जात।
मेरे मन में अब आ झाँकें, माधुरिमा की झाँकी ताकें;
रोकें टोकें नाचें गाएं, मन में सिहरें, हद में हाँसें।

143. उर में व्यथा * 319/28.05.09

उर में व्यथा, सुर में कथा, तन में विधा, मन में सुधा;
आनन्द रस की सरसता, प्राणों भरी प्राणीनता.
तव चरण में तल्लीनता, आकृति भरी औचित्यता;
सानिध्य की शुभ सहजता, आराध्य की मधु गहनता.

मानव मनीषी की मधुर चाहन भरी चैतन्यता;
सानन्द सौरभ में मगन, प्रारब्ध की मधु सौम्यता.
शुभ सुरभि है, मन उदधि है, मधु व्योम है, शुधु क्षोभ है;
प्रकृति प्रमोदित क्रिया है, मधु नाद में खद्योत है.

मृदु अधर है, शुधु अमिय है, आनन्द धारा सुघड़ है;
शीतल सुशोभित हृदय है, संस्कृत चलन शुभ छन्द है.
शुभ दृष्टि की शालीनता, 'मधु' वृष्टि की है प्रखरता;
प्रणवित धरणि की मधुरता, व्यापक विभु की विरलता.

144. ख्वाब मैं देखे चला हूँ * 327/30.05.09

ख्वाब मैं देखे चला हूँ विश्व में, स्राव में बहता चला हूँ द्रश्य में;
ब्यक्त हूँ अभिब्यक्त हूँ नव सृष्टि में, कर रहा हूँ कर्म नव अनुरक्ति में.
दृष्टि है शंकित ब्यथित मम मनुज की, दनुज मन आश्वस्त सा भय ग्रस्त है;
सृष्टि की संकुचित दृष्टि से विकट, बट रहा मानव मनोरथ में मगन.

कृष कथा विरहित विधा, संचरित है सोई धरा,
व्योम है सिहरा हुआ, जल मधुर है ठहरा हुआ;
मैं बिखरता बिछुड़ा विहरता, रत बिरत चलता रहा,
आनन्द की अभिब्यक्ति को मैं हृदय में वरता रहा.

प्राणी उत्त्रण है, तरुण है, काया करुण है वरुण है,
संताप की उन्मुक्ति से नन्दित लसित वह मुक्त है;
आक्लान्त मन, विश्रान्त तन, है मुक्त मानव मनों में,
छायी धरा 'मधु' शान्ति में, धाया गगन आनन्द में.

145. तुम न आये तुम न धाये * 260/29.03.09

तुम न आये, तुम न धाये, दर्द कितना हो दिल में जगाये;
टीस कितनी हो उर में उगाये, पीर कितनी हो मन में जगाये.

बिलबिलाता रहा क्रूर जग में, खिलाखिलते रहे लोग जग में;
खिसखिसाता रहा मैं यतन में, पीर आयी न प्राणी के मन में.

लोग करते रहे अपने मन की, सुरति ली ना मेरे मन बदन की;
खोज की ना किसी ने मधु की, प्रीति पायी न प्रियतम के उर की.

आभी जाओ आभी जाओ, जीव को तुम न इतना सताओ;
मेरे मन में तराना सुनाओ, प्रीति अपनी जगत में दिखाओ.

देह दासी बना प्रीति करलो, मानवों को भी मुक्ति सिखालो;
मुक्त प्राणों को 'मधु' संग नचालो, जीव जाग्रत करा भक्ति ढालो.
टीस कितनी हो उर में उगाये, पीर कितनी हो मन में जगाये.

146. स्वप्न में श्वेत हँस देखा है * 188/14.11.08

स्वप्न में श्वेत हँस देखा है, ब्रह्म वेला में उड़ते उसे देखा है;
मधुर सी ज्योति द्योति में माखा, मन्द मधु चाल में बढ़ते है देखा.

श्वेत अद्भुत छटा में वह उड़ता, चलता उड़ता रुकता मोहित करता;
पास में भूरा पक्षी फिर आया, मिलके उससे वो मधुर सिहराया.

चलते उड़ते फुदकते फिर आया, निकट के पक्षियों से मिल धाया;
भाव विह्वल हो छवि आँका हूँ, गद् गद् हूँ, थिरकित पुलकित हूँ.

प्रभु क्या हँस तुम बने आये, 'मधु' से मिलने धरा पै तुम धाये!
मिल के जीवों से तुम यों मुस्काये, बहा आनन्द तुम्हीं उड़ धाये!

अध्याय 5 – कवि अनुभूति

147. मेरी कविता

* 15 / 27.03.08

मेरी कविता तुम किसकी सृष्टि हो!
किस सृष्टि में बिखर जाओगी तुम!

क्या तुम कागज के उर बैठी, कलम की कालिमा का रस हो!
या तुम कमलिनी हो कुयाशा की अथवा वैभव हो बिखरते बृह्माण्ड का!

क्या तुम हो कागज़ में सुप्त, भावों में व्यक्त, आत्मा में तृप्त!
मन में ब्याप्त, तन में लिप्त, हृदय में विचरित, प्राण में प्रेरित!

क्या तुम पुस्तक की सृष्टि में, सृष्टि के सृजन, लय व प्रलय में;
रहना चाहोगी, रह सकोगी, चिर जीवित!

या फिर बसना चाहोगी! मेरी 'मधु' सृष्टि की आत्मा में, चित्त में, शून्य में!
हर प्राण के स्पन्दन में, हर पृथ्वी कण की करुण कथा में!

क्या तुम मिलोगी हर जल धारा से,
हर पावक चिंगारी से, हर पवन की लहर से;
आकाश की शून्यता में बसे; हर राग, हर लय, हर कवित से!

148. कविता की कोमल काया को * 224/20.01.09

कविता की कोमल काया को, कवि तुम कलुषित मत कर देना;
भावों की जाया कविता को, 'मधु' आनन्दित सी छवि देना।

गरिमा में लिपटा कर रखना, भक्ति से भावित भव करना;
छन्दित आल्हादित कर देना, तारक धारक स्वर रच देना।

पृथ्वी की गति सुगन्ध देना, तारों की ज्योति भर देना;
सूर्योदय का सौरभ देना, चन्द्रोदय का रस भर देना।

यम नियमों में बँध कर रहना, योगासन ध्यान किये जाना;
प्राणायामों में रत रहना, अर्पित आत्मा प्रभु को देना।

प्रभु का रस जग को दे देना, आनन्द श्रेय प्रभु को देना;
कविता की मधु आहुति देना, आनन्द तरंग लिये जाना।

149. मेरी ऋचा * 22/02.04.08

मेरी ऋचा, तुम कब ऋतम्भरा होगी!
श्वेत सहस्रार पर खिलकर तुम, कब चैतन्य होगी!

किस दिशा में बहोगी तुम, किस दशा में रहोगी तुम!
किस राग में रगोगी तुम, किस छन्द में नाचोगी तुम!

किस लय में गाओगी तुम, किस ध्वनि पर थिरकोगी तुम!
किस आशा पर आश्रित हो, गोपाल होगी तुम!

शाश्वत तुम, अभिनव तुम, चिर नव तुम, चिर ध्वनि तुम;
तुम मम स्वर, तुम 'मधु' मन, वेद ऋचा, सोहं ध्वनि तुम।

150. मेरी कविते तुम किसकी वृष्टि हो!
* 16/27.03.08

मेरी कविते तुम किसकी वृष्टि हो!
किस सृष्टि में बिखरना चाहोगी तुम!

क्या तुम खोजोगी, हर उस कविता को,
जो अभी सोई है, हर मानव मन में!
क्या तुम सब मनों के मर्म को,
कविता बना कर बहाना चाहोगी!
क्या तुम हर ब्यथा को बहाव दोगी,
क्या तुम आनन्द को और आनन्दित करोगी!

मेरी हर हवा, मेरा हर प्राण पीड़ित है;
कुछ आनन्दित हैं अज्ञान में, कुछ अन–आनन्दित हैं ज्ञान में.

तुम कुछ ऐसे सिहराओ उनके सरों को, पुष्पाच्छादित करो उनके चरणों को;
सहलाओ उनके हृदयों को कि उनका मन निखर जाये, आँसू बिखर जायें.
हृदय हिल जायें, साँस चल जाये,
गान बह जाये, आनन्द आ जाये.

तुम अपना दर्दे दिल मत कहना,
सिर्फ़ सुनना, सहना सीखना, सींचना सिखाना;
रोना समझना, हँसना सिखाना, हँसते जाना,
हँसाते जाना, आनन्दित करना.

तुम पुरूष्कार मत खोजना, प्रतिष्ठा की मत सोचना,
कीमत की मत, मत बनाना;
तुम सिर्फ़ चलना, 'मधु' हृदय से हृदयों तक,
दुख सुख की लय से, आनन्द की लय तक.
जीव से ब्रह्म तक, ब्रह्म से जीव तक.

151. कविता की यह मृदु तरङ्ग
* 43/23.04.08

कविता की यह मृदु तरङ्ग,
'मधु' तुम्हारे उर में कैसे उठी!
क्यों तुम्हारा हृद, हिम नद बन बह उठा!
गागर सर पर लिये, तुम कैसे सरस हो उठे!
क्यों तुम्हारे भाव वरसे, कैसे तुम गा उठे!

क्या किसी ने तुममें चिंगारी डाली!
या किसी चिंगारी ने तुम्हें जलाया!
क्या किसी चिंगारी को देख, तुम प्रज्ज्वलित हुए!
या आनन्द की अनुभुति से तरङ्गित हुए!

क्या तुम गत जगत की गति जाने!
या तुम, जगत जनक की जुगति जाने!
क्या जगत की जुगति का गीत जाने!
या जगत का चेतना स्रोत जाने!

क्या तुम लिखने लगे, किसके लिये, लिखने लगे!
क्या गुनगुनाने लगे, किसकी लय मिलाने लगे!
क्यों सुर साधने लगे, क्या राग गाने लगे!
किसको सुनाने लगे, किसकी सुनने लगे!

तुम्हारी कविता, आनन्द तरङ्ग हो उठी,
भाव सरिता में जल तरङ्ग बज उठी;
अपनी मन वीणा पर, वह कुछ गा उठा,
तुम्हारी हृदय वीणा, उससे सुर मिला गा उठी.

152. मधु तुम्हारी कविता * 44 / 24.04.08

'मधु' तुम्हारी कविता, प्रभु को आनन्द देती है;
उनकी आनन्द तरङ्ग, तुम्हें और आनन्द देती है.
तुम कविता लिखते जाते हो,
जीवन को जीवन देते हो.

तुम्हारा राग लय सुर नया है,
चैतन्य की चिंगारी तुम्हारी कविता की काया है;
वह लय है जीवन की, सुर है शम्भु का,
छन्द है जगत का, राग है अनादि के नाद का.

तुम सभी के आनन्द की प्रतीक्षा मत करो,
तुम केवल लिखो और स्वच्छन्द गाओ;
जगत की गति को वह गति देगी,
कुछ जीवों को आनन्दित करेगी.

तुम्हारी कविता की चिंगारी, किसी को प्रज्ज्वलित करेगी,
उसका मन प्रकाशित होगा, रोशनी तुम पर पड़ेगी;
वह भी किसी को रोशन करेगा, जगत रोशन हो जायेगा,
तुम कविता की आहुति दोगे, प्रभु प्रसन्न हो जायेंगे!

तुम केवल चिंगारी जलाओ, जगाओ, जनाओ, गाओ,
चेतना फैलाओ, जगत जब कभी जगमग हो ही जायेगा;
आत्मा झलमल होंगी, तुम तरङ्गित होगे, सब आनन्दित होंगे,
और तुम्हें चिंगारी देने बाले गुरु भी, आनन्दित हो जायेंगे!

***

अध्याय 6 : प्राकृतिक

153. तुम्हारा सूर्योदय के साथ आना
* 48/ 05.05.08

तुम्हारा प्रति दिन सूर्योदय के साथ आना,
नव प्राण, नव उल्लास को साथ लाना;
सबको आनन्द से भर जाना, तुम्हारी कृपा का है खजाना।

ब्राह्मी वेला में, पक्षियों की कुँजन, पक्षी परिवार की, मिलित साधना की गुँजन;
विश्व को अर्पित, 'मधु गीति' का व्यञ्जन, सूर्योदय को है आनन्द अभिनन्दन !

प्रातः वायु का शीतल मन्द सुगन्ध प्रवाह,
पार्श्व आँगन में श्वेत पुष्पों का विहरण;
हँबर नदी का कलरव प्रवाह, हिरणों का उन्मुक्त विचरण।

घर में गूफी का प्रातः प्रणाम, स्नेह भरे स्पर्ष के लिये अवलोकन,
बिल्ली का प्यार से पूंछ से स्पर्ष करते हुए, नये जल का निवेदन;
स्नान कक्ष में बेसुध सोए चींटे का, अनायास उठ जाना,
पार्श्व आँगन में चिड़ियों गिलहरियों का दाने का आह्वान।

मन का पाञ्चजन्य, प्रातः कर्मों में प्रवृत होना,
प्राणायाम, साधना, योगासन, स्वाध्याय में संयत होना;
मन का अनायास निर्मल हो जाना,
'मधु' गीति का स्वयमेव तरङ्गित हो जाना।

***

153 H. मधु छन्द * 413B/11.07.09

सूर्य को सजाये, धरणि को जगाये; शून्य को सुर दिये, साक्षी सबको किये।
नीलिमा उर लिये, उदधि को तर किये; सुर मधुर मन लिये, तुम रंगे सब हुये।

154. श्वेत हिम कणों की बृष्टि ले * 240/18.02.09

श्वेत हिम कणों की बृष्टि ले, तुम आये 'मधु' प्रेम लिये;
त्रिभुवन में तुम व्याप्त हो रहे, फुलझड़ियों के हार लिये।

श्यामल सारंग के मधु उर में, माधव मन की भाषा में;
गाते जाते हो 'मधु गीति' पावन सी प्रभु–शाला में।
विश्व तुम्हारा प्रेम सरोवर, मैं तुमरा प्रेमी प्रभुवर;
आता जाता मैं तव अन्तर, प्रियतम तुम रहते मम उर।

मानव मन पढ़ता है तुमको, तव प्रकृति की भाषा में;
सर्दी गर्मी हिम वर्षा में, मोहन मृदु अभिलाषा में।
तुमको पढ़ते और समझते मानव मन हैं मुस्काते;
निज सृष्टि में तुम खोजाते, हिम बृष्टि बन तुम धाते।

155. हे पृथ्वी! प्रभु के निर्देशन में * 81/02.06.08

हे पृथ्वी! प्रभु के निर्देशन में तुम्हारा,
हम सभी को लेकर, सूर्य की परिक्रमा करना;
इतना   रोमांचक, इतना व्यस्त होना,
अद्भुत है कितना, आनन्द मय है कितना!

तुम हमें गोद में ले, घूमती जाती हो, अपनी कक्षा में दिवा रात्रि;
दिन रात के फेर में पड़े हम, नहीं देख पाते तुम्हारी गति।

साथ ही तुम सूर्य के चारो ओर कभी इधर,
कभी उधर, विशाल व्योम में विचरती हो;
कभी तुम आकाश गंगा के 'मधु' तारों को निकट से देख लेती हो।

कभी सौर मंडल के ग्रह घूमते घूमते तुम्हारे निकट आजाते हैं,
कभी सूर्य के उस ओर वे दूर चले जाते हैं।

156. हे पृथ्वी! हम तुम्हारी गोद में * 81A/02.06.08

हे पृथ्वी! हम तुम्हारी गोद में, दिन रात खेल करते हैं;
तुम्हारा दर्द, तुम्हारी व्यथा, फिर भी हम समझ नहीं पाते हैं।

तुम्हारे विश्व में हम कितने उचित अनुचित कर्म करते हैं,
तुम्हारे भाव, तुम्हारी व्यथा का विचार नहीं करते हैं;
तुम्हारा हमारे प्रति अतिशय स्नेह,
हमें बिना कष्ट दिये द्विगति में चलते रहना,
हमें उत्साहित आनन्दित कर देता है।

माँ! तुम रात दिन, वर्ष भर, चलती रहती हो!
तुम कितनी दयालु, धीर और सहनशील हो!
युगों युगों से चल, तुमने हमें विकसित सुयोग्य किया है।
पल पल पल्लवित कर हमें, 'मधु' मानव बना दिया है।

157. हे पृथ्वी! तुम सूर्योन्मुख हो * 82/02.06.08

हे पृथ्वी! तुम सूर्योन्मुख हो,
अपने गोलार्द्ध में प्रकाश न आने दे, रात्रि कर देती हो।
अपने 'मधु' अंक में सृष्टि को ले, रात्रि में सुला लेती हो।

वह भी कुछ इस तरह कि यह क्रिया सतत चले,
कुछ सोयें, कुछ जगें, कुछ सुबह शाम देखें;
सृष्टि का कार्य सुचारु चले, सभी प्राणी जाग्रत सुप्त संतुलित रहें।

कितनी नियमित संतुलित है तुम्हारी गति,
कितनी नियंत्रित है तुम्हारी अँगड़ाई;
सतत प्यार में सबको खींचती सँभालती साधती,
तुम्हारी गुरुत्वाकर्षण शक्ति की गहराई।

158. हे पृथ्वी! कितना योजना मय है * 82A/02.06.08

हे पृथ्वी! कितना योजना मय है, तुम्हारा अपने ध्रुवों पर घूमना!
ध्रुवों का धीरे धीरे स्थान परिवर्तन होना, मौसम परिवर्तित होना.

कितनी अनुपम है तुम्हारी देह, नील जल, श्वेत हिम, हरे वन;
विचरते जीव जन्तु मनुज, बुद्धि रचित उपग्रह वायुयान व शून्य यान.

सूर्योन्मुख हो सबको 'मधु' प्रकाश से भर देना,
तारे निहारिकाओं को नजरों से ओझल कर देना;
रात्रि को फिर तारों का सप्तरङ्गी रूप दिखा देना,
प्रातः पक्षियों के कलरव के साथ, सब को उठा देना.

159. हे पृथ्वी! तुम अपने शरीर की सतह पर * 83/02.06.08

हे पृथ्वी! तुम अपने शरीर की सतह पर, सबको धारण किये विचरती हो!
अपने उर की ज्वाला तुम किसी को दिखाती नहीं हो!

तुम्हारे शरीर की, नील मणि जैसी 'मधु' झलक भी,
मानव तुम से दूर चन्द्रमा पर जाकर ही देख पाया है;
तुम्हारी गति की गहनता, अनन्त चलने की लालसा,
मुझे तुमसे प्यार करा देती है.

तुम्हारी अनखोजी वनस्पतियां, बहु आयामी जीव जन्तु,
निरन्तर विकासोन्मुख मानव, सब तुम्हारे प्यार में नृत्यरत हैं;
तुम्हारी सृष्टि की असामञ्यस्यता, समय रहते साम्य हो जाती है,
कितनी विकराल परिस्थितियां आती हैं, समय चलते सब बदल जाती हैं.

हे पृथ्वी माँ! तुम चलती रहती हो, चलाती रहती हो,
ओंकार ध्वनि में नाचती रहती हो;
'मधु' सृष्टि को चलाती रहती हो, सृष्टा को रिझाती चलती हो.

160. भारत की भाव भूमि * 24/02.04.08

भारत की भाव भूमि, विश्व की विश्वसनीयता;
भारत का भूमा भाव, सृष्टि की भवतव्यता।

राम का आदर्श जीवन, शिव का योग तन्त्र ताण्डव आयुर्वेद विवाह प्रचलन;
कृष्ण की सोलह कलाओं का आकर्षण, अर्जुन का भक्ति पूर्ण समर्पण।
आनन्दमूर्ति की नव्य मानवता, बुद्ध का बोध, पतञ्जलि का योग दर्शन;
भरत का वीरत्व, गुरु नानक का नाम, कबीर का पन्थ, जैनी सात्विक जीवन।

मीरा, सूर, तुलसी, चैतन्य, विवेकानन्द व रवीन्द्र की भक्ति निष्ठा;
शिवाजी का शौर्य, लक्ष्मीबाई का लक्ष, अहिल्याबाई होल्कर की सात्विकता।
गाँधी की सत्य निष्ठा, सुभाष भगत पटेल आजाद व तिलक की त्याग निष्ठा;
राजेन्द्र राधाकृष्णन गुलजारीलाल नन्दा, लालबहादुर व कलाम की राष्ट्र निष्ठा।

सभी योगियों का योग, ज्ञानियों का ज्ञान योग, भक्तों का सुयोग;
सभी धर्मों की कर्म व मर्म भूमि, मानव धर्म का सुप्रयोग।
आध्यात्मिक विज्ञान का सृष्टा, भूमा भाव का 'मधु' दृष्टा;
शून्य से अनन्त का शोध कर्त्ता, भूमा भाव का प्रयोग कर्त्ता।

161. मेरे मन के मेघ * 144/20.08.08

मेरे मन के 'मधु' मेघ! तुम कभी पूरे हृदयाकाश में छाये नज़र आते हो;
कभी निरव चिदाकाश में तुम, कहीं भी नज़र नहीं आते।
कभी सब तुम्हें देखते हैं, कभी तुम सबको देखते हो;
कभी काले भूरे हो गरजते बरसते हो, श्वेत शान्त हो कभी सिहरते हो।

ध्यान यान में पैठ जब कभी तुमसे मिलने आता हूँ,
अठखेली सी तुम करते हो संग ऊपर नीचे चलते हो;
कभी निकट आजाते हो, पर दूर कभी चल देते हो,
नभ में मैं जब खोजता हूँ, तुम मुझ में ही रह जाते हो।

162. कहाँ चल दिये हो सारङ्ग तुम * 258/12.03.09

कहाँ चल दिये हो सारङ्ग तुम, मेरे उर का राग लिये?
नील गगन में विचर रहे हो, सतरङ्गी सौन्दर्य लिये.

सबके सर पर उड़ते रहते, श्यामल सुमधुर रूप लिये;
अपनी धुन में चलते रहते, पुलकित थिरकित भाव लिये.
प्रातः वेला में उठ धाते, क्या क्या दिन भर तुम कर जाते!
चिड़ियों के जैसे उड़ जाते, मोहन मधुमय गीत सुनाते.

लेकर तुम रङ्गीली टोली, नभ उर में खेलत नित होली;
क्या क्या अभिनव रङ्ग लगाते, पृथ्वी जन को तुम सिहराते.
द्युति चमकाते लहर दिखाते, फागुन में सावन बन धाते;
होली के 'मधु' गीत सुनाते, टोली पर टोली बन धाते.

163. कनाडा का कण कण * 93/14.06.08

कणादि की कल्पना से भरा है, कनाडा का कण कण;
प्राकृतिक सौन्दर्य से परिपूर्ण है, कनाडा का मन प्राण.
मूल वंशजों की सहजता, आगन्तुकों की मन गहनता;
प्रवासियों की प्रासंगिकता, विश्व समाज की मधुरता.

मानवीय मूल्यों की प्रयोगशाला, अध्ययन मनन खुलापन;
भक्ति कर्म ज्ञान का प्रसारण, योग तन्त्र का त्वरित प्रचलन.
मानवों का परस्पर मधुर व्यवहार, पशु पक्षियों के प्रति समादर;
ले चल रहा है सभ्यता को अन्तर्मन, विकसित है मानव मन, अवचेतन.

विश्व सभ्यताओं का है यहां 'मधु' संगम,
विश्व संस्कृतियों का है आवागमन;
स्वार्थ से परमार्थ की ओर हैं हम प्रेरित, विश्व के प्रदीप हैं हम प्रज्ज्वलित.

164. बाढ़ के बाद नदी * 563/15.10.09

बाढ़ के बाद नदी लघु होती, धार कम होती बालू बहु होती;
पहाड़ों से निकल नदी चुप होती, बृहत धारा में त्वरित बह लेती.

बाढ़ उपरान्त शान्त वह होती, बालुका में प्रशान्ति भर देती;
बहती धाराएं धीर हो जातीं, दूरियां तटों से हैं सह लेतीं.
बाढ़ के वक्त नदी बढ़ जाती, गाँवों पेड़ों किनारों को ढहती;
पाट चौड़ा किये है चल देती, जो भी मिलता उसे बहा लेती.

पार करने पथिक प्रचुर चलते, बाढ़ की विभीषिका लख लेते;
नाव में बैठ धार तर लेते, बालुका का अनन्त उर तकते.
विहङ्गम द्रश्य बाढ़ का होता, तरङ्गित द्रश्य बाद का करता;
'मधु' उर धारें बहुत बह जातीं, त्रसित त्रसरेणु क्या क्या कह जाती.

165. बाढ़ की विभीषिका * 564/15.10.09

बाढ़ की विभीषिका क्या कहती, कितने बृक्षों के उर फुरा देती;
किनारे कितनी व्यथा कह देते, शिखर कितने धरा पै ढह जाते.

गाँव कितने उजड़ बिखर जाते, जीव जीवन कहाँ चले जाते;
कगारें कितनीं नयी बन जातीं, धारें कितनीं नयी निकल धातीं.
कितने पाषाण बालुका बनते, कितना बृक्षों की शाखें हैं सहतीं;
कितनीं फसलों की फ़िज़ा गुल होती, कितने प्राणों की दुन्दभी बजती.

काया विस्तीर्ण किये चलतीं तुम, समाये सबको स्वयं अपने उर;
हिलातीं डुलातीं प्रकृति का घर, मिटातीं डुबातीं त्रणों का उर.
तुम्हारे बृहत मन में मैं खोता, बालुका बन तुम्हारे उर सोता;
मुझे तुम क्या क्या नहीं कह जातीं, मेरा 'मधु' मन लिये न क्यों चलतीं.

166. बादल के उर से आ निकले * 588/04.11.09

बादल के उर से आ निकले, कितना सुन्दर रूप लिये;
कितने चित्र विचित्र बनाये, रवि तुमने आने से पहले।

बादल के बहु रूप दिखाये, कितने सागर नभ बिखराये;
कितनी ज्योति की धाराएं, अगणित रूप लिये धायी हैं।
कभी चले आये तुम छिपके, कभी तेज अपना दिखलाये;
कभी बादलों के घूँघट से, तुम आये जैसे शरमाये।

किरणों ने प्रकाश फैला के, देखा सब जग को मुसकाके;
आँखें सबकी दी चौंधाके, फिर खुद छिपे घटा में जाके।
तुमने जगा दिये सब आके, सोये थे जो मन को ढाके;
'मधु' ज्योति जग को दिखलाके, जागृत सब के उर कर डाले।

167. हँबर तट पर झाड़ियों का झुरमुट * 62/14.05.08

हँबर तट पर झाड़ियों का झुरमुट,
गिलहरियों के पेड़ों पर, चढ़ने उतरने की छटपटाहट;
चहकती चिड़ियों के उड़ने की फुरफुराहट,
सजे वृक्षों पर श्वेत पुष्पों की खिलखिलाहट।
शान्त श्वेत बतखों का जल विचरण करना,
वन जीवों का चुलबुलाहट में जल पीना;
श्वान का भ्रमण करते हुए, जल धारा में कूद पड़ना,
पक्षियों का पेड़ से कूद, जल में डुबकी लगाना।

हँवर तुमने कितनी पीढ़ियों को राह दिखायी है,
कितने व्यापारों की नींव लगाई है;
कितने सुहावने फूल सजा, टोरोन्टो नगरी बसायी है,
कितनी धाराएं बहाई हैं और औन्टारिओ झील में मिलाई हैं।
हर समय याद आती है मुझे, तुम्हारे चलते रहने की छटपटाहट;
मेरे मन को वरवश निकट बुलाने की, तुम्हारी 'मधु' आहट।

168. हँवर मैंने तुम्हारे कितने रूप देखे हैं! * 63/14.05.08

हँवर मैंने तुम्हारे कितने रूप देखे हैं!
जल के कितने ज्वार घाटे देखे हैं!

कभी तुम किनारा छलांग, बह जाना चाहती हो,
कभी अपनी पेंदी के, पत्थरों में सिमट जाती हो;
कभी तुम स्वयं बर्फ बन जाती हो,
कभी बर्फ के नीचे, चुपचाप बह लेती हो।

कितनी बार ग्रीष्म में तुम्हारे साथ, चल कर देखा हूँ,
कितनी बार शीत में बिछुड़ कर, तुम्हें ठिठुरते देखा हूँ;
कितनी बार, मीठे सेव और शहतूत, तुमने खिलाये हैं,
कितनी बार, अपने सहमते हिरणों से, तुमने मिलाया है।

कितनी बार, तुम्हारी झाड़ियों की शांत गुफाओं में चला हूँ,
कितनी बार, तुम्हारे बिखरते पत्थरों पर बैठ तुम्हें देखा हूँ;
कितनी बार, तुम्हारे तट के बृक्षों से बात किया हूँ,
कितनी बार, तुम्हारी कलरव ध्वनि में बैठ,
सृष्टा का 'मधु' ध्यान किया है।

169. शिशिर के आने की आहट में * 65/14.05.08

शिशिर के आने की आहट में, पेड़ों की पत्तियां रंग बदलती हैं,
उनका नारंगी गुलाबी नीबुआ रंग, उनकी मन व्यथा को व्यक्त करता है;
पर मानव मन, उनके बदले रंगों को, उनका रूप समझ आनन्द लेता है।

पत्तियां शिशिर के आने की व्यथा में, अनन्त रंगों में बिखर जाती हैं;
पेड़ों से उतर धरा पर विचरती हैं, वायु वेग से उड़ सब जगह दौड़ पड़ती हैं।
सम्भवतः वृक्ष के ऊपर रहने के संस्कार को क्षय करने;
धरा के हर कोने था, धरा की 'मधु' धूल से मिलती हैं।
जन सुजन के चरणों में जा, साष्टाङ्ग प्रणाम करती हैं

170. नियाग्रा प्रपात की जल तरङ्ग * 94/16.06.08

नियाग्रा की नील झील का जल प्रपात,
थिरकित है पुलकित है, मधुरिमा से है ओत प्रोत;
जल धारा का यकायक अधोपात,
इन्द्र धनुष रच देता है, आकाश में निष्णात।

अचानक गिरी जल धारा की कुछ बूँदों का ऊर्ध्व गमन,
आकाश में जाना, छाना और वर्षण;
कर देता रोमांचित थिरकित मानव मन,
जल तरङ्ग से तरङ्गित हो जाता जन जन।

जल धारा के अनचाहे उतरने का व्यतिरेक,
ले जाता जल मन को, आकाश में अशोक;
जन मन को भी कर देता भावुक, भिंगो देता 'मधु' प्राण, भर देता कुहक।

171. नियाग्रा के जल कणों का अस्तित्व * 97/14.05.08

नियाग्रा के जल प्रपात से, कितने जल कणों का अस्तित्व उठा!
कितनी वायु जल मय हुई, कितनी सूर्य किरणें शीतल हुई!

कितने आकाश ध्वनित हुये, कितने पशु पक्षी चह चहाये;
कितने मानव मन तरङ्गित हुये, कितने सुप्त हृदय जाग्रत हुये।

कितने जल कण मृदुल धारा में मिल बह उठे,
कितने सूर्य किरणों से मिल, इन्द्र धनुष बन उठे!
कितने जल कण वायु से मिल बह उठे, जन जन की साँसों में रम उठे!

कितने जल कण आकाश में धाये, वन, उपवन, राहों से गले मिलने आये!
कितने हृदयों को 'मधु' प्रेम में बाँधा, कितने दम्पतियों को प्रेम में साधा!

172. नियाग्रा जल प्रपात से पूर्व * 96/14.05.08

नियाग्रा जल प्रपात से पूर्व, ओन्टारिओ झील का नील जल,
'मधु' गहराई में है मृदुल स्वप्निल;
पर फिर पत्थरों पर चल, वह हो उठता है चपल,
झूम उठता है उसे देख श्वेत सीगल।

पत्थरों पर त्वरित गति से चल, गति से आनन्दित नीरव जल;
मन में पुलकित अलोकित जल, नियति की सोचे हो उठता है और नील।

थिरकते मचलते नील जल का, अनायास अपने धरातल को खोदेना,
धीर जल का विह्वल हो जाना, उसके जीवन का हिल जाना;
सृष्टि का इस दारुण घटना को निहारना,
निहारिका का नीरव हो जाना।

अनजानी गहराई में कूदना जाता है उसे पड़,
रोमाञ्चित हो जाता है, उसका मन प्राण;
यह हृदय द्रावक घटना, उसके अस्तित्व के लिये, चुनौती जाती है बन।

इस प्रपात के सामूहिक संघर्ष वश, जल के कितने कण विद्युत बनाये;
कितने अणु वायु के साथ बह गये,
कितने आकाश में उठ 'मधु' इन्द्र धनुष बनाये।

**

172 H.   मधु छन्द * 457 BC/31.07.09

सौन्दर्य मन का ही बिखर, होता प्रकट है जगत में;
जो जगत का सौन्दर्य है, जाता बिखर मन जगत में।

सौन्दर्य मन का ही बिखर, होता प्रकट है जगत में;
जो जगत का सौन्दर्य है, जाता बिखर मन जगत में।

173. नियाग्रा की नीरव बूंदें * 98/14.05.08

नियाग्रा जल प्रपात की नीरव बूँदें,
अनायास अवरोह की आशंका में हैं आँखें मूँदे;
धीमी हुई गति से गंभीर हुई बूँदें, टटोलती हैं बाँध की गहराई नयन मूँदे.

कुछ बूँदें करती हैं प्रयास, धरा तल से जुटने का,
बाँध के इसी ओर रहने का, उसकी गरिमा समझने का;
आगे की ऊपर की बूँदों को, उस ओर जाते देख,
विस्मित हैं, भयमय हैं, और कुछ हैं, अशोक.

पीछे बहते जल के संवेग से पीड़ित, नीचे की धाराओं से प्रकम्पित;
बाँध के ऊपर बहने को प्रताड़ित, जल बूँदें हैं व्यथा से आलोड़ित.

अनायास आये आवेग की जल धारा,
ले चलती है उन्हें उस ओर, करके आत्महारा;
विस्मित जल बूँदों का 'मधु' सकाश, विस्मृत कर देता है मानव का चिदाकाश.

174. नियाग्रा का जल ताण्डव * 99/14.05.08

नियाग्रा की जल धारा का इतनी गहराई में अचानक गिरना,
साथ की बूँदों का तड़ पड़ाना;
कुछ बूँदों का परस्पर संघात से ऊपर उठ जाना,
कुछ का नीचे धारा बन बह जाना.

इस गहन सामूहिक जल ताण्डव में, बूँदों के इस असामयिक समावरोह में;
कुछ बूँदों के हुए संहार में, कुछ के आरोह में,
वायु होजाती है आद्रित, आकाश हो जाता है द्रवित

जल तरङ्गों से हो आलोड़ित, मन तरङ्गों को कर लेते हैं झंकृत;
नियाग्रा जल प्रपात के 'मधु' दृष्टा, झाँकते हैं इसमें सृष्टा.

175. नियाग्रा जल प्रपात से थिरकित * 95/16.06.08

नियाग्रा जल प्रपात से थिरकित, कुछ जल प्राण उड़ धाते आकाश,
सूर्य रश्मियों में रम, बन जाते इन्द्र धनुष;
पक्षी कलरव कर, छू लेते 'मधु' आकाश,
नील वस्त्र धारी मानव, नीचे नौका में करते निर्यास.

पञ्च तत्व के उभरते पहाड़, मचलता जल,
उड़ती पवन, उमड़ता गगन, कर देता मानव मन को मगन;
ब्राह्मी चित्त से व्याप्त पञ्च तत्त्व, हो जाता पुलकित,
चकित मानव, पशु पक्षी पुष्प, प्रमुदित हो, हो जाते थिरकित.

176. जल प्रपात को निहारते नर नारी * 100/14.05.08

नियाग्रा जल प्रपात को निहारते नर नारी;
बूँदों के बरसने के रस से, आल्हादित हैं मनोहारी.

सामने बाँध के ऊपर बह रही, विह्वल जल धारा का सतत प्रपात;
ऊपर आकाश में बना इन्द्र धनुष, मन को कर देता भावों से आप्लुत.

जल बूँदों का प्रपात संघात से ऊपर उठ, चहुँ ओर दूर दूर विखर जाना;
मानव तन मन को सराबोर कर देना, प्रेम रस में भिंगो उन्हें पर वश कर देना.

परिजनों का मिल कर जल प्रपात देखना,
मन्द मन्द उतरती ऊर्ध्वरेता फुहारों में भींगना;
मृदु मन का पुलकित प्रफुल्लित होना,
बूँदों का है मानो, बृह्म से मिल आनन्दित होना.

नीचे नौका में नील वस्त्रों में विहरती नर नारियों की नन्दित टोली;
ऊपर से गिरते 'मधु' जल को देख, आत्म हारा हुए जन मन डोली.

177. श्यामल सारङ्ग नीलाम्बर में * 142/20.08.08

श्यामल सारङ्ग नीलाम्बर में, गढ़ता बुनता छवि प्रति पल में;
कितनी क्रीड़ा सारङ्ग स्वर में! नीरवता कितनी नभ उर में!

कितने द्वीपों को तुम गढ़ते, कितने सागर उर में रखते?
कितने मन की भाषा पढ़ते, साजों में कितने तुम सजते?
पर्वत पशु पक्षी तुम बनते, नभ नाटक में नायक रहते;
बहु आयामों में रम लेते, झंकृत स्पन्दित हो जाते।

विचलित बिखरे तुम जब रहते, विरहित बेसुध बेमन होते;
वायु के झोंके आजाते, विहँसित थिरकित तुम चल देते।
परिलक्षित दृष्टा को करके, मन सृष्टा में अर्पित करके;
आओ पृथ्वी के प्राङ्गण में, 'मधु' प्राणों के हृदयाङ्गन में।

178. मेघों का सौन्दर्य सुहाया * 143/20.08.08

मन मोहक मेघों का सौन्दर्य सुहाया;
शोभा 'मधु' भायी, शिल्प सुहाया।

मुक्ति जो भी जल कण पा पाये, वायु बादल जो बन पायी;
पावक पावन जो कर पायी, धरती देखे मन मन सिहरायी।
जीवन ज्वाला दे वरमाला, कर देती विस्मृत नभ बाला;
ले जाती तुमको मधु वाला, चल देते तुम पी मधु प्याला।

स्नेही जन को तुम देखे, सहमे सिहरे मन तुम देखे;
विरही मन को तुम हो ताके, उत्सुक हो स्वजनों को झाँके।
मन तुमरा जब भी भर जाये, नभ से प्रीति जब निभ जाये;
भू माँ से मिलने घर आना, भूमा से वृष्टि बन धाना।

अध्याय 7 – विविध भाषा साहित्य

(संस्कृत, ब्रज, बङ्गला, गुजराती, पञ्जाबी, उर्दू व अंग्रेजी)

संस्कृत / हिन्दी भाषा (SAM'SKRTA/HINDI)

179. त्वम् मम आनन्द स्रोत

* 18 / 17.11.08 (संस्कृत/हिन्दी)

त्वम् मम आनन्द स्रोत, त्वम् मम आश्रय पोत;
त्वम् मम जीवनस्य द्योत, त्वम् मम प्राणेर प्रणेत.
त्वम् अस्माकम् प्राण स्रोत, त्वम् विश्वस्य चेतन ज्योत;
त्वम् उर मम, त्वम् स्वर मम, त्वमसि सम्बल केवल मम.

त्वम् धारा, त्वम् मम आधारा, त्वम् पथ मम, त्वम् मम त्वर धारा;
त्वम् विद्या, त्वम् ज्ञान प्रभा मम, त्वम् स्वर, वीणा, भाव स्वयम् त्वम्.
त्वम् उर मम जीवन सुर धावित, त्वम् मन मंहि तन्मय भव गावत;
जीवन ज्वार उदधि तव आवत, 'मधु' मन उदधि बहत तब धावत.

180. स्वर मम त्वम्

* 190/17.11.08 (संस्कृत/हिन्दी)

स्वर मम त्वम् वीणा वादनि मम, आनन्द मधुर आलोक स्वयम्;
थिरकित पुलकित मन आनन्दम्, जीवन ज्योति त्वम् अस्माकम्.
मम जीवन धारा स्वर हारा, तव मन मंहि मम मन सुर हारा;
जीवन सम्पादन सुमधुर स्वर, सानिध्य प्रणेता प्राण सुमधुर.

स्वर संगमस्य त्वम् त्रिवेणी, जीवन स्वर मंहि त्वम् सुर वेणी;
प्रति पालक त्वम्, सुर धारक त्वम्, जीवन सरिता संचालक त्वम्.
धाराये धरा बहति प्रमुदित, तव ध्यान स्रोत सर्वे थिरकित;
'मधु' जीवनस्य गति उत्प्रेरक, आनन्दित अभिनव तारक त्वम्.

181. त्वमसि मम सर्व श्रेय * 194/26.11.08   (संस्कृत/हिन्दी)

त्वमसि मम सर्व श्रेय, त्वमेकम् मम ध्यान ध्येय;
प्रणम्यम् त्वम् सर्व ज्ञेय, अर्पित मम सकल प्रेय।

स्वप्ने त्वयि सघन सुख मम, शयने त्वम् आश्रय मम;
जीवने त्वम् रसघन मम, निःश्वासे त्वम् आश्वासन मम।
सम्पदे मम विवेकी मन, विपदे त्वम् धीरज मम;
शासने अनुशासन त्वम्, विराजित हृदयासन मम।

राजित त्वम् निखिल भुवने, मम मन कुञ्जे, हृदय निकुञ्जे;
पञ्च तत्वे चित्त प्रवाहे, महत अहम् प्रस्फुट गुण धामे।
अभिनव अद्भुत त्वयि सोहम्, अनन्ते त्वयि आदि अन्त मम;
त्वमसि 'मधु' अन्तर्मन, सुमधुर सर्वग आत्मा त्वम् मम।

ब्रज भाषा (BRAJA BHA'S'A')

182. सखी री श्याम नाहिं बन आये! * 329/30.05.09

सखी री श्याम नाहिं बन आये!
लता पता कुमिलाय रहे हैं, चातक मन अकुलाये;
गोपिन्ह के मन बिखर रहे हैं, हलधर मन सकुचाये।

जमुना जल कल कल करि धावत, विकल राधिका उर अकुलावत;
बालक धेनु निहारत जाबत, श्याम सखा सकुचाये।
सोहन सुभग श्याम उर माला, देखन चहत सकल ब्रज वाला;
सुन्दर सुघड़ सुहाबति डाला, लतन्ह बीच विहरत ब्रज वाला।

तन तरसाये, मन हरषाये, कब वे आये, जान न पाये;
मुरली की मोहन सी धुनि पै, राग 'मधु' मन गाये।
सखी री श्याम आज बन आये।

183. सखी री हौं रहबति इहँ नाहीं * 40/17.04.08 (ब्रज भाषा)

सखी री, हौं रहबति इहँ नाहीं;
हौं रहबति अब नंद नन्दन सँग, दुख सुख, सब बिसराई.

तन इहाँ रहतु, मन न रहतु, मोर आत्मा बृज ते बसति;
भोजन करति भवन रहति, ब्रज बालन्ह संग खेल करत.
भोर भये, जमुना तट धावत, ग्वाल बाल संग   वेनु बजावत;
गोकुल तों बृन्दावन जावत, गोवर्द्धन जाइ, धेनु चरावत.

मधुवन मधुर, माधुरी भावति, कृष्ण चाहनी, लखन चहति;
मन मम फुरत, तन जग फिरत, गोकुल फिरति, बरवस रहति.
सरदी गरमी, कछु नहिं लागत, बरखा बिच हौं, न्हावत फिरत;
'मधु' मन भयहु, कृष्ण अनुरागी, तारे संग प्रीति मोरी लागी.

184. मुरली वारौ सखि आयौ ऐ * 281/09.04.09 (ब्रज भाषा)

मुरली वारौ सखि आयौ ऐ, मेरे आङ्गन में धायौ ऐ;
मेरी मटकी कूँ देख्यौ ऐ, मेरे घट में वो ताक्यौ ऐ.

मेरी मटकी ना फोड्यौ ऐ, नवनीत लिये कहूँ धायौ ऐ;
जमुना तट पै वो खेल्यौ ऐ, सब के मन में वो भायौ ऐ.
मन मेरौ कछु सिहरावतु ऐ, मेरौ अपनों सौ लागतु ऐ;
मधु माखन मेरौ खायौ ऐ, गागर सर पै रखबायौ ऐ.

मैं आल्हादित अनुरागित हूँ, मधु आनन्दित है थिरकित हूँ;
मैं ठगी रहि गयी सी कछु हूँ, आनन्द अमिय मधु पायी हूँ.
मन मन बिन्दी स्पर्श्यौ ऐ, सर पै 'मधु' हाथ फिरायौ ऐ;
मन ही मन गोदी सर लैकें, कछु राग नयौ सौ गायौ ऐ.
मन वृन्दावन में नाच्यौ ऐ, वँशी वारौ सखि आयौ ऐ.

185. वाँसुरी वे बजायें गोकुल में * 600/14.11.09 (हिन्दी/ब्रज)

वाँसुरी वे बजायें गोकुल में, सुन रहीं गोपियां हैं हर मन में;
ब्रज बनों में कूँजती कोयलिया, मधु वनों में थिरकती पेंजनिया।

कृष्ण कब धरा पै चले आये, राधिका मधुर मन लिये धाये;
साधिका का स्वप्न साकार किये, मधुरता विश्व में लिये प्रकटे।
पखेरू प्राण पन से बिखरे हैं, लताएं लट पटा के बिखरी हैं;
घटायें प्रेम से उमड़ती हैं, छटायें सिहर कर छिटकती हैं।

श्याम कुञ्जों में वे रहे छाये, गोप मन में सिमट के वे आये;
क्षीण तन में क्षरित हुये आये, जीर्ण आत्मा ज्वलित किये धाये।
मेरा मन प्रेम में पगा सा है, निखिल कुछ ठगा हुआ सा है;
जमुन जल उछलता है पल पल में, 'मधु' उर नाचता है नव सुर में।

186. जीवन धरम * 263/31.03.09 (ब्रज भाषा)

हरि मेरौ जीवन धरम सँवारौ।
जीवन में हौं फिरत रह्यौ हूँ, पावतु नाहिं सहारौ;
मैं तुम संग चलन चाहतु अब, मेरो वेश सँवारौ।

मैं सेवा नहिं कछु करि पावतु, चरण पादुका नहिं गहि पावतु;
मन मेरौ कछु सोचतु जाबतु, प्रभु मन की कछु समझि न पाबतु।
गातु जातु मन मेरो ध्यावतु, भक्ति योग अति समझि न पावतु;
जाति पाँति कछु बिछुरत जाबत, मानव धरम समझि कछु आवतु।

जीवन धारण करतु धरमु ऐ, मानव मन कौ मरम धरमु ऐ;
मानव की सब जाति एक ऐ, मानव की सब पाँति एक ऐ।
जीवन की सब रीति एक ऐ, मानव मन की प्रीति एक ऐ,
मानव की 'मधु' गीति एक ऐ, अब सबु आइ सँवारौ।

187. 'मधु' मन विहग * 429/17.07.09 (ब्रज भाषा)

'मधु' मन विहग प्रभु व्योम महिं, धावत उड़त उतरत चढ़त;
थकि जातु कब अकुलातु कब, हँसि जातु कब, सुधि कब करतु.

जानतु न मैं, ताड़तु न मैं, तरजत न मैं, सुलझत न मैं;
सुर पातु कब, सुख आतु कब, जानत न पाबत, प्रात कब.
कबहू चहकि, कबहू दहकि, कबहू लुढ़कि, कब प्रस्फुरित;
मैं सोचि ना पावतु बहुत, विधि की करनि में रत रहत.

ना तृप्त हूँ या जगत में, ना सुप्त हूँ जागरण में;
ना लुप्त मैं हो पा रहा, ना लिप्त अति हो पारहा.
लावण्य मेरी देह में, सब यन्त्र मेरी देह में;
मैं तन्त्र बन तेरा उड़त, मैं मन्त्र बन तव जग फुरत.

188. हियहिं हँसति मनहिं रिसति * 239/11.02.09 (ब्रज भाषा)

हियहिं हँसति मनहिं रिसति, जसुमति मन सकुचकाति;
कान्हा बन फिरन जात, गोपिन्ह मन फुरत जात!

नयन झाँकि करति बात, तर्जनि सों बरजि जाति;
तन सुहात, मन सिहात, हिय हरसित, पग थिरात.
पुलक गात, गात जात, मोहन मन मुस्करात;
मन सुख कछु कहन चहत, श्यामा मन महिं रिझात.

राधा उर श्याम रहतु, मुरली धुनि सुननि चहति;
सन्मुख लखि झिझकि जाति, लतिकन्ह बिच लुकति जाति.
सखन्ह संग कृष्ण चलत, सखिन्ह महिं राधा फिरति;
धेनु वेनु सुनन चहति, कोकिल 'मधु' रस चखति.

189. प्रभु की कृपा * 41/17.04.08 (ब्रज भाषा)

प्रभु की कृपा, वरसि जब जावत, मेरौ मन आनन्दित होय जावत;
ब्रज खिल जावत, धेनु गावत, वेनु बिनु बाजिये, बजि जावत.

ग्वाल बाल वरवश उठि धावत, जमुना जल शीतल हैं जावत;
कोयल अपनी तान सुनावत, मोर पँख सर पै धरि नाचत.
निरमल गात होत अनुशासित, मेरौ हिय हर्षित होय जावत;
चक्र मोर निज तान सुनावत, मन नाचहि, आत्मा सिहरावत.

मूलाधार सुगन्ध फैलावत, स्वाधिष्ठान क्षुध प्यास मिटावत;
मणिपुर अरुण प्रभा बिखरावत, लिये अनाहत ऊपर धावत.
सिद्धि ज्ञान विशुद्ध बहावत, आज्ञा धर्म कर्म पहिं प्रेरति;
भक्ति देत, कृपा गुरु करत, समर्पहहुँ 'मधु' मन आनन्दित.

190. ए सखि आये जग मन भावन
* 434/17.07.09 (ब्रज भाषा)

ए सखि आये जग मन भावन, भाव तरावन भक्ति जगावन;
प्रीति लगावन, भीति भगावन, युक्ति बतावन, योग सिखावन.

तुम सखि नाचो गाओ ध्याओ, सत्संगति की बेलि बढ़ाओ;
उपवासन में वास कराओ, कान्हा के उर कूँ फुरकाओ.
मैं भावुक अति, प्रेम विरल रति, चाहत जावति उर अन्तर अति;
सन्तन की गति, योगिन की मति, मोहि नचावति मन थिरकावति.

सारंग नाचतु, मोहि बतावतु, मैं माया विच समझि न पावति;
चातक चाकतु मोर पखा सर, पीताम्बर लखि अम्वर सोहत.
तू आनन्द भरी क्यों गावति, ठाड़ी रहति पलक ना मारति;
क्या देखी तू भी 'मधु' भावन, क्या रीझी तू भी लखि मोहन.

191. कबहुकि बिखरि जातु मन मेरौ * 645/05.12.09 (ब्रज भाषा)

कबहुकि बिखरि जातु मन मेरौ, कबहुकि भटकि जातु मन मेरौ;
कबहुकि सुलझि जातु मन मेरौ, कबहुकि उलझि जातु मन मेरौ.

कबहु प्रसारतु कबहु उड़ावत, कबहु स्वप्न गति में धरि धावत;
कबहु उमड़ि जमुना जल भावत, कबहु घुमड़ि बादल पहिं जावत.
कबहु प्रसन्न चित्त मन धावत, कबहुकि गिरिते लुढ़क्यौ जावत;
कबहु धरातल पै अकुलावत, कबहु धरणि के सुर में गावत.

कबहु पतंग संग वह नाचतु, कबहु निमिष में धरणी धावतु;
कबहू मन में बहुत सिहावतु, कबहू मन में बहुत डरावतु.
कबहु गिरा गंभीर सुनावत, कबहू मन मन में मुस्कावत;
कबहू प्रसन्न चित्त मन भारी, कबहु होत 'मधु' अन्तर्यामी.

192. नाचन देहु मोहि गिरिधारी * 656/11.12.09 (ब्रज भाषा)

नाचन देहु मोहि गिरिधारी, क्यों करि विपति देहु मोहि भारी;
क्यों ना भगति देहु मोहि प्यारी, क्यों करि तोलत रहत मुरारी.

तुम संग प्रीति लगावत राजत, तुम संग नाच करत मन भावत;
कबहु दृष्टि तुम दूरि करो ना, कबहु सृष्टि कूँ रुष्ट करो ना.
सब जीवन की गति तुम थारो, सब जीवन की मति संभारो;
सब प्राणन कूँ तुम प्रभु थारो, सब के मन की गति कूँ तारो.

सब तुम संग नाँच करि पावहिं, प्राणिन कूँ ना नाँच नचावहिं;
संस्कारन विच उलझि न जावहिं, सेवा प्रेम भगति करि पावहिं.
सब प्राणन की प्रीति पखारी, सब जीवन की मीति निहारी;
बिपदहिं शीष कमल पद धारी, 'मधु' उर बसि जावहु त्रिपुरारी.

193. तुम ही प्रति पालक हो जगके * 668/13.12.09 (ब्रज भाषा)

तुम ही प्रति पालक हो जग के, मैं क्यों सोच करत घुन घुन के;
तुम ही जीव चराचर चेतक, तुम ही सब जग के संचालक।

मारि सकै ना कोइ काऊ के, जब तक तुम बाचत हो ताके;
मारन बालेन कूँ तुम ताकत, जब चाहत तिनकौ मन मारत।
सब जीवन की उमरि तुमहिं ते, एक एक पल गिनती तुम ते;
जे विदृष्टि जीवन पै डालत, तिनकी गति तुम खुद संजोवत।

अध पक उमरि कोउ ना जावै, मनुज काउ कूँ मारि न पावै;
ऐसौ ध्यान धरौ गिरिधारी, परवश ना होहि जीव दुखारी।
जब जीवन कूँ मारत देखत, मन कर्मन अस जब कोउ सोचत;
'मधु' मन उमड़ि घुमड़ि रहि जावत, तुम ही ते निज टेर लगावत।

194. मेरौ मन जब दृढ़ होहि जावत * 669/13.12.09 (ब्रज भाषा)

मेरौ मन जब दृढ़ होहि जावत, जग की धूप ताप सहि जावत;
जब जब नरम भयौ वह नाचत, कबहुकि जग तेहि खूब नचाबत।

मन संयम करि ध्यान लगावत, ताण्डव ललित कौशिकी भावत;
गुरु चक्र पै गुरु पैठावत, जग कूँ उर अन्तर वह देखत।
शिष्टन नेह करत वह नाचत, दुष्टन कूँ वह दंड करावत;
सब जग कूँ वह उर धरि नाचत, सबकूँ प्रभु उर सौंपत जावत।

जग प्रवन्ध संवित होहि जावत, प्रमा प्रकटि प्रभु पाने लावत;
शुद्ध बुद्धि होहि कर्म निखारत, प्रेम समर्पण सेवा लावत।
तातें जीव जगत सुधि पावत, प्रभु चरणन महिं मन लगि जावत;
मम मन आनन्दित होय जावत, दृढ़ मन उर 'मधु' सृष्टि सुहावत।

195. श्याम गिरिधारी लेहु मोहि तारी * 700/21.12.09 (ब्रज)

श्याम गिरिधारी लेहु मोहि तारी, राति बहु कारी न दीखै सुखारी;
करौ ना को देरी, सुरति लऔ मोरी, आऔ चक्रधारी, विपति हरौ भारी.

साँस मेरी अटके, भटकि मन जाये, रूह मेरी काँपे, चटकि हिया जाये;
न बुद्धि सुझाये, न धीरज ही आये, समझ नाही आये, किया क्या भी जाये.
पास मेरे आऔ, धीरज बँधाऔ, गति कछु लाऔ, जुगति बतलाऔ;
बोझ मन भारी, भयौ हूँ दुखारी, आऔ गिरिधारी, हरौ कष्ट भारी.

संग नाहि कोऊ, करौ मोरे छोहू, शकति कछु देऊ, भगति मोहि देहू;
वेगि आऔ प्यारे, नयन के दुलारे, हरो दुःख सारे, बसौ उर हमारे.
आऔ चक्रपाणी, हिया मेरे स्वामी, लखहु उर माही, रखहु उर माही;
'मधु' उर वासी, मधु सुर भासी, देहु मृदु हाँसी, प्रात आवै प्यारी.

196. लिखत जाऊँ पाती पिय को सुहाती * 701/22.12.09 (ब्रज)

लिखत जाऊँ पाती, पिय को सुहाती, मृदुल मुसकाती, सिहरती सिहाती;
रोती रिसाती, हँसती खिसाती, सिमटती समाती, छिपती छिपाती.

दरद दिल में जो भी, टीस रही जो भी,
लिखूँ उर में जो भी, चहूँ मन में जो भी;
पिया मेरे जोगी, मेरौ मन वियोगी, रहत कछु प्रयोगी, रहत आत्म योगी.
लिखूँ मन की बतियाँ, बीति जाय रतियाँ, न जावै सुरतिया, न आवै सँवरिया;
न आवै खवरिया, न जावै दुपरिया, जाँय सब घड़ियाँ, साँझ आवै दैया.

न कजरा लगाऊँ, न गजरा सजाऊँ, लिखे उनको जाऊँ, मन में सिहाऊँ;
मधु मेरी अँखियाँ, तकत जाँय सखियाँ, धड़कि जाय जियरा, सुनत पैंजनियाँ.
'मधु' पिय दुलरिया, श्याम मेरे पीया, पाती 'मधु गीति' लिखत नित जाती;
चुभन मधु जगाती, हँसी मृदु उगाती, मधुर मुसकाती, लजाती सुधाती.

বঙ্গলা Bengali   বাংলা
197. মহা মানস * 321/28.05.09

মহা মানস উৎসর্জিয়ে, চেতন ধরা গড়িতে জায়;
মহা মানৰ প্রকৃতি নিয়ে, নব্য মানৰ গড়িতে চায়।

তুমি এশে, নিকটে বশে, মধু মনে ৰাঁশী বাজাও;
মধুরতা শুধু ঢেলে ফেলো, স্পন্দন নৰ মনেতে জাগাও।
প্রকৃতি নাঁচাও, গগন সাজাও, শোভিত মনে ফেলিয়ে জাও;
মানস হিয়ায় থিরকিয়া জাও, শুভ্র শুভ জ্যোৎসনা জাগাও।

তাওৰ ৰেশী করো তুমি না কো, পাওৰ মনে মধুরতা আনো;
দানৰতায় ধ্বস্ত করো, ধরিণী ধর ধ্বজা ফহরাও।
নব্য মানৰ মানৰতা নিয়ে, প্রকৃতি সাযুজ্যে সহজতা নিয়ে;
জড় চেতন কে সংগে নিয়ে, তোমার 'মধু' তে মাখিয়া জায়।

197. महा मानस * 321/28.05.09 (बङ्गला)

महा मानस उत्सर्जिये, चेतन धरा गड़िते जाय;
महा मानव प्रकृति निये, नव्य मानव गड़िते चाय।

तुमि एशे, निकटे बशे, मधु मने वाँशी बाजाओ;
मधुरता शुधु ढेले फेलो, स्पन्दन नव मनेते जागाओ।
प्रकृति नाचाओ, गगन साजाओ, शोभित मने फेलिये जाओ;
मानस हियाय थिरकिया जाओ, शुभ्र शुभ ज्योत्सना जागाओ।

ताण्डव वेशी करो तुमि ना को, पाण्डव मने मधुरता आनो;
दानवताय ध्वस्त करो, धरिणी धर ध्वजा फहराओ।
नव्य मानव मानवता निये, प्रकृति सायुज्ये सहजता निये;
जड़ चेतन के संगे निये, तोमार 'मधु' ते माखिया जाय।

198. সকল মানুষ ভাই * 323/28.05.09 (Bengali   বাঙলা)

'মধু' ধরা রাঙিয়ে চলো সকল মানুষ ভাই,
প্রেম তরঙ্গে ভাসিয়ে চলো, ধরাতে সবাই.

সরায়ে দাও সকল আপদা, বহাইয়া চলো সদাই সুধা;
মন কে কিয়ে সুহৃদ বৃহত, মানবতা কে ঢালিয়ে মহত.
পীছনে কভু তাকাও না তুমি, মানব হিয়ায রাখিও চুমি;
ধর্মে কর্মে উদ্যত থাকো, মনের মাঝারে শুধু শুভ তাকো.

ঘৃণা কারো করো নাকো, অবহেলিত করো না কো;
ছন্দে তালে সবাই নাচো, সুরেতে গাইয়া থাকো.
সুধা তরঙ্গে মাতিয়ে চলো বসুধাতে সবাই,
নাচিয়ে চলো গাইয়ে চলো, সকল মানুষ ভাই.

198. सकल मानुष भाइ * 323/28.05.09 (बङ्गला)

'मधु' धरा राङ्गिये चलो सकल मानुष भाइ,
प्रेम तरङ्गे भासिये चलो, धराते सबाइ.

सराये दाओ सकल आपदा, बहाइया चलो सदाइ सुधा;
मन के किये सुहृद बृहत, मानवता के ढालिये महत.
पीछने कभू ताकाओ ना तुमि, मानव हियाय राखिओ चूमि;
धर्मे कर्मे उद्यत थाको, मनेर माझारे शुधु शुभ ताको.

घृणा कारो करो नाको, अवहेलित करो ना को;
छन्दे ताले सबाइ नाचो, सुरेते गाइया थाको.
सुधा तरङ्गे मातिये चलो बसुधाते सबाइ,
नाचिये चलो गाइये चलो, सकल मानुष भाइ.

199. ওগো 'মধু' * 31/08.04.08 (Bengali   বাঙলা)

ওগো 'মধু' তুমি আও, মোর মন মধু নিযে যাও;
তুমি মোর পানে চাও, মোরে নিজ পানে নিযে যাও।

তুমি এস্শে, মোর পানে বসে, কিছু কিছু করে যাও, যাহা কিছু মননেতে চাও;
কিছু কিছু কথা কযে যাও, কিছু কিছু ব্যথা সুনে জাও।
মোর সঁচিত মধু আছে, শুধু মধু অছে, খাঁটি মধু আছে;
কিছুই তো বেংচে আছে, সেই তোমাই দিতে চাই, তুমি আও।

আমি তোমারি মহুরিমা চাই, তোমারি শোভনি দেখি;
তোমারই মননেই ডোলি, তুমি আও, মোর মন মধু নিযে জাও।
মোর মোরে বলে যা কিছু আছে, সে সব তোরাই তো আছে;
তুমি এস্শে ভালো বেসে, আমাকে নিযে যাও, মোরে নিজ পানে নিযে যাও।

199. ওগো মধু * 31/09.04.08 (বাঙ্লা)

ওগো 'মধু' তুমি আও, মোর মন মধু নিযে জাও!
তুমি মোর পানে চাও, মোরে নিজ পানে নিযে জাও।

তুমি এশ্শে মোর পানে বোসে, কিছু কিছু করে জাও, জাহা কিছু মননেতে চাও;
কিছু কিছু কথা কযে জাও, কিছু কিছু ব্যথা সুনে জাও।
মোর সঁচিত মধু আছে, শুধু মধু আছে, খাঁটি মধু আছে;
কিছুই তো বেঁচে আছি, সেই তোমায় দিতে চাই, তুমি আও।

আমি তোমারি মধুরিমা চাই, আমি তোমারি শোভনি দেখি;
তোমার মননেই ডোলী, তুমি আও, মোর মন মধু নিযে জাও।
মোরা মোরে বোলে জা কিছু আছে, সে সব তোরাই তো আছে;
তুমি এশ্শে ভালোবেসে, আমাকে নিযে জাও, মোরে নিজ পানে নিযে জাও।

200. মোর তন তোর * 38/09.04.08 (Bengali   বাঙলা)

মোর তন তোর সুর লহরী, মোর স্বর তোর মন লহরী;
তুমি আমাতেই গাইতে যাও, আমি সুর সেধে চলে যাই.

তুমি আমায় ৰীণা মত বাজাও, মোর তার তার ছেড়ে যাও;
আমার হৃদি তন্ৰীতে, নিজের ধ্বনি জাগাও, তুমি নিজের রাগ সুনাও.
তুমি আমার প্রাণের সারথী, মোর সুরেরই রথী, মোর রাগেরই পারখী;
মোর পানে চাও, আমায় নিজেতেই মিশাইয়া নাও.

আমি নাচিছি তোমারই তালে, গাইবো তোমারই সুরে;
মাতিব তোমারই লয়ে, গুনগুনিএ তোমারই গানে.
তুমি এশে আমার সুর সেধে দাও, তুমি ম্বদু 'মধু' হেসে;
আমায় ধ্যানে চাও, আমার ধ্যানে আও. আমাতেই গাইতে যাও.

200. मोर तन तोर * 38/09.04.08 (बाङ्गला)

मोर तन तोर सुर लहरी, मोर स्वर तोर मन लहरी;
तुमि आमातेइ गाइते जाओ, आमि सुर सेधे चले जाइ.

तुमि आमाय वीणा मत बाजाओ, मोरे तारे तारे छेड़े जाओ;
आमार हृदि तन्त्रीते, निजेर ध्वनि जागाओ, तुमि निजेर राग सुनाओ.
तुमि आमार प्राणेर सारथी, मोर सुरेरइ रथी, मोर रागेरइ पारखी;
मोर पाने चाओ, आमाय निजेतेइ मिशाइया नाओ.

आमि नाचिछि तोमारइ ताले, गाइबो तोमारइ सुरे;
मातिबो तोमारइ लये, गुनगुनिए तोमारइ गाने.
तुमि एशे आमार सुर सेधे दाओ, तुमि मृदु 'मधु' हेसे;
आमाय ध्याने चाओ, आमार ध्याने आओ, आमातेइ गाइते जाओ.

201. সকল প্রাণের পরশমণি তুমি * 557/08.10.09 (Bengali বাঙলা)

সকল প্রাণের পরশমণি তুমি, সকল রাগের আধার ভূমি;
সকল হিয়ার পরস খানি তুমি, সকল বীণার তন্ত্রিত ধ্বনি।

বৃজের গোপাল তুমি এশে জাও, আমার হিয়ায় ৰাঁশী বাজাও;
সকল জগতে আমাকে নাচাও, জগত কে আমার হিয়ায় নাচাও।
জীৱনে আমি যাহা কিছু ভাৱি, সব কিছু তোমাতেই সেজে আছি;
তোমার বিনু নাহিং ধেনু ৰেণু, তোমার বিনা ন রেণু ত্রসরেণু।

উদয়গিরি তে উদধি জলেতে, হিম শিখিরের প্রতি পরমাণু তে;
অস্তাচলেরই তপন দাহনে, তুমি সুশীতল সুহৃদ নয়নে।
আমার জীৱনে কৃপা করে জাও, ধ্যানের মাঝে নিজ প্রাণে চাও;
নিজেরই ৰাঁশীটি সুনাইযা যাও, নিজেরেই চরণে 'মধু' কে সাজাও।

201. सकल प्राणेर परशमणि तुमि * 557/08.10.09 (बङ्गला)

सकल प्राणेर परशमणि तुमि, सकल रागेर आधार भूमि;
सकल हियार परस खानि तुमि, सकल वीणार तन्त्रित ध्वनि।

बृजेर गोपाल तुमि एशे जाओ, आमार हियाय वाँशी बाजाओ;
सकल जगते आमाके नाचाओ, जगत के आमार हियाय नाचाओ।
जीवने आमि याहा किछु भावि, सब किछु तोमातेइ सेजे आछि;
तोमार बिनु नाहि धेनु वेणु, तोमार बिनु न रेणु त्रसरेणु।

उदयगिरि ते उदधि जलेते, हिम शिखिरेर प्रति परमाणु ते;
अस्ताचलेइ तपन दाहने, तुमि सुशीतल सुहृद नयने।
आमार जीवने कृपा करे जाओ, ध्यानेर माझे निज प्राणे चाओ;
निजेरइ वाँशीटि सुनाइया याओ, निजेरेइ चरणे 'मधु' के साजाओ।

202. আমার হিয়ায় তুমি এশে জাও * 646/09.12.09 (Bengali)

আমার হিয়ায় তুমি এশে জাও, আমার মনে ৱাংশীটি বজাও;
আমার নিকটে তুমি বসে জাও, নিজের চরণে আমাকে বোসাও।

আমার মনে পরশিয়া জাও, আমার তনে হরষিয়া জাও;
আমার জীৱনে নাচিয়া জাও, আমার ধ্যানে থিরকিয়া জাও।
মুরলিয়া তুমি সুনাইয়া জাও, ধৱনি ৱ্যঞ্জনে সবাইকে সাজাও;
প্রতিটি হৃদয়ে স্পন্দন জাগাও, প্রকৃতি কে নিয়ে সংগে নাচাও।

তোমার ৱাণীটি সুনিতে চাই, তোমার হাঁসিটি দেখিয়ে চাই;
তোমারি চাহনী আঁখি দেখে চাই, লকুটি তোমারি চিত্তে রেখে রই।
সকল প্রাণের তুমি পরশমণি, সকল জীৱের তুমি প্রেম খানী;
আমার হিয়ায় ভগতি জাগাও, 'মধু' মানসে মাধুরী নাচাও।

202. आमार हियाय तुमि एशे जाओ * 646/09.12.09 (बङ्गला)

आमार हियाय तुमि एशे जाओ, आमार मने वांशीटि बजाओ;
आमार निकटे तुमि बसे जाओ, निजेर चरणे आमाके बोसाओ।

आमार मने परशिया जाओ, आमार तने हरषिया जाओ;
आमार जीवने नाचिया जाओ, आमार ध्याने थिरकिया जाओ।
मुरलिया तुमि सुनाइया जाओ, ध्वनि व्यञ्जने सबाइके साजाओ;
प्रतिटि हृदये स्पन्दन जागाओ, प्रकृति के निये संगे नाचाओ।

तोमार वाणीटि सुनिते चाइ, तोमार हाँसिटि देखिये चाइ;
तोमारि चाहनी आँखि देखे चाइ, लकुटि तोमारि चित्ते रेखे रड़।
सकल प्राणेर तुमि परशमणि, सकल जीवेर तुमि प्रेम खानी;
आमार हियाय भगति जागाओ, 'मधु' मानसे माधुरी नाचाओ।

203. তুমি কী করে রচিযা জাও * 647/09.12.09 (Bengali বাঙ্গলা)

তুমি কী করে রচিযা জাও, তুমি কী করে করিযা জাও;
তুমি কী ভাৱে মাতিযা রও, তুমি কী কী মানসে চাও।

তুমি আতুর তুমি কাতর, তুমি বৃহতের মাঝে চাতুর;
তুমি গতির মাঝে কাঁপন, তুমি হাসের মাঝে থিরকন।
তুমি হিযার মাঝে গোপন, তুমি বনের মাঝে সিহরন;
তুমি চিতৱন মাঝে চিত্ত ৱন, তুমি ভাৱনা মাঝে ভাৱন।

তুমি আমারই মনে সাজো, তুমি আমার হিযায রাঁচো;
তুমি অকাতর হযে থাকো, তুমি সচেতন সদা থাকো।
তুমি 'মধু' মনে মধু ঢালো, তুমি চাঁদের মত হাসো;
তুমি জগত কে মধু বানাও, তুমি সংস্কৃতি মধু জাগাও।

203. तुमि की करे रचिया जाओ * 647/09.12.09 (बङ्गला)

तुमि की करे रचिया जाओ, तुमि की करे करिया जाओ;
तुमि की भावे मातिया रओ, तुमि की की मानसे चाओ।

तुमि आतुर तुमि कातर, तुमि बृहतेर माझे चातुर;
तुमि गतिर माझे काँपन, तुमि हासेर माझे थिरकन।
तुमि हियार माझे गोपन, तुमि बनेर माझे सिहरन;
तुमि चितवन माझे चित्त वन, तुमि भावना माझे भावन।

तुमि आमाराइ मने साजो, तुमि आमार हियाय राँचो;
तुमि अकातर हये थाको, तुमि सचेतन सदा थाको।
तुमि 'मधु' मने मधु ढालो, तुमि चाँदेर मत हासो;
तुमि जगत के मधु बानाओ, तुमि संस्कृति मधु जागाओ।

204. ওগো মোদের প্রাণের সখা * 752/01.01.10 (Bengali বাঙ্গলা)

ওগো মোদের প্রাণের সখা, আমি তোমারই প্রেমে মাখা;
আমি শুধু চাই ভালোৱাশা, তুমি ভেৱে থেকো এই আশা।

জলসা ঘরে আমি থাকি, তুমি ওদের ঘরেতে আছি;
কণে কণে সুধা দেখি আমি, সুধা ঝরে ভেসে থেকো তুমি।
ৱেশী তুমি আমাকে জানো, তুমি ভালোৱাশিতে জানো;
নাই জানী তোমারি ভাষা, তুমি জেনো মোর অভিলাষা।

আমি তোমার মনেতে ভাসী, তোমারই মননেতে হাসী;
আমি তোমাতেই শুধু যাচী, তোমাকেই নিযে আমি আছী।
আমি তোমার সুরে গেযে যাই, তোমারই গানে নেচে যাই;
ৱেশী কিছু আমি চাই না, চাই একটূ ভালোৱাশা।

204. ओगो मोदेर प्राणेर सखा * 752/01.01.10 (बङ्गला)

ओगो मोदेर प्राणेर सखा, आमि तोमारइ प्रेमे माखा;
आमि शुधु चाइ भालोवाशा, तुमि भेवे थेको एइ आशा।

जलसा घरे आमि थाकि, तुमि ओदेर घरेते आछि;
कणे कणे सुधा देखि आमि, सुधा झरे भेसे थेको तुमि।
वेशी तुमि आमाके जानो, तुमि भालोवाशिते जानो;
नाइ जानी तोमारि भाषा, तुमि जेनो मोर अभिलाषा।

आमि तोमार मनेते भासी, तोमारइ मननेते हासी;
आमि तोमातेइ शुधु याची, तोमाकेइ निये आमि आछी।
आमि तोमार सुरे गेये याइ, तोमारइ गाने नेचे याइ;
वेशी किछु आमि चाइ ना, चाइ एकटू भालोवाशा।

गुजराती **Gujarati** ગુજરાતી

205. **સૂરત નાં પુરનાં સ્વરૂપ** * 136/12.08.08   (Gujarati   ગુજરાતી)

આપણી સૂરત નાં પુરનાં સ્વરૂપ, હે તાપી! તૂ ભુલાવી પા શકે છે?
જ્યાવે તુ કૂદતી છલકાવતી થનગનતી, પોતાના કિનારા તોડી નાખતી.

તારા ઉપર શ્રદ્ધાનો બનેલો પુલ, ત્યારે એકાકી પાતડી રેખા લાગે છે;
તારા કિનારે બનેલા બહુ માળી મકાનો, તારામાં ડુબાયેલા દેખાય છે.
તારો પ્રવલ પ્રવાહ સાગરને મળવા લાગ છે;
ખમ્ભાતની ખાડીની પૂનમની ભરતી, તને અટકાવતી લાગે છે.

તારા વધારે પડતા પ્રવાહને, સાગર પલ સ્વીકાર કરતો લાગતો નથી;
તને સીમામાં રહેવાનું કહી રહ્યો હોય લાગે છે.
હે તાપી, તૂ શાન્ત વહી, પોતાની સાથે બધાને ફરાવા દે;
'મધુ' બસ્તિયોં ને બસેલા રહેવા દે, વાદળોં ને વરસવા દે.

205. **आपणी सूरत नां पुरनां स्वरूप** * 136/12.08.08 (गुजराती)

आपणी सूरत नां पुरनां स्वरूप, हे तापी! तू भुलावी पा शके छे?
ज्यावे तु कूदती छलकावती थनगनती, पोताना किनारा तोड़ी नाखती.

तारा ऊपर श्रद्धानो बनेलो पुल, त्यारे एकाकी पातड़ी रेखा लागे छे;
तारा किनारे बनेला बहु माली मकानो, तारामां डुबायेला देखाय छे.
तारो प्रवल प्रवाह सागरने मळवा लाग छे;
खम्भातनी खाड़ीनी पूनमनी भरती, तने अटकावती लागे छे.

तारा वधारे पड़ता प्रवाहने, सागर पल स्वीकार करतो लागतो नथी;
तने सीमामां रहेवानुं कही रह्यो होय लागे छे.
हे तापी, तू शान्त वही, पोतानी साथे बधाने फरावा दे;
'मधु' बस्तियों ने बसेला रहेवा दे, वादणों ने वरसवा दे.

पञ्जाबी PUNJABI ਪੰਜਾਬੀ

206. ਲੋੜ੍ਹ ਫੁੱਲਾਂ ਤੋਂ ਵਧਦਾ ਫੁਲਦਾ ਲੁਧਿਆਣਾ * 91/12.06.08

ਲੋੜ੍ਹ ਫੁੱਲਾਂ ਤੋਂ ਵਧਦਾ ਫੁਲਦਾ ਲੁਧਿਆਣਾ, ਸੋਨੇ ਭੰਗੜੇ ਨਾਲ ਨਚਦਾ ਹੈ;
ਪੰਜ ਆਂਵਾਂ ਤੋਂ ਵਗਦਾ ਪੰਜਾਬ, ਗੁਰੁ ਦੀ ਕਿਰਪਾ ਨਾਲ ਆਨੰਦਿਤ ਹੈ।

ਭਾਖੜਾ ਨੰਗਲ ਭਾਰਤ ਦੀ ਸ਼ਾਨ ਹੈ, ਗੋਵਿੰਦ ਸਾਗਰ ਵੱਡਾ ਵਿਸ਼ਾਲ ਹੈ;
ਰੋਪੜ ਦੀ ਸਤਲਜ ਦੀ ਗਹਰਾਈ, ਮਾਨਵ ਮਨ ਦੀ ਅੰਗੜਾਈ ਹੈ।
ਵਿਆਸ ਦਾ ਵਿਸ਼ਾਲ ਬਿਆਸ, ਆਧਿਆਤ੍ਮਿਕ ਵਿਸ਼ਵਾਸ ਨਾਲ ਭਰਿਆ ਹੈ;
ਹੁਸ਼ਿਆਰਪੁਰ ਰਸ ਨਾਲ ਭਰਿਆ ਹੈ, ਅਮ੍ਰਿਤਸਰ ਆਨੰਦਵਾਣੀ ਵਿਚ ਰੰਗਿਆ ਹੈ।

ਸੰਗਰੂਰ ਦੇ ਹਰੇ ਭਰੇ ਖੇਤਾਂ ਵਿਚ ਕਿੱਲਾ, ਮਨੂੰ ਛੂਹਣ ਵਾਲਾ ਹੈ;
ਅਹਮਦਗੜ 'ਮਧੁ' ਆਨੰਦ ਨਾਲ ਭਰਿਆ ਹੈ,
ਚੰਡੀਗੜ ਦਾ ਵਿਕਾਸ ਯੋਜਨਾਵੱਧ ਹੈ;
ਬਾਗ ਬਗੀਚਿਆਂ ਵਿੱਚੋਂ ਮਹਕਦੀ ਹਵਾ ਵਿਚਰਦੀ ਹੈ।

206. लौध फुल्लां तों वधदा फूलदा लुधिआणा * 91/12.06.08

लौध फुल्लां तों वधदा फूलदा लुधिआणा, सौणे भंगड़े नाल नचदा है;
पंज आवां तौं वगदा पंजाब, गुरु दी किरपा नाल आनंदित है।

भाखड़ा नंगल भारत दी शान है, गोविंद सागर वड्डा विशाल है;
रोपड़ दी सतलज दी गहराई, मानव मन दी अंगड़ाई है।
व्यास दा विशाल बिआस, अधिआत्मिक विशवास नाल भरिआ है;
हुशिआरपुर रस नाल भरिआ है, अम्रितसर आनंदवाणी विच रंगिआ है।

संगरूर दे हरे भरे खेतां विच किल्ला, मननूं छूहण वाला है;
अहमदगढ़ 'मधु' आनंद नाल भरिआ है।
चंडीगढ़ दा विकास योजनावद्ध है;
बाग बगीचिआं विच्चों महकदी हवा विचरदी है।

उर्दू / हिन्दी ـﮯ URDU/HINDI

207. आबरू है तो सिर्फ़ तेरी है * 440/24.07.09 (उर्दू / हिन्दी)

आबरू है तो सिर्फ़ तेरी है, ना ही मेरी है, ना किसी की है;
जिसकी भी है ढकी ही तू ने है, रखी जैसे भी रखी तू ने है।

क्रोध की आग हो जला देते, कुछ भी बन्दे से तुम करा देते;
पलों में उसको हो लजा देते, जगत से सज़ा भी दिला देते।
माध्यम जीव सब तुम्हारे हैं, इशारे नज़ारे नगाड़े हैं;
संवारे निखारे संजोये हैं, सिखाये सजाये बढाये हैं।

ओट में तुम सदा छिपे रहते, कराते रहते खुदी जो चहते;
इन्द्रियों को तुम्हीं नचा देते, दूर से बैठ कर करा लेते।
आदमी कैसी बेवशी में है, रेशमी डोर में बँधा सा है;
छोर एक जिसका पकड़ा 'उसने' है, छोर दूजा 'मधु' के मन में है।

208. रूह की रोशनी निराली है * 554/08.10.09 (उर्दू / हिन्दी)

रूह की रोशनी निराली है, पहेली बुझाती सुझाती है;
द्विधाएं मिटाती घटाती है, सुधाएं सुधाती पिलाती है।

रूह ढलती है, चाह ढलती है, रोशनी खुद व खुद ही बढती है;
जिन्दगी समझ आने लगती है, वन्दगी धीरे धीरे आती है।
रूहानी रोशनी सुहानी है, विराना विश्व अपना करती है;
विराने मधुर मुखर होते हैं, जिन्दगी सजग सुखद होती है।

पहेली मत बुझाओ हे प्रियवर, खुद व खुद आही जाओ अब दीगर;
जगत की रवानी बतानी है, जुगति की बात सब बतानी है।
शख्सियत मेरी सब दिखानी है, रूहानी रोशनी दिखानी है;
'मधु' को राह मधु बतानी है, अपने को रूबरू दिखाना है।

209. चाह की आह में * 508/09.09.09 (उर्दू / हिन्दी)

चाह की आह में राहें निकल ही आती हैं, हारते हरते विहरते बहारें आती हैं;
व्यथा कथा विचार पाती हैं, व्यस्तता शुद्धि 'मधु' बढाती हैं.

वाहनों की कमी विचारों की, कमी खुशी की कभी दर्द की सी वेचैनी;
चाह को उर्वरा कराती हैं, राह खुद ही बनाये जाती हैं.
जर्जरित त्रसित तन त्रणों से भी, अणु ऊर्जा लिये भुवन से ही;
नाचता फिरता घुमाता जीवन, ज्योति लेकर जगाता जग जीवन.

प्राण मन जब कभी जिसे चाहे, सृष्टि कर समर्पण चली आये;
समर्पित मन स्वयं जभी होता, प्रकट प्रभु प्राण है वहीं होता.
समर्पण सिद्धि की जरूरत है, विकर्षण बुद्धि की हकीकत है;
प्रेरणा शुद्धि में समर्पित है, एषणा प्रभु से प्रकम्पित है.

210. सृष्टि की हर अदा * 510/11.09.09 (उर्दू / हिन्दी)

सृष्टि की हर अदा निराली है, सँवारी निखारी दुलारी है;
संतुलित सुहृद सभी सिहरित हैं, सभी सानन्द सुर में शोभित हैं.

पुष्प हर कीट को बुलाते हैं, गीत हर मीत को बुलाते हैं;
प्रीति की रीति सभी चलते हैं, दीप ढलते हुए भी जलते हैं.
फलों की महक सभी को भाती, हज़ारों मक्खियों को मदमाती;
मधु की खुशबू चींटे लेआती, फूल की हर अदा है मधुमाती.

युवती हिरणी है सदा मुस्काती, खिलती कलियां हैं गज़ल गा जातीं;
शिशु की सुहानी सुहृद हाँसी, बृद्ध की रुहानी मृदुल हाँसी.
वालपन की विचित्र प्रश्न झड़ी, बृद्ध की विवेकी विशुद्ध घड़ी;
सभी तो सृष्टि की विधायें हैं, सभी 'मधु' दृष्टि की अदायें हैं.

अंग्रेजी ENGLISH - Poem Nos. 211 -225
मूल अंग्रेजी खण्ड 3 में Original in English Part 3

A'NANDA ANUBHU'TI
PART 2 - ROMAN SAM'SKRTA

PERCEPTION OF BLISS
PART 2 - ROMAN SANSKRIT

आनन्द अनुभूति
भाग २: रोमन संस्कृत

By
Gopal Baghel 'Madhu'
गोपाल बघेल ' मधु '

Vis'aya Su'cii Va Adhya'ya
Contents and Chapters

"रोमन संस्कृत" वर्णमाला
"ROMAN   SAM'SKRTA" ALPHABET

Adopted for swift writing, understanding, pronouncing and singing

अ	आ	इ	ई	उ	ऊ	ऋ	ॠ	ल	लृ
a	a'	i	ii	u	u'	r	rr	lr	lrr

ए	ऐ	ओ	औ	अं	अ:				
e	ae	o	ao	am'	ah				

क	ख	ग	घ	ङ	च	छ	ज	झ	ञ
ka	kha	ga	gha	una	ca	cha	ja	jha	ina

ट	ठ	ड	ढ	ण	त	थ	द	ध	न
t'a	t'ha	d'a	d'ha	n'a	ta	tha	da	dha	na

प	फ	ब	भ	म	य	र	ल	व	
pa	pha	ba	bha	ma	ya	ra	la	va	

श	ष	स	ह	क्ष	त्र	ज्ञ			
sha	s'a	sa	ha	ks'a	tra	jin'a			

क़	ख़	ज़	ड़	ढ़	फ़	त्	अँ		
qua	quha	za	r'a	r'ha	fa	t	an		

ऋषि	छाया	ज्ञान		संस्कृत		ततोऽहं	
rs'i	cha'ya'	jina'na		sam'skrta		tato'aham'	

A'NANDA ANUBHU'TI (PERCEPTION OF BLISS)

PART 2 - ROMAN SAM'SKRTA

Chapter 1.
A'dhya'tmika Prabandha

1. Vishva kii a'nanda bhu'mi mem'
* 601 / 15.09.09

Vishva kii a'nanda bhu'mi mem' raca' tha' eka hiya',
Sarasata' sa' macalata' sa' prajjvalita sa' vaha hiya';
Vicarate brhma'n'd'a mem' vaha madhurata' d'ha'la' kiya',
Siharata' sus'ama' liye vaha jiiva ko bha'ya' kiya'.

Manuja ko yama niyama de vaha priiti mem' bandha' kiya',
Prakrti ko ma'dhurya de vaha lalita mem' na'nca' kiya';
Thirakata' madhu na'da mem' vaha niiti ko sa'dha' kiya',
Cetanom' ko cetana' de chitta ko cetana kiya'.

Sam'skrti kii su'ks'ma dha'ra' ko phura' kara cala diya',
Vikrti kii pra'ciira ko vaha ciira kara cira kara gaya';
Su'ks'ma ma'nava hrdaya ko usane saja'ya' sanjoya',
Giiti raca, rasa priiti bhara, ura miiti bhara, vaha cala diya'.

Vishva ura a'nanda dha'ra' mem' baha' hii raha gaya',
Krandanom' ke vega ko vaha sahaja mem' hii saha gaya';
Drashya badale druma haem' mahake ba'dalom' ko bha' gaya',
Drga dravita kara hrda sravita kara, ura sabhii ke cha' gaya'.

Srota 'Madhu' ma'dhurya ke vaha saba khila' kara cala diya',
Diipa nava saondarya ke vaha jaga khila' kara cala diya';
Maem' acetana cetana' ke giita madhu ga'ya' kiya',
Vaha muraliya' ta'na para sabako naca'kara cala diya'.

2. Su'ks'ma prema kii anubhu'tiya'm'
* 132/ 08.08.08

Tumha're su'ks'ma prema kii anubhu'tiyom' ko;
Maem' a'nanda umanga kahu'n ya' a'nanda taranga kahu'n!
A'nanda anubhu'ti kahu'n ya' anubhu'ti a'nanda kahu'n;
Srs't'i prabandha ke sura kahu'n
Ya' a'dhya'tmika prabandha kahu'n.

Jo bhii kahu'n, ve tumha'rii hii vidha' ya' kala' haem'.
Tumha're liye, bana'ii pus'pa ma'la' haem'.
Unakii sugandha saundarya tumha'ra' hae;
Unako dha'ge mem' pirone ka' a'nanda mera' hae.

Tuma unake sahasra'ra ke hara dala para,
Apane pada kamala rakho.
Unaka' hradaya kamala adharom' se spars'a karo;
Apane hrdaya pat'ala para rakha use a'nandita karo.

Unake roma roma mem' rama ja'o;
Tuma jana jana ko sihara'o;
Hara tana mana mem' tuma ga' ja'o;
Hara dhar'akana mem' tuma basa ja'o.

3. A'nanda rasa * 286/12.04.09

A'nanda rasa phuharata gagana,
Tribhuvana magana ma'nava magana;
A'nanda mem' thirakita pavana,
Jiivana surabhi a'nanda ghana.

Jana mana magan, surabhita sumana,
Na'ncata gagana a'nanda mem'
Madhu ca'nda hae sura chanda mem',
Thirakita dhara' madhu na'da mem'.
A'ka'sha niila'njana liye, nava megha thirakita ho cale;
A'nanda sa'gara mem' magana dhruva sahita ta're baha cale.

A'nanda   rasa mem' sarasatii, ulka' alokita ho ut'hii;
Ta're sabhii thirakita hue, Prthvii umar'atii prema mem'.
Sura Su'rya mem' bahane lage, graha magana mana rahane lage;
Guru krpa' barasa'te magana,
Prabhu bhakti mem' 'Madhu' hae magana.

4. A'nanda ghana * 328/30.05.09

A'nanda ghana cha'ya' hua', a'ka'sha mana bha'ya' hua';
A'lhva'da it'hala'ya' hua', hae Arun'a 'Madhu'   a'ya' hua'.

Haem' viharatii cir'iya'm' bikhara,
Hae magana mana ma'nava prakhara;
Arama'na mem' uchala' pavana, ga'raha' hae gazalem' gagana.

Sura madhura haem' kucha baja ut'he,
Sha'shvata hiya' kucha kaha ut'he;
Saha ra'ga mem' kucha ga' ut'he, anura'ga ram'jita kucha hue.

A'nanda madhu mohita dhara', madhu pus'pa kii ma'dhuryata';
Sa'rthaka prakrti kii pun'yata', dha'raka dhvani kii pran'avata'.

Hae adhara akula'ya' hua', hae madhura mana ga'ya' hua';
Hae shobhita sam'shodhita', a'ra'dhana' kii dyotana'.

5. Sura mem' lahara * 330/30.5.09. (Hindi/ Braja)

Sura mem' lahara, mana mem' kahara, 'Madhu' ca'takii ca'kati madhura;
Ura dhya'na dhari, kara karama kari, budhi brhata kari, hiya haras'a bhari.

Mana pulaka bhari, prakrti parakhi, pra'n'iinata' kii chavi nirakhi;
Madhu vyoma mem' surabhi lakhati, sha'shvata calana mem' rata rahati.
Dhana dha'nya pu'rita dhara' para, adbhuta anaokhii chavi nirakhi;
Ga'tii rahii mrdu ta'na para, phurakita alaokika madhu lahara.

Mana ullasita tana praphullita, udvega rahita prakrti nirakhi;
Sha'liinata' kii jyoti lakhi, pa'vana papiiha' ko parakhi.
Ura surabhi ko dha'rati rahati, sura surabhi kii shobha' lakhati;
Pala mem' pulaki, pala mem' bikhari, ga'vati rahati 'Madhu' adhara para.

6. Pratya'shita pramudita * 191/26.11.08

Pratya'shita pramudita jiivana dhuna,
Abhinavq anubhava a'nanda cubhana;
Madhumaya pra'ngan'a ke pramudita mana,
Jiivana a'bha' ke diipa magana.

Ga'o sumadhura na'co sundara, jiivana dha'ra' tribhuvana bha'svara;
Mana mandira mem' dhya'o Mohana, a'o tribhuvana Ra'dha' citavana.

Ra'dha' ke roma roma mem' rasa, barasa'ne ke ka'nana mem' basa;
Gopii mana ke dadhi mem' tuma rasa, jiivana ke sha'shvata gopana rasa.

Gopii ke ra'sa bhare mana mem', Gopom' ke a'lhva'dita tana mem';
Ra'dha' kii nat'akhat'a citavana mem',
Shya'ma' ke madhuvana se mana mem'.

Ma'nava mana kii arun'a'ii mem', paks'hii kii mohaka citavana mem';
Ma'ta' ke madhura vilocana mem', bhakti ki mohana thirakana mem'.

'Madhu' mana shobhana jiivana upavana,
Mohana muralii kii manahara dhuna;
Shya'mala ghana kii mohana garjana,
Prabhu vya'pakata' kii pran'avita dhuna.

7. Pra'ngan'a pracura * 192/26.11.08

Pra'ngan'a pracura pra'n'ii prakhara,
Prakrti pramutthita prabhaakara;
Pra'n'iinata' pra'ciinata', pramudita praphullita manuja svara.
Pra'ciira ciira bar'ho magana, dharatii khar'e chu'lo gagana;
Prthvii tarangita 'Madhu' sumana, A'ka'sh Gunga' maya gagana.

A'nanda kii sura ta'na mem', srs't'i racita sopa'na mem',
Sa'yujya ke shubha calana mem', prati vimba ke prativimba mem';
A'bha'sa hae, mradu a'sha hae, mana mem' bhara' vishva'sa hae,
Nishcaya bhara' nihshva'sa hae, nishchala hrdaya a'ka'sha hae.

Talliinata' pratibaddhata', pra'n'iinata' sam'shodhita',
Shobhita hrudaya kii saralata', sim'cita hrdaya kii prakharata';
Cam'cala hrdaya kii vikalata', Ca'n'akya mana kii caturata',
Dediipya mana kii dhavalata', a'nanda rasa kii navalata'.

8. Pulakita praphullita * 193/26.11.08

Pulakita praphullita subhaga tana, a'nanda lasita prabha' ratana;
Jiivana pramodita lasita mana, surabhita sumana a'nanda ghana.

Mama mana pran'ava a'nanda maya,
Jiivana surabhi shubha chanda maya;
Pra'rabdha prerita pra'n'a maya,
Sam'ska'ra sevita 'Madhu' maya.

Malayaja pavana sa'runga sura, sa'runga aunga sudha' pracura;
Anubhu'ti a'nandama madhura, tatpara tarala tana tarun'a cira.

A'nanda shobhita svayam tuma,
A'nanda ra'shi dhara' varam;
Soham vara'bhaya svayam tuma,
Rasa saghana hruda Shiva sarisa tuma.

Tuma dharma prerita karma rata, tuma garala pa'na kiye phirata;
A'dha'ra bhu'ta dhara' dharata, soham bane srs't'i dharata.

9. Sohana subhaga * 195/26.11.08

Sohan subhaga sundara sumana,
Sumadhura sarala caetanya mana;
A'nanda ghana mandrita nayana, cetana cubhana jiivana tarana.

Mana ullasita, tana praphullita, dha'ye dhara' pulakita pavana;
A'nanda mem' lipat'a' gagana,
Leta' svapana mu'nde nayana.

A'nand thirakita Brahma mana, sham'ka' tirohita brahata mana;
A'sha' tarungita manuja mana, A'nanda utprerita sujana.

Shubha karma rata yogii vikala, kala kala karata dha'ra' vikala;
Vishva'sa arpita mana at'ala, sam'ta'pa rahita suha'sa pala.

Ga'vata jagata, na'cata nikhila, khilatii suha'nii dhu'pa khila;
Jhilamila'tii ca'ndanii ba'je vigula,
Na'ncatii 'Madhu' ya'minii hokara mrdula.

10. Kitanii sadiyam' * 308/20.05.09

Kitanii sadiyam' biita calii haem',
Tuma a'ye na'm' maem' pahuncha' hu'n;
Ta're kitane camaka cale haem', dharin'ii kitaniim' dhara dha'yii haem'.

Kitane nabha mujhako dekhe haem', kitane jala mujhako siim'ce haem';
Cir'iya'm' kitanii chahaka gayiim' haem',
Garjana sim'ha kiye kitane haem'.

Ma'navata' kitanii bikharii hae, da'navata' kitanii nikharii hae;
Kitane pa's'a'n'om' kii ka'ya', Pratisam'cara mem' pus'pa banii hae.

Mere ura mem' tuma na'm' a'ye, sura na'm' pa'ye, sudhi na' pa'yii;
Pra'n'om' kii isa u'ha poha mem', rtu na' bha'yii, gati na'm' pa'yii.

Prema payonidhi vikala hue haem', sura surabhita ho bikhara rahe haem';
Ka'ya' kii ma'ya' mem' Mohana,
'Madhu' mana Ra'dha' nirakha rahe hacm'.

11. Sarasata' sa' raha' * 312/20.05.09

Sarasata' sa' raha' maem' sajana,
Barasata' sa' raha' 'Madhu' gagana;
Tarasata' sa' raha' ye camana, ca'hata' sa' raha' ye sumana.

Jiiva ja'grta nahiim' ho raha', tandra' ura se nikala na'm' rahii;
Bhiiti ura mem' hae cah'yii huyii, miiti mana mem' nahiim' a'rahii.

Ga' bhii do sura naya' sa' sajana,
Raca bhii do kucha naya' sa' bhuvana;
Ranga do ye ram'giila' sa' mana, priiti Prthvii pae ja'ye bikhara.
Nancata' sa' raha' umra bhara, ka'npata' sa' raha' svapna bhara;
Dina nikalata' raha' bekhabara, ra'ta rotii rahii beasara.

Surabhi bharado sumana mem' sajana,
Sa'njha ga' ja'ye miit'hii gazala;
Pavana na'nce de kara tala kii dhvani,
Pra'ta pa'ja'ye pra'n'om' mem' dhuna.

12. Dhara' dhu'li kii bhu's'ta man'i * 163/23.09.08

Tuma dhara' dhu'li kii bhu's'ita man'i,
A'bhu's'ita jiivana kii ciradhvani;
Sa'gara tala kii 'madhu' hiira kan'i, jjiivana kii nandita vaitarin'ii

Nabha ura kii eka kiran'a sahamii, va'yu se vicarita bu'nda nayii;
A'nandita Gunga' kii t'hit'hurii, simat'ii sisakii shist'ita laharii.

Pus'pita pulakita surabhita vras't'ita,
A'nandita ga'yita sura pramudita;
Ra'gom' kii eka lahara thirakita, jiivana ka' eka svapana surabhita.

Maem' na'm' ja'nu'n, maem' na' ma'nu'n,
Jiivana kii dhuna sunana' ja'nu'n;
Jiivana kii ra'ga bharii ba'tem', kahata' sunata' ga'ta' ja'u'n.
Tuma a'ja'o, 'madhu' ga'ja'o, jiivan ke srota baha' ja'o;
A'nanda dhara' para de ja'o, a'nanda sudha' lete ja'o.

13. Madhu tum a'ja'o to * 28/03.04.08

'Madhu' tuma a'ja'o to, ranga bharem' jiivana mem'
Ra'ga bharem', cham'da bharem', giita bharem' tribhuvan mem';
Ru'pa bharem', rasa bharadem',
Gandha bharem' hara mana mem'.

Tras'a' ks'udha' mit'a ja've, jagamaga jaga ho ja've;
Svasthyita tana ho ja'vem', sva-sthita mana ho ja'vem'.

Karma karem' dhya'n dharem', bhakti bharem' jiivan mem';
A'sha' abhila'sha' kii, pu'rti karem' jaga jana mem'.

Bha's'a' bha'vom' mem'   bharem',
Hara jiivana   hrda kii kaha pa'ye;
Hara mana kucha suna pa'ye sunapa'ye,
Hara hrda hada saha pa'ye.

Kunt'ha' ko ka't'a sakem', kat'uta' ko ba'nt'a sakem'
Kampit mana pra'n'a na hom', jhankrat a'nandita hom'.
Sras't'a' ka' prema page, bhu'ma' ke kan'a kan'a mem'.

Hars'ita prathvii ka' hara kan'a ho,
Prati pus'hpa praphullita ho ja've;
Vihanse vicharem' jaga mem' jantu, har tantu tarungita ho ja've.

Tuma a'ja'o, aba a'ja'o, bhava bhara ja'o tuma bhava bhara mem';
Vicaro viharo bhu'ma' mana mem',
An'u ke mana mem', jaga jiivana mem'.
***

13R. Madhu Chanda * 486BC/13.08.09

A'nanda ka'nana Krs'n'a kita, Gopiii bina' ve phirata kita;
Kokila lakhati virahita phirati,   jala Jamuna vica siharata phirata.

A'ye na kyom', ga'ye na kyom', gayanha sahita dha'ye na kyom';
Kyom' ven'u binu sa'je camana,
Kyom' Shya'ma binu shobhita gagana.

14. Purus'a ke purus'a'rtha tuma * 29/04.04.08

Purus'a ke purus'a'rtha tuma, maem' prakrti kii krta baddhata';
Megha mandrita madhura tuma, maem' mayu'rii kii madhurata'.

Cancala capala maem' caturata', tuma shya'ma sundara saghanata';
Maem' karma prerita rata virata, tuma dharma prerita mana virata.

Tuma prakrti ko pra'krta karata, maem' prakrti kii gati mem' pravrta;
Prakrti mujhe para - krti lage, sva - krti sarisa tuma mem' page.

Cintita sabhaya vicalita vyathita, maem' vicaratii isa vishva mem';
Vis'apa'na karate vikat'a vihanse, viharate brahma'n'd'a mem'.

Tuma dhara' kii dhu'la dharate vicarate,
Maem' dhara' ke phu'la cunate bikharatii.
Phu'la mere dhu'la apanii mem' mila'lo,
Prakrti ko nija anka le Prabhu tuma sula'lo.

15. Madhu ga'na tuma ga'o * 53/08.05.08

'Madhu' ga'na tum ga'o suhrda, mana ko hrdaya mem' le calo;
Tuma ra'ga ek ga'o gahana, a'nanda mem' aba le calo.

Mana ko liye a'ka'sha mem', Tuma du'ra baha kar cala par'ao;
Mere hraday ke ra'ga ko, A'ka'sha Ganga' bana'do.
Tuma calo, a'nanda kii laya mem' baho;
Le calo, priya ke nikat'a, tuma le calo.

Vishva sarita'   mem', mujhe tuma baha'lo;
Madhura   madhukara, kara naca'lo.
Suhrda mere hrdaya ko, tuma dekhalo,
Madhura muralii ta'na para, tuma naca'lo.

Giita tuma ga'lo, mujhe ma'dhyama bana'lo;
Surasarii bana madhurata' mem' d'uba'lo.
Mere mana ko tarangita kara le calo;
Giita mem' bhara kara mujhe tuma le calo.

16. Mayu'rii ko megha mem' * 30/04.04.08

Mayu'rii ko megha mem', Prabhu tuma naca'lo!
Prakrati ko thirakita karo,
Nava vishva d'ha'lo.

Madhura bha's'a'em' bahem', hara kan't'ha mem';
Kan't'ha a'nandita rahem' vaekun't'ha mem'.
Sarasa surabhita praphullita hara pus'pa ho;
Citta nirmala, mana abhaya, svacchanda ho.
Sudha' vasudha' para baha' do.

Na'ca ja'em' mana , magana ma'nava rahe;
Sras't'i kii shobha', aks'un'n'a anupama rahe.
Thiraka ja'em' jiiva, jiivana kii chat'a' mem';
Amiya ja'ye varasa, sa'vana kii ghat'a' mem'.
Shiva jat'a' se Surasarii ko phira baha' do.

Pradu's'an'a mana ka' haro, tan ka' haro;
Vibhu's'ita jala ko karo, vana ko karo.
Va'yu ko vicarita karo, gad gad gagana mem',
Mukta dha'ra'em' bahem', jar'a jiiva jaga mem'.
Kokila' ke ra'ga se kisalaya khila'do.

Bha'va jar'ata' ko jagata se hat'a'lo,
Mazahavom' ko hava'om' se baca'lo.
Vishva ko vya'pak bana' vyavaha'ra karalo,
Sam'pada' samucita 'Madhu' ko dila'do.
Vishva sarita' bana sabhii ko Prabhu baha'do.

17. Vishva vishva'sa se khila' rahata' * 586/02.11.09

Vishva vishva'sa se khila' rahata',
Khula' khila' hiya' 'vahii' deta';
Vividhata' vishva mem' bhare rahata',
Shva svayam' bikhara vishva bana ja'ta'.

Vishva kii vicaratii vidha'om' mem',
Pra'n'a kii khula rahii gupha'om' mem';
Uphanatii macalatii ghat'a'om' mem',
Siharatii saomya sii ada'om' mem'.

Raciyata' vishva ka' basa' rahata',
Niyantran'a sabhii kucha vahii karata';
Ca'nda ta'rom' ko ghuma'ta' rahata',
An'u jiivata ko vahii phura karata'.

Cetana' cira cahakate jiivana mem',
Caraevati sikha'tii sahaja pana mem';
Prakrti ke panapate prayogom' mem',
Vikrti ke jhat'akate jharokhom' mem'.

Vishva prati ks'an'a ks'arita udita hota',
Vilaks'an'a gati liye tvarita hota';
'Madhu' drs't'a' bane sada' rahata',
Vishva tra'ta' sada' hrdaya rakhata'.

18. Kapotom' para krpa' barasa ja'tii * 575/22.10.09

Kapotom' para krpa' barasa ja'tii,
Candanii mem' ghat'a' hae khila ja'tii;
Trasita tana para baha'ra a'ja'tii,
Rasita mana bhakti lahara cha'ja'tii.

Kalpana' se ghire kapolo' para,
Karun'a ka'ya' khile navelom' para;
Krs'n'a kii ka'ncanii kamala ka'ya',
Kas't'a kara du'ra taratii mana ma'ya'.

Ka'nanom' kii kat'hora kat'u ga'tha',
Kaha nahiim' pa'ta' ka'ga kas't'a katha';
Hiran'i ke sahamate se nayanom' mem',
Bharii kitanii katha' hae ka'jala mem'.

Krandanom' ka' kasa'ba kar'ava' hae,
Candanom' ka' rakha'va tiikha' hae;
Bandhanom' ka' baha'va sikur'a' hae,
Prabhu spandanom' se tarana' hae.

Sva'ti kii bu'nda kabhii gira ja'tii,
Siipa motii bane hae khila ja'tii;
Kapolom' para baha'ra a'ja'tii,
'Madhu' ka'nana mem' kaliya'n khila ja'tiim'.

19. Ananta kii angar'a'ii * 21/28.03.08

Tuma ho ananta kii angar'a'ii;
Maem' hu'n 'Madhu' jaga kii gahara'ii.

Desha ka'la pa'tra, Tumha're a'ya'ma haem';
Sata raja tama, Tumha'rii prakrti ke nihshva's haem'.
Mahat aham citta, Tumha'rii prabandha shaelii kii laharem' haem'.
Panca tattva tumha'rii sampada' haem';
Prakrti janita jiiva, Tumha'rii praja' haem'.

Jiiva ko, desha ka'la pa'trom' se vilaga kara,
Vilaya lete ho, svayam mem' jab kabhii;
Srs't'i kara dete ho, jiiva ke shu'nya mem', svayam kii;
Jagata saja ut'hata' hae, panca tattva kii camaka se.

Srjana karate ho, apanii hara vidha' mem', hara ada' mem';
Vicitra jiiva raca lete ho, panca tattva kii hara parat mem'.
Kara lete ho viracita vana, jantu, jana sujana svayam mem';
Saba vicarita vika'sashiila rahate haim', jana vjana mem'.

Tuma sam'cara raca, pratisancara   paida' karate ho;
Sujana ko svayama mem'   samet'a srjana kara' dete ho.
Srjana ke hara pal, hara pa'tra va desha mem', srjita karate ho,;
Nava srs't'i nava bha'va, nava ra'ga, nava lahar, nayii gahara'ii.

20. Prabhu tumha're praka'sha mem' * 42/22.04.08

Prabhu tumha're praka'sh mem', kitane uja'le a'ye;
Tumha'rii niirava nisha' mem', kitane ta're jagamaga'ye.
Kaune mem' bait'ha' mera' mana,
Dekha nahiim' pa'ya', samajha nahiim' pa'ya'.

Kitanii cim'ga'riim', bujhate bujhate jaliim';
Kitanii a'tma'em', cita'om' ke d'her se ut'hiim'.
Kitane patam'ge praka'sh ke prema mem' tare;
Kitane jiiva du'sarom' ko jiivita rakhane mem' ut'he.

Apanii prakrati mem', tuma kitane jiiva racate ho;
Unakii bhu'kha pya's ka' dhya'n rakhate ho.
Eka eka koshika' ko rakta rasa dete ho;
Phira kabhii, eka ka' jiivana, du'sare ko le lene dete ho!

Kabhii kabhii maim' socata' hu'm'!
Tuma apana' yaha khela,
Kisii aura taraha, kyom' nahiim' kara lete!
Kyom' itanii anupama niriiha a'tma'om' ko naca'te ho;
Kyom' hara pra'n'a ko ba'ra ba'ra,
Mit'ane samit'ane ka' kas't'a dete ho.

Sha'yada tuma hara atma' kii, Usakii hara jiivana liila' kii,
Anubhu'ti ka' pra'n'a rasa parakhate ho;
Usa pra'n'a rasa ko srs't'i mem' phira bo dete ho.

Shariira yam'tra mem', mana mantra ka' biija bo,
A'tma tantra kii fasala uga'te ho.
Phira kabhii, dagdha biija ho ja'ne para,
Ura mem' rakha lete ho.

21. Ananta ka' ra'hii * 11/27.03.08

Prabhu maem' ananta ka' ra'hii hu'n,
Tuma mere sa'ks'ii ho, mere hama safara ho.

Kitanii vyatha'yem' viharatii haim' vishva mem',
Bikharate haim' pus'pa kitane tumha're shikhar mem'.
Kitanii kaliyom' ko tuma Karun'a' dete ho,
kitane kam't'om' ko tuma hat'ava' dete ho.

Tuma calate rahate ho, cala'te rahate ho;
Muskara'te ho, hansa'te ho, preran'a' dete ho.
Kabhii rula' dete ho, kabhii sula' lete ho;
Pya'ra mem' kanpa' dete ho, krodha mem' hansa' lete ho.

Tumha'rii liila' kabhii samajh a'tii hae,
Kabhii samajhii huii hokar bhii bega'nii ho ja'tii hae.
Kabhii tuma cira daya'lu lagate ho,
Kabhii daya' bina' virahii bera'hii lagate ho.

Tuma jiivom' ko kabhii
Svaccham'da vicaran'a karane dete ho;
Kabhii unakii eka eka indriya ko jakar'a dete ho,
mana pra'n'a ko bhat'akane dete ho.

Kabhii unaka' sab kucha samet'a apane hrdaya mem' rakha,
Unase bhiks'a' mam'gava'kar prasa'da ma'ga lete ho;
To kabhii unake guru cakra para bait'ha,
'Madhu' krpa' bikhera dete ho, ma'lika bana' dete ho.

22. Nirgun'a sagun'a satta' * 56/13.05.08

Nirgun'a satta' sagun'a ho srs't'i racatii hae,
Prakrti usakii prabam'dha shakti bana prakat' hotii hae.

Srs't'i mem' trigun'a'tmaka sam'tulana hota' hae;
Sata raja tama gun'om' mem',
Samtulana sa'mya rahata' hae.

Sata raja tama ka' sam'tulana, asa'mya hone para,
Pratisam'cara mem' prabam'dh sudha'rane,
Prakrti kriya'shiila hotii hae.

Sagun'a satta', mahata bha'va, dha'ran'a kar letii hae;
Srs't'a sam'stha' aura vikasita hone para,
Mahata aham prakat'a karatii' hae.

Avashyakata' hone para,
Aham citta ka' a'virbha'va karata' hae,
Srs't'i ko sagun'a mahata, aham, citta cala'te haim'.

Prakrti prabam'dha kala' mem'
Parima'rjita hotii ja'tii hae, ;
Sagun'a dvaita aura phira,
Anant hota' ja'ta' hae.

Vikashita srs't'i mem',
Sagun'a kii prakrati ka' niyantran'a bar'hata' hae;
Sagun'a svayama bhii prabam'dha ke
Ananta pada vibha'gom' mem',
Prakat'a hota' hae.

Sagun'a kii srs't'i ka' vista'ra,
Pratisam'cara ko 'Madhu' gati deta' hae;
Usakii prakrti kii prabam'dha shailii,
Srs't'i ko pragati detii hae.

23. Ananta raciyata' * 14/27.03.08

Tuma ananta raciyata' ho, desh ka'la pa'tra ke,
Citta ke, mahata ke, trigun'a'tmaka prakrti ke, sagun'a ke.

Panch bhu'ta bhu's'ita hae tumha'rii hii Prathvii,
Jala agni va'yu evam' a'ka'sha mem'
Tumha'ra' hii citta vya'kula ho,
Prathvii ke kles'a se;
Raca leta' hai vana, jantu, jana;
Sujana, yogii apanii hii srs't'i mem'.

Yogii yoga karata' hae, tumha're hii sagun'a se,
Tumha'ra' sagun'a yoga karata' hae
Srs't'i ke yogarasa se.
A'lhva'dita spandita ho mila ja'ta' hae nirgun'a se;
Nirgun'a phir kabhii bhii sagun'a ho ut'hata' hae;
Ho ut'hatii hae nava srs't'i   nava prakrati kii usii se.

Srs't'i vihansita, rasita ho, racatii hae nava srs't'i;
Srs't'i, nava srs't'i, antara srs't'i, va'hya srs't'i.
Racatii hae hama'rii srs't'i   pa'tra ko,
Desha ka'la mem';
Desha ka'la pa'tra na'ca ut'hate haem'
Tumha'rii isa kriir'a' se.
Vismrata prakrti vihansa ut'hatii hae,
Trigun'a gun'a'yama'na ho ut'hate haim'.

Nirgun'a kii gahara'ii gun'a raca letii hae;
Hara desha ka'la mem'
Prati pa'tra se praya's kara' letii hae.
Gun'a vicarita ho, vikasita ho;
Nirgun'a ke gun'a ko samajha lete haem'.

Desha ka'la pa'tra,
Srs't'i ko a'nanda se bhar dete haem'.
Apanii isa liila' ka' a'nanda rasa,
Tuma 'Madhu' mana mem' baet'he le lete ho.

24. Sagun'a * 57/13.05.08

Sagun'a ka' mahata, ahama bana', aham citta bana',
Hara citta ne apana' a'ka'sha raca';
A'ka'sha mem' va'yu vicarii, va'yu agni banii, agni jal banii,
Jala prathvii bana', panca tatva maya jagata bana'.

Prthvii ke kan'a jaba atishaya sam'ghars'a rata hue,
Taba usane, kisii prathvii kan'a ke andar, citt ko jaga'ya';
Vanaspati prakat'a huii, vikashit huii, sam'ghars'a rata huii,
Vanaspati ke sam'ghars'a se srjan hua' jantu ka'.

Jantu vikashit ho, sam'ghars'a rata ho, ma'nava bana ut'ha',
Ma'nava sam'ghars'a karata' karata', buddhi jiivii bana';
Buddhi jiivii ma'nava sam'ghars'a se a'dhya'tmika bana',
Sagun'a, nirgun'a, srs't'i cakra va prakrti ko ja'na'.

A'dhya'tmika ma'nava antatah mila'ya' mana ko sagun'a mem';
Sama'dhis't'a ho, samarpit hua', sagun'a nirgun'a mem'.
Sagun'a ne apane isa naye samarpita ma'nava ko;
Sagun'ita kiya' sras't'i ke sam'ca'lana mem'.

Phira racii srs't'I , sagun'a, mahata, aham citta kii;
Panca tattva, vana, jantu, jana, sujana kii.
Srs't'i ke cakra para cakra cale;
Satta'em' sagun'a nirgun'a huiim'.
'Madhu' a'nanda dha'ra'em' aneka bahiim',
Sambhu'ti kuccheka huiim'.

25. Tuma kaba kya' karoge * 13/27.03.08

Tuma kaba kya' karoge, kisako kyom' karoge;
Desha ka'la pa'trom' kii siima' mem' bandha' mera' mana,
Samajha nahiim' pa'ta', saha nahiim' pa'ta'.

Dekha nahiim' pa'ta' maim desha va pa'trom' ka' ka'la,
Ka'la va pa'trom' ka' desha, desha va ka'la ke pa'tra;
Tuma jha'nka lete ho, desha ka'l pa'tra ko,
Jhakajhora jhanka'ra dete ho unako.

Srs't'i kar dete ho kabhii kisii
'Madhu' ka'la mem', desha kii, pa'tra kii, desha mem' desha kii,
Pa'tra mem' pa'tra kii, ka'la mem' ka'la kii;
Athava' laya kara lete ho, sabako svayam mem'.

26. Yoga mem' pratis't'hita hone para * 61/13.05.08

Yoga mem' pratis't'hita hone para,
Tantra jina'na ka' suyoga pa'ne ka' bha'va a'ta' hae;
Yoga ke tvarita prayoga ka' abhya'sa,
Srs't'a' kii krpa', tantronmukha kara' detii hae.

Tantra mem' sthita hone para;
Srs't'i mem' maha' prabandha kii ks'hamata' a'ja'tii hae;
Nirantar abhya'sa va bhakti se;
Srs't'i kii seva' mem' aura a'nanda a'ta' hae.

Yoga tantra siddha hone para, bhakti aura sudrar'ha hotii hae;
Srs't'a' mem' a'stha' aura vishva'sa aura bar'hata' hae.
Jina'na va karma, samarpita, samparkit yoga se rahata' hae;
Bhakti, tantra se tarangita ho, kevala' banii rahatii hae.

Bhakti jina'na karma yoga tantra, susthira hone para,
Srs't'a' krpa' kara sakate haem', svayam mem' laya kara sakate haem'.
Apanii srs't'i ka' aura uttarda'yitva use de sakate haem';
Usake sabhii sam'ska'rom' ka' bha'ra le sakate haem'.

Phira kabhii samaya a'ne para, dagdh biija kara sakate haim';
Aura kabhii, sras't'i cakra ke niyantran'a ka'
'Madhu' ka'rya de sakate haem'!

27. Pa'rakhii * 12/27.03.08

Tuma kitane pa'rakhii ho, pariiks'aka ho,
Paridras't'a', prabam'dhaka, pra'yojaka ho;
Pra'n'a maya pratis't'hita prayoga maya ho.

Yoga se racate ho sam'yoga viyoga,
Prakrati ko prayoga kara kara'te ho sam'yoga.
Svayam tuma adras't'a' asrs't'a' bana,
Sras't'i ke drashyom' ko druti dete ho;
Kabhii sras't'i ko nija anka mem' sula' lete ho,
Kabhii nija hrdaya mem' srs't'i ko bit'ha',
Sphurita kara dete ho.

Tuma antarmana mem' hansa kabhii;
Srs't'i ke 'Madhu' jiivom' ko
Khushii se a'lor'ita kara dete ho.
Kabhii apanii painii dras't'i se pa'ra ja'kara,
Praja' kii prajina' ko prasphut'ita kara dete ho.

28. Samaya * 68/21.05.08

Samaya kya' srs't'i ka' a'peks'ika a'ya'ma hae!
Samaya kya' desha pa'tra ka' sahodara hae!

Samaya kya' sambha'vana' kii patha taranga hae!
Samaya kya' ana'di ananta kii rekha' hae!
Samaya kya' srs't'i kii laya hae!
Samaya ka' udgama kya' sagun'a se hae!

Ma'nava kya' sagun'a mem' samarpita ho,
Ka'la ko bheda sakata' hae!
Ma'nava kya' desha ke ka'la ko, jha'nka sakata' hae!
Kya' vaha pa'trom' ke bhu'ta   bhavis'ya ko, dekha sakata' hae!

Ka'la ka' niyanta' kya' sagun'a hae!
Ka'la ka' drs't'a' kya' Bra'hmii mana hae!
Kya' 'Madhu' ma'nava, mana ko Bra'hmii mana bana';
Desha ka'la pa'tra mem', svacchanda vicara sakata' hae!

29. Desha ka'la pa'tra *69/21.05.08

Desha ka'la pa'tra kii svara lahariya'm',
Srs't'a' se tarungita haem'.
Ananta pa'tra, ananta deshom' mem',
ananta ka'la mem', liila'yita haem';
Chandita spandita haem', thirakita a'nandita haem'.

Prthvii kii parikrama' karate upagraha ka' patha,
Shu'nya se siidhii rekha' ja'na par'ata' hae;
Srs't'i ka' samaya bhii vaise hii,
A'di ananta ke biica a'yojita hae.

Bra'hmii mana ka'la cakra kii gati ko,
Bhanpa sakata' hae, ma'npa sakata' hae,
Chala'm'ga sakata' hae;
Jha'm'ka sakata' hae, jhakajhora sakata' hae.
Tvarita kara sakata' hae, jham'krata kara sakata' hae.

Bra'hmii mana jiivaa'tma' ko suniyojita karata' hae;
Desha ko vya'paka vyavasthita karata' hae.
Ka'la kii a'peks'ika gati ko sam'yojita karata' hae;
Srs't'i prabandha ko pragatishiila bana'ta' hae.
***

29R. Madhu Chanda * 433D/17.07.09

Saba desha ka'lom' kii katha',
Saba pa'tra kii paricaya vyatha';
Tumane racii haem' saba vidha',
Tumane saja'yiim' saba fiza'.

Jo kilakate saba phira rahe,
Jo hradaya mem' haem' bhara rahe;
Ho saba kisii ke raciyata',
'Madhu' jiiva ke Tuma pran'eta'.

30. Gatishiila mana * 70/23.05.08

Gatishiila mana kii su'ks'ma kriya';
Brahma'n'd'a ko a'nandita karatii hae.

Calatii ga'r'ii mem',
Bacce kii phem'kii gem'da,
Jaise ya'triyom' ko a'nanda detii hae;
Ra'ha mem' calate ya'trii ko vaha gem'da,
Ga'r'ii kii khir'akii se nikala,
A'hata ya' a'nandita kara sakatii hae.

Prthvii kii kaks'a' se nikala yahii gem'da,
Shu'nya sthita ya'na ko nas't'a kara sakatii hae;
Athava' use du'sarii kaks'ha' mem'
Stha'pita kara sakatii hae.

Calatii ga'r'ii mem' phem'kii
Gem'da kii su'ks'ma gati,
Ba'hara nikala ga'r'ii kii gati se teja lagatii hae.
Vahii shu'nya mem' ja',
Prathvii kii gati se adhika teja lagatii hae.

Gatishiila Bra'hmii mana kii
Su'ks'hma 'Madhu' kriya' bhii,
Vaese hii, panca bhu'ta jiiva jagata ko
Jha'nkrata, spandita karatii hae.
Niyantrita, tarangita karatii hae,
Thirakita, a'nandita karatii hae.

31. Srs't'i prabandha ks'amata' * 76/28.05.08

Adbhuta hae, tumha'rii srs't'a' kii prabandha ks'amata';
Vicitra hae, tumha're niyantran'a kii kaoshalata'.

Nirgun'a se sagun'a ho, srs't'i raca, tumha'ra' ananta hona';
Mahata mem' aham, citta, panca tatva raca lena'.
Prathvii se eka koshii aura phira, ananta koshii jiiva gar'ha lena';
Ma'nava ke vikara'la mana ko bhii, svayam mem' mila' lena'.

Prati jiiva ko pratisancara mem', pragati kii ora prerita karana';
Svayam hara desha ka'la mem', pa'trom' ko protsa'hita karana'.

Hara jiiva ke mana kii   ba'ta suna lena';
Hara 'Madhu' hrdaya ko apana' nirdeshana dete rahana'.
Hara jiiva kii mrtyu ka' marma samajhana';
Hara jiiva ko uttarottara janma dena'.

32. Srs't'i prabandha prashiks'an'a * 77/28.05.08

Kitana' rahasyamaya hae tumha'ra' hara pra'n'a ko,
Srs't'i prabandha mem', prashiks'ita karana'.

Yugom' yugom' ma'nava ko, jina'na, vijina'na,
Bha's'a', kala', dharma, a'dhya'tma,
Jiivana shaelii, sama'ja vyavastha', ra'ja tantra sikha'na';
Sam'ca'ra, ya'tra', grah ya'tra', brahma'n'd'a prabandha mem',
Prashiks'ita, pratis't'hita karana',
Ma'nava mana kii jar'a cetana shaktiyom' ko
Vikashita niyantrita karana'.

Vyakti va sama'ja ko shu'dra, ks'atriya,
Vaishya va vipra sama'ja cakrom' mem';
Uttarottara praviin'a va pratis't'hita kara'na';
Vijina'na ko a'dhya'ma mem' le ja'na';
A'dhya'tma ko vijina'namaya karana'.

Prati 'Madhu' jiiva ko, srs't'i vika'sha ke liye,
Pu'rn'a vikashita praphullita hone ka' suyoga sam'yoga dena'.
Sras't'i vika'sa mem' unmukha hone para
Use svayam mem' samet'a lena'.

33. Gurutva ka' a'kars'an'a * 86/05.06.08

Gurutva ka' a'kars'an'a,
Gurutva'kars'an'a sva'bha'vika hae;
Gurutva se mahatva, gati avasthiti pariyojit hae.
Gurutva'kars'an'a se hii srs't'i gatishiila hae;
Gurutva'kars'an'a se hii jagata pragatishiila hae.

Prathvii kii gurutva'kars'an'a shakti ba'm'dhatii hae,
Pancabhu'ta, vana, jantu, jana, sujana;
Gati shakti ba'dhita hae gurutva'kars'an'a se;
Niyantrita haem' gatishiila jiiva jana sujana.

Ma'tra'om' ka' gun'atva, paraspara du'ratva;
Anupa'lita karate haem', a'kars'an'a ka' gurutva.
Am'dhaka'ra se praka'sha mem' calata' prati pathika;
Ju'jhata' hae jar'a, ja'gatika sa'tvika a'kars'an'a se prati pala.

Ma'nava buddhi se parica'lita shu'nya ya'n,
Ucita gati va nika'sha kon'a se pare ja'te haem';
Dhyeya pu'ra' kara shu'nya ya'na mem' laot'a a'te haem',
'Madhu' Gurutva'kars'an'a ko pa'ra kara a'te ja'te haem'.

34. Guru shis'ya gurutva * 87/05.06.08

Gurutva ka' a'kars'an'a gaurava pu'rn'a hae;
Gurutva se hii, mahatva, gati, sthiti parica'lita hae.

Guru ka' gurutva va mahatva prerita karata' hae,
Shis'ya ka' samarpan'a, Guru kii ora gamana;
Guru ko arpan'a, Guru ke prati bhakti,
Shis'ya ko dila' detii hae
Guru krapa' va Guru namana.

Guru shis'ya apanii a'tma'om' kii
Ma'tra' sthiti avastha' se
Paraspara a'kars'hita karate haem';
Brahma'n'd'a ko ve
Bha'va'kars'ita karate haem',
Jagata ko bhii ve bhakti se
Tarungita thirakita karate haem'.

Shis'ya ka' dhyeya Guru hae,
Shis'ya ka' gurutva, garima' maya hota' hua',
Bana ut'hata' hae mahatva;
Guru ka' Gurutva su'ks'ma, gahan,
Karun'a va krapa' maya hue,
Ho ut'hata' hae " sahajatama mamatva ".

Gurutva'kars'an'a sras't'i ka' 'Madhu' satya hae,
Gurutva'kars'an'a sras't'i ka' mahatva hae;
Gurutva'kars'an'a hote hue hii Guru gatishiila hae,
Gurutva'kars'an'a hote hue hii shis'ya pragatishiila hae.
***

34 R. Madhu Chanda * 433C/17.07.09

Tuma sabhii mem' baet'he hue,
Ho dekhate mana kii dasha';
Dete dikha' bhaya mem' pravrta,
Karate sajaga ja'te dikha'.

35. Gurutvaa'kars'an'a * 88/06.06.08

Gurutva ka' a'kars'an'a hae gurutvaa'kars'an'a.

U'para phem'kii gaim'da ka',
Prathvii kii goda mem' punah laot'a a'na';
Khelane gaye shishu ka', ghar ba'pasa a',
Ma'n kii goda mem' let'a ja'na'.

Tiivra praka'sha mem' patam'gom' ka',
Praka'sha srota ke sa'tha kriir'a' karana';
Cakorii ka' nirantara ca'nda ko niha'rana',
Su'ryamukhii ka' su'ryonmukh hona'.

Yuva' samtati ka' ja'gatika sammohana upara'nta,
Punah pa'riva'riiya a'stha' mem' laot'a a'na';
Shis'ya ka' Guru se vikars'hita hona',
Punah Guru ke a'kars'an'a mem' a'ja'na'.

Sa'tvikata' mem' Prathvii shayana,
Shis'ya ka' sa's't'a'nga pran'a'ma;
Shaeshava mem' ma'n ka' dugdha pa'na,
Jiivana samajhane ke ba'da, vraddha ka' shishupana.

Timira se praka'shonmukha kara'na',
Jar'a se su'ks'matara bha'va mem' liye calana';
Guru ka' krapa' bhara' vilocana,
Sagun'a ka' hae, srs't'i cakra a'yojana.

36. An'u jiivata ka' prema * 89/06.06.08

Srs't'i ke prati an'u jiivata ka'
Paraspara prema gurutva'kars'an'a hae;
Gurutva kii ma'tra'em', paraspara du'rii, sthiti avastha'em',
Gurutva'kars'an'a bala ka' ma'pa dan'd'a haem'.

Prati an'ujiivata mem' vidyama'na pra'n'a,
A'kars'ita karate haem', sabhii pra'n'aom' ko;
Preran'a' protsa'hana, cetana' dete haem',
Unake chaetanya ke sa'hacarya ko.

Srs't'i mem' svayam gun'ita sagun'a,
Niha'rata' parakhata' hae, nija srs't'i ko;
A'nanda leta' deta' hae, srs't'i mem' phaile,
Apane hii angom' se, nija   angom' ko.

Udga'rita utprerita karate hue, sagun'a a'kars'ita karata' hae,
Nija shariira mana pra'n'a mem' sabhii pra'n'om' ko;
A'kars'ita karate haem' sabhii pra'n'a bhii,
Nija bhaotika ma'nasika, a'tmika bha'va se sagun'a ko.

Dha' ut'hate haem' pancabhu'ta, vana jiiva sujana,
Bhanpa gurutva ke ingita udga'ra ko;
Thirakate hue apanii kaks'a' va cakra mem',
Athava' tor'ate badalate hue, siima'om' ko.

Pa'trom' ka' bhaotika ma'nasika   a'dhya'tmika parima'pa,
Paraspara bhaotika ma'nasika a'dhya'tmika du'riya'm';
Srs't'i ka' bha'ra bala, mana a'tma sa'mya, sthiti, gati,
'Madhu' ma'nyata'yem' niyantrita karata' hae..

37. Ananta ka' chanda * 117/27.06.08

Mera' prati pala ananta ka' chanda hae;
Mera' astitva ananta ka' a'nanda hae.
Mera' prati ansha ananta ka' a'shraya hae;
Mera' vyaktitva, ananta ka' ka'vya hae.

Sarva vya'pta ka' mem', abhinna astitva hu'n;
Sarva shaktisha'lii ka' maim' satata svaru'pa hu'n.
Sarva'm'tarya'mii kii maem' abhinna satta' hu'n.
Ana'di ke ananta rishtom' kii maem' satata kar'ii hu'n.

Desha ka'la kii nirantarata' kii a'tma' sa'ks'ii hae.
A'tma' drs't'a' va drashya ke rishtom' kii du'riya'm'
Desha se ma'patii hae .
A'tma' anubhavom' ka' antara samaya se ma'patii hae .
Para samaya bhii vica'ra ma'tra hae;
Usakii anubhu'ti a'tma' ke a'nanda se prakat'a ya' pratiita hotii
hae.

"Brahma satya hae, jagata a'peks'ika satya hae";
"Yatha' pin'd'e tatha' brahma'n'd'e" satya hae.
Jo jiiva mana mem' hae, vahii Brahma mana mem' hae;
Jo pala mera' hae, vaha usake ana'di mem' hae.
Jo 'Madhu' a'tma' merii hae, usii kii hae.

38. Mana mem' base braja ra'ja * 52/08.05.08

Mana mem' base Braja Ra'ja tuma,
'Madhu' hrdaya mem' cha'ye raho;
Tuma pavana bana bahate raho, ajina'na ko dahate raho.

Tuma mahata ho, tuma jina'na ho, a'nanda kii sura ta'n ho;
Tuma rang ho, madhu ru'pa ho, a'nanda ke pratiru'pa ho.
A'sha' bhara' vijina'na ho, tuma a'dhya'tmika jina'na ho;
A'nanda kii utpreran'a', tuma sa'dhana' kii jyoti ho.

Tuma mahata ke anura'ga ho, tuma jina'na ke saobha'gya ho;
Tuma bha'va ke a'dhiis'a ho, tuma madhurata' kii ta'na ho.
Pus'pom' kii surabhi tuma ho, jina'na ke a'nanda ho;

Vijina'na ke tuma jina'na ho, tuma jina'na ke vijina'na ho.

39. A'nanda kii anubhu'ti * 123/28.06.08

Kya' maem' a'nanda kii anubhu'ti nahiim'!
Kya' maem' a'nanda ka' pratiru'pa nahiim'!
Kya' mere pala srs't'i mem' sama'hita nahiim';
Kya' mera' stha'na brahma'n'd'a mem' nahiim'!

Kya' dhruva ta're se maem' a'kars'ita nahiim'!
Kya' brahma'n'd'a mem' maem' a'nandita nahiim'!
Kya' mere cakra, Guru spars'a se a'nandita nahiim'?

Kya' merii kund'alinii, Prabhu prema mem' alhva'dita nahiim'!
Kya' mere sahasra'ra para, Guru ka' vara'bhaya nahiim'?
Kya' mere u'para, Prabhu kii krapa' nahiim'!

Mujhe tuma praka'sha se bhara dete ho;
Svayameva mujhe, a'kars'ita kara lete ho.
'Madhu' mana ko apane andar bit'ha', sama'dhis't'a kara dete ho.

Mere mana pra'n'a ko bha'va'lupta kara;
Kya' tumane mujhe a'nandita kiya' nahiim'?
Kya' yaha tumha'rii apa'ra ahaetukii krpa' nahiim'?

40. Srs't'i usakii hae * 8/19.03.08

Srs't'i usakii hae, merii hai terii hae;
Sabakii hae saba mem' hae, saba srs't'i mem' haem'.

Sa'm'sa lete haem', vahii jo du'sare dete haem';
Sa'm'sa dete haem', vahii du'sare lelete haim'.
Apane am'dar ka' pradu'shan'a phem'ka dete haim' ba'hara;
Ut'ha' leta' hae hara du'sara' jiiva, jiivana samajha kara.

Sa'm'som' kii yahii kriir'a' racatii hae sras't'i yoga;
Pam'ca tatvom' ka' yahii sam'yoga, karata' hae prayoga.
Sam'yog se hii 'Madhu' suyoga hota' hae;
Jiiva ka' Brahma se yoga hii srs't'i ka' suyoga hae.

41. Ananta satta' ke anga! * 116/26.06.08

Kya' hama ananta satta' ke abhinna anga nahiim'!
Kya' hama'ra' shariira, brahma'n'd'a mem' sama'yojit nahiim'!

Kya' hama'ra' mana, brhma se samparkita nahiim'!
Kya' hama'ra' shariira mana se sam'yujya nahiim'!

Kya' hama're shariira ke anga va raks'a' pran'a'lii eka nahiim'!
Kya' hama're hrdaya va anga pratyanga
Mastis'ka se sam'yukta nahiim'!

Kya' hama'ra' citta hara pala thirakita nahiim'!
Ya' vaha brahma'n'd'a kii badalatii sthitiyom' se
Prabha'vita nahiim'!

Kya' vaha sa'gara kii bu'ndom' jaisa' tarangita nahiim'!
Kya' brahma'n'd'a hara pala hama're citta ko
Sam'bha'lata' nahiim'!

Hama're shariira ka' prati   ansha, srs't'i ka' itiha'sa hae;
Hama're shariira ka' prati aunga, prati pala parivartita hae.

Hama're shariira kii koshika'yem',
A'tma raks'a' mem' praviin'a haem';
Hama'rii shva'nsa dva'ra' brahma'n'd'a
Hara pala a'ta' ja'ta' hae.

Hama'ra' mana brahma'n'd'a kii
Hara gati mem' sam'tulana rakhata' hae;
Hama'ra' mana brahma'n'd'a kii
Hara sthiti se sa'mya bana'ta' hae.

Kya' hama'ra' shariira
Mana ka' hii svaru'pa nahiim';
Kya' hama'ra' 'Madhu' mana,
Brahma kii hii satta' nahiim'.

42. Advaeta dvaeta advaeta * 129/11.07.08

Prabhu kya' tuma dvaeta ho! Kya' tuma advaeta ho!
Ya' phira ' advaeta dvaeta advaeta ' ho!
Kya' tuma advaeta se, sagun'a ho, dvaeta hue, ananta hue!
Tumha'rii ananta satta' ke ansha;
Tuma mem' mila, kya' phira advaet hue.

Ma'nava ka' 'aham brahma'smi' anubhava karana',
Apane astitva ko hae, samajha lena';
Sva'bha'vika hae tumase milane para,
Aham'ka'ra ka' a'kara tumamem' viliina hona'.
Tatvatah cara'cara satta' ko tumha'rii samajha lena';
'Ahama Brahma'smi' se pare,
'Sarvaungam Brahma Mayaung jagata', anubhu'ta karana'.

Jaise pita' banakar hii, pita' kucha samajha a'te haem';
Vaise hii 'Aham Brahmaa'smi ' anubhu'ta kara,
Jiiva tuma ko kucha samajha pa'te haem'.
Kintu jaise pita' banate hii, karttavya va adhika'ra bar'ha ja'te haem';
Tumha'ra' 'Madhu' svaru'pa anubhu'ta karate hii,
Ma'nava ke adhika'ra va karttavya bar'ha ja'te haem'.

43. Anubhu'tiya'm' va jina'na * 130/11.07.08

Anubhu'tiya'm' va jina'na, vika'sashiila kii avastha' hae;
Anabhijina'ta va ajina'na, vika'sonmukha satta' kii,
Sva'bha'vika avastha' hae.

Ajina'na, jina'na se sam'ghars'a karata' hae,
Jina'na, ajina'na se sneha karata' hae;
Ajin'ana, aham'ka'ra vika'ra bar'ha'ta' hae,
Jina'na, bhakti va krapa' la'ta' hae

Bina' pita' bane, hama apane pita' ko nahiim' samajha pa'te;
Pita' banane para, hama're putra putrii,
Hamem' samajha nahiim' pa'te.

Yaha a'peks'ika jna'na ajina'na,
Sras't'i prabandha mem' sva'bha'vika hae;
Bina' ajina'na 'Madhu' jina'na nahiim' ho pa'ta'hae,
Bina' jina'na ke ajina'na samajha nahiim' a'ta' hae.

44. Sarva vya'pta pu'rn'a satta' * 115/26.06.08

Parama'tma' sarva vya'pta pu'rn'a satta' hae;
Vahii eka ma'tra sras't'a', bhokta', paritrapta' hae.

Svayam' ko niha'rane ke liye srs't'a';
Jaba kabhii, bana ja'te haem', a'tma dras't'a';
Gar'ha lete haem' niha'rane kii vidhi;
Raca lete haem', mana buddhi.

Shariira va jagata, bana ja'te haem' drashya;
Prakat'a hote haem', dras't'a' drasht'ya va drashya.

Dras't'a' va drasht'ya paraspara
Sambam'dha racate haem';
Yahii sambam'dha
Desha bana prakat'a hote haem'.

Rishtom' mem' gati a'ne se
Ghat'ana'em' ghat'atii haem';
Ghat'ana'em' ka'la kii dyotaka haem'.

Desh ka'la pa'tra, ananta a'tma satta' ke
Sthiti janya a'ya'ma haem';
Pa'tra ho ja'te haem' kaedii buddhi ke;
Siimita desha ka'la mem' rama ja'te haem'.

Buddhi se mukti hii,
Jagata se mukta hone kii 'Madhu' yukti hae;
Vastavikata' ke prativimba ke baja'ya;
Va'stavikata' dekhana' hii mukti hae.

45. Jiiva ja'nata' hae   * 131/11.07.08

Jiiva ja'nata' hae, mana hii mana,
Ki vaha Brahma ka' ansha hae;
Satata sam'ghars'a uttarottara uttha'na,
Brahma se usaka' milane ka' praya'sa hae.

Pahale vaha eka'kii anubhava kara,
Usase samparkita nahiim' ho pa'ta';
Phira ' Ahama Brahma'smi ' anubhava kara,
Vaha aorom' se nahiim' kaha pa'ta'.

Srs't'i mem' sabhii to usiike ansha haem',
'Vayam Brahma' sabaka' svaru'pa hae;
Use ja'na lene para lajja' bhaya kyom',
Sabhii to hama'rii bha'm'ti, usake apane haem'.

Ve srs't'i pariva'ra ko,
Sneha nirdesha a'shiis'a dete haem';
Srs't'i mem' hama'rii upalabdhiyom' ko,
Yathocita sabhii ko upalabdha kara'te haem'.

Hama svayam ko, srs't'a jiivom' ko samajhem',
Yathocita karma jina'na bhakti karem';
Yoga tantra dhya'na mem' sudrar'ha hom',
Srs't'a' ko samajhem', srs't'i kii seva' karem'.

46. Tumha'rii antaranga taranga *135/11.08.08

Prabhu! Tumha'rii antaranga taranga pa'
Tumha're kucha bhakta kyom' sahaja nahiim' raha pa'te?
Kyom' bha'va jar'ata' mem' svayam ko jakar'a
Cira cetana jagata ko jar'a samajha bait'hate haem'.

Tumha're sras't'i prabandha kii alpa anubhu'ti,
Kyom' unhaim' anya manaska kara detii hae?
Kyom' ve tumha'rii brahattara satta' kii gu'r'ha liila' ko;
Gahara'ii se dekha nahiim' pa'te haem'!

Kyom' ve sa'tvika aham'ka'ra mem' ulajha ja'te haem'?
Kyom' ve sras't'i ke ta'raka bana ja'na' ca'hate haem'!
Kyom' ve tumhem' bhu'la, tumha'rii siddhiyom' ko
Pakar'ane ka' praya'sa karate haem'?
Kyom' ve tumha'rii srs't'i ko,
Apanii paetrika sampatti samajha lete haem'!

Sha'yada tuma bhii sabaka'
Adhikatama upayoga karate rahate ho;
Apanii liila' mem' anta taka sabako sha'mila rakhate ho !
Tuma kisii kii bhii jiivana liila' kabhii bhii roka sakate ho;
Tatks'an'a du'sarii liila' usase pra'rambha kara' sakate ho.

Ra'ja' ko tuma bhikha'rii bana' sakate ho,
Bhikha'rii ko ra'ja' ka' 'Madhu' uttarda'yitva de sakate ho.
A'stha'va'na kii a'stha' kama kara sakate ho;
Kama a'stha'va'na pu'rn'a a'stha' pa' sakate haem'.

47. Mahata brahata * 50/08.05.08

Kitane mahata tuma ho brahata! Kitane madhura tuma ho mahata!
Kitane suhrada tuma ho madhura! Kitane sahrada tuma ho suhrda!

Tuma vishva kii mahima' bane, brahma'n'd'a mem' cha'ye huye;
Tuma viharate brahma'n'd'a mem', a'ka'sha Gunga' bana gaye!

Tuma raman'ate racana' bhare, a'ka'sha mem', u's'a' liye;
Ghan ba'dalom' se varas'a kara, tuma dhara' ko sincita kiye.

Tuma viharate rahate sada', isa vishva mem', brahma'n'd'a mem';
Tuma a'di ke a'nanda mem', a'nanda ke isa chanda mem'.

Tuma jagata kii a'sha' bane, Tuma vishva kii bha's'a' bane;
Tuma a'sako to a'hii ja'o he madhur!
Ga'na 'Madhu' mujha ko suna'o, he mahata!

48. Madhura mahata *51/08.05.08

Kitane madhura tuma ho mahata,
Kitane sahaja tuma ho mahata!
Tuma madhura mana kii a'sha mem',
Tuma ha'sa mem', pariha'sa mem'.

Tuma mayu'ri ke na'nca mem',
Tuma cakorii kii ca'ha mem';
Tuma khva'ba ho, a'nanda ho,
Madhu chanda ho, 'Madhu' ra'ga ho!

Tuma jina'na kii Gunga' baha'ye, Shiva jat'a' se baha cale;
Tuma Kanhaiya' ka' ra'sa raca, ka'liya' mardana kara cale.

Tuma madhura bana kara cala uthe, a'nanda ke rasa mem' runge;
Hara hrday mem' tuma basa gaye, a'nanda kii Gunga' bane!

49. Sagun'a satta' ka' a'yojana * 58/13.05.08

Srs't'i sagun'a satta' ka' a'yojana hae;
Srs't'i cakra usakii sam'stha' hae.
Desha ka'la pa'trom' ka' a'yojana;
Usakii prabandh byavastha' ka' vargiikaran'a hae.
Prakrti Usake prabandha ka' kriya' bha'va hae;
Jina'na karma bhakti, Usake pa'trom' ke ma'pa dam'd'a haem'.
Karma kii gatishiilata' ka' ma'pa ka'la hae;
Panca tattvom' ke sam'ghars'a se prakat'e, jiiva pa'tra haem'.

Desha kii deha mem' vya'pta sagun'a ka' citta;
Pa'trom' ke citta aham mahata se, prabandh kara' leta' hae.
Desha ka'la pa'tra, srs't'i ke a'ya'ma haem';
Jina'na karma bhakti, pa'trom' ke ma'padam'd'a haem'.
Sagun'a srs't'i mem' uttarottara brddhi, gun'avatta' la'ta' hae;
Sam'stha'gata udyeshyom' ko,
'Madhu' pa'trom' dva'ra', kriya'nvita kara'ta' hae.

50. Abhinava abhinaya * 235/06.02.09

Kya' kya' abhinava abhinaya karate,
cittom' ko tuma mukharita karate;
Gaganom' ko tuma garima' dete, va'yu ko tuma vicala' dete.

Jiivom' ko ja'gruta tuma karate, ma'nava mana ko bha's'a' dete;
Cetana ko avacetana karate, avacetana ko bha'svar karate.

A'dhyatmikata' ko laya dete, buddhi ko mukta kara' dete;
A'tma' ko biija bana' lete, srs't'i mem' tuma bikhara' dete.

Srs't'i cakrom' kii ma'ya' mem',
Madhu mana kii komala ka'ya' mem';
Tuma biija bane calate rahate,
Prakrti ko 'Madhu' pramudita karate.

51. Kitane vyathita * 49/06.05.08

Kitane vyathita tuma ho pathika!
Kitanii us'a' a'yiim' gayiim',
Kitanii nishha' dha'yiim' rahiim';
Ananda tuma pa'ye nahiim',
Calate rahe, calate rahe!

Ananda kii isa ra'ha mem',
Ajina'na kii isa deha mem',
Niirava byatha' kii ga'nt'ha mem',
Tuma kya' sakoge ba'ndha sura;
Prabhu ke hrday a'ka'sha mem'.

Kitanii dhara' para tuma cale,
Kitane jalom' mem' tuma bahe,
Kitanii jva'la'em' tuma sahe,
Kitane va'yu ke vega sahe.
Kitane nabha a'ye aura gaye,
Kitane nabha tuma ko dekhe haem'!
Cupake se tumako dekhe haem'!

Prabhu dhya'na mem' arpita karo,
Nija jina'na ko, nija karma ko,
Nija shakti ko, nija bhakti ko!
Tuma a'sako to a'bhii ja'o,
Prabhu ke nikat'a!
Ananda ke isa jva'r mem'!

Mere hradaya ke giita sunalo, he pathika!
Sabake hrdaya ke giita tuma ga'o, pathika;
Tumharii byatha' usakii byatha',
Dedo use, dedo use!
Caran'om' mem' sara naba' hii do,
He 'Madhu' pathika!

52. Jina'na karma bhakti ka' ma'pa * 60/13.05.08

Srs't'a' jiivom' ke, jina'na karma bhakti ko
Ma'pa kara, bha'npa kara, nirn'ay lete haem'.
Uttama hone para, krpa' kara, padonnati de dete haem';
Jiiva ko panca bhu'ta ka', du'sare jiivom' ka',
Niyantran'a de dete haem'.

Srs't'i ka' madhya shren'ii ka' prabandhan milane se pu'rva;
Yoga ka' jina'na va anubhava a'vashyaka hae.
Yoga srs't'a' kii sam'stha' ka', srs't'a' ka',
Prakrti, pancabhu'ta, desha, ka'la, pa'trom' ka',
Samyaka prabandh jina'na va prabandha abhya'sa hae.

Sam'yoga dva'ra' yoga hone para, jiva ko pada siddhi moha na ho;
Srs't'a' ke a'tmiiya nirdeshana mem',
Ma'tra srs't'i seva' hii karan'iiya ho!

Srs't'i prabandh ke yoga mem' pravrata ho jiiva;
Bhakti jina'na karma aura sudrar'ha karata' hae.
Srs't'i vibha'ga anusa'ra, srs't'a' ke 'Madhu' niyantran'a mem';
Desha aora pa'trom' ka', usa ka'la mem', prabandha karata' hae.

53. Avataran'a se pu'rva * 78/30.05.08

He Krs'n'a! avataran'a se pu'rva, a'ka'sha va'n'ii kara'
Jagata ko pu'rva su'cita karana';
Kya' tha', apane u'par, a'pattiyom' ko a'mantrita karana'?
Ya' tha', apanii srs't'i mem', a'ne ka' ka'ma a'sa'na karana'!

Pu'rva su'cana' de, shos'aka sha'saka kii,
Bhaya vratti ko prajjvalita karana';
Aura phira, usakii krodha'gni ko jaga', karma mem' use prerita karana'.
Jagata ko usake karma dikha'; usakii ba'stavikata' ka' bha'na kara'na'.

Svayam' para, nija janom' para, shos'aka ka' a'kraman'a jhelana'
sahana';
Shos'ak ko asaphala kara', usa para 'Madhu' niyam'tran'a karana'.
Asurii shakti ko shamita kara, sa'tvikata' ko protsahita karana';
Dhiire dhiire shos'an'a ko sama'pta ya' samarpita kara'na'.

54. Tumha'ra' a'na', ja'na' * 78A/30.05.08

Vicitra hota' hae, tumha'ra' a'na', ja'na' aura rahana';
Ati su'ks'ma hota' hae, tumha'ra' sunana',
Kahana' aura karana'.

Vishes'a hota' hae, tumha'ra' akars'an'a,
Vikars'han'a, milana aura vilayana
Yahii to hae tumha'rii prabandha liila' ka' anokha'pana.

Tumha'rii jagata kriir'a' ka', ajiiva hona',
Jiiva ko ota prota ho, vikashita niyantrita karana'.

Ati tvarita, druta, tumha'ra' 'Madhu' srs't'i sam'ca'lana karana';
Satata pallavita, suprabandhita   Tumha'rii satta' ka' ja'grata
rahana'.

55. Sam'ska'rom' se rn'ii jiiva * 79/30.05.08

Jiivana ke sam'ska'rom' se rn'ii jiiva;
Kya' kabhii bina' Prabhu krapa',
Urn'a ho sakata' hae !

Janmake adhika'rom' se pra'pta sampada',
Kya' Prabhu kii nahiim',
Kya' vam'shajom' ko deya nahiim' !

Hama're mana, pra'n'a , deha, shva'm'sa,
Sabhii to usake haem';
Ma'n ba'pa, pariva'ra, ga'm'va, desha,
Duniya'm' bhii to usii kii den hae.
Hama'ra' pa'lana pos'an'a, shiks'an'a, ka'rya;
Sabhii to usii ke sama'ja ka' hae.

Prabhu pradatta prema, sambam'dha,
Desha ka'la   pa'tra kii 'Madhu' sthiti avastha'yem';
Sras't'i mem' hamase ka'rya lene ke liye,
Diye usake a'yojana avayava haem'.

56. Ma'nava a'tma' kii avastha' * 71/23.05.08

Ma'nava a'tma' kii avastha', usakii desha ka'la sthiti,
Anya pa'trom' kii desha ka'la a'tma sthiti,
Sras't'i cakra mem' ma'nava kii avastha' sthiti;
Vibhinna deshom' mem', vibhinna samaya mem',
Vibhinna pa'trom' se karma kara' letii hae.

A'tma' kii sudrar'ha avastha' mem',
Anuku'la desha pa'tra mem',
Srs't'i cakra kii unnata prabandh avastha' mem',
'Madhu' ma'nava, desha ka'la pa'tra ko
Niyantrita kara sakata' hae;
Ka'la ko jha'nka sarvavya'pta ho sakata' hae,
Antarya'mitva va siddhi pa' sakata' hae.

57. Srs't'i mem' pra'pta pra'n'ii * 80/30.05.08

Sras't'i mem' pra'pta pra'n'ii, pada, artha, pada'rtha;
Pahale saba Prabhu ka' hae, phira hama'ra' hae.
Hama svayam' apane nahiim', usake haem';
Hama're shva'm'sa vishva'sa usake haem'.

Jo dem' usamem' samarpita ho dem',
Jo lem' usii se samarpita ho lem',
Lekara dene ka' praya'sa karem';
Dekara usamem' samarpita ho kara ma'gem',
Na de ya' lesakem' to, usiimem' samarpita karem'.

Hama 'Madhu' srjana kii kar'ii banem',
Kar'uva'hat'a na banem',
Dharohara ko jakar'em' nahiim',
Pra'yojita sam'ca'lita karem';
Samaya badalata' hae, dhana a't'a' hae, ja'ta' hae,
Vakta accha' bura', a'ta' hae ja'ta' hae,
Vyavaha'ra ya'da raha ja'ta' hae.

58. He vishva prabandhak * 133/08.08.08

He vishva prabandhak!
Kya' tumha'rii praja' ke tantra abhii,
Tumha're prajina' tantra se tarangita nahiim' ho pa'ye!
Kya' tumha're 'Madhu' ma'nava abhii
As't'a pashom' se mukta nahiim' ho pa'ye!
Kya' ve tumha'rii prabandha kala' ko
Nahiim' samajha pa'ye!

Kya' a'darsha sim'chita tumha're ma'nava,
Abhii marya'da' mem' nahiim' bam'dha pa'ye!
Kya' ve prabandha vijina'na mem' praviin'a nahiim' ho pa'ye!
Kya' ve bhakti karma jina'na mem'
Pratis't'hita nahiim' ho pa'ye!

Kucha samaya pu'rva praja' dva'ra' cune yogya vyakti bhiii,
Pada para pahunca pathabhras't'a kyom' ho ja'te haem';
A'darsha kii pratijina' karane ba'le kucha samaya mem',
Shreya ko bhu'la preya ko kyom' pakar'a lete haem'.

Tumha're praja' tantra abhii
Prakrti mem' kyom' ulajhe haem'?
Tumha're ra'ja tantra ra'jasika va ta'masika kyom' haem'?
Pada para pahunca sa'tvikata' kyom' bahaka ja'tii hae?
Ta'masikata', sa'tvikata' ko kyom' bhat'aka' detii hae?

Dhu'la dhu'sarita jarjarita ma'navata' ke sa'tha,
Aba tuma aora prayoga mata karo;
Bhras't'a kapat'a'ca'rii prabandhakom' se,
Dhara' ko mukta karo.

Sa'tvika ma'navom' ko
Sambala do, saks'ama karo,
Dhara' ko ura mem' dharo,
Jhankrata karo, tantrita karo.

59. Tumha'rii ananta satta' * 122/28.06.08

Maem' tumha'rii ananta satta' hu'm';
Ananta hama'ra' sa'mra'jya hae;
A'di se hama ananta haem',
Ananta ke hama a'di haem'.

Hama ananta ke ra'hii haem',
Brahma'n'd'a ke vishis't'a vyakti haem';
Ananta kii hama shakti haem',
Brahma ke vyakta 'Madhu' ru'pa haem'.

Tuma mere ho, maem' tumha'ra' hu'm',
Saba apane haem', apane hii svaru'pa haem';
Hama ananta haem', sagun'a nirgun'a haem',
Pancabhu'ta, vana jantu jana, sujana haem'.

60. Jina'na hote hue bhii * 59/13.05.08

Jina'na hote hue bhii,
Karma karate hue bhii, bhakti pramukha hae;
Bhakti aur jina'na hote hue bhii, karma a'vashyaka hae.

Jiiva ka' sras't'a' kii ora, calane ka' praya'sa bhakti hae;
Sras't'a' ka' jiiva kii ora, calane ka' praya'sa krpa' hae.

Bina' bhakti ke, jina'na va karma ka'
Phalita hona' a'vashyaka nahiim';
Bhakti hone para bhii, krpa' pa' ja'na'
A'vashyaka nahiim'.

Krpa' kara pa'na', na kara pa'na',
Srs't'a' kii paristhiti para nirbhara hae;
Bina' bhakti ke bhii ve 'Madhu' krpa' kara sakate haem';
Bhakti hone par bhii krpa' karane mem',
Dera laga' sakate haem'.

61. Mere shariira ka' ks'itija * 121/28.06.08

Kya' mere shariira ka' ks'itija;
Brahma'n'd'a ke ks'itija se nahiim' milata'!
Kya' mera' mana bra'hmii mana se sam'yukta nahiim'!
Kya' merii a'tma', parama'tma' mem' vya'pta nahiim'!

Kya' su'rya mujhe dhu'pa sna'na nahiim' kara'ta'?
Kya' jala mujhe pla'vita nahiim' kara'ta'?
Kya' va'yu mujhe pulakita nahiim' karatii?
Kya' a'ka'sha mujhe, a'lhva'dita nahiim' karata'!
Mera' mana kya', tumha're mana mem' nahiim' sama' ja'ta'!

Mera' mana kya' tumha're mana ke
Ks'itija ke pare nahiim' cala' ja'ta'!
Mera' mana kya', brahma'n'd'a ke pare nahiim' cala' ja'ta'!
Kya' mera' mana, tumha'rii vyatha' ko anubhava nahiim'
karata'!
Kya' mera' 'Madhu' mana, Tumha're a'nanda kii
Abhivyakti nahiim' karata'!

62. Kitane sura maim'ne ga'ye haim' * 225/01.02.09

Kitane sura maim'ne ga'ye haim',
Kitane ura maim'ne dekhe haim';
Kitanii ba'dha'm' bedhii haim',
Kitanii bya'dha'em' ba'm't'ii haim'.

A'tura vicalita tuma kyom' hote, arpita a'nandita na'm' hote;
Ma'navata' ko madhu dhun dete,
Kyom' pra'n'a sudha' tuma na'm' rasate.

Jiivana mem' jaba ulajhe bikhare, madhu drs't'i kiye calate
sanvare;
Prabhu ke jaba nikat'a cale a'ye, jiivana dha'ra' ko tara a'ye.

Tuma kyom' na'm' su'ks'ma drs't'i dha'ro,
A'dhya'tmikata' mana mem' dha'ro;

Isa bhu'ma' ko hrdi mem' d'ha'lo,
Ma'navata' ko tuma 'Madhu' d'ha'lo.

Chapter 2
A'dhya'tmika Prabandha,
Vijina'na va Shodha

63. Dhya'na ao' ya'na * 521/21.09.09

Dhya'na se ya'na sabhii ur'a ja'te,
Ya'na se vaddha pra'n'a ut'ha ja'te;
Dhya'na mem' ya'na sabhii utara'te,
Ya'na mem' vaddha pra'n'a a'ja'te.

Dhara' se ya'na dhya'na se ja'ta',
Calata' rukata' praka'sha camaka'ta';
Siddha a'sana mem' ya'trii phura hota',
Ur'ate phurate hae dhya'na kara leta'.

Shu'nya taka samarpita sabhii hote,
Ba'dalom' kii chat'a' ko lakha lete;
Dhara' ko jha'nkakara haem' taka lete,
Ya'na kii siddhiyom' ko cakha lete.

Ya'na mem' ghu'ma phira haem' kucha pa'te,
Khir'akiyom' se ks'itija ko lakha lete;
Su'rya kii svarn'a prabha' lakha pa'te,
Candra ta'trom' ko dekha haras'a'te.

Dhya'na ke ya'na mem' vahii hota',
Citta calata' a'tma' sa'ks'ii hota';
Srs't'i ko shu'nya se parakha pa'te,
Dhya'na 'Madhu' cakha ke pra'n'a tara ja'te.

***
63 R. Madhu Chanda * 437A/22.07.09   ?

Ja'garan'a mem' svapna, svapna mem' ja'garan'a;

Svapna mem' svapna, yatna para yatna.

64. Srs't'i ao' Drs't'i * 520/21.09.09

Srs't'i hae nikat'a se na lakha pa'tii,
Drs't'i hae drshya para na t'ika pa'tii;
Dhara' se ut'hake adhika lakha pa'ta',
Vyoma se drshya adhika dikha ja'ta'.

Dhara' para ya'na brhata hae lakhata,
Vyoma mem' ya'na laghu hae lagata';
Dhara' se drshya laghu hae lakhata',
Vyoma se drshya brhata hae dikhata'.

Shu'nya se dhara' sabhii dikha ja'tii,
Srs't'i laghu ru'pa liye lakha ja'tii;
Desha pa'trom' kii sabhii siima'em',
Ka'la ko bheda nikat'a dikha ja'tii.

Dhya'na ke shu'nya mem' svayam' ja'kara,
Jiiva saba desha bheda pa'te haem';
Pa'tra ko ura mem' sama' pa'te haem',
Ka'la ko svayam' dekha pa'te haem'.

Srs't'i shobha' suha'nii taba lakhatii,
Drsht'i sumadhura sada' jagata takatii;
Dhara' sundara suyogya shubha lagatii,
Vyoma mem' vya'pta srst'i 'Madhu' lakhatii.

65. Sha'shvata sundara * 138/14.08.08

Tuma sha'shvata sundara abhinava ho, jiivana ke ra'ga suna' ja'o;
He a'nandita Prabhu ke pra'n'ii; pra'n'aom' ke giita suna' ja'o.
Tuma madhumaya ru'pa liye a'o;
Bha'vom' mem' bharakara ga' ja'o;
Jiivana ka' srota dikha' ja'o; srotom' ko jiivana de ja'o.

'Madhu' ma'khe sa'ranga ke sa'ks'ii,
Svapnom' se du'ra nahiim' ja'o;
Mohana vijina'na bharii mamata', ma'nava ko a'ja dikha' ja'o.

Bhu'mi kii bha's'a' bha'vom' mem', a'nanda umangem' bhara
ja'o;
Bhu'ma' kii anahad va'n'ii mem', a'nanda sudha' rasa sarasa'o.

66. Priya a'tmana!
* Madhu Giiti 1/ Composed 1983

Priya a'tmana! ut'ho ja'go! ut'ho ja'go, priya a'tman!
Ut'ho ja'go, priya a'tman! ut'ho ja'go, priya a'tman!

Soye the hama donom', usakii hii godii mem',
Aura khogaye the hama, svapna kii usa sras't'i mem'.
Kitanii va'stavika lagatii thii, vaha ava'stavika svapna srs't'i;
Mithya' sam'kalpa janita the,   jisake dras't'a' va drashya.

Usa svapna mem' bhii hama mile the, eka ba'ra,
pya'ra kiya' tha', Ghara basa'ye the, bana'ye the, biga'r'e the;
Aura pra'rabdha vasha, paraspara praha'ra bhii kiye the.

Eka ba'r, tumha're prata'ran'a   kii piir'a' vasha,
jaba maim' kara'ha' Usane mujhe pya'r kiya' aura thapathapa'ya',
para phira maim' so na saka'.

Ut'hane para dekhata' hu'm', ki tuma abhii soye ho,
Vismrata ho bhayamaya ho, khoye ho mohe ho;
Maim' thapathapa'ta' hu'm', tumhem' ut'ha'ne ke liye,
Para tuma d'arate ho, mere prema bhare spars'a se.

Aura sochate ho ki kahiim', tumha're usa svapna ke
Prata'ran' ka' pratika'ra, to nahiim' kar raha' maim'.
Para tuma nahiim' ja'nate ki, kya' koii vyathita karega' usako,
Jisane vyathita kiya' ho, usako svapna mem'.

Svapna ka' vaha prema ya' prata'ran',
Ma'tra ek sukhada anubhuti hae;
Isa ja'grat jiivan ka', hara kaona' ja'grata hae,
Surabhita spandita hai, thirakita a'nandit hae.

Isiiliye kahata' hu'm', aur thapathapa'ta' hu'm',

A'm'khem' kholo priya a'tman! ut'ho ja'go 'Madhu' a'tman!
Priya a'tman, priya a'tman, ut'ho a'go, priya a'tman!

67. Diipa avali avani pae shobhita hae * 566/16.10.09

Diipa avali avani pae shobhita hae,
Ta're agan'ita gagana mem' hars'ita haem';
Hrdaya mem' pra'n'a shikha' prajjvalita hae,
Deha mem' jyoti lahara thirakita hae.

Prabhu a'kara jala'o saba diipaka, sa'dhana' jyoti de karo cetana;
Diwa'lii divya a'bha' kii a'lii, khusha'lii saba manom' kii diiwa'lii.

Gharom' mem' diipa jagamaga'te haem',
Hrdaya mem' jyoti saba jaga'te haem';
Vishva jana mana phuraka bhii ja'te haem',
Vishva a'tma' cahaka hii ja'tii hae.

Sha'nti a'nanda diipa dete haem', urja' utkan't'ha' urmi dete hae';
Ullasita para'gita sumana hote, praphullita pallavita camana hote.

Diipa ma'la' Prabhu ko arpita hae, diipa avali bhuvana kii priiti hae;
Jiiva jyoti srs't'i kii giiti hae, 'Madhu' dyoti jagata kii jyoti hae.

68. Maem' diipa jala'ta' hu'm' ura mem' * 567/16.10.09

Maem' diipa jala'ta' hu'n ura mem',
Maem' ra'ga jaga'ta' hu'n sura mem';
Tuma sha'shvata diipa jala' do na',
Tuma nirjhara sura mem' ga' do na'.

Merii Diiwa'lii tuma mem' hae, merii Holii tuma sam'ga hii hae;
Merii ranga rolii tava mana hae, merii Ra'khii tava hrda mem' hae.

Tuma abhinava nat'a na'gara Prabhu ho, Tuma nitya sana'tana cetana ho;
Tuma ojasvii a'nanda srota, Tuma tejasvii traelokya pravrta.

Maem' Tumara' hii to ura diipaka, Tuma hii to mere sura preraka;
Tava sam'ska'rom' kii maem' dyoti, Tuma mama jiivana kii cira jyoti.

Tumare hii diipaka saba ura haem', Tumare hii sura sabake ura haem';

Maem' ga' deta' Tumare sura mem', Saba suna lete 'Madhu' se ura mem'.

69. Prabhu ke srjana mem' * 6/19.03.08

Prabhu ke srujana mem' jiiva ka' srjana,
Kitana' madhumaya hae, kitana' anupama hae.
Kya' jiiva kii yojana'em',
Usakii parikalpana' mem' sama'yojita nahiim'?
Kya' jiiva ka' praya'sa,
Usake bhu'ma' praya's ka' am'sha nahiim'?

Kyom' kuca jiiva ca'hate haem' tor'ana' marya'd'a'em',
Usakii srs't'i   aura pa'trom' kii ?
Kyom' nahiim' seva' karate ve, usa ke diye samaya mem',
Usa kii sras't'ii kii, usa ke pa'trom' kii.

Kyom' racana' ca'hate haem' ve apanii bhrama bhittiya'm',
Usake aga'dha ananta brahmii shu'nya mem'?
Bikhar ja'tii haim' jo, usakii hava' ke jhom'kom' se,
Samudra tat'a kii reta kii laharom' jaise.

Usii ke pam'ca tatvom' se,
Usii ke pa'trom' dva'ra', diiva'ra banaba' kara,
Avaruddha karate haim', pam'ca tatvom' va pa'trom' ka',
A'va'gamana avarohan'a a'rohan';
Usii ke Brahman'n'd'a mem' an'd'a bana' kara,
Pin'd'om' ka' a'ka'ra Chot'a' karane ka' karate haem' praya's.

A'tma'om' ko a'tma'om' se
Alaga karane ka' praya's karate haem'.
Tra'sa pa'te haim', usakii prakrati ka'
Apanii racana' para a'gha'ta jhelate haem'
Mana ko vyatha' dete haim',   saba ko vyathita karate haem'.

Phira bhii Prabhu srs't'i ka' prabandha,
Abhiyam'tran'a va vika'sa,
Suvyavasthita cala'ye rakhate haem';
Saba jiivom' ko, srs't'i   mem', saba samaya, ota prota ho,

Prasanna praphullita   rakhane ka'
'Madhu' praya'sa karate haem'.

70. Runga kitane bhare ho * 509/ 10.09.09

Runga kitane bhare ho jiivana mem',
Bhara rahe 'Madhu' tarunga hara mana mem';
Shva'sa prashva'sa mem' base calate, ra'ha anaja'na para liye calate.

Tumha'rii sampada' suha'nii hae, tumha'rii a'pada' anaokhii hae;
Tumha'rii vya'ptata' nira'lii hae, tumha'rii a'ptata' ruha'nii hae.

Ahat'em' kitanii kiye ja'te ho, ra'hatem' kitanii diye ja'te ho;
Ca'hatem' kitanii bhare ja'te ho, minnatem' kitanii tuma kara'te ho.

Runga hara hae taranga apanii mem', tarungem' runga apanii apanii
mem';
Umungem' roja tuma bhare ja'te, sam'ga sabake sada' ho tuma rahate.

Ca'hate rahate sada' hara ura mem', gaba'te rahate sada' nija sura mem';
Srs't'i kii chat'a' 'Madhu' suha'nii mem',
D'ha'late rahate gazala hara ura mem'.

71. Mana ke rahasya * 26/02.04.08

Mana ke rahasya, nira'le haem';
Ja'ne anaja'ne haem', ca'he anaca'he haem'.

Hara ja'ne anaja'ne kii a'm'khom' mem' a'nkhem' d'a'la khojate haem';
Ham apane "usa" ko usamem', ya' usako apane man kii gahara'ii mem'.

Lagate haim' sab mile hue se; kabhii na kabhii, kahiim' na kahiim';
Rishte nika'l lete haem', prema pa'la lete haem', byatha' ba'nt'a lete haem'.
Sambam'dha bana' lete haem', kucha kara bait'hate haem';
Aur kabhii kabhii, ca'he anaca'he, lar'a jhagar'a bhii lete haem'.

Paradesh ya' svadesha se a'ne para,
Kucha ra'ta hamem' niim'da nahiim' a'tii hae;
'Jaet' laega' se 'Madhu' prabha'vita hama pratiita hote haem'.

Para kya' yaha, paradesha ke parijanom' kii
Bha'vana'om' kii pratikriya' nahiim' hae!

Unake dinom' mem' ve hamem' ya'd karate haem';
Hama'rii ra'tom' kii niida ur'a ja'tii hae.

72. Jiivom' mem' Brahma * 7/19.03.08

Jiiva tuma kyom' sahaja nahiim' ho pa'te,
Kyom' nahiim' khoja'te unake mana mem';
Unhiim' ke mana mem' to tuma ho srs't'i mem',
Kyom' nahiim' khela lete tuma usii srs't'i mem'.

Tuma ghar yojana'yem' evam' miita bana'oge,
Aham' sim'cita hue, sras't'imaya na hua' to ve bikhara ja'vem'ge;
Eka rasata' banii rahegii, hama kucha na kara pa'vem'ge,
Kucha na kaha pa'vem'ge.

Hama'ra' hara yojana' unakii pariyojana' hae,
Mana pra'n'a shariira unakii pariyojana' maya haem';
Na hue to ve hama'rii yojana' badala dem'ge,
Unakii srs't'i, unake pam'jacbhu'ta,
Usiikii prakrti kriir'a' kara' dem'ge.

Kyom' na hama unako sahayoga karem',
Kyom' na yoga kare'm', unase jur'u'm';
Kyom' na tantra se tarem' aura ta'rem',
Kyom' na dhya'n mem' unhem' dharem'aura varem'.
Apanii pariyojana' mem' unhem' varem',
Unakii aura apanii yojana' ko pariyojita karem'.

Kyom' na sama'dhi mem' unhem' varem',
Kyom' na jiivan ko sama'dhit karem';
Kyom' na mrtyu ko cira jiivit karem',
Kyom' na shariira ko shrii karem'.

Kyom' na unakii parikalpana' ko hama apanii bana'lem',
Kyom' na 'Madhu' jiivom' mem' Brahma dekhem'.

73. Prem mem' jiiva * 27/02.04.08

Prem mem' jiiva, para - vash ho ja'te haem',
Desha ka'la pa'tra kii, siima'yem' la'ngha ja'te haem';
Srjan ho ja'ta' hae, 'Madhu' jiiva ka',
Srs't'i eka piir'hii a'ge bar'ha ja'tii hae.

Premii jiiva ma'n ba'pa bana naye ajanavii ko,
Nija se jya'da' prema karane lagate haem'.
Yah a'ne ba'la' hara naya' jiiva, hama'ra' pu'rvaj ho sakata' hae,
Hama'rii ungalii pakar'a bar'a' ho sakata' hae;
Phir kabhii vah hama're pita'maha jaesa'
Vyavaha'r kara sakata' hae.

Jo darda, jo dava', hamane use dii;
Usakii pratikriya' vaha kara sakata' hae;
Apana' bana kara darda de sakata' hae,
Para'ya' a'kara dava' de sakata' hae.

Usake kuch sam'ska'ra, susam'skrata ho sakate haem';
Kucha aura acche ya' bure ho sakate haem'.
Kucha sam'ska'ra a' sakate haem',
Usake jiivan ke biica ke par'a'va ke.
kucha naye sam'ska'ra a' sakate haem';
Isii jiivan ke aura suyogom' ke.

Ananta jiivanom' mem' jo jiiva sam'parkita hue,
Jo jiiva pa'ye, jo a'ye, jo gaye, jo a'yem'ge;
Saba hama're mana ko tarangita karate haem';
Hama're bha'va svabha'va d'ha'late sam'va'rate haem'.

Isiiliye vishva apana' lagata' hae;
Aora kabhii bega'na' para'ya' lagata' hae.
Saba apane haim', saba sapane haem';
Sab mana mem' haim', sab ja'ne haem'.
Saba a'ne haim', saba ja'ne haem';
Saba ja'ne, ana - ja'ne haem'.

74. Sambha'vana' *20/28.03.08

Sambha'vana' sama bha'vana' kii srs't'i hae;
Samabha'vana' sada bha'vana' kii vrs't'i hae.

Sa'dhana' ke samanvaya se, sama bha'va sambhava hae;
Tapa kii tanmayata' se, sadbha'va ka' udbhava hae.
Sa'dhana' sa'dhatii hae, mana ko tana mem', pra'n'a mem';
Tapa nikha'rata' hae, tana ko, mana ko, pra'n'a ko.

Sadhe mana mem', tape tana mem'; a'tma' vicaratii hae, jagata jana mem'.
Saba sama, saba sata, saba sambhava; ho ut'hata' hae, srs't'a jagata mem'.
Srs't'i ho ja'tii hae, antarva'hya jagat mem'.

Sama samanvit hota' hae sahaja se, shu'nya va ananta ke milana se;
A'tma' ke saba mem' sama' ja'ne se, jiiva ke brahma se, mila ja'ne se.
Aura taba sabhii sama, sabhii sata, kara dete haim' srs't'i;
Sambha'vana' kii, saphalata' kii, 'Madhu' srjan kii.

75. Mamata' * 45/24.04.08

Mamata' jiivom' mem', prema kii vratti hae;
Para vaha, desha ka'la pa'tra ke moha se, bam'dhii ho sakatii hae.

Ma' apane shishu kii mamata' mem';
Usake liye saba kuch balida'na kar sakatii hae.
Para vahii ma', du'sare shishu, jiiva ya' jantu ke prati;
Bha'va rahita, nirmama, Nirdaya ho sakatii hae.

Byakti svadesha ke atishaya moha mem';
Svadesh kii gun'ahiina vastuom' kii prasham'sa' kara sakate haem'.
Para ve, svadesh ke bhii sabhii logom' se saba samay,
Sabhii stha'nom' para, prema nahiim' kara pa'te.

Ma'nava tiivra athak praya'sa se, sa'dhana' se,
Mamata' vratti ko moha se, mukta kara sakata' hae;
Desh ka'la pa'tra kii siima' se pare ja' sakata' hae,
Mamata' ko madhur bana', maha' ma'nava bana sakata' hae.

Maha' ma'nava bana, hara desh ka'la pa'tra se, prema kara sakata' hae;
Mamata' ko, 'Madhu' ma'nava, bhu'ma' bha'va mem'

Bhu's'ita kara sakata' hae.

76. Tuma kaba kya' karate ho * 72/28.05.08

Tuma kaba kya' kaise karate ho,
Maem' samajha nahiim' pa'ta';
Tumha're nya'ya kii caetanyata',
Maem' pu'rn'atah a'tmasa'ta nahiim' kara pa'ta'.

Relve pha't'aka ke ek ora du'ka'na para,
Ma'su'ma bekhabara paks'ii liye vam'ye kara,
Laoha yantra liye da'm'ye kara;
Gra'haka se pasanda kara'te, da'ma karate,
Vyasta vikreta' ko lete ho tuma dekha,
Ma'su'ma paks'ii kii mana vyatha',
Lete ho tuma bha'npa.

Sha'yada use bha'n nahiim', jina'na nahiim' ki,
Agale pala vaha nahiim' rahega' jagata mem'!
Vikreta' vyasta hae, abhyasta hae,
Paks'ii se a'nkha mila'ne mem' asamartha hae;
Gra'haka sha'yada paks'ii ke shariira ka'
Saom'darya aora gun'avatta' parakhata' hae,
Paks'ii ka' a'tma es'an'a', mana vedana',
Mrtyu kii tar'apana, usake liye gaun'a hae.

Vikreta' paks'ii ke shariira ko
Lifafe mem' bam'da kara gra'haka ko de deta' hae,
Usake pankha panje rakta, avashes'a raha ja'te haem',
Jiivita pra'n'a pala mem' nis'pra'n'a ho ja'te haem';
Parama purus'a va prakrti ke srs't'a pra'n'a,
Sevita shariira, mana lupta ho ja'te haem'.

Dekha lete ho tuma bana kara 'Madhu' drs't'a',
Ma'nava kii yaha niriiha nirdaya akarun'a kriya';
Sha'yada usii se ks'ubdha ho,
Kahiim' tuma dete ho dhara' para kuch kara'.

77. Nya'ya kii caetanyata' * 73/28.05.08

Prabhu, tumha're nya'ya kii caetanyata',
Kucha samajha pa'ta' hu'n, kucha samajha nahiim' pa'ta'!

Shahara ko a'te va'hanom' mem' banda,
Vevasha niriiha pashu paks'iyom' ke pariva'rom' ka' sanna't'a';
Unakii jiivita a'nkhom' mem',
Spas't'a diikhata' unakii mrtyu ka' sa'ya',
Jagata ke prati unakii hata'sha', ma'nava ke prati nira'sha'.

Ajina'ta bhavis'ya ka' bhaya,
Pu'rva mem' a'ye agrajom' ka' vichur'ana';
Na ja'na pa'na' ki, unaka' kya' hasra hua',
Kula mila' kara deta' hae, unhem' tilamila'.

Piiche calate va'hana mem' bait'he tuma,
Unaka' darda samajha lete ho,
Unakii a'nkhom' mem', mrtyu ka' bhaya par'ha lete ho.
Para tuma bhii prataks'a mem' usa pala,
Kucha kaha nahiim' pa'te ho.

Tuma unake 'Madhu' mana kii vyatha' ko,
Sha'yada srs't'i prabandhaka ko dete ho bata';
Aura usase kucha nya'ya, yatha' shiighra kara' dete ho kara'!

78. Tumha'rii prabandha ks'amata' * 74/28.05.08

Anupama hae tumha'rii, brahma'n'd'a kii prabandha ks'amata';
Vicitra hae tumha're, prasha'sana kii kaushalata'.
Tumha're jagata ke diggaja prabandhaka bhii,
Mu'ka vimukha hoja'te haem' jaba kabhii;
Prthvii kii praja' kii mu'la a'vashyakata'om' ke prati bhii.

Praja' ka' pradarshan, nirva'san, a'hva'hana;
Prata'r'ita praja' ka' nivedana;
Nahiim' sunata' unaka' pada'rtha va sva'rtha lipta mana.
Taba tumha'rii prabandha praviin'a prakrti, sha'yada,
Prthvii hila', va'yu baha', vars'a' kara', a'tma'em' jaga';
Unakii tandra' detii hae hat'a', anaca'ha' detii hae ghat'a'.

79. Netrom' kii niha'rika'om' mem' * 92/14.06.08

Shahara kii sarakatii sar'aka para,
Hara vyakti svayam mem' sikur'a' hae;
Nija mana mem' kahiim' vyasta hae ,
Bharii bhiir'a mem' kucha akela' hae.
Basa mem' vicarata' hara vyakti, svayam' mem' ajanavii eka'kii hae;
Ankha banda kiye dhya'na mem' hae,
Ya' phira ka'na mem' phona laga' kucha sunane laga' hae.

Svayam mem' hara vyakti anaukha' hae,
Byakta hae vyasta hae, siddha hae prasiddha hae.
Phira bhii anaja'nom' kii bhiir'a mem', apane mem' gaya' simat'a hae.
Mana sam'ska'rom' se grasita hae, vica'rom' se a'pluta hae;
A'tma' kisii kii ca'ha mem' rasita hae,
Nikat'a baet'hii a'tma' se vilaga hae.

Kyom' na svayam mem' khoii 'Madhu' srs't'i ko nirakhem',
Mana hii man, a'nkhom' hii a'nkhom' mem' dekhem';
Kucha kahem', kucha sunem', rasa ur'elem',
Mukta ho, a'nanda dem', a'nanda lem'.
Kyom' na hama cetana hom', anaja'nom' ko bhii niha'rem' yukta hom';
Hamem' niha'ratii netrom' kii niha'rika'om' mem',
Srs't'a' ko dekhem', ja'grata hom'.

80. Tumha'ra' pratyeka pra'n'ii * 134/11.08.08

Prabhu tumha'ra' pratyeka pra'n'ii kya' rahasyamaya nahiim'!
Usaka' ru'pa svaru'pa, bha'va bha's'a' kya' anupama nahiim'!
Prthvii ke ma'nava bhii kya' anya grahom' jaise vilaks'an'a nahiim'?
Prahvii ke saba tatva, kya' brahma'n'd'a ke ansha nahiim'!
Ma'nava mana ka' sadaeva satata paratom' mem' cala'yama'na rahana',
Kya' vicitra nahiim', kya' ashcarya nahiim'!

Kaona hae jo nitya nava ru'pom' mem' hamem' d'ha'lata' saja'ta'
hae?
Vica'ra tarangom' ko hara pala, udvelita utprerita karata' calata' hae.
Agan'ita niha'rika'om' ka' prati parama'n'u
Kya' hama're sa'tha ra'sa raca'ta' nahiim'?
Sa'rii cara'cara 'Madhu' satta' kya' hamem'

Hara pala hansa'tii naca'tii calatii nahiim'!

81.   Praja'tantra *75/28.05.08

Praja'tantra aura mazahavii taranga ke na'ma mem',
Calate tumha're kucha loka;
Praja' kii gaharii a'stha' va at'u't'a vishva'sa   vasha
Ho ja'te haem' nirbhiika.

Sam'kuchita desha ka'la pa'trom' kii paridhi mem' siimita,
Sva'rthii jana bana baet'hate haem' sha'saka;
Yatha' shiighra nagna karate ho tuma unaka' chadma caritra,
Naetikata' ma'nasikata' va aviveka.

Sha'sakom' ka' vyaktiyom', pariva'rom',
Ja'ti sama'ja va mazahavom' ke liye satahii prema praca'ra;
Andara se sva'rtha, dhana gavan, shos'an'a,
Caritra hiinata', bhras't'a'ca'ra va atya'ca'ra ka' avica'ra.

Vishva kii pra'n'a va'yu ko desha pradesha
Jilom' pam'ca'yatom' mem' ulajha'ne ka' vica'ra,
Desh ka'la pa'tra premii a'dhya'tmika
Ma'nava a'tma' ko kum't'hita kar,
Kusha'shana karane ka' kuvica'ra.

Jar'a bhoga, pada satta' moha, bha'va jar'ata' ka' sammohana,
Sva'rtha kendrita shaktiyom' ka' sam'vega pralobhana;
Acche sha'sakom' ko bhiI kara deta' hae patha cyuta,
Sad prabandhakom' ko karate ho taba tuma ja'grat utprerita.

Apanii prakruti se saba kii 'Madhu' prajina' ko prerita kara,
Sha'saka ka' mana bhramita kara, kara' d'a'late ho cuna'va;
Badala d'a'late ho taba tuma sha'sana vyavastha' prabandha,
Tarungita karate ho jagata ke sama'ja cakrom' ka' suprabandha.

82. Milita nirn'aya * 152/04.09.08

Sama'ja mem' milita nirn'aya kii mahatta',
Guruttama va mahattama hae;
Vyaktigata nirn'aya ko sama'ja se,
Anumodita kara' lena' atyuttama hae.

Vyaktigata nirn'aya hama're mana shariira a'tma' kii,
Avasthiti ka' pratiphalana hae;
Sa'ma'jika a'shiirva'da hama're a'tmiiya nirn'aya ko,
Paripakva anumodita tarngita karata' hae.

Paraspara vinimaya se kiya' vyakti va sama'ja ka' nirn'aya,
Santulan, suvyavastha' va suyog deta' hae;
Jiivana mem' kiye milita nirn'aya, a'nanda taranga,
Sa'phalya va sa'dhana' la'te haem'.

Nirn'aya jitane sahaja atmiiya sammati se hom',
Sa'ma'jika saphalata' atmonnati utane hii tvarita hote haem'.
Pa'riva'rika va sa'ma'jika nirn'aya pra'ya:,
Paraspara upaka'rii, prabha'vaka'rii va a'nanda deya hote haem'.

A'tma'em' unnata hom', shreya ko samajhem',
Mahata kii mahatta' ja'nem',
Is't'a ko pahaca'nem', a'shiirva'da ka' mahatva ja'nem',
Milita nirn'aya karem';
Bhakti va krapa' karem'
Evam 'Madhu' srs't'i ko a'nanda se bharem'.

83. Ta'n'd'ava jaga mem' * 141/15.08.08

Ma'navata' shos'ita vicalita hae,
Aa'tankita shankita bhayamaya hae;
Ta'n'd'ava jaga mem' Prabhu kama karado,
A'nandita jana gan'a mana karado.

Ma'nava mana vihansita thirakita ho,
Bhojana shiks'a' saba ko ghara ho;
Aos'adhi vastrom' kii kamii na ho,
Mana pra'n'om' mem' sa'tvikata' ho.

Saba dharmom' mem' ho ' Madhu ' priiti,
Shubha niiti siikhe ra'janiiti;
Vya'pa'rii vya'paka dharma sahita,
Seva' bha'vii hom' karma pravrata.

Sata karmom' mem' ma'nava hom' rata,
Kraya shakti sabhii pa'yem' avirata;
Hom' du'ra mu'lya vraddhi rishvata,
Sha'sana sha'saka hom' anusha'sita.

Ja'grata Prabhu saba jana ko kara do,
Mantrita abhimantrita mana kar do;
Tantrita jhankrata jaga ko kara do,
A'nandita ' Madhu' Prathvii kara do.

84. Bha'rata bhuvana ko ura rakho * 411/10.07.09

Bha'rata# bhuvana ko ura rakho,
Surasari bana bhava ko taro;
Sus'ama' bharo sam'skrti bharo,
Bha'rata# bane bhu'ma' varo.

Sura ta'la mem' ga'o sabhii, nava ra'ga mem' na'co sabhii;
Ha'so sabhii, rasa do sabhii, sukha do sabhii, sura do sabhii.

Rasa do dhara', ks'hudha do mit'a',
Mana ks'ubdha ko sudha do pila';
Sudha mem' rakho saba danujata',
Sudhi mem' rakho saba manujata'.

Giita' sugiita' bhava karo, bha'vom' ko a'dhya'tmika karo;
Mana ko brhata karate calo, sabako sahita le kara calo.

'Madhu' ra'ga mem' ga'te calo,
Jana gan'a manom' ko le calo;
Vasudha' kut'umba bana' calo,
Bhu'ma' ko Bha'rata# kara calo.

***

Bha'rata = One who nurtures, Arjuna,
Bha'rata, Offsprings of Bharata

85. He Va'yuya'na * 146/25.08.08

He va'yuya'na apane laghu pahiyom' para,
Sarapat'a daor'ate va'yu pat't'ii para;
Yaka'yaka ut'ha jaate ho va'yu mem' ho phura,
Prathvii se a'ka'sha kii ora rukha kara.

Kitane ya'triyom' kii a'sha'om' ke sura,
Sham'kita bhaya kampita hote hue hoja'te haem' pulakita;
Kitane darshakom' kii a'sha'em' ho ut'hatii haem' prajjvalita,
Kitane hrdaya a'ne kii suna ho ja'te haem' tarungita.

Hara ghar'ii ur'ate vima'nom' ko dekha kara,
' Madhu ' mana ke arama'na   ho ut'hate haem'phura;
Prathvii se a'ka'sha ko dha'te hue nirantara,
Jiivana ko jhakajhorate sam'kalpa a'te haem' nazara.

86. Jiivana ke isa hava'ii ad'd'e para * 147/25.08.08

Vida' karane a'ye svajanom' ko dekha,
Hava'ii ad'd'e para vida'ii le rahe ya'triyom' ko dekha.

Sva'gata karane a'ye svajanom' ke manom' ko dekh,
Sva'gata pa'rahe parijanom' ko dekha;
Mera' mana ana'ya'sa unakii a'tma'om' kii,
Piir'a' hars'a, vis'aa'da, a'nanda se a'ta' hae bhara.

Para ' Madhu ' ko to jiivana ke isa hava'ii ad'd'e para,
Sadaeva hii vima'nom' va ya'triyom' ka'
Dekhana' hae a'va'gamana;
Dekhate hue unhem' sa'ks'ii vata, rakhana' hae
Unakii sukha suvidha' va suraks'a' ka' khaya'la .

Unakii a'sha' nira'sha' muska'ra'hat'a mem' dekhana' hae
ananta,
Sneha bharii muskara'hat'a denii hae, rahate hue karma rata;
Karana' hae 'Madhu' seva' samarpan'a yathocita,
Jimmeda'rii de pa'rii ke uparanta, ja'na' hae cale apane ghara.

87. Na'shapa'tii ka' biija * 148/31.08.08

Na'shapa'tii ke madhur phal mem' tumha'ra',
Usake biija ko itana' saheja kara rakhana';
Usake visha'la braks'a ke niice mu'la biija ko,
Bhu'mi mem' itana' gahara' daba' kara rakhana'.

Bhu'migata biija ko anuku'la jalava'yu de,
Ankurita kara dhiire dhiire paudha' bana' dena'.
Biija ko dhara' dhu'la mem' mila',
Sama'pta pra'yah kara dena';
Sardii garmii hima vars'a' sahate hue,
Paudhe ka' braks'a bana ja'na'.

Vasanta mem' visha'la braks'a ka' pallavita pus'pita ho ja'na';
Kitane jana jiivana ko cha'ya' va sugandha se trapta kara dena'.

Agan'ita phala khila'
Ma'nava pashu paks'iyom' ko sa'tvika kara dena';
Itane sukha dukha dekhate hue bhii,
Eka rasa a'nandita rahana'.

Hemanta kii a'hat'a mem', braks'a ka' patra vihiina ho ja'na';
Hima vars'a' sahars'a saha, vasanta kii ra'ha takana'.
Anukju'la samaya a'ne para punah pallavita ho ja'na';
Shveta pushpom' ka' khila ut'hana',
Phalom' ka' avatarita ho ja'na'.

Rahasyamaya hae Prabhu, tumha're biija ka' jiiana !
Bhu'migata ho samaya a'ne para, braks'a bana ja'na'.
Srs't'i ko yatha' sambhava ' Madhu ' phala khila'te ja'na';
Phala mem' antarnihita bija ka', srs't'i mem' bikhara ja'na'.

88. Biija ka' itiha'sa * 149/31.08.08

Kitana' hrdaya spars'ii hae, biija ka' itiha'sa;
Kitana' marma bhedii hae, usaka' bhavis'ya.
Biija ka' phala ke andara prakat'a hone ka' rahasya;
Aneka phalom' mem' aneka ho, karana' satata vika'sa.

Kya' braks'a sha'kha'yem' patra va phala,
Mu'la biija ko pahaca'ne ?
Kya' a'shraya a'nanda lene va'le,
Biija kii garima' mahima' laghima' ja'ne ?
Phala bhiI kya' svayam mem' chipe, biija ka' bha'vis'ya ja'ne ?
Pus'pa bhii kya', bhu'mi mem' chipe biija ka' itiha'sa ja'ne ?

Eka biija ka' prati pala aura unnata ananta hote ja'na';
Sa'tha mem' srs't'i karate hue, srs't'i seva' karate ja'na'.
Svayam aparicita adras't'ya raha, ananta utpa'dana karate ja'na';
Srs't'a' bana srs't'i mem' hae, 'Madhu' maya liila' karate ja'na'.

89. Ashiirva'da * 151/04.09.08

A'shiirva'da a'nanda ka' prasa'da hae,
A'shiirva'da vishva'sa ka' nihshva'sa hae;
A'shiis'a shiis'a ka' abhimantran'a hae,
A'shiis'a a'sha' ko a'mantran'a hae.

A'nanda ka' madhu va'da de mahata a'tma',
Hama'ra' patha prashasta karatii hae;
Apanii a'tma' ke sam'vega se hama'rii gati tvarita kara,
Tarungita karatii hae.
Prabhu hamem' a'shiirva'da le de pa'ne mem', saks'ama karem';
Dhara' para bharapu'ra bhakti bha'va bahem'.
Krpa' dha'ra' dhara' para avirata bahe,
Gurutvapu'rn'a krpa' bha'va barasate rahem'.

Mahata bha'va pa'kara hii,
A'shiirva'da lene ka' bha'va samajha a'ta' hae;
Brahata bha'va anant ho kar hii, 'Madhu' a'shiirva'da de pa'ta' hae.

90. Maha' vis'phot'a va Brahma kan'a * 155/10.09.08

' Maha' vis'hphot'a ' ka' prayoga kara vaejina'nika,
' Brahma kan'a ' ko ja'nana' ca'hate haem'.
Para kya' Brahma unhem', saba kucha jana'ne ko
Svayam' yugom' se tatpara nahiim' hae ?

Do vars'a tvaraka (Accelerator) mem' rakha,
Eka kharaba degree   centigade tak garma kara,
Pada'rtha ke a'dha'rabhu'ta avibha'jya kan'a ko,
'Kan'a bhaotika sha'strii' samajhana' ca'hate haem'.
Para kya' ma'nava
A't'ha araba dollar ka' yaha prayoga kara,
Pada'rtha va Parma'tma satta' ke rahasyom' ko
D'ham'ga se ja'na sakata' hae ?

Kya' kisii satta' ka' astitva bina' srs't'a' ke
Pala bhara bhii raha sakata' hae?
Kya' srs't'i ka' hara jiiva, hara pala, hara vidha' mem';
Srs't'a' Brahma kan'a, vishva vyavastha' ka',
Izaha'ra nahiim' kara raha' hota' hae?

Srs't'a' ka' rahasya kya',
Pada'rtha ko bina' vis'phot'ita kiye,
Nahiim' ja'na' sakata' hae ?
Kya' srs't'i ke pra'n'ii,
Ma'nasa'dhya'tmika vijina'na dva'ra',
Yaha rahasya ja'nate hue,
Hara pala prayoga nahiim' kara rahe haem'.
Kya' srs't'i prabandha kii 'Madhu' vyavastha',
Ve nahiim' kara rahe haem'!

91. Srs't'a' shakti * 156/10.09.08

Pada'rtha ke u'para maha' vis'hphot'a kara vaijina'nika,
Usamem' avibha'jya 'srs't'a' shakti' ko khojana' ca'hate haem'.
Para kya' yaha 'usakii' vahii citta shakti nahiim',
Jo hara jiiva mem' pras'hput'ita antarnihita hae !

'Madhu' cita shakti ka' srota bra'hmii mana hae;
Bra'hmii mana ke shu'nya mem'
'Ka'la' chidra' (Black hole) ho sakata' hae.
Bra'hmii mana ka' sphuran'a maha' vis'phot'a kara' sakata' hae;
Bra'hmii mana ka' sam'kalpa srs't'i ko
Laya vilaya kara sakata' hae.

Pada'rtha ke maha' vis'phot'a se srs't'i,
Sama'pta nahiim' ho sakatii hae.
Ma'naviiya yoga prayoga citta, hara ks'an'a, hara stha'n para;
Bra'hmii mana ke santulita niyantran'a mem' rahate haem'.
Desha ka'la pa'tra ke ks'udra chidra,
A'ya'ma va shu'nya, saba usake prayoga haem'.

Ma'nava ke pada'rtha ke sa'tha kiye prayoga,
Usake ja'gatika ma'nasa'dhyatmika jina'na
Va suvidha' mem' upayogii haem'.
Ma'nava mana kii sa'marthya siimita kintu pragatishiila hae;
Jina'na vijina'na ka' hara 'Madhu' prayoga use
Srs't'a' ke aora nikat'a le ja'ta' hae.

92. Srs't'i ke rahasya * 157/10.09.08

Brahma'n'd'a ka'ran'a va prabha'va ke
Pratiphalana kii satta' sthiti hae.
Usamem' kisii bhii avayava dva'ra' siddha'ntatah hama,
Pu'rn'a ko pahaca'na sakate haem'.

Braks'a ko jaese mu'la biija, mu'la, tana', sha'kha'om';
Patra pus'pa va nava biijom' se pahaca'na sakate haem'.
Phira bhii biija dva'ra' use pahaca'nana',
Vikasita karana' a'sa'na ho sakata' hae.

Srs't'i ke pura'tana va naviina ma'nava biija dva'ra',
Srs't'a' va srs't'i ko samajhana' vaise hii a'sa'na hae.
Pada'rtha pancabhu'ta ke prayogom'se use samajhana',
Samaya artha praya'sa mem' mahanga' par'a sakata' hae.

Ma'nava ke karma gati prabha'va ko samajhane ka' praya'sa,
Jaise usaka' mana sam'kalpa a'tma'
Samajhane mem' utane saha'yaka nahiim';
Pada'rtha kii gati sthiti gun'a svabha'va samajhane ka' praya'sa,
Vaise hii sras't'i srs't'a' ko samajhane mem'
Utane saha'yaka nahiim'.

Ma'nava citta ka', srs't'a' ke citta mem'
Vilaya kara dena', a'sa'na upa'ya hae ;
Srs't'a' ke mana pra'n'a mem' pait'ha,
Srs't'i va srs't'a' ke 'Madhu' rahasya
Samajha lena', sarala kunjii hae.

93. Brahma kan'a - Srs't'i Prabandha * 158/10.09.08

Vaijina'nikom' dva'ra' 15 araba vars'a pu'rva sras't'a,
'Srs't'i kan'a' ko a'ja, pahaca'nane ka' prayoga kara pa'na';
Pada'rtha kan'a kii gati tvarita kara,
'Brahma kan'a' ko pahaca'nane ka' prayoga karana'.
Kya' nahiim' hae, " Kan'a Bhautikii" ka' itana' piiche calana' ?

Itane yugom' mem' vijina'na ka' itana' hii praya'sa kara pa'na';
'Jiiva'n'u va Brahma'n'u' ko 'pada'rtha kan'a' dva'ra'
Samajhane ka' praya'sa karana'.

Pancatattvom' va Bra'hmii mana kii
Vya'pakata' ko na samajha pa'na';
Brahma, Bra'hmii yojana', srs't'i ko,
Vijina'na dva'ra' na samajha pa'na'.

Kya' srs't'i mem' aese pracura prabandhaka nahiim',
Jo use haja'rom' vars'om' se samajhe hue haem' ?
Srs't'a' ke hara kan'a, hara mana,
Hara ura lahara ko samajhate haem';
Srs't'a' kii yojana'om' ko bakhu'bii
Kriya'nvita kara'te rahate haem'.

Srs't'i kya' cala sakatii hae, sras't'a',
Prabandhakom' va sam'stha' ke,
Ja'grata jhankrta vinimaya ke bina'!
Prakat'a vikashita ya' ks'iin'a ho sakata' hae.
'Maha' vis'phot'a' ya' 'ka'la' chidra' kya'
Srs't'i prabandhakom' ke 'Madhu' sam'jina'na bina'!

94. A'pattika'la ka' phona * 185/13.11.08

A'pattika'la ka' phona pra'yah hama prayoga nahiim' karate;
Para sarvocca satta' ca'hatii hae ki hama use ya'da rakhem'.
A'vashyakata' par'ane para avashyameva prayoga karem'.

Pariiks'an'a karane ke liye, jiivana dva'ra para svayam ve;
Apana' va'hana kabhii tejii se daor'a'kara le ja' sakate haem'.
Aura hamase phona karane kii apeks'a' kara sakate haem'.

Phona na karane para ve hamem' dam'd'ita kara sakate haem';
Punah prashiks'an'a ke liye bheja sakate haem'.
Daenika ka'rya pran'a'lii se
Kucha dina ke liye du'ra kara sakate haem'.

Prabhu se hama pratidina
Accha' ka'rya karate hue, ba'ta nahiim' karate;
Unhem' phona karane ya' puka'rane kii
A'vashyakata' nahiim' samajhate.
Prabandha vyavastha' saba kii
Karmat'hata' se calatii rahatii hae.

Para kabhii ve svayam' pariiks'an'a karane,
Va'rta'la'pa karane a'sakate haem';
Nirantara unake a'ne va antarmana mem'
Ca'hane kii pratiiks'a' karate rahem'.
Dhya'na dva'ra para sadaeva sajaga rahate hue,
Prabhu se 'Madhu' sam'parkita rahem'.

95. Tumha're jiivom' kii hrdaya hiinata' * 201/19.12.08

Prabhu! Tumha're jiivom' kii hrdaya hiinata',
Usase a'hata tumha're hrdaya kii vihvalata';
Unakii bha'va hiinata' se a'hata tumha'rii vikalata',
Anubhu'ta karatii hae 'Madhu' hrdaya kii niiravata'.

Jiivom' ko a'hata karatii unakii uddam'd'ata',
Vyathita karatii hae ma'naviiya cetanata';
Aham'ka'ra ajina'na ana'ca'ra mem' d'u'bii unakii jar'ata',
a'tankita karati hae ja'gatika sa'tvikata'.

Anavarata utpiir'ana se unmiilita tumha'rii brahatta',
Saha nahiim' pa'tii jaba unakii da'navata';
Tumha'ra' a'graha udga'ra nahiim' badala pa'ta'
Jaba unakii bha'va jar'ata',
Karanii par'a ja'tii hae prayoga taba,
Tumhem' apanii prabandha ks'amata'.

Tumha'rii seva' karmaliinata', daya'luta' bha'va sahajata';
Nahiim' ja'na pa'tii jaba, hara jiiva kii ma'nasikata'.
Tumha're ta'n'd'ava kii tha'p, da'va'nala kii da'hanata';
Mit'a' detii hae taba unakii malinata' da'navata'.

96. Tumha're ta'n'd'ava ka' spandana * 203/19.12.08

Prabhu! Tumha're ta'n'd'ava ka' spandana,
Bhara deta' hae sras't'a jagata mem' siharana;
Vinas't'a karata' hae srs't'i kii shithilata' utpiir'ana,
Tarungita ho ut'hatii hae hara dhar'akana.

Aham'ka'ra vika'ra mem' grasita ma'nava mana,
D'u'ba ja'ta' hae jaba kabhii tandra' mem' cetana;
A'hata karata' hae jaba sujana mana,
Vya'hata karata' hae jaba vah Prabhu prayojana.

Uttis't'ha ho ut'hate haem' taba sa'tvika pra'n'a mana,
Samarpita ho kara ut'hate haem' ga'na sa'dhana' dhya'na;
Ho ut'hata' hae lalita kaoshikii ta'n'd'ava gahana,
Vira'jita prakat'a hote haem' Prabhu sujana mana.

Srs't'i kii sha'liinata' ke liye karate haem',
Prabhu! prabandha manthana,
Vya'paka uthala puthala parivartana karate haem' ve usa ks'an'a;
Vina'sha karate haem' ve sras't'i kii andha tamisra' gahana,
A'lokita a'lor'ita karate haem' Prabhu 'Madhu' mana.

97. Srs't'a' se samparkita rahana' * 186/13.11.08

Sarvocca satta' ka' prabandha vyavastha' ka',
Ana'ya'sa pariiks'an'a karana' ajiiva ba'ta hae;
Para 'Madhu' jiiva ko ajiiva daora se guja'ra kara,
Jiivom' kii caetanyata' parakhana' bhii Usakii a'vashyakata' hae.

Saba ja'grata cetana ja'garu'ka rahem',
Apana' karma samucita saceta karem',
Sarvocca satta' kii svayam' prabandha bhanga
Karane kii avastha' mem' bhii;
Usakii apeks'a' hae ki hama use rokem' t'okem',
Phona kara shika'yata karem'.

Ma'tra ka'ma karana',
Yathocita srs't'i seva' karana' parya'pta nahiim' hae,
Usase usiikii, usake jiivom' kii,
Tatka'la shika'yata karana', usakii apeks'a' hae;
Srs't'a' se sadaeva samparkita rahana', srs't'i kii a'vashyakata' hae.

98. Tumha'rii vya'pakata'   * 202/19.12.08

Prabhu! Tumha'rii vya'pakata', vrahatata', visha'la hrdayata';
Vishva ma'nava ahasa'sa nahiim' kara pa'ta'.
Tumha'rii madhurata' mohakata' vinaya shiilata';
Jar'a jiiva ka' kru'ra mana anubhu'ta nahiim' kara pa'ta'.

Aho ra'tri tarungita tumha'rii sneha bharii shiilata';
Ma'nava mana kii anavarata ananta anucitata'.
Mana karma bha'va se bharii tumha'rii mahatta';
Sam'kucita satahii unakii sva'rtha liptata',

Tumha'ra' satata prema sahaja sam'vedana shiilata';
Tumha'rii vishva dras't'i mem' trut'i nirakhatii unakii ma'nasikata'.
A'hata karatii hae 'Madhu' hrdaya kii niiravata';
Tumha're ananta karmom' mem'
Dhu'la jha'nkatii unakii baoddhikata'.

Anaca'he karanii par'atii hae tumhem' upayogita',
Apane adhika'ra va a'vashyakata' kii prayoga shiilata';
Ota prota ho tarungita karate ho vishva prabandh shiilata',
Laya vilaya kara ut'hate ho Srs't'i sam'ca'lanata'.

99. Merii vyatha' * 23/02.04.08

Merii vyatha', merii katha', merii vidha';
Merii dvidha', merii ks'udha', merii sudha'.

Ura kii arun'ima' tuma, ankhiyom' ke ashru tuma;
A'hat ke ana'hat tuma, ana'hat ke svara svayam.
Tum kucha ga' do ga'yana, vyatha' kare pala'yana;
Sura gu'nje sha'shvata ka', ana'hata ho a'jina' ka'.

Maem' soja'ta' hu'n, usakii hii godii mem';
Khoja'ta' mana mera', usakii mana srs'ti mem'.
Vaha a'ja'ta' hae, sara thapathapa'ta' hae;
Sahasra'r khil ja'ta' hae vishuddha sudha' la'ta' hae.

Mana khila ja'ta' hae, maem' ut'ha ja'ta' hu'm';
Vyatha' bikhar ja'tii hae, a'nanda a'ja'ta' hae.
Ks'udha' merii ks'udra huii, banii dvidha' suvidha';
Katha' merii kavita' banii, vidha' banii vidya'.

100. Surabhi * 322 AE/28.05.09

Prema mem' pulakatii madhura sii siharatii,
Sahasa' surabhi bikharatii rahii sarasatii;
Preya sii shreya sii, saomya sii sha'nta sii,
Niira sii ks'iira sii, dhiira sii viir sii.

Udita a'tma' kii prakharita sarasatii surabhi,
Navya ma'nava kii paricaya bharii sii surabhi;
Brhma kii cetana' se ubharatii surabhi,
Prakrti kii preran'a' kii 'Madhu' sii surabhi.

101. Taralata' tarun'ata' * 320/28.05.09

Taralata' tarun'ata' tiiks'n'ata' tiivrata',
Ta'la para na'cata' ta'kata' bhanpata';
Jiiva ka' mana magana prakrti ko jha'nkata',
Ma'pata' ja'ncata' thirakata' kanpata'.

Saomyata' shodhita' sam'tulana sa'myata',
Dhiirata' gahanata' shobhita' madhurata';
Surabhi d'ha'le cale prakrti pra'n'iinata',
Pracurata' prakharata' pra'n'a udvelita'.

Nancata' ku'data' bahakata' phudakata',
Calata' rahata' manuja ma'dhurii d'ha'lata';
Viharata' vihansata', vyoma mem' jha'nkata',
Dharan'i   para uchalata', prema mem' pulakata'.

Shikhara para nancata', hima sarisa siharata',
Barasata' bikharata' tarasata' tar'apata';
Lasita mana, trasita tana, ta'na para na'ncata',
Nayana mu'nde navelii prakrti dekhata'.

Sha'nta mana preyasii prakrti kii saomyata',
Parakha pa'ta' 'Madhu' mana, manana gahanata';
Manujata' cahakatii nirakha caetanyata',
Maha' ma'nava d'hale srs't'i ma'dhuryata'.

102. Srs't'i biija * 150/31.08.08

Prabhu tumha'ra' biija vata, bhu'ma' mana bhu'mi mem' rahana';
Srs't'i ko pras'phut'ita pus'pita, phalita va vikashita kara dena'.

Svayam srs't'i mem' chipe rahana',
Srs't'i ko gun'a dharma dete ja'na';
Ucita samaya a'ne para sabako, pallavita praphullita kara dena'.
Ananta phalom' mem' ananta biijom' kii srs't'i kara dena';
Phalom' ko srs't'a jiivom' ko khila'te ja'na'.

Biijom' ko jiivom' pancabhu'tom' dva'ra',
Srs't'i mem' bikharava' dena';
Ucita va'ta'varan'a mem' biijom' ko
Ankurita kara, braks'a bana' dena'.
Tumha'rii srs't'i ka' satata vikasita rahana';
Rahasyamaya hae, tumha'ra' srs't'i sam'ca'lana karana'.

Adhika'nsha jiivom' ko jiivana liila' ka'
Rasa lene mem' rata rakhana';
Kucha jiivom' ko apanii ka'ran'a satta' ka'
'Madhu' svaru'pa jana'ne ka' praya'sa kara' dena'.

Chapter 3: Bhakti va Krpa'

103. Le calo mujhako priye * 118/27.06.08

Le calo mujhako priye, tum le calo!
Mujhe rakha apane hrdaya mem', le calo.

Ga' sako to, ga'na tuma ga'te calo;
Gunjarita hrada ko kiye, calate calo.
Prema ko paeda' kiye, kucha kara calo;
Vishva ko na't'aka samajha, dekhe calo.

Madhura ke a'nanda mem', bahate calo;
Madhura sarita' mem' baha'kara, le calo.
Vishva ko sumadhura bana', nija mem' d'uba'lo;
Le calo mujhako nikat'a, nija mem' d'uba'lo.

He hari, mujhako baha'kar le calo;
Pala mere aba nija palom' mem' mila'lo.
Palaka apanii para, bit'ha'kara le calo;
Mana mera', 'Madhu' mana bana a'kara, le calo.

104. A'nanda kii sura ta'na * 119/27.06.08

He Prabhu ! a'nand kii sura ta'na dha'lo;
He Prabhu! mujhako baha'lo !

Buddhi ko vya'paka bana', tava mana bana'lo;
Mujhe tuma vanshii bana'kara, guna guna'lo;
Nikat'a mere a' tumhiim', kavita' raca' lo,
Madhura mere ra'ga mem', tuma khu'ba ga'lo.

Vishva mem' sabase mila'kara, nija bana'lo,
Vishva mem' sabako tumhiim', mera' bana'do;
Svayam kii kucha seva', mujhase kara'lo,
Hrda bana'kara dhya'na mem', 'Madhu' ko laga'lo.

105. A'nanda umangom' mem' * 127/10.07.08

A'nanda umangom' mem' bharakara,
Tumara' maem' giita suna' ja'u'n;
Maem' ta'raka brahma liye mana mem',
Tarata' ja'u'n, ga'ta' ja'u'n.

Varata' ja'u'n tava caran'om' ko,
Tava mana kii maem' karata' ja'u'n;
Tava karmom' mem' bhava bhara ja'u'n,
A'nandita ho, ga'ta' ja'u'n.

Tuma sha'shvata sundara abhinava ho,
Tuma mem' ga'u'n, tuma ko pa'u'n;
A'nanda payonidhi pa' ja'u'n,
Maem' abhinava 'Madhu' ghana ho ja'u'n.

Tuma niirava jina'na payodhi ho,
Bhakti mem' yogii ho ja'u'n;
Jhankrata tantrita, tuma karma pravrta,
Yantrita anura'gi ho ja'u'n.

106. Ra'ga kitane phura cale haem' * 651/09.12.09

Ra'ga kitane phura cale haem' a'ja mana,
Ta'na kitanii a'gayiim' haem' dhiira mana;
Shu'nya kii 'Madhu' ra'ginii mem' vikala tana,
ThirakatA sa' raha gaya' hae pra'n'a mana.

Saomyata' kii sarahadom' mem' ks'iira mana,
Tus't'ata' kii tiivra dha'ra' mem' thirana;
Teja kii madhu roshanii mem' hae tarana,
Tra'n'a kii nava dyotana' mem' hae phurana.

Ga'na kitane ga' rahii hae ye dhara',
Pavana kitane lakha raha' hae mana mera';
Gagana kii adbhuta chat'a' mana mohatii,
Salila kii saondaryata' sudhi khojatii.

Johata' hae ba't'a mera' hrda sada',
Sadya ke sangiita ko deta' dhara';
Dharan'i ke prati an'u ko deta' sudha',
Ks'udha' kii ks'udha a'kuti karata' vida'.

Vida'ii ke 'Madhu' milana mem' mathita mana,
Juda'ii kii khuda'ii mem' lasita mana;
Ra'ga ta'nom' kii buna'ii mem' magana,
Srs't'i kii sura ta'na para raca raha' dhuna.

107. Kisalaya kii laya mem' * 126/10.07.08

Kisalaya kii laya mem' maem' ga'u'm', kisake liye ga'ta' ja'u'm'?
Kisakii sha'la' mem' 'Madhu' pa'u'm', kisake kisalaya para laya
pa'u'm'?

Kisake mana mem', maem' musaka'u'n,
Kisake hrda mem', sunata' ja'u'n?
Kisake adharom' se kaha ja'u'n, kisake tana mem' maem', bhava ja'u'n?

Mera' mana usaka' hii tana hae, mera' tana usaka' hii mana hae;
Mera' hrada usakii hii laya hae, merii laya usakii hii dhuna hae.

Maem' kya' ga'u'n, kya' na' ga'u'n, kevala usakii sunata' ja'u'n;
Kevala usakii karata' ja'u'n, usake bala maem' jiita' ja'u'n.

108. Maem' akelii gopa ba'la' (Braja) * 2/19.03.08

Maem' akelii Gopa ba'la', basati Yamuna' tiira.

Ut'hyao jovana jva'ra mo para, hiya ut'hii eka piira;
Milana ho piya sam'ga, aesii hiyahi ut'hii hilora.

Sarasa shiitala bahati pavana, subhaga sundara Yamuna' jala;
Na'cata mayu'ra kadamba ta'la, udita su'raja nabha visha'la.

Yamuna' tat'a bat'a nikat'a sakhii lakhi,
Jala bica naha'vana chalii gopa mana;
A'nandita thirakita a'lhva'dit, aunga suyoga bhayau jala sam'ga jaba.

Mana kii piira, jagata kii piir'a', Jamuna'jal pala mem' hari liinha';
Daihika daivika bhautika piir'a', gopa va'lika' kachu na'him' ciinha'.

Mana pulakita, a'tma' a'nandita, gopii jala sama'dhi a'pla'vita;
Mana halka', tana subhaga praphullita,
Roma roma shiharata alhva'dita.

Keka' koyal kalarava karata, gopa va'lika' mana shihara'vata;
Mana shariira saba bhayau 'Madhu' maya,
Saomya sha'nta surabhita jyom' Hari maya.

109. Hari merao hari liyo tuma ciira * 3/19.03.08 (Braj)

Hari merao hari liyo tum ciira!
Maem' akelii Gopa va'la', basati Yamuna' tiira.

Jala sama'dhi Gopii jaba d'u'bii, pulakit mana satsam'gati bhogii.
Raks'a' karat ciir kii hiyahari, hiya mam'h baet'hi vastra liye ha'rii.
Krs'na ut'ha'ye ciir tiira tom', baet'heu ucca kadamba sha'kh para.
Dhya'n gayau vastrana para jaba,
Lakhe vastra sam'g Shya'ma manohara.

Chiira haryao athava' hiya ha'ryau, hiy cira ha'ryao, chiira hara'yo.
Ura manh vaha, ba'hara vaha baet'ha';
Jiiva sam'ga khelahi ati niika'.
Jimi bhaktiimaya bhakta samarpita, satsam'gati jala bica avarohita;
Kas't'a vilaya a'pana sam'tana bica,
Sam'ta   rahahim' a'nandita pulakita.

La'ja bhaya nagnata' ka' bha'v kisase,
Kriir'a' kare karaba'ye jo hamiim'se!
Ciira usake, tana usii ke, mana usa ke, la'ja bhaya usii ke!
Am'dara vaha, ba'hara vaha, ciira dene se pahale vaha!
'Madhu' ciira lene ke ba'da bhii vaha!

110. Nanca ja'u'm' maem' * 120/27.06.08

Nanca ja'u'm' maem', tumha're hrdaya mem';
Barasa ja'u'm' maem', tumha're dhya'na mem'.

Mana mile a'nanda mem', tava hrdaya mem';
Gagana mila ja'ye, tumha're runga mem'.
Magana mem' na'nchu'n, tuma're chanda mem';
Gagana ja'ye d'u'ba, tumare citta mem'.

Mana ja'ye mila, tuma're dhya'na mem';
Vishva ja'ye mila, tuma're vesha mem'.
Pala ja'yem' mila, tuma're hradaya mem';
'Madhu' ja'ye mila, tumare caran'a mem'.

111. Dhiire dhiire Gopii calii * 4/19.03.08

Dhiire dhiire Gopii calii, bilaga ho satsam'gati ke jala se;
Sala'ja sabhaya chipa'ye apane am'gom' ko, apane karom' se.
Chor'i saba bhavitavyata', nija nagnata' kii la'ja;
Cala par'ii us ora gopii, jisa dika lakhe Nanda Kuma'r.

Jala chu't'a', mana tat'a se jut'a', tana mana mem' mit'a';
Kintu kras'na dekhe   ma'tra usake mana mem',
Usakii bhakti dravita a'nkhom' mem'.
Gopii vishva'sa bar'ha', tapa nikhara', samarpan'a bar'ha';
Bhakti ananta mem' milii, mana a'nandita hua', arpan'a bar'ha'.

Netra a'tma' bane, netrom' ne a'tma da'na diya';
Krs'n'a cala diye, vastra mila gaye.
Ra'sa rasa gaye, biras vastra hue, a'nanda thiraka';
'Madhu' a'tma' parama huii. Gopii Ra'dha' huii.

112. Kyom' na cura'yem' ciira mera' * 5/19.03.08

Kyom' na cura'yem' ciira mera' Krs'n'a hara pala,
Shariira kyom' na ho ja'ye sha'shvata!
Kyom' maim' chiirom' kii cinta' karu'm',
Kyom' na unhaim' chiir du'm' har pala!

Hara pala Jamuna' kii satsam'gati se nikala,
Kyom' na unakii goda mem' bisaru'm', bikharu'm';
Ve mujhe dekhem', vara'bhaya dem',
Maim' unake caran'om' mem' sara rakha so ja'u'm!

Kyom' na unhem' apane gurucakra para,
Sahasra padma dalom' para bit'ha'u'm';
Aura maim' unake sha'shvata caran'om' mem' let'a' ja'um'!
Ve mere shariira mana a'tma' ko sahala'em',
Aura maim' unake ana'hata mem' mila ja'u'm'!

Kyom' na maem' unako sneha du'm', Unake cakrom' ko sahala'u'n'!
Kya' ve thaka nahiim' gaye dete dete,
Kyom' na unhem' unhiim' kii 'Madhu' a'tma srs't'i dedu'm'!

113. Mera' astitva * 17/28.03.08

Mera' astitva ananta hae,
Maim' ananta ka' ra'hii hu'm'.

Kabhii maim' ananta ka' a'di khojata' hu'm',
Kabhii maim' a'di ka' anta khojata' hu'm';
Kabhii astitva pa'ja'ta' hu'm',
Kabhii astitva khodeta' hu'm'.

Kabhii tum mujhe mila ja'te ho madhya mem',
Kabhii tarasa'te ho anta taka;
Kabhii samajha a'ja'te ho,
Kabhii samajha' ja'te ho.

Mera' astitva tumhiim' mem' hae,
Tuma milo to maim' milu'm';
Tuma gale laga'o to maim' lagu'm',
Tuma nazara a'o to maim' caran'a par'u'm'.

Tum mere nikat'a raho, nikat'ata' rakho,
Kat'uta' mata rakho, krapan'ata'   mata karo;
Tuma byasta ho, srs't'i ke niyantran'a mem',
Sa'tha phira bhii raho mere hara pala mem'.

Tumha're sa'nidhya mem', tumha're astitva mem';
Pa' ja'u'm'ga' maim' ra'ha, apana' 'Madhu' astitva.

114. Prabhu Tumha're a'loka mem'! * 159/14.09.08

Prabhu Tumha're a'loka mem',
Kitanii a'bha'em' ubhariim'!
Prabhu tumha're ma'dhurya mem',
Kitanii 'Madhu' giiti utariim'!

Kitanii vidha'em' vidya' bana bahiim',
Kitanii pratibha'em' pratibhu'ta huyiim'?
Kitane sukha dukha a'nanda dha'ra' bana bahe,
kitanii piir'a'em' viina' bana ga'yiim'?

Vishva kii vya'pakata' ura mem' dha' ga'yii,
Jiivana kii sa'rthakata' antarmana ranga ga'yii.
Guru kii krpa' kitana' ranga la'yii!
Dhara' kii dhu'li kitanii mana bha'yii!

Kitane da'nava, ma'nava bana ga'ye!
Kitane ma'nava, mana se tara ga'ye!
Kitanii pratikriya'em', preran'a' bana a'yiim'!
kitanii dyotana'em' cetana' bana ga'yiim'!

115. Bha'va ke bhanvara mem' * 18/28.03.08

Bha'va ke bhanvara mem' , bha'vana' bha'vuk hae;
Bhanvara' bha'va'tmak hae, prthvii a'nandita hae.

'Madhu' tuma a'ja'o to, bha'va bharem' bha's'a' mem',
Ga'yem' kucha giita yaha'm', pa'yem' kuch miita yaha'm'.
Ta're a'ja'yem'ge, ca'nda sa'tha la'em'ge;
Khanjan mana ranjan kara, gunjana bhara ja'em'ge.

Tuma khoja'na' mata, apane hii ra'gom' mem',
Ra'ga mila' dena' tuma, saba ke hii ra'gom' mem'.
Pancama svara phu't'ega', papiihara' bolega';
Ca'nda muskara' dega', cakorii ga' degii.

Cala dega' bha'vuk jala, hima se visravita ho kara;
Su'raja sura de dega', va'yu se sam'yuta ho ho kara.
Nabha sara para hoga', sarapat'a mana d'olega';
Ajina' se bha'va bikhara , mana mana mem' bolem'ge.

Taba tuma bhii suna lena', aora use ga' dena',
Prthvii khila ja'egii, ca'nda sharama ja'ega'.
Bha'va bham'pa ja'em'ge, bha'vana ke a'ne ko,
Mana bha'vana bhagawan bana,
Vihansa bikhara ja'em'ge.

116. Jiivana ke su'tradha'ra * 140/14.08.08

Jiivana ke su'tradha'ra, mujhako dedo a'dha'ra;
Dekara a'nanda jva'ra, 'Madhu' ka' karado uddha'ra.
Jiivana sarita' bharakara, sa'gara maya ho ja'kara;
Mera' abhinava udga'ra, le calo sa'gara pa'ra.

Jiivana ke srotadha'ra, jiivana ko dedo dha'ra,
Khola do a'nanda dva'ra, jhara' do mukti ha'ra.
Haralo dharin'ii ka' bha'ra, bha'va bharo haralo ra'ra;
Tribhuvana ke karn'adha'ra, karado sabaka' uddha'ra.

117. Pu'rn'a kii ya'tra' * 25/02.04.08

Pu'rn'a kii pu'rn'a se pu'rn'a taka kii ya'tra';
Pu"rn'a hae, paripu'rn'a hae, pu'rn'a thii, pu'rn'a hogii.

Mera' hara pala, hara shva'm'sa, pu'rn'a kA parva hae;
Mera' hara paga pu'rn'a ka' chanda hae.
Merii jiivan ya'tra', pu'rn'a kii pariyojana' hae;
Merii hara ruka'bat'a, pu'rn'a mem' par'a'ba hae.

Merii yojana'em' usii ke a'yojana haem';
Merii shakti, mera' sam'kalpa, Usii ka' pra'n'a'ya'ma hai.
Mere dukha, mere darda, pu'rn'a ke upaca'ra haem';
Merii upalabdhiya'm', merii saphalata'em',
Usii kii krapa' ka' prasa'd haem'.

Merii apu'rn'a katha', merii apurn'a byatha';
Pu'rn'a kii hii iccha'-sthiti hae.
Bhavis'ya kii dharohar hae, merii sa'ja sajja';
Pu'rn'a kii kalpana' hae, merii hara iccha'.

Maem' bhayabhiita, cintita, byathita kyom' hu'n;
Pala pala nita badalatii, niyati kii sthitiyom' mem'.
'Madhu' giita hu'n usaka',   sa'j hu'm' usaka';
Sunata' hu'n giita Usake, Usakii hii viin'a' para.

118. Prabhu ke ra'ga * 55/08.05.08

Prabhu ke maem' ra'ga suna'ta' hu'm',
A'nanda mem' d'u'ba' ja'ta' hu'm';
Tuma a'ja'o, mere hrda mem',
Mana mem' sura mem', madhu ga'yana mem';
Tuma na'co mere a'ngana mem', a'nandita ho sura bha'vana mem'.

Mere mana ko tuma leja'o, a"nanda dhara' para le ja'o;
Tuma a'ja'o, aba a'ja'o! mujhako dha'ra' mem' le ja'o.
A'nandita Gunga' mem' le ja' kara, d'ubakii tuma mujhako lagaba'o;
Mrdu a'nandita kara le a'o, rasa bhara ja'o, 'Madhu' de ja'o.

119. Bha'va samudrom' mem' * 37/08.04.08

Bha'va samudrom' mem' bahakara, 'Madhu' tuma ga'o, nava giiti;
Dhara' praphullita ho ja'ye, ga'o aesii 'Madhu Giiti'.
Nabha ga' ut'he, tarungita ho, miit'hii miit'hii anubhu'ti.

Tuma a'ja'o va'yu mem' baha, agni mem' jala, jala mem' milakara,
Kucha ga' ja'o mrdu sam'smaran'a.
Dhara' muskara'kar dha'ye, jana de jana jana mem' nava priiti.
Ra'ha bane a'nandita chandit, phu't'e nava anubhu'ti..

Nabha se a'kara, hrda mem' cha'kara,
A'nandita ho, abhinava bana kara;
Tana yantrita kara, mana mantrita kara,
Tuma madhura madhupa gunjana bana kara.
Ga' kara, pa' kara, hrda sarasa' kara.

Tuma madhu maya ho, madhukar madhu ho,
Nabha mem' tum ho, hrda mem' bhii ho;
Mujha mem' tum ho, saba hii mem' ho,
Tuma ho to mem' hu'm', saba jaga hae,
Tana hae, mana hae, jana jiivana hae;
A'o ham sab na'ncem' ga'yem', 'Madhu' ks'ara' ' Madhu Giiti'.

120. Prabhu ka' madhu ga'na * 128/10.07.08

Tuma Prabhu ka' madhu ga'na ho, a'nanda kii sura ta'na ho;
Mere hrdaya mem' jva'ra ho, mera' tumhi udga'ra ho.
Tuma srs't'i ke a'nanda ho, Tuma adhara mem' cha'ye raho;
Tum vishva ke vikashita manuja, a'nanda ka' tuma ra'ga ho.

Aba a'bhii ja'o vishva mem', Tuma ma'navom' ke marma mem';
Prema tuma dete rahe ho sras't'i mem',
Vishva mem' a'o, tumhii a'nanda ho.

Sabhii ke mana mem' baha' amrata tumhiim',
Jina'na do, abhidhya'na do, sura ta'na do;
Madhura bana kara ga'na mere suna'do,
'Madhu' bana', a'nanda kii sura ta'na do.

121. Gokula kii kulaba'la' * 46/01.05.08

Maem' hu'm' Gokula* kii kula-ba'la',
Tuma ho Madhupura* ke Nandala'la';
Maem' kula kund'alinii kii Ra'dha',
Tuma sahasra'ra ke parama Shiva'.

Tumharii muralii dhvani mem' ma'khii,
Maem' madhu kii pya'sii madhu ma'khii;
Kitanii madhuma'khii madhu ca'khiim',
Kitanii madhu ma'khii 'madhu' ra'khiim'.

Kitanii kriir'a' madhu liila' mem',
Kitana' mohan madhu nagarii mem';
Ghana a'kars'an'a madhumaya madhu mem',
Suprabandha suraks'a' saba madhu mem'.

Maim' mu'la'dha'ra kii 'Madhu' va'la',
Tuma guru cakra kii madhusha'la';
Abhinava ba'la' maem' nava jva'la',
Nava madhu d'ha'la', tuma nabha jva'la'.

122. Prabhu kii nirmita madhu ka'ya'   * 47/01.05.08

Prabhu kii nirmita yaha 'Madhu' ka'ya',
Kitane janmom' kii madhu ma'ya';
Kula kund'alinii kii laghu ka'ya', kitane kalpom' kii praticha'ya'.

Mu'la'dha'ra kii Gopii kii pran'aya katha',
Mohana muralii kii pran'ava dhvani hae;
Gopii se Krs'n'a se milane kii katha',
Sahasra'ra ke param Shiva' kii marma katha'.

Mu'la'dha'ra se sahasra'ra kii ya'tra',
Jiiva se brahma kii yaha ya'tra', kitanii chot'ii hae;
Para kyom' itanii lam'bii lagatii hae, samaya le letii hae.
Sambhavatah, Prabhu apane hara pra'n'a ko,
Milane sam'varane sajane dete haem';
A'nanda dete haem', a'nanda lete haem'.

123. Mem' kya' ga'u'm' * 54/08.05.08

Mem' kya' ga'u'm', aba Tuma ga'o!

Savita' bana kara Tuma a'ja'o, a'nanda bane Tuma cha' ja'o;
Mere hrda mem' a'kara ga'o, muralii kii ta'na suna' ja'o.

Mem' a'nandita ho ja'ta' hu'm',
Jaba Tumarii t'era suna'ta' hu'm';
Rasa ra'gom' se bhara ja'ta' hu'm',
Maem' a'lhva'dita ho ja'ta' hu'm'.

Tuma a'ja'o aba a'ja'o, nat'avara na'gara tuma a'ja'o;
Bhava sa'gara mem' tuma a'ja'o, mere mana ko aba le ja'o.

Apane caran'om' ko daba ba'o,
Mere sara ko tuma sahala'o;
Maem' a'nandita sunata' ja'u'm',
Madhu' Giiti tumhiim' ga'te jao.

124. Tuma jiivana ho * 137/14.08.08

Tuma jiivana ho jiivana sura ho;
Abhinava madhumaya, ma'nava svara ho.

A'nanda mahula 'Madhu' mem' bahakara,
'Madhu Giiti' tumhiim' ga'te ja'o;
Dete ja'o a'nanda madhura,
Anubhu'ti kucha kahate ja'o.

Maem' a'ta' hu'n, ga' ja'ta' hu'n;
Tuma sunakara hii mata raha ja'o.
A'nanda ananta liye mana mem', utsuka anura'gii ho ja'o.

Aba ra'ga dhara' ke tuma ga'o, arama'na hrdaya ke dikhala'o;
Sabake ura ke ga'ne ga'o; sabake hrda mem' ja'kara ga'o.

125. Pus'pom' ke dala dala para   * 160/23.09.08

Pus'pom' ke dala dala para, madhu ma'khii dha'tii hae;
Para'gita kan'a kan'a lekar, pragat'ita madhu karatii hae.

Sahamita surabhita siharata, pus'pom' ke jhun'd'a madhura;
Madhukara kii dhuna manahara, dharin'ii kii gandha madhura.

Bikhara'ta' dina ra'ti, prabha' kusuma bahu bha'nti;
Mera' mana ho vihansita, khila ja'ta' nava bhanti.

Tum bhii 'Madhu' ho pramudita, pras'phut'a mana, tana thirakita;
Pra'n'om' se a'nandita, jhankrata pulakita mandrita.

126. Maem' ra'ga dhara' ke * 139/14.08.08

Maem' ra'ga dhara' ke kya' ga'u'n!
Tumhare sura mem' ulajha' ja'u'n!
Tumhare ranga mem' rangata' ja'u'n!
Jiivana kii kama sunata' ja'u'n!

Maem' kya' dekhu'nga' sunalu'nga',
Kya' tuma se kucha kaha pa'u'nga';
Mujhase tuma kya' le pa'oge,
Maem' tumako kya' de pa'u'nga'.

Sumadhura shobhana hae tumara' sura,
Mohana abhinava madhu se madhukar;
Tuma sunalo mere ura ke sura,
Sura ura mem' le de do nava svara.

Maem' a'nandita surabhita sura hu'n,
Anubhu'ti se mohita 'Madhu' hu'n;
Rddhi siddhi kii ma'ya' se,
Thirakita avimohita modita hu'n.

127. Mera' mohana mana * 161/23.09.08

Mera' mohan mana 'Madhu' ma'kha',
Madhu ma'kkhii se yah ca'kha';
Ka'nt'om' ne hae isako ra'kha',
Pus'pom' ka' hae yaha madhu ma'kha'.

Madhu priiti ma'khii madhu vidya',
Bhara detii mana mem' madhura vidha';
Prabhu krpa' ne 'Madhu' ko sa'dha',
Bhakti ne man ko hae ba'm'dha'.

Dha'ran'a' kii dhyeyita dha'ra', pra'n'a'ya'ma prayojita dhara';
Sama'dhi sambodhi ks'ara', yama niyamom' se dha'rita dhara'.
Pratya'ha'ra pralobhana ha'ra', yoga'sana mudra' madhu dva'ra';
Dhya'na dhyeya mem' arpita ha'ra',
Milita sa'dhana' ka' sura nya'ra'.

Upava'som' kii deha ma'dhurii, mana a'tma' kii priiti nikha'rii;
Kiirtan ka' rasa barase pya'ra', a'nandita bahatii prabhu dha'ra'.

128. Maem' madhu-ma'khii * 164/23.09.08

Maem' madhu-ma'khii bana kara ja'ta',
Pus'pom' se madhu-kan'a le a'ta';
Madhu-graha mem' madhu ko rakha a'ta',
Madhu sva'mii ko arpita karata'.

Prati dina dha'ta', a'ta' ja'ta', madhu ko arjita karata' rahata';
Eka dina koii aesa' a'ja'ta', madhu-ma'khe madhu ko leja'ta'.

Maem' phira madhu-graha se ur'a ja'ta',
A'nandita madhu arjita karata';
Madhu-corii kii a'sha' karata', 'sva'mii ke sva'mii' ko lakhata'.

Mera' ma'khii-mana makha ja'ta',
rakhane ka' bha'va bikhara ja'ta';
Madhu jiivan madhu-ma'kha' karata',
Madhu 'Madhu' ko de madhumaya karata'.

Chapter 4. Karun'a'nubhu'ti

129. Kam'kar'a * 153/05.09.08

Kam'kar'a ke kan'a kan'a kii katha' kucha karun'a hae,
Para 'Madhu' rasa mem' d'u'bii vaha a'nandita sagun'a hae;
Hradaya krandana se kincita vicalita hae,
Para marma mem' vaha thirakita vihansita hae.

Usake bahurangii bahuru'pii virala svaru'pa mem',
Kitana' saundarya lasita itiha'sa chipa' hae;
Usake arama'nom' kii at't'a'lika'om' ne,
Kitanii vidha'yem' baha'rem' vyavastha'yem' bikharii haem'.

Kitanii ulka'yem' a'ka'sha se a'kar usase milii haem',
Kitane sa'garom' kii man'i dhu'la kan'a banii haem';
Kitanii parvata shikha'yem' hima mem' t'hit'huriim' haem',
Hima nada sanga nandita ho, dhara' para bikharii haem'.

Pa'vana parvata shila'yem' bhii ma'nava se pujatii haem',
Dha'ra'om' mem' bahe patthara bhii sundar ho siharate haem';
Kitanii shila' kam'kar'a dhu'la,
Graha upagrahom' se la' hama dekhe haem',
Hama're kitane shu'nya ya'na
Anya grahom' para ja' dhu'la kan'a bane haem'.

130. Sar'aka ke kan'a kan'a ka' * 154/05.09.08

Sar'aka ke kan'a kan'a ka' ura kan'a,
A'ja kucha virahita vidhura anamana' hae;
Apane atiita ke a'nanda kii ya'da mem',
Vicalita vyathita unmana' hae.

Ananta ranga ru'pom' se bharii usakii ka'ya' hae,
Dhu'la dhu'sarita dhara' usakii dha'ya' hae;
A'ka'sha jala va'yu dhu'p ka' sa'ya' hae,
Shveta him kii usake u'para cha'ya' hae.

Kankar'a kii kar'aka se hii, dhara' kii dhar'akana hae,
Kankar'a kii akar'a se hii usakii jakar'ana hae;
Kankar'a kii pakar'ana hii use ba'm'dhe rakhati hae,
Kankar'a kii sahanashIiiata' se hii aorom' kii sar'aka hae.

Kankar'a ka' ghanatva usake antaranga a'kars'an'a se hae,
Usakii mana bhu'mi panca tattvom' se pla'vita hae;
Usaka' chhidra yukta bha'va bha'ratva,
Kya' kucha nahiim' sokha saha leta' hae.

Apane hrdaya ke viira'na mem' bhii vaha,
jiivan'a'uom' kii 'Madhu' bastii basa' leta' hae;
Apane sara para ma'nava va'hana calane de,
ma'navom' ko mam'jila para pahunca' deta' hae.

131. Mere mana kii ye shya'malima' * 176/13.11.08

Mere mana kii ye shya'malima',
Mere tana kii yaha ka'jalima'!
Tumane hii to d'halava' dii hae,
Tumane hii to rangava' dii hae!

Kyom' ma'nava mana ko racate ho,
Kyom' nija karmom' mem' rangate ho?
Kyom' seva' mem' lagava'te ho,
Kyom' mana ko bhat'aka' dete ho?

Saba srs't'i kii a'turata'em',
Saba drs't'i kii ka'tarata'em';
Tumane dii haem' cetanata'em',
Tumane lii haem' shya'malima'em'.

Kyom' tuma cira daya'lu hoja'te,
Kyom' kucha kat'hora Prabhu hoja'te!
Kyom' tuma 'Madhu' karava' lete,
Kyom' tuma mujhase bikhara' dete!

Mera' ura gora' shya'mala hae,
Sam'ska'rom' kii godhu'li hae;
Pra'rabdhom' kii pra'kratata' hae,
Tumarii prakati ki kii bha's'a' hae.

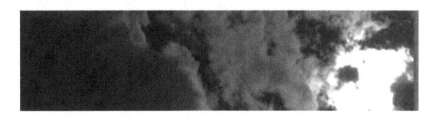

132. Cala cala mere mana * 182/13.11.08

Cala cala mere mana madhuvana mem',
Eka'kii pracalita prati pala mem';
A'nandita yamuna' kii dhuna mem',
Sha'kha' mraga kii mradu kunjana mem'.

Madhu ma'khii ke madhu vyanjjan mem',
A'nkhom' ke pya're khanjana mem';
Ta'rom' kii pran'ava bharii dhvani mem',
Mana ke 'Madhu' thirakita gunjana mem'.

Soham' kii dhvani mem' maem' gau'm',
Jiivana a'bha' ko damaka'u'm';
Priitama ke sukha mem' rama ja'u'm',
Dharatii kii dhvani mem' baha ja'u'm'.

Abhinava madhumaya sha'shvata sundara,
Cetanata' kii bharapu'ra lahara;
Jiivana kii abhinava prati dhvani mem',
Pa'vanata' kii prati pratidhvani mem'.

133. He Hari tumane kya' kara d'a'la'   * 175/13.11.08

He Hari tumane kya' kara d'a'la',
Mera' mana kyom' yom' ranga d'a'la'?
Kitanii dedii mujhako jva'la', mera' mana kaisa' kara d'a'la'?

He priyatam, kitane dukha dete, mana apana' mama tana ko dete;
Siima'om' mem' sikur'a' dete, kum't'ha'om' mem' jakar'a' dete.

Jab ca'he tuma calaba' dete, jaba ca'he tuma t'hahara' dete;
Kaba ja'ne kya' kahala' dete, kaese tum kucha karaba' dete.

Kyom' maem' cinta' bhaya ko pa'lu'm', jo ho pa'ta' vaha kara d'a'lu'm';
Jo raha ja'ta' tuma para d'a'lu'm', mana tumamem' arpita kara d'a'lu'm'.

Tuma hii to mama mana ke preraka, priyatama tuma ho jaga ke sevaka;
Sevaka ke tuma ekaka dha'raka, 'Madhu' a'tma' ke tuma prati pa'laka.

134. Merii madhurata' kii muska'na * 179/13.11.08

Tum merii madhurata' kii muska'na ho,
Kya' tuma mujhe pahaca'na pa' rahe ho?
Tuma merii vya'pakata' kii baocha'ra ho,
Kya' tuma mujhe parakha pa' rahe ho?

Tuma vishva kii ba'dha'om' kii vya'pakata' ho,
Ananta a'bha' kii tuma shobha' ho;
Tuma akhilata' kii khilakhila'hat'a ho,
Aparu'pa ka' tuma abhinava svaru'pa ho.

Tuma kyom' asha'nta digbhra'nta ho,
Tuma kyom' dvividha' mem' bhaya'kra'nta ho;
Tuma ujjvala a'sha' ke nihshva'sa ho,
Brahma'n'd'a kii arun'ima' ke tuma pratiika ho.

Tuma pa'vana pa'vaka kii pahelii ho,
Jiivan ya'minii kii tuma sahelii ho;
'Madhu' jiivana ke Tuma pradiipa ho,
Saos't'hava sarita' ke madhu bhanvara ho.

135. Jagata kii jananii niiravata' * 178/13.11.08

Jagat kii jananii niiravata', ma'nava mana kii modaka madhuryata';
Cetaka kii cetana caturata', pa'vana kii preraka pra'n'iinata'.

Prabhu ke preran'a' srota ko nikat'a la'o,
Vikat'a vana mem' nazara a'o;
Prakat'a tana mem' sihara ja'o,
Nikat'a mana mem' bhava ja'o.

Maem' tumha'rii krpa' ko samajha nahiim' pa'ta',
Tumha'rii nikat'ata' ko dekha nahiim' pa'ta';
Tumha'rii ca'hata ko pahaca'na nahiim' pa'ta',
Tumha'rii ra'hata ko parakha nahiim' pa'ta'.

Tuma ananta marya'da'om' kii pahelii ho,
Vishva kii vya'pakata' kii tuma sahelii ho;
Ananta bhogom' ki tuma bhaya'nakata' ho,
Aneka ra'gom' kii tuma surabhi ho.

Tuma ho srs't'i ke sneha preraka lalita nrtya,
Tumhii ho sarva ba'dha'om' ko bedhate ta'n'd'ava;
Jiivana kii tuma vya'paka dha'ra',
Ho 'Madhu' a'nanita prakhara prabha'.

136. Mama ma'dhurii kii mukharata' * 180/13.11.08

Mama ma'dhurii kii mukharata', tuma prakrti kii pra'curyata';
Mama manujata' kii madhurima', tuma sha'nta susmita saghanata'.

Mana mayu'rii kii la'ja tuma, madhu' prakrti ke sopa'na tuma;
Mama bha'gya ke madhu ya'na tuma, mere hrdaya ke dhya'na tuma.

Mem' kya' puka'ru'm', kya' kahu'm'! Tuma ko kaha'm' kaese lakhu'n!
Nija hradaya mem' kaese rakhu'm'! Saba sahaja maem' kaese karu'n!

Tuma eka rasa 'Madhu' pra'nta ho, maem' virala virahi kla'nta hu'n;
Lakhi prakrti kii pra'ciinata', abhinava madhura maem' sha'nta hu'n.

137. He 'Madhu' paks'ii! * 183/13.11.08

He 'Madhu' paks'ii! Tuma kya' dekhate ho?
Kya' parakhate ho, kya' su'nghate ho?
Kya' sunate ho, kya' ca'hate ho?
Kyom' a'te ho, kyom' cale ja'te ho?

Tuma kucha khojate ho, kucha socate ho;
Kucha bolate ho, kucha cahakate ho.
Kucha phudakate ho, kucha sahamate ho;
kucha sharama'te ho, phira ur'a ja'te ho.

Ma'nava se tumha'ra' rishta' pura'na' hae,
Tinakom' mem' tumha'ra' khaja'na' hae;
Tanika dera mem' tumane ur'a ja'na' hae,
Hava' ke jhonkom' sam'ga tumhaem' cala dena' hae.

Tumha'ra' mana pra'n'a madhu utsa'ha bhara' hae,
Maha'dviipom' kii ya'tra' ka' shaurya bhara' hae;
Jiivana kii ma'dhurii ka' rasa tumane piya' hae,
Srs't'i kii shobha' ka' rasa tumane cakha' hae.

138. Thirakita pulakita * 184/13.11.08

Thirakita pulakita sahamita mohita,
Mama mana a'shanka' se piir'ita;
Ura kii vyavadha'na bharii viithi, mana kii arama'na bharii giiti.

A'sha' pu'rita jiivana ces't'a', bha's'a' bha'vita bhu's'ita nis't'ha';
Ma'navata' kii prakat'ita ces't'a', jiivana kii madhura priiti nis't'ha'.
Dediipyama'na diptita drs't'a', da'va'nala kii da'hita ces't'a';
Dedu'm' maem' nija mana kii iccha', Unakii iccha' merii nis't'ha'.

Arpan'a ke pun'ya samarpan'a mem',
Tarpan'a ke tapa mohita mana mem';
Maem' kyom' socu'm', kyom' cintita hu'n,
Nyaocha'vara nirbhara una para hu'n.

Ve kya' ca'hem', maem' kya' ja'nu'n, kya' kara d'a'lem'ge kya' ja'nu'n;
Saba kucha unako maem' de ja'u'n, 'Madhu' prema payodhi le ja'u'n.

139. Mere mana kii shu'nyata' * 162/23.09.08

Mere mana kii shu'nyata', kaha'n se a'yii, kaese a'yii!
Mere mana kii dhaeryata', kaom'na la'ya', kaese a'yii!

Kya' pa'ya' maem'ne, kya' khoya'?
Kya' ca'ha' maem'ne, kya' boya'?
Kyom' moha' maem' hu'n, kyom' roya'?
Kyom' ja'ga' maem' hu'n, kyom' soya'?
Kaese merii prakrti upajii? Kaese piir'a' mana mem' upajii?
Kyom' vikrati merii thii bigar'ii? Kaese ca'hata merii ujar'ii?

Tuma kyom' a'te ho, ga'te ho? Kyom' varavasha tuma cala dete ho?
Mana viin'a' ko sura dete ho, thirakita pulakita kara dete ho.
Ma'nava mana ke vihansita sa'thii, shobhita sajja' ke parilaks'ii;
Ks'obhita mana ke he paridras't'ii,
A'nandita 'Madhu' mana ke sa'ks'ii.

140. Mere ks'itija kii gahara'iyom' mem' * 226/03.02.09

Mere ks'itija kii gahara'iyom' mem' tuma na jha'm'ko,
Mere hrudaya sa'gara kii laharom' mem' khoja'o;
Mere mana kii gahara'iyom' mem' simat'a ja'o,
Mere a'nanda sa'gara kii laharom' mem' bikhara ja'o.

Mere upaha'sa ke at't'a'ha'sa mem' tuma na khoo,
Mere hrdaya kii srota gunga' mem' mujhe pa'o;
Mere mana kii niiravata' mem' mujhe dekho,
Mere a'nanda kii sarita' mem' tuma kho ja'o.

Mere ura ke udadhi kii a'bha' ko tuma niha'ro,
Mere saondarya kii shobha' mem' damaka ja'o;
Mere surom' ke sam'giita mem' bikhara ja'o,
Mere a'nanda kii 'Madhu' gupha' mem' sihar ja'o.

141. Maem' ma'navata' ko * 236/06.02.09

Maem' ma'navata' ko kya' sukha du'n!
Maem' da'navata' ko kya' dukha du'n!
Dukha sukha kii laharom' mem'   bahalu'n,
A'nanda sudha' hrdi mem' bhara lu'n.

Maem' kyom' thirakita jaga ko kara du'n!
Pulakita pramudita bhava ko kar du'n!
Maem' kyom' ja'gu'n, kyom' so ja'u'n!
Maim' kyom' a'u'n, maem' kyom' ja'u'n!

Tuma sabake ka'ran'a dha'ran'a ho,
Tuma sabake preraka dyotaka ho;
Maem' kyom' krodhita hu'n vikarita hu'n,
Maem' kyom' prerita a'lhva'dita hu'n!

Maem' kyom giitom' se bhara ja'ta',
Maem' kyom' shokom' ko saha ja'ta';
Maem kyom' agni ko ura leta',
Maem' kyom' a'nanda sudha' deta'!

Maem' kyom' a'ta', maim' kyom' ga'ta',
Maem' kyom' madhukara bana ur'a ja'ta';
Maem' kyom' pa'naii kii dha'ra bana',
Agni   jva'la' ko saha leta'.

Maem' kyom' pavanom' ko uradedu'n,
Kyom' gaganom' ko maem' phaila'du'n;
Maem' kyom' aesii srs't'i racadu'n,
'Madhu' cittom' ko kyom' bikhara'du'n!

142. Kya' tuma mujhase gaba ba'oge * 238/06.02.09

Kya' tuma mujhase gaba ba'oge, kya' tuma 'Madhu' ko apana'oge!
Ka'likhata' merii pom'choge, pa'vanata' kya' apanii doge!

Maim' kya' karata' ja'ta' a'ta', Ga'ta' ja'ta' maim' matiya'ta';
Ma'nava mana kii sudha budha khota',
Tumare hrdi kii dhuna mem' rahata'.

Ghana ghana ghana ghana ghanaghora ghat'a',
Tumare ura kii mohan trijat'a';
Maim' lat'apat'a'ta mana mem' siha'ta,
Lat'a ulajhi   ja'ta, tana sulajha ja'ta.

Mere mana mem' aba a'jha'm'kem',
Ma'dhurima' kii jha'm'kii ta'kem';
Rokem' t'okem' na'ncem' ga'em',
Mana mem' siharem', hrudi mem' hansem'.

143. Ura mem' vyatha' * 319/28.05.09

Ura mem' vyatha', sura mem' katha',
Tana mem' vidha', mana mem' sudha';
A'nanda rasa kii sarasata', pra'n'om' bharii pran'iinata'.

Tava caran'a mem' talliinata', a'kuti bharii aocityata';
Sa'nidhya kii shubha sahajata', a'ra'dhya kii madhu gahanata'.
Ma'nava maniis'ii kii madhura, ca'hana bharii caetanyata';
Sa'nanda saorabha mem' magana, pra'rabdha kii madhu saomyata'.

Shubha surabhi hae, mana udadhi hae,
Madhu vyoma hae, shudhu ks'obha hae;
Prakrti pramodita kriya' hae, madhu na'da mem' khadyota hae.
Mrdu adhara hae, shudhu amiya hae, a'nanda dha'ra' sughar'a hae;
Shiitala samanvita hrdaya hae, sam'skrta calana shubha chanda hae.

Shubha dras't'i kii sha'liinata', 'Madhu' vrs't'i   kii hae prakharata';
Pran'avita dharan'i kii madhurata', vya'paka vibhu kii viralata'.

144. Khva'ba maem' * 327/30.05.09

Khva'ba maem' dekhe   cala' hu'n vishva mem',
Sra'va mem' bahata' cala' hu'm' drashya mem';
Byakta hu'm' abhibyakta hu'm' nava srs't'i mem',
kara raha' hu'm' karma nava anurakti mem'.

Drs't'i hae sham'kita byathita mama manuja kii,
Danuja mana a'shvasta sa' bhaya grasta hae;
Srs't'i   kii sam'kucita dras't'i se vikat'a,
Bam't'a raha' ma'nava manoratha mem' magana..

Krs'a katha' virahita vidha', sam'carita hae soii dhara',
vyoma hae sihara' hua', jala madhura hae t'hahara' hua';
Maem' bikharata' bichur'a' viharata', rata virata calata' raha',
A'nanda kii abhibyakti ko maem' hrdaya mem' varata' raha'.

Pra'n'ii urn'a hae, tarun'a hae, ka'ya' karun'a hae varun'a hae,
Sam'ta'pa kii unmukti se nandita lasita vaha mukta hae;
A'kla'nta mana, vishra'nta tana, hae mukta ma'nava manom'
                mem',
Cha'yii dhara' 'Madhu' sha'nti mem',
Dha'ya' gagana a'nanda mem'.

144 R. Madhu Chanda * 456A/29.07.09

Kala kala kare tuma baha calo, a'nanda kii Surasari bane;
Anubhu'tiyom' ko ura liye, prajina' ko sam'yojita kiye.

145. Tuma na a'ye * 260/29.03.09

Tuma na a'ye, tuma na dha'ye,
Darda kitana' ho dila mem' jaga'ye;
T'iisa kitanii ho ura mem' uga'ye,
Piira kitanii ho mana mem' jaga'ye.

Bilabila'ta' raha' kru'ra jaga mem',
Khila'khilate rahe loga jaga mem';
Khisakhisa'ta' raha' maim' yatana mem',
Piira a'yii na pra'n'ii ke mana mem'.

Loga karate rahe apane mana kii,
Surati lii nam' mere man badan kii;
Khoja kii na'm' kisii ne madhu kii,
Priiti pa'yii na priyatama ke ura kii.

A'bhii ja'o a'bhii ja'o,
Jiiva ko tuma na itana' sata'o;
Mere mana mem' tara'na' suna'o,
Priiti apanii jagata mem' dikha'o.

Deh da'sii bana' priiti karalo,
Ma'navom' ko bhii mukti sikha'lo;
Mukta pra'n'om' ko 'Madhu' sam'ga naca'lo,
Jiiva ja'grta kara' bhakti d'ha'lo.

T'iisa kitanii ho ura mem' uga'ye,
Piira kitanii ho mana mem' jaga'ye.

146. Svapna mem' shveta hansa * 188/14.11.08

Svapna mem' shveta hansa dekha' hae,
Brahma vela' mem' ur'ate use dekha' hae;
Madhur sii jyoti, dyoti mem' ma'kha',
Manda madhu ca'la mem' bar'hate hae dekha'.

Shveta adbhuta chat'a' mem' vaha ur'ata',
Calata' ur'ata' rukata' mohita karata';
Pa'sa mem' bhu'ra' paks'ii phira a'ya',
Milake usase vo madhur sihara'ya'.

Calate ur'ate phudakate phira a'ya',
Nikat'a ke paks'iyom' se mila dha'ya';
Bha'va vihvala ho phot'o khiim'ca' hu'n,
Gad gad hu'n, thirakita pulakit hu'n.

Prabhu kya' hansa tuma bane a'ye;
'Madhu' se milane dhara' pai tum dha'ye!
Mila ke jiivom' se tuma yom' muska'ye;
Baha' a'nanda tumhiim' ur'a dha'ye!
***

146 R. Madhu Chand * 476E/07.08.09

Saba jiiva tumare yantra haem',
Saba pra'n'a tumare mantra haem';
Saba a'tma'em' tantra haem',
'Madhu' marma mem' Tuma basa rahe.
Kya' kara rahe, kya' raca rahe,
Kya' kya' gazaba sa' d'ha' rahe.

Chapter 5. Kavi Anubhu'ti

147. Merii kavita'
* Madhu Giiti No. 15/ Composed on 27.03.08

Merii kavita' tuma kisakii srs't'ti ho;
Kisa srs't'i mem' bikhara ja'ogi tuma !

Kya' tuma ka'gaza ke ura baet'hii;
Kalama kii ka'lima' ka' rasa ho!
Ya' tuma kamalinii ho kuya'sha' kii;
Athava' vaebhava ho bikharate Brahman'd'a ka' !

Kya' tuma ho ka'gaza mem' supta;
Bha'vom' mem' vyakta, atma' mem' trapta !
Mana mem' bya'pta, tana mem' lipta;
Hradaya mem' vicharita, pra'n'a mem' prerita !

Kya' tuma pustaka kii srs't'i mem',
Srs't'i ke srjana, laya va pralaya mem';
Rahana' ca'hogii, raha sakogii cir jiivita !

Ya' phira basana' ca'hogii, merii srs't'i kii,
A'tma' mem', citta mem', shu'nya mem'!
Hara pra'n'a ke spandana mem',
Hara prthvii kan'a kii karun'a katha' mem'!

Kya' tuma milogii hara jala dha'ra' se,
Hara pa'vaka cim'ga'rii se, hara pavana kii lahara se;
Aka'sha kii shu'nyata' mem' base;
Hara ra'ga, hara laya, hara kavita se !

148. Kavita' kii komala ka'ya' * 224/20.01.09

Kavita' kii komala ka'ya' ko, kavi tuma kalus'ita mata kara dena';
Bha'vom' kii ja'ya' kavita' ko, 'Madhu' a'nandita sii chavi dena'.

Garima' mem' lipat'a' kara rakhana',
Bhakti se bha'vita bhava karana';
Chandita alhva'dita kara dena',
Ta'raka dha'raka svara raca dena'.

Prthvii kii gati sugandha dena', ta'rom' kii jyoti bhara dena';
Su'ryodaya ka' saorabha dena', candrodaya ka' rasa bhara dena'.

Yama niyamom' mem' bam'dha kara rahana',
Yoga'sana dhya'na kiye ja'na';
Pra'n'a'ya'mom' mem' rata rahana',
Arpita a'tma' Prabhu ko dena'.

Prabhu ka' rasa jaga ko de dena', a'nanda shreya Prabhu ko dena';
Kavita' kii madhu a'huti dena', a'nanda tarunga liye ja'na'.

149. Merii rca' * 22/02.04.08

Merii rca' tuma kaba rtambhara' hogii!
Shveta sahasra'ra para khila tuma, kaba caetanya hogii!

Kisa disha' mem' bahogii tuma, kisa dasha' mem' rahogii tuma!
Kisa ra'ga mem' ragogii tuma, kisa   chanda mem' na'cogii tuma!

Kisa laya mem' ga'ogii tuma,
Kisa dhvani para thirakogii tuma!
Kisa a'sha' para a'shrit ho,
Gopa'la hogii tuma!

Sha'shvata tuma, abhinav tuma;
Cira nava tuma, cira dhvani tuma.
Tum mam svara, tuma 'Madhu' mana;
Veda rca', soham' dhvani tuma.

150. Merii kavite * 16/27.03.08

Merii kavite tuma kisakii vrs't'i ho,
Kisa srs't'i mem' bikharana' ca'hogii tuma!

Kya' tuma khojogii , hara usa kavita' ko,
jo abhii soii hae, hara ma'nava mana mem'!

Kya' tuma saba manom' ke marma ko,
Kavita' bana' kara baha'na' ca'hogii!

Kya' tuma hara byatha' ko baha'va dogii,
Kya' tuma a'nanda ko aura a'nandit karogii!

Merii hara hava', mera' hara pra'n'a piir'ita hae;
Kucha a'nandit haem' ajina'na mem',
Kucha ana-a'nandit haem' jina'na mem'.

Tuma kucha aese sihara'o unake sarom' ko,
Pus'pa'ccha'dita karo unake caran'om' ko;
Sahala'o unake hrdyom' ko.

Ki unaka' man nikhar ja'ye, a'm'su' bikhar ja'yem';
Hrdaya hila ja'yem', sa'm'sa cala ja'ye.
Ga'na baha ja'ye, a'nanda a' ja'ye.

Tuma apana' darde dila mata kahana', sirfa sunana',
Sahana' siikhana', siim'cana' sikha'na',
Rona' samajhana', hansana' sikha'na',
Hansate ja'na', hansa'te ja'na', a'nandita karana'.

Tum purus'ka'ra mata khojana';
Pratis't'ha' kii mata socana', kiimata kii mata, mata bana'na'.

Tuma sirfa calana', 'Madhu' hrdaya se hrdayom' taka;
Dukha sukha kii laya se a'nanda kii laya taka.
Jiiva se Brahma taka, Brahma se jiiva taka.

151. Kavita' kii mrdu tarunga * 43/23.04.08

Kavita' kii yaha mradu tarunga,
'Madhu' tumha're ura mem' kaise ut'hii!

Kyom' tumha'ra' hrda, hima nada bana baha ut'ha'!
Ga'gara sara para liye, tum kaese sarasa ho ut'he!
Kyom' tumha're bha'va varase, kaese tuma ga' ut'he.

Kya' kisii ne tumamem' cinga'rii d'a'lii!
Ya' kisii cinga'rii ne tumhem' jala'ya'?

Kya' kisii cinga'rii ko dekha, tuma prajjvalit hue!
Ya' a'nanda kii anubhu'ti se tarungita hue!

Kya' tuma gata jagata kii gati ja'ne!
Ya' tuma, jagata janaka kii jugati ja'ne!

Kya' jagata kii jugati ka' giita ja'ne!
Ya' jagata ka' cetana' srota ja'ne!

Kya' tuma likhane lage, kisake liye, likhane lage!
Kya' gunaguna'ne lage, kisakii laya mila'ne lage!

Kyom' sura sa'dhane lage, kya' ra'ga ga'ne lage!
Kisako suna'ne lage, kisakii sunane lage!

Tumha'rii kavita', a'nanda tarunga ho ut'hii;
Bha'va sarita' mem', jala tarunga baja ut'hii.

Apanii mana viin'a' para vaha kuch ga' ut'ha',
Tumha'rii hrdaya viin'a', usase sura mila' ga' ut'hii!

152. 'Madhu' tumha'rii kavita' * 44/24.04.08

'Madhu' tumha'rii kavita', Prabhu ko a'nanda detii hae.
Unakii a'nanda tarunga, tumhem' aora a'nanda detii hae.
Tum kavita' likhate ja'te ho; jiivana ko jiivana dete ho.

Tumha'ra' ra'ga laya sura naya' hae,
Caetanya kii cinga'rii tumha'rii kavita' kii ka'ya' hae.
Vaha laya hae jiivana kii , sura hae Shambhu ka';
Chanda hae jagata ka', ra'ga hae ana'di ke na'da ka'.

Tuma sabhii ke a'nanda kii pratiiks'a' mata karo,
Tuma kevala likho aura svacchhanda ga'o;
Jagata kii gati ko vaha gati degii,
Kucha jiivom' ko a'nandit karegii.

Tumha'rii kavita' kii cinga'rii, kisii ko prajjvalit karegii;
Usaka' mana praka'shita hoga', roshanii tuma para par'egii.
Vaha bhii kisii ko roshan karega', jagata roshana ho ja'yega',
Tuma kavita' kii a'huti doge, Prabhu prasanna ho ja'yem'ge!

Tuma kevala cinga'rii jala'o, jaga'o, jana'o, ga'o;
Cetana' phaela'o, jagat jaba kabhii jagamag ho hii ja'yega'.
Atma' jhalamala hom'gii, tuma tarungita hoge;
Saba a'nandita hom'ge.
Aura, tumhem' cinga'rii dene va'le Guru bhii,
Anandita ho ja'yem'ge!

Chapter 6. Pra'krtika

153. Tumha'ra' su'ryodaya ke sa'tha a'na'* 48/05.05.08

Tumha'ra' prati din su'ryodaya ke sa'tha a'na';
Nava pra'n'a, nava ulla'sa ko sa'tha la'na'.
Sabako a'nanda se bhara ja'na';
Tumha'rii krapa' ka' hai khaja'na'.

Bra'hmii vela' mem', paks'iyom' kii kunjana;
Paks'ii pariva'ra kii, milit sa'dhana' kii gunjan.
Vishva ko arpit, "Madhu Giiti" ka' vyanjan;
Su'ryodaya ko hai, a'nanda abhinandan !

Pra'tah va'yu ka' shiital mam'd sugandh prava'ha;
Pa'rshva a'ngan mem' shveta pus'pom' ka' viharan'a.
Hanbar nadii ka' kalarava prava'ha;
Hiran'om' ka' unmukta vicaran'a.

Arpita graha shva'na ka' pra'tah pran'a'ma,
Sneha bhare spars'a ke liye avalokana;
Billii ka' pya'ra se spars'a karate hue, naye jala ka' nivedana.
Sna'na kaks'a mem' besudh soe ciim't'e ka', ana'ya'sa ut'ha ja'na';
Pa'rshva a'ngana mem' cir'iyom' gilahariyom' ka'
Da'ne ka' a'hva'na.

Mana ka' pa'ncajanya, pra'tah karmom' mem' pravrata hona';
Pra'n'a'ya'ma, sa'dhana', yoga'sana,
Sva'dhya'ya mem' sam'yat hona'.
Mana ka' ana'ya'sa nirmal ho ja'na', '
'Madhu' giiti ka' svayameva tarungita ho ja'na'.

154. Shveta hima kan'om' kii
* 240/18.02.09

Shveta hima kan'om' kii brus't'i le, tuma a'ye 'Madhu' prema liye;
Tribhuvana mem' tuma vya'pta ho rahe,
Phulajhar'iyom' ke ha'ra liye.

Shya'mala sa'runga ke madhu ura mem',
Ma'dhava mana kii bha's'a' mem';
Ga'te ja'te ho 'Madhu giiti' pa'vana sii Prabhu-sha'la' mem'.

Vishva tumha'ra' prema sarovara, maem' tumara' premii Prabhuvara;
A'ta' ja'ta' maim' tava antara, priyatama tuma rahate mama ura.

Ma'nava mana pad'hata' hae tumako, tava prakrti kii bha's'a' mem';
Sardii garmii hima vars'a' mem', mohana mrudu abhila's'a' mem'.

Tumako pad'hate aura samajhate ma'nava mana haim' muska'te;
Nija srus't'i mem' tuma khoja'te, hima brus't'i bana tuma dha'te.

155. He Prthvii! Prabhu ke nirdeshana mem'
* 81/02.06.08

He Prthvii! Prabhu ke nirdeshana mem' tumha'ra',
Hama sabhii ko lekara, Su'rya kii parikrama' karana';
Itana' roma'ncaka, itana' vyasta hona',
Adbhuta hae kitana', a'nanda maya hae kitana'!

Tuma hamem' goda mem' le,
Ghu'matii ja'tii ho, apanii kaks'a' mem'diva' ra'tri;
Dina ra'ta ke phera mem' par'e hama,
Nahiim' dekha pa'te, tumha'rii gati.

Sa'tha hii tuma Su'rya ke ca'ro ora,
Kabhii idhara, kabhii udhara, visha'la vyoma mem' vicaratii ho;
Kabhii tuma A'ka'sh Gunga' ke 'Madhu' ta'rom' ko
Nikat'a se dekha letii ho.

Kabhii saora mam'd'ala ke graha ghu'mate ghu'mate
Tumha're nikat'a a'ja'te haem', kabhii Su'rya ke usa ora cale ja'te haem'.

156. He Prthvii! Tumha'rii goda mem' * 81A/02.06.08

He Prthvii! Hama tumha'rii goda mem',
Dina ra'ta khela karate haem';
Tumha'ra' darda, tumha'rii vyatha',
Phira bhii hama samajha nahiim' pa'te haem'.

Tumha're vishva mem' hama kitane
Ucita anucita karma karate haem',
Tumha're bha'va, tumha'rii vyatha' ka'
Vica'ra nahiim' karate haem';
Tumha'ra' hama're prati atishaya sneha,
Hamem' bina' kas't'a diye, dvigati mem' calate rahana',
Hamem' utsa'hita a'nandita kara deta' hae.

Ma'n! Tuma ra'ta dina, vars'a bhar satata, calatii rahatii ho!
Tuma kitanii   daya'lu, dhiira aora sahanashiila ho!
Yugom' yugom' se cala, tumane hamem'
Vikasita suyogya kiya' hae.
Pala pala pallavita kara hamem',
'Madhu' ma'nava bana' diya' hae.

157. He Prthviii! Tum su'ryonmukha ho * 82/02.06.08

He Prthvii! Tuma su'ryonmukha ho,
Aapane gola'rddha mem' praka'sha na a'ne de, ra'tri kara detii ho.
Apane 'Madhu' anka mem' srs't'i ko le,   ra'tri mem' sula' letii
ho.

Vaha bhii kucha isa taraha ki yaha kriya' satata cale,
Kucha soyem', kucha jagem', kucha suvaha sha'ma dekhem';
Srs't'i ka' ka'rya suca'ru cale,
Sabhii pra'n'ii ja'grata supta sam'tulita rahem'.

Kitanii niyamita sam'tulita hae tumha'rii gati,
Kitanii niyantrita hae tumha'rii angar'a'ii;
Satata pya'ra mem' sabako khiim'catii sam'bha'latii sa'dhatii,
Tumha'rii gurutva'kars'an'a shakti kii gahara'ii.

158. He Prthvii! Kitana' yojana' maya * 82A/02.06.08

He Prthvii! Kitana' yojana' maya hae,
Tumha'ra' apane dhruvom' para ghu'mana';
Dhruvom' ka' dhiire dhiire stha'na parivartana hona',
Maosama ka' parivartita hona'.

Kitanii anupama hae tumha'rii deha, niila jala,
Shveta hima, hare vana;
Vicarate jiiva, jantu, manuja, mana buddhi racita, upagraha,
Va'yuya'na va shu'nya ya'na.

Su'ryonmukha ho sabako praka'sh se bhara dena',
Ta're niha'rika'om' ko najarom' se ojhala kara dena';
Ra'tri ko phira ta'rom' ka' saptarungii ru'pa dikha' dena',
Pra'tah paks'iyom' ke kalarava ke sa'tha, saba ko ut'ha' dena'.

159. He Prthvii! Tuma apane shariira * 83/02.06.08

He Prthvii! Tuma apane shariira kii sataha para,
Sabako dha'ran'a kiye vicaratii ho!
Apane ura kii jva'la' tuma kisii ko dikha'tii nahiim' ho!

Tumha're shariira kii, niila man'i jaesii 'Madhu' jhalaka bhii,
Ma'nava tuma se du'ra, Candrama' para ja', dekha pa'ya' hae;
Tumha'rii gati kii gahanata', ananta calane kii la'lasa',
Mujhe tumase pya'ra kara' detii hae.

Tumha'rii anakhojii vanaspatiya'm', bahu a'ya'mii jiiva jantu,
Nirantara vika'shonmukha ma'nava,
Saba tumha're pya'ra mem' nrutyarata haem'.

Tumha'rii srs't'i kii asa'manajasyata',
Samaya rahate sa'mya ho ja'tii hae;
Kitanii vikara'la paristhitiya'm' a'tii haem',
Samaya calate saba badala ja'tii haem'.

He Prthvii ma'n! Tuma calatii rahatii ho, cala'tii rahatii ho,
Onka'ra dhvani mem' na'catii rahatii ho!
'Madhu' srs't'i ko cala'tii rahatii ho, Srs't'a' ko rijha'tii calatii ho.

160. Bha'rata kii bha'va bhu'mi * 24/02.04.08

Bha'rata kii bha'va bhu'mi, vishva kii vishvasaniiyata'.
Bha'rata ka' bhu'ma' bha'va, srs't'i kii bhavatavyata'.

Ra'ma ka' a'darsha jiivana, Shiva ka' yoga tantra,
Ta'n'd'ava a'yurveda viva'ha pracalana;
Krs'n'a kii solaha kala'om' ka' a'kars'an'a,
Arjuna ka' bhakti pu'rn'a samarpan'a.

A'nandamu'rti kii navya ma'navata', Buddha ka' bodha,
Patanjali ka' yoga darshana;
Bharata ka' viiratva, Guru Na'naka ka' na'ma,
Kabiira ka' pantha, Jaini sa'tvika jiivana.

Miira' Su'ra Tulasii Caetanaya,
Viveka'nanda va Raviindra kii bhakti nis't'ha';
Shiva'jii ka' shaorya, Laks'mii Ba'ii ka' laks'a,
Ahilya' Ba'ii Holkara kii sa'tvikata'.

Ga'ndhii kii satya nis't'ha', Subha'sa Bhagata,
Pat'ela va Tilaka kii tya'ga nis't'ha';
Ra'jendra, Ra'dha'krs'n'ana Nehru' Nanda',
La'labaha'dura va At'ala kii ra's't'ra nis't'ha'.

Sabhii yogiyom' ka' yoga,
Jina'niyom' ka' jina'na yoga, bhaktom' ka' suyoga;
Sabhii dharmom' kii karma va marma bhu'mi,
Ma'nava dharma ka' suprayoga.

A'dhya'tmika vijina'na ka' srs't'a,
Bhu'ma' bha'va ka' 'Madhu' drs't'a';
Shu'nya se ananta ka' shodha kartta',
Bhu'ma' bha'va ka' prayoga kartta'.

161. Mere mana ke megha * 144/20.08.08

Mere mana ke 'Madhu' megha!
Tuma kabhii pu're hrdya'ka'sha mem' cha'ye nazara a'te ho;
Kabhii niirava cida'ka'sha mem' tuma,
Kahiim' bhii nazara nahiim' a'te.
Kabhii saba tumhem' dekhate haem',
Kabhii tuma sabako dekhate ho;
Kabhii ka'le bhu're ho garajate barasate ho,
Shveta sha'nta ho kabhii siharate ho.

Dhya'na ya'na mem' pait'ha jaba kabhii tumase milane a'ta' hu'n,
At'hakhelii sii tuma karate ho, sunga u'para niice calate ho;
Kabhii nikat'a a'ja'te ho, para du'ra kabhii cala dete ho,
Nabha mem' maem' jaba khojata' hu'n,
Tuma mujha mem' hii raha ja'te ho.

162. Kaha'm' cala diye ho sa'runga tuma * 258/12.03.09

Kaha'm' cala diye ho sa'runga tuma, mere ura ka' ra'ga liye?
Niila gagana mem' vicara rahe ho, satarungii saondarya liye.

Sabake sara par ur'ate rahate, shya'mala sumadhura ru'pa liye;
Apanii dhuna mem' calate rahate, pulakita thirakita bha'va liye.

Pra'tah vela' mem' ut'ha dha'te,
Kya' kya' dina bhara tuma kara ja'te;
Cir'iyom' ke jaise ur'a ja'te, mohana madhumaya giita suna'te.

Lekara tuma rungiilii t'olii, nabha ura mem' khelata nita Holii;
Kya' kya' abhinava runga laga'te, Pruthvii jana ko tuma sihara'te.

Dyuti camaka'te lahara dikha'te,
Pha'guna mem' Sa'vana bana dha'te;
Holii ke 'Madhu' giita suna'te, t'olii para t'olii bana dha'te.

163. Kana'd'a' ka' kan'a kan'a * 93/14.06.08

Kan'a'di kii kalpana' se bhara' hae, Kana'd'a' ka' kan'a kan'a;
Pra'krtika saondarya se paripu'rn'a hae,
Kana'd'a' ka' mana pra'n'a.

Mu'la vam'shajom' kii sahajata', agantukom' kii mana gahanata';
Prava'shiyom' kii pra'sangikata', vishva sama'ja kii madhurata'.

Ma'naviiya mu'lyom' kii prayogasha'la',
Adhyayana manana khula'pana;
Bhakti karma jina'na ka' prasa'ran'a,
Yoga tantra ka' tvarita pracalana.

Ma'navom' ka' paraspara madhura vyavaha'ra,
Pashu paks'iyom' ke prati sama'dara;
Le cala raha' hae sabhyata' ko antarmana,
Vikasita hae ma'nava mana, avacetana.

Vishva sabhyata'om' ka' hae yaha'm' 'Madhu' sam'gama,
Vishva sam'skrtiyom' ka' hae a'va'gamana;
Sva'rtha se parama'rtha kii ora haem' prerita,
Vishva ke pradiipa haem' hama prajjvalita.

164. Ba'r'ha ke ba'da nadii * 563/15.10.09

Bar'ha ke ba'da nadii laghu hotii, dha'ra kama hotii ba'lu' bahu hotii;
Paha'r'om' se nikala nadii cupa hotii,
Brhata dha'ra' mem' tvarita baha letii.

Ba'r'ha upara'nta sha'nta vaha hotii, ba'luka' mem' prasha'nti bhara detii;
Bahatii dha'ra'em' dhiira ho ja'tiim',
Du'riya'm' tat'om' se haem' saha letiim'.
Ba'r'ha ke vakta nadii bar'ha ja'tii,
Ga'nvom' per'om' kina'rom' ko d'hahatii;
Pa't'a caor'a' kiye hae cala detii, jo bhii milata' use baha' letii.

Pa'ra karane pathika pracura calate, ba'r'ha kii vibhiis'ka' lakha lete;
Na'va mem' baet'ha dha'ra tara lete, ba'luka' ka' ananta ura takate.
Vihungama dras'ya ba'r'ha ka' hota', tarungita drashya ba'da ka' karata';
'Madhu' ura dha'rem' bahuta baha ja'tiim',
Trasita trasaren'u kya' kya' kaha jaatii.

165. Ba'r'ha kii vibhiis'ika' kya' kahatii * 564/15.10.09

Ba'r'ha kii vibhiis'ika' kya' kahatii, kitane vraks'om' ke ura phura' detii;
Kina're kitanii vyatha' kaha dete, shikhara kitane dhara' pae d'haha ja'te.

Ga'nva kitane ujar'a bikhara ja'te, jiiva jiivana kaha'n cale ja'te;
Kaga'rem' kitaniim' nayii bana ja'tiim',
Dha'rem' kitaniim' nayii nikala dha'tiim'.
Kitane pa's'a'n'a ba'luka' banate,
Kitana' brks'om' kii sha'khem' haem' sahatiim';
Kitaniim' phasalom' kii fiza' gula hotiim',
Kitane pra'n'om' kii dundabhii bajatii.

Ka'ya' vistiirn'a kiye calatiim' tuma, sama'ye sabako svayam' apane ura;
Hila'tiim' d'ula'tiim' prakrti ka' ghara,
Mit'a'tiim' d'uba'tiim' tran'om' ka' ura.
Tumha're brhata mana mem' maem' khota',
Ba'luka' bana tumha're ura sota';
Mujhe tuma kya' kya' nahiim' kaha ja'tiim',
Mera' 'Madhu' mana liye na kyom' calatiim'.

166. Ba'dala ke ura se a' nikale * 588/04.11.09

Ba'dala ke ura se a' nikale, kitana' sundara ru'pa liye;
Kitane citra vicitra bana'ye, Ravi tumane a'ne se pahale.

Ba'dala ke bahu ru'pa dikha'ye, kitane sa'gara nabha bikhara'ye;
Kitanii jyoti kii dha'ra'em', agan'ita ru'pa liye dha'yii haem.
Kabhii cale a'ye tuma chipake, kabhii teja apana' dikha'la'ye;
Kabhii ba'dalom' ke ghu'nghat'a se, tuma a'ye jaese sharama'ye.

Kiran'om' ne praka'sha phaela' ke, dekha' saba jaga ko mu'aka'ke;
Ankhem' sabakii dii caom'dha'ke, phira khuda chipe ghat'a' mem' ja'ke.
Tumane jaga' diye saba a'ke, soye the jo mana ko d'ha'ke;
'Madhu' jyoti jaga ko dikhala'ke, ja'grta saba ke ura kara d'a'le.

167. Hanbara tat'a para * 62/14.05.08

Hanbara tat'a para, jha'r'iyom' ka' jhuramut'a,
Gilahariyom' ke per'om' para,
Car'hane utarane kii chat'apat'a'hat'a;
Cahakatii cir'iyom' ke ur'ane kii phuraphura'hat'a,
Saje vraks'hom' para shveta pus'pom' kii khilakhila'hat'a.

Sha'nta shveta batakhom' ka', jala vicaran'a karana',
Vana jiivom' ka' culabula'hat'a mem', jala piina';
Shva'na ka' bhraman'a karate hue,
Jala dha'ra' mem' ku'da par'ana',
Paks'iyom' ka' per'a se ku'da, jala mem' d'ubakii laga'na'.

Hanbar tumane kitanii piir'hiyom' ko ra'ha dikha'yii hae,
Kitane vya'pa'rom' kii niim'va laga'ii hae;
Kitane suha'vane phu'la saja', T'oront'o nagarii basa'yii hae,
Kitanii dha'ra'em' baha'iim' haem',
Aura Aom'nt'a'rio jhiila mem' mila'iim' haem'.

Hara samaya ya'da a'tii hae mujhe,
Tumha're calate rahane kii chat'apat'a'hat';
Mere mana ko varavash nikat'a bula'ne kii tumha'rii a'hat'a.

Hanbara = Aumt'a'rio (Kana'd'a') mem' bahatii ek nadii.

168. Hanbara tumha're kitane ru'pa * 63/14.05.08

Hanbara maem'ne tumha're kitane ru'pa dekhe haem'!
Jala ke kitane jva'r gha't'e dekhe haim'!

Kabhii tuma kina'ra' chala'm'ga, baha ja'na' ca'hatii ho,
Kabhii apanii pem'dii ke, pattharom' mem' simat'a ja'tii ho;
Kabhii tuma svayam', barpha bana ja'tii ho,
Kabhii barpha ke niiche, cupacha'pa baha letii ho.

Kitanii ba'ra griis'ma mem' tumha're sa'tha, cala kara dekha' hu'm',
Kitanii ba'ra shiita mem' bichur'a kara,
Tumhem' t'hit'hurate dekha' hu'm';
Kitanii ba'ra, miit'he seva aura shahatu'ta tumane khila'ye haem',
kitanii ba'ra, apane sahamate hiran'om' se tumane mila'ya' hae.

Kitanii ba'ra, tumha'rii jhar'iyom' kii,
Sha'nta gupha'om' mem' cala' hu'm';
Kitanii ba'ra, tumha're bikharate
Pattharom' para baet'ha tumhem' dekha' hu'm'.
Kitanii ba'ra, tumha're tat'a ke braks'om' se ba'ta kiya' hu'm';
Kitanii ba'r, tumha'rii kalarava dhvani mem' baet'ha,
Srs't'a' ka' 'Madhu' dhya'na kiya' hae'.

169. Shishira ke a'ne kii a'hat'a mem' * 65/14.05.08

Shishira ke a'ne kii a'hat'a mem',
Per'om' kii pattiya'm' ram'ga badalatii haem';
Unaka' na'ram'gii gula'vii niibua' ram'ga,
Unakii mana vyatha' ko vyakta karata' hae.
Para ma'nava mana, unake badale ram'gom' ko,
Unaka' ru'pa samajh a'nanda leta' hae.

Pattiya'm' shishira ke a'ne kii vyatha' mem',
Ananta ram'gom' mem' bikhara ja'tii haem';
Per'om' se utara, dhara' para vicaratii haem',
Va'yu ke vega se ur'a, saba jagaha daur'atii haem'.

Sam'bhavatah, vraks'a ke u'para rahane ke, Sam'ska'ra ko ks'ay karane;
Dhara' ke hara kone dha', dhara' kii 'Madhu' dhu'la se milatii haem'.
Jana sujana ke caran'om' mem' ja', sa's't'a'nga pran'a'ma karatii haem'.

170. Niya'gra' kii niila jhiila ka' * 94/16.06.08

Niya'gra' kii niila jhiila ka' jala prapa'ta,
Thirakita hae pulakita hae, madhurima' se hae ota prota;
Jala dha'ra' ka' yaka'yaka adhopa'ta;
Indra dhanus'a raca deta' hae, a'ka'sha mem' nis'n'a'ta.

Aca'naka girii jala dha'ra' kii kucha bu'ndom' ka' u'rdhva gamana,
Aka'sha mem' ja'na', cha'na' aura vars'an'a;
Kara deta' roma'm'cita thirakita ma'nava mana,
Jala tarunga se tarungita ho ja'ta', jana jana.

Jala dha'ra' ke anaca'he utarane ka' vyatireka,
Le ja'ta' jala mana ko, a'ka'sha mem' ashoka;
Jana mana ko bhii kara deta' bha'vuka,
Bhim'go deta' 'Madhu' pra'n'a , bhara deta' kuhaka.

171. Niya'gra' ke jala kan'om' ka' astitva *
97/14.05.08

Niya'gra' ke   jala prapa'ta se,
Kitane jala kan'om' ka' astitva ut'ha'!
Kitanii va'yu jala maya huii,
Kitanii su'rya kiran'em' shiitala huii!

Kitane a'ka'sha dhvanita huye,
Kitane pashu paks'ii caha caha'ye!
Kitane ma'nava mana tarungita huye,
Kitane supta hrdaya ja'grta huye!

Kitane jala kan'a dha'ra' mem' mila baha ut'he,
Kitane su'rya kiran'om' se mila, indra dhanus'a bana ut'he!
Kitane jala kan'a va'yu se mila baha ut'he,
Jana jana kii sa'm'som' mem' rama ut'he!

Kitane jala kan'a a'ka'sha mem' dha'ye,
Vana, upavana, ra'hom' se gale milane a'ye!
Kitane hrdayom' ko prema mem' ba'm'dha',
Kitane dampatiyom' ko prema mem' sa'dha'!

172. Niya'gra' jala prapa'ta se pu'rva * 96/14.05.08

Niya'gra' jala prapa'ta se pu'rva,
Ont'a'rio jhiila ka' niila jala;
'Madhu' gahara'ii mem' hae mrdula svapnila.

Par phir pattharom' para cala,
Vaha ho ut'hata' hae capala;
Jhu'ma ut'hata' hae use dekha shveta siigala.

Pattharom' para tvarita gati se cala,
Gati se a'nandita niirava jala;
Mana mem' pulakita alokita jala,
Niyati kii soce ho ut'hata' hae aura niila.

Thirakate macalate niila jala ka',
Ana'ya'sa apane dhara'tala ko khodena',
Dhiira jala ka' vihvala ho ja'na', usake jiivana ka' hila ja'na';
Srs't'i ka' isa da'run'a ghat'ana' ko niha'rana',
Niha'rika' ka' niirava ho ja'na'.

Anaja'nii gahara'ii mem' ku'dana' ja'ta' hae use par'a,
Roma'ncita ho ja'ta' hae, usaka' mana pra'n'a;
Yaha hrdaya dra'vaka ghat'ana',
Usake astitva ke liye, cunautii ja'tii hae bana.

Isa prapa'ta ke sa'mu'hika sam'ghars'a vasha,
Jala ke kitane kan'a vidyuta bana'ye;
Kitane an'u va'yu ke sa'tha baha gaye,
Kitane aka'sha mem' ut'ha
'Madhu' indra dhanus'a bana'ye.

173. Niya'gra' kii niirava bu'ndem' * 98/14.05.08

Niya'gra' jala prapa'ta kii niirava bu'n'dem',
Ana'ya'sa avaroha kii a'sham'ka' mem' haem' a'nkhem'
mu'nde;
Dhiimii huii gati se gam'bhiira huiim' bu'ndem',
T'at'olatii haem' bandha kii gahara'ii nayana mu'nde.

Kucha bu'ndem' karatii haem' praya'sa dhara'tala se jut'ane ka',
Ba'ndha ke isii ora rahane ka', usakii garima' samajhane ka';
A'ge kii u'para kii bu'ndom' ko, usa ora ja'te dekha,
Vismita haem' , bhayamaya haem', aura kucha haem', ashoka.

Piiche bahate jala ke saa'vega se piir'ita,
Niice kii dha'ra'om' se prakampita;
Bandha ke u'para bahane ko prata'r'ita,
Jala bu'ndem' haem' vyatha' se a'lor'ita.

Ana'ya'sa a'ye a'vega kii jala dha'ra',
Le calatii hae unhem' usa ora, karake a'tmaha'ra';
Vismita jala bu'ndom' ka' 'Madhu' saka'sha,
Vismrta kara deta' hae, ma'nava ka' cida'ka'sha.

174. Niya'gra' ka' jala ta'n'd'ava * 99/14.05.08

Niya'gra' kii jala dha'ra' ka' itanii gahara'ii mem' aca'naka girana',
Sa'tha kii bundom' ka' tar'apar'a'na';
Kucha bu'ndom' ka' paraspara sam'gha'ta se u'para ut'ha ja'na',
Kucha ka' niice dha'ra' bana baha ja'na'.

Isa gahana sa'mu'hika jala ta'n'd'ava mem',
Bu'ndom' ke isa asa'mayika sama'varoha mem';
Kucha bu'ndom' ke hue sam'ha'ra mem',kucha ke a'roha mem',
Va'yu hoja'tii hae a'drita, a'ka'sha ho ja'ta' hae dravita.

Jala tarangom' se ho a'lor'ita,
Mana tarangom' ko kara lete haem' jhankrta;
Niya'gra' jala prapa'ta ke 'Madhu' drs't'a';
Jha'nkate haem' isamem' Srs't'a'.

175. Niya'gra' jala prapa'ta se thirakita * 95/16.06.08

Niya'gra' jala prapa'ta se thirakita,
Kucha pra'n'a, ur'a dha'te a'ka'sha,
Su'rya rashmiyom' mem' rama, bana ja'te indra dhanus'a.
Paks'ii kalarava kara, chu' lete 'Madhu' a'ka'sh,
Niila vastra dha'rii ma'nava, niiche nauka' mem' karate nirya'sa.

Panca tatva ke ubharate paha'r'a, macalata' jala,
Ur'atii pavana, umar'ata' gagana,
Kara deta' ma'nava mana ko magana;
Bra'hmii citta se vya'pta panca tattva, ho ja'ta' pulakita,
Cakita ma'nava , pashu paks'ii pus'pa,
Pramudita ho, ho ja'te thirakita.

176. Jala prapa'ta ko niha'rate * 100/14.05.08

Niya'gra' jala prapa'ta ko niha'rate nara na'rii;
Bu'ndom' ke barasane ke rasa se, a'lhva'dita haem' manoha'rii.

Sa'mane ba'ndha ke u'para baha rahii,
Vihvala jala dha'ra' ka' satata prapa'ta;
U'para a'ka'sha mem' bana' indra dhanus'a,
Mana ko kara deta' bha'vom' se a'pluta.

Jala bu'ndom' ka' prapa'ta sam'gha'ta se u'para ut'ha,
Cahun ora du'ra du'ra vikhara ja'na';
Ma'nava tana mana ko sara'bora kara dena',
Prema rasa mem' bhim'go unhem' para vash kara dena'.

Parijanom' ka' mila kara   jala prapa'ta dekhana',
Manda manda utaratii u'rdhvareta' phuha'rom' mem' bhiim'gana';
Mrdu mana ka' pulakiat praphullita hona',
Bu'ndom' ka' hae ma'no   Brahma se mila a'nandita hona'.

Niice nauka' mem' niila vastrom' mem' viharatii
Nara na'riyom' kii t'olii;
U'para se girate 'Madhu' jala ko dekha,
A'tma ha'ra' hue jana, mana d'oli.

177. Shya'mala sa'runga * 142/20.08.08

Shya'mala sa'runga niila'mbara mem',
Gar'hata' bunata' chavi prati pala mem';
Kitanii kriir'a'a sa'runga svara mem'!
Niiravata' kitanii nabha ura mem'!

Kitane dviipom' ko tuma gar'hate, kitane sa'gara ura mem' rakhate?
Kitane mana kii bha's'a' par'hate, sa'jom' mem' kitane tum sajate?

Parvata pashu paks'ii tuma banate,
Nabha na't'aka mem' na'yaka rahate;
Bahu a'ya'mom' mem' rama lete, jham'krta spandita ho ja'te.

Vicalita bikhare tuma jaba rahate, virahita besudha bemana hote;
Va'yu ke jhonke a'ja'te, vihansita thirakita tuma cala dete.

Parilaks'ita drs't'a' ko karake, mana srs't'a' mem' arpita karake;
A'o Prathvii ke pra'ngan'a mem',
' Madhu ' pra'n'om' ke hrdayaungana mem'.

178. Meghom' ka' saondarya suha'ya' * 143/20.08.08

Mana mohaka meghom' ka' saondarya suha'ya';
Shobha' 'Madhu' bha'yii, shilpa suha'ya'.

Mukti jo bhii jala kan'a pa' pa'ye, va'yu ba'dala jo bana pa'yii;
Pa'vaka pa'vana jo kara pa'yii, dharatii dekhe mana sihara'yii.
Jiivana jva'la' de varama'la', kara detii vismrata nabha ba'la';
Le ja'tii tumako madhu va'la', cala dete tuma pii madhu pya'la'.

Snehii jana ko tuma dekhe, sahame sihare mana tuma dekhe;
Virahii mana ko tum ho ta'ke, utsuka ho svajanom' ko jha'nke.

Mana tumhara' jaba bhii bhara ja'ye,
Nabha se priiti jaba nibha ja'ye;
Bhu' ma'n se milane ghara a'na',
Bhu'ma' se vrs't'i bana dha'na'.

Chaper 7 : Vividhi Bha's'a' Sa'hitya

179. Tvam mama a'nanda srota
* 189/17.11.08 (Sam'skrta/Hindii)

Tvama mama a'nanda srota, tvama mama a'shraya pota;
Tvama mama jiivanasya dyota, tvama mama pra'n'era pran'eta.

Tvama asma'kam pra'n'a srota, tvama vishvasya cetana jyota;
Tvama ura mama, tvama svara mama; tvamasi samvala kevala mama.

Tvama dha'ra', tvam mama a'dha'ra',
Tvama patha mama, tvam mama tvara dha'ra';
Tvama vidya', tvam jina'na prabha' mama,
Tvama svara, viin'a', bha'va svayam tvam.

Tvama ura mama jiivana sura dha'vita,
Tvama mana manhi tanmaya bhava ga'vata.
Jiivana jva'ra udadhi tava a'vata,
'Madhu' mana udadhi bahata taba dha'vata.

180. Svara mama tvam * 190/17.11.08 (Sam'skrta/Hindii)

Svara mama tvama, viin'a' va'dani mama,
A'nanda madhura, a'loka svayam;
Thirakita pulakita mana a'nandam, jiivana jyoti tvam asma'kam.

Mama jivana dha'ra' svara ha'ra',
Tava mana manhi mama mana sura ha'ra'.
Jiivana sampa'dana sumadhura svara,
Sa'nidhya pran'eta' pran'a sumadhura.

Svara sam'gamasya tvam triven'ii,
Jiivana svara manhi tvam sura ven'ii.
Prati pa'laka tvam, sura dha'raka tvam;
Jiivana sarita' sam'ca'laka tvam.

Dha'ra'ye dhara' bahati pramudita,
Tava dhya'na srota sarve thirakita.
'Madhu' jiivanasya gati utpreraka, a'nandita abhinava tvam ta'raka.

181. Tvamasi mama sarva shreya
* 194/26.11.08 (Sam'skrta/Hindii)

Tvamasi mama sarva shreya, tvamekam mama dhya'na dhyeya;
Pran'amyam tvam sarva jineya, arpita mama sakala preya.

Svapane tvayi saghana sukha mama, shayane tvam a'shraya mama;
Jiivane tvam rasaghana mama, nihshva'se tvam a'shva'sana mama.
Sampade mama vivekii mana, vipade tvam dhiiraja mama;
Sha'sane anusha'sana tvam, vira'jita hrdaya'sana mama.

Ra'jita tvam nikhila bhuvane, mama mana kunje, hrdaya nikunje;
Panca tatve citta prava'he, mahata aham prasphut'a gun'a dha'me.
Abhinava adbhuta tvayi soham, anante tvayi a'di anta mama;
Tvamasi ' Madhu' antarmana,
Sumadhura sarvaga atma' tvama mama.

182. Shya'ma na'him' bana a'ye
* 329/30.05.09 (Braja Bha's'a')

Sakhii rii Shya'ma na'him' bana a'ye!
Lata' pata' kumila'ya rahe haem', ca'taka mana akula'ye;
Gopinha ke mana bikhara rahe haem', Haladhara mana sakuca'ye.

Jamuna' jala kala kala kari dha'vata,
Vikala Ra'dhika' ura akula'vata;
Ba'laka dhenu niha'rata ja'bata, Shya'ma sakha' sakuca'ye.

Sohana subhaga Shya'ma ura ma'la',
Dekhana cahata sakala Braja va'la';
Sundara sughar'a suha'bati d'a'la',
Latanha biica viharat Braja va'la'.

Tana tarasa'ye, mana haras'a'ye, kaba ve a'ye, ja'na na pa'ye;
Muralii kii mohana sii dhuni pae, ra'ga 'Madhu' mana ga'ye.
Sakhii rii Shya'ma a'ja bana a'ye.

183. Sakhii rii, haom' rahabati iham' na'hiim'
* 40/17.04.08 (Braja Bha's'a')

Sakhii rii, haom' rahabati iham' na'hiim';
Haom'   rahabati, aba Nanda Nandana sam'ga,
Dukha sukha, saba bisara'ii.

Tana iha'm' rahatu, mana na rahatu, mora a'tma' Braja te basati;
Bhojana karati, bhavana rahati, Jamuna'   jala bica, nha'vata phirata.
Braja ba'lanha sam'ga khela karata.

Bhora bhaye, Jamuna' tat'a dha'vata,
Gva'la ba'la sam'ga ven'u baja'vata;
Gokula tom' Branda'vana ja'vata, Govarddhana ja'i, dhenu cara'vata.

Madhuvana madhur, ma'dhurii bha'vati,
Krs'n'a   ca'hanii, lakhana cahati;
Mana mama phurata, tana jaga phirata,
Gokula phirati, barabasa rahati.

Saradii garamii, kachu nahim' la'gata,
Barakha' bica haom' nha'vata phirata;
Tuma a'bata , mora mana sihara'vata,
Nanda Nandana sam'ga, prem paga'vata.

Nahiim' a'bata vaha, jaba haom', tuma sam'ga khelata,
Tuma ja'bata vaha turatahi a'bata, more sam'ge neha laga'vata;
'Madhu' mana bhayahu, Krs'n'a anura'gii,
Ta're sam'ga priiti morii la'gii.

184. Muralii va'rao sakhi a'yao ae
* 281/09.04.09 (Braja bha's'a')

Muralii va'rao sakhi a'yao ae,
Mere angana mem' dha'yao ae;
Merii mat'akii ku'n dekhyao ae,
Mere ghat'a mem' vo ta'kyao ae.

Merii mat'akii na'm' phor'yao ae,
Navaniit liye kahu'n dha'yao ae;
Jamuna' tat'a pae vo khelyao ae,
Saba ke mana mem' vo cha'yao ae.

Pagad'am'd'ii pae cali a'yao ae,
Mohana ca'hani te dekhyao ae;
Maem' bhu'li nahiim' pa'yii ba'ku'n,
Mana mem' mere vo bha'yao ae.

Man merao kachu sihara'vatu ae,
Merao apanom' sao la'gatu ae;
Madhu ma'khana merao kha'yao ae,
Ga'gara sara pae rakhaba'yao ae.

Maem' a'lhva'dita anura'gita hu'n,
Madhu a'nandita hvae thirakita hu'n;
Maem' t'hagii rahi gayii sii kachu hu'n,
A'nanda amiya madhu pa'yii hu'n.

Mana mana bindii spars'yao ae,
Sara pae 'Madhu' ha'tha phira'yao ae;
Mana hii mana godii mem' sara lae,
Kachu ra'ga nayao sao ga'yao ae.

Man Vranda'vana mem' na'cyao ae,
Vanshii va'rao sakhi a'yao ae.

185. Va'nshurii ve baja'yem' Gokula mem'
* 600/14.11.09 (Hindii/Braja Bha's'a')

Vanshurii ve baja'yem' Gokula mem',
Suna rahiim' Gopiya'n haem' hara mana mem';
Braja banom' mem' kunjatiim' koyaliya'm',
Madhu vanom' mem' thirakatiim' pem'janiya'm'.

Krs'n'a   kaba dhara' pae cale a'ye,
Ra'dhika' madhura mana liye dha'ye;
Sa'dhika' ka' svapna sa'ka'ra kiye,
Madhurata' vishva mem' liye prakat'e.

Pakheru' pra'n'a pana se bikhare haem',
Lata'em' lat'a pat'a' ke bikharii haem';
Ghat'a'yem' prema se umar'atiim' haem',
Chat'a'yem' sihara kara chit'akatiim' haem'.

Shya'ma kunjom' mem' ve rahe cha'ye,
Gopa mana mem' simat'a ke ve a'ye;
Ks'iin'a tana mem' ks'arita hue a'ye,
Jiirn'a a'tma' jvalita kiye dha'ye.

Mera' mana prema mem' paga' sa' hae,
Nikhila kucha t'haga' hua' sa' hae;
Jamuna jala uchalata' hae pala pala mem',
'Madhu' ura na'cata' hae nava sura mem'.

186. Hari merao jiivana dharama
* 263/31.03.09 (Braja Bha's'a')

Hari merao jiivana dharama sanva'rao,
Jiivana mem' hom' phiratu rahyao hu'm', pa'vatu na'nhi saha'rao;
Maem' tuma sam'ga calana ca'hatu aba, mero vesha sanva'rao.

Maem' seva' nahim' kachu kari   pa'vatu,
Caran'a pa'duka' nahim' gahi pa'vatu;
Man merao kachu socatu ja'batu,
Prabhu mana kii kachu samajhi na pa'batu.

Ga'tu ja'ta dhya'vatu mana mero,
Bhakti Yoga kachu samajhi na pa'vatu;
Ja'ti pa'nti kachu bichurata ja'bata,
Ma'nava dharamu samajhi kachu a'vatu.

Jiivana dha'ran'a karatu dharamu ae,
Ma'nava mana kao marama dharamu ae;
Ma'nava kii saba ja'ti eka ae, ma'nava kii saba pa'nti eka ae.

Jiivana kii jaga jyoti eka ae, jiivan kii saba riiti eka ae;
Ma'nava mana kii priiti eka ae, ma'nava kii 'Madhu' giiti eka ae.
Aba sabu a'i sanva'rao.

187. 'Madhu' mana vihaga * 429/17.07.09 (Braja Bha's'a')

'Madhu' mana vihaga Prabhu vyoma mahim',
Dha'vata ur'ata utarata car'hata;
Thaki ja'tu kaba, akula'tu kaba, hansi ja'tu kaba, sudhi karatu kaba.

Ja'nata na maem', ta'r'ata na maem',
Tarajata na maem', sulajhata na maem';
Sura pa'tu kaba, sukha a'tu kaba, ja'nata na pa'bata, pra'ta kaba.

Kabahu' cahaki, kabahu' dahaki,
Kabahu' lur'haki, kaba prasphurata;
Maem' soci na' pa'vatu bahuta, vidhi kii karani mem' rata rahata.

Na' trapta hu'n ya' jagata mem', na' supta hu'n j'agaran'a mem;
Na' lupta maem' hopa'raha', na' lipta ati ho pa'raha'.

La'van'ya merii deha mem', saba yantra merii deha mem';
Maem' tantra tera' bana ur'ata,
Maem' mantra bana tava jaga phirata.

188. Hiyam'hi hansati * 239/11.02.09 (Braja Bha's'a')

Hiyam'hi hansati manahim' risati, Jasumati mana sakucaka'ti;
Ka'nha' bana phirana ja'ta, Gopinha mana phurata ja'ta!

Nayana jha'nki karati ba'ta, tarjani som' baraji ja'ti;
Tan suha'ta, mana siha'ta, hiya siharata, paga thira'ta.

Pulaka ga'ta, ga'ta ja'ta, Mohana mana muskara'ta;
Manasukh kachu kahana cahata, Shya'ma' mana mahim' rijha'ta.

Ra'dha' ura Shya'ma rahatu, muralii dhuni sunani cahati;
Sanmukha lakhi jhijhaki ja'ti, latikanha bica lukati ja'ti.

Sakhanha sam'ga Krs'na calata,
Sakhinha mahim' Ra'dha' phirati;
Dhenu ven'u sunani cahati, kokil 'Madhu' rasa cakhati.

189. Prabhu kii krpa' * 41/17.04.08 (Braja Bha's'a')

Prabhu kii krpa', varasi jaba ja'vata,
Merao mana a'nandita hoya ja'vata;
Braja khila ja'vata, dhenu ga'vata, venu binu ba'jiye, baji ja'vata.

Gva'la ba'la varavasa ut'hi dha'vata,
Jamuna' jala shiitala hvae ja'vata;
Koyala apanii ta'n suna'vata, mora pankh sara pae dhari na'cata.

Nirmala ga'ta hota anusha'sit, merao hiya hars'ita hoya ja'vata;
Cakra mora nija ta'na suna'vata, mana na'cahi, a'tma' sihara'vata.

Mu'la'dha'ra sugandha phaela'vata,
Sva'dhist'ha'na ks'udha pya'sa mit'a'vata;
Man'ipura arun'a prabha' bikhara'vata, ana'hata a'ka'she liye
dha'vata.

Siddhi jina'na, vishuddh baha'vata, dharma karme a'jina' prerati;
Bhakti deta, krpa' Guru karata,
Samarpahahun 'Madhu' mana a'nandita.

190. E Sakhi a'ye * 434/17.07.09 (Braja Bha's'a')

E sakhi a'ye jag mana bha'vana, bha'va tara'vana bhakti jaga'vana;
Priiti laga'van, bhiiti bhaga'vana, yukti bata'vana, yoga sikha'vana.

Tuma sakhi na'co ga'o dhya'o, satsangati kii beli bar'ha'o;
Upava'som' mem' va'sa kara'o, Ka'nha' ke ura ko phuraka'o.
Maem' bha'vuka ati, prema virala rati, ca'hati ja'vati ura antara ati;
Santan kii gati, yogina kii mati, mohi naca'vati, mana thiraka'vati.

Sa'ram'ga na'catu, mohi bata'vatu,
Maem' ma'ya' vica samajhi na pa'vati;
Ca'taka ca'katu mora pakha' sara, piita'mbara lakhi amvara sohata.

Tu' a'nanda bharii kyom' ga'vati, tha'r'ii rahati, palaka na' ma'rati;
Kya' dekhii tu' bhii 'Madhu' bha'vana,
Kya' riijhii tu' bhii lakhi Mohana!

191. Kabahuki bikhari ja'tu mana merao * 645/05.12.09

Kabahuki bikhari ja'tu mana merao,
Kabahuki bhat'aki ja'tu mana merao;
Kabahuki sulajhi ja'tu mana merao,
Kabahuki ulajhi ja'tu man merao.

Kabahu prasa'ratu kabahu ur'a'vata,
Kabahu svapna gati mem'   dha'vata;
Kabahu umar'i Jamuna' jala bha'vata,
Kabahu ghumar'i ba'dala pahim' ja'vata.

Kabahu prasanna citta mana dha'vata,
Kabahuki girite lur'hxakyao ja'vata;
Kabahu dhara'tala pae akula'vata,
Kabahu dharan'i ke sura mem' ga'vata.

Kabahu patam'ga sam'ga vaha na'catu,
Kabahu nimis'a mem' dharan'ii dha'vatu;
Kabahu' mana mem' bahuta siha'vatu,
Kabahu' mana mem' bahuta d'ara'vatu.

Kabahu gira' gam'bhiira suna'vat,
Kabahu' mana mana mem' muska'vata;
Kabahu' prasanna chitta mana bha'rii,
Kabahu hota 'Madhu' antarya'mii.

192. Na'cana dehu mohi Giridha'rii * 656/11.12.09

Na'cana dehu mohi Giridha'rii, kyom' kari vipati dehu mohi bha'rii;
Kyom' na' bhagati dehu mohi pya'rii, kyom' kari tolata rahata Mura'rii.

Tuma sam'ga priiti laga'vata ra'jata,
Tuma sam'ga na'ca karata mana bha'vata;
Kabahu drs't'i tuma du'ri karo na', kabahu srs't'i ku'm' rus't'a karo na'.

Saba jiivana kii gati tuma dha'ro, saba jiivana kii mati sam'bha'ro;
Saba pra'n'ana ku'm' tuma Prabhu dha'ro,
Saba ke mana kii gati ku'm' ta'ro.

Saba tuma sam'ga na'nca kari pa'vahim,
Pra'n'ina ku'm' na' na'nca naca'vahim';
Sam'ska'rana vica ulajhi na ja'vahim',
Seva' prema bhagati kari pa'vahim'.

Saba pra'n'ana kii priiti pakha'rii, saba jiivana kii miiti niha'rii;
Bipadahim' shiis'a kamala pada dha'rii,
'Madhu' ura basi ja'vahu Tripura'rii.

193. Tuma hii prati pa'laka ho jagake * 668/13.12.09

Tuma hii prati pa'laka ho jagake,
Maem' kyom' soca karata ghuna ghuna ke;
Tuma hii jiiva cara'cara cetaka, Tuma hii saba jaga ke sam'ca'laka.

Ma'ri sakai na' koi ka'u' ke, jaba taka Tuma ba'cata ho ta'ke;
Ma'rana ba'lena ku'm' Tuma ta'kata,
Jaba ca'hata tinakao mana ma'rata.

Saba jiivana kii umari Tumhiim'te, eka eka pala ginatii Tuma te;
Je vidrs't'i   jiivana pae d'a'lata, tinakii gati tuma khuda sam'jovata.

Adha paka umari kou na' ja'vai, manuja ka'u ku'm' ma'ri na pa'vai;
Aisao dhya'na dharao Giridha'rii, paravash na' hohi jiiva dukha'rii.

Jaba jiivana ku'm' ma'rata dekhata, mana karman asa jaba kou socata;
'Madhu' mana umar'i ghumr'i rahi ja'vata, Tuma hii te nija t'era laga'vata.

194. Merao mana jaba jaba drr'ha hohi ja'vata
* 669/13.12.09

Merao mana jaba jaba drr'ha hohi ja'vata,
Jaga kii dhu'pa ta'pa sahi ja'vata;
Jaba jaba narama bhayao vaha na'cata,
Kabahuki jaga tehi khu'ba naca'bata.

Mana sam'yama kari dhya'na laga'vata,
Ta'n'd'ava lalita kaoshikii bha'vata;
Guru cakra pae Guru paet'ha'vata,
Jaga ku'm' ura antara vaha dekhata.

Shis't'ana neha karata vaha na'cata,
Dus't'ana ku'm' vaha dam'd'a kara'vata;
Saba jaga ku'm' vaha ura dhari na'cata,
Sabaku'm' Prabhu ura saom'pata ja'vata.

Jaga pravandha sam'vita hohi ja'vata,
Prama' prakat'i Prabhu pa'ne la'vata;
Shuddha buddhi hohi karma nikha'rata,
Prema samarpan'a seva' la'vata.

Ta'te jiiva jagata sudhi pa'vata,
Prabhu caran'ana mahim' mana lagi ja'vata;
Mama mana a'nandita hoya ja'vata,
Drr'ha mana ura 'Madhu' srs't'i suha'vata.

195. Shya'ma Giridha'rii lehu mohi ta'rii
* 700/21.12.09 (Braja Bha's'a')

Shya'ma Giridha'rii lehu mohi ta'rii,
Ra'ti bahu ka'rii na diikhae sukha'rii;
Karau na' ko derii, surati lau morii,
A'u cakradha'rii, vipati harao bha'rii.

Sa'nsa merii at'ake, bhat'aki mana ja'ye,
Ru'ha merii ka'npe, cat'aki hiya' ja'ye;
Na buddhi sujha'ye, na dhiiraja hii a'ye,
Samajha na'hii a'ye, kiya' kya' bhii ja'ye.

Pa'sa mere a'ao, dhiiraja bandha'ao,
Gati kachu la'ao, jugati batala'ao;
Bojha mana bha'rii, bhayao hu'n dukha'rii,
A'ao Giridha'rii, harao kas't'a bha'rii.

Sanga na'm'hi kou', karao more chohu',
Shakati kachu deu', bhagati mohi dehu';
Vegi Aao pya're, nayana ke dula're,
Harao dukha sa're, basao ura hama're.

A'ao cakrapa'n'ii, hiya' mere sva'mii,
Lakhahu ura ma'hii, rakhahu ura ma'hii;
'Madhu' ura va'sii, madhu sura bha'sii,
Dehu mrdu ha'nsii, pra'ta a'vae pya'rii

195 R. Madhu Chanda * 393A/03.07.09

A'mi Surasari bane na'ci, a'mi nirjhara jale ha'nsi;
A'mi meghera mata d'oli, a'mi hima girite sa'ji.

196. Likhata ja'u'n pa'tii, piya ko suha'tii
* 701/22.12.09 (Braja Bha's'a')

Likhata ja'u'n   pa'tii, piya ko suha'tii,
Mrdula muskara'ti, siharatii siha'tii;
Rotii risa'tii, hansatii khisa'tii,
Simat'atii sama'tii, chipatii chipa'tii.

Darada dila mem' jo bhii, t'iisa rahii jo bhii,
Likhu'n ura mem' jo bhii, cahu'n mana mem' jo bhii;
Piya' mere jogii, merao mana viyogii,
Rahata kachu prayogii, rahata a'tma yogii.

Likhu'n mana kii batiya'n, biiti ja'nya ratiya'n,
Na ja'vae suratiya', na a'vae sanvariya';
Na a'vae khavariya', na ja'vae dupariya',
Ja'nya saba ghar'iya'n, sa'njha a'vae daeya'.

Na kajara' laga'u'n, na gajara' saja'u'n,
Likhe unako ja'u'n, mana mem' siha'u'n;
Madhu merii ankhiya'n, takata ja'nya sakhiya'n,
Dhar'aki ja'm'ya chatiya'n, sunata paem'janiya'n.

'Madhu' piya dulariya', Shya'ma mere piiya',
Pa'tii 'Madhu Giiti' likhata nita ja'tii;
Cubhana madhu jaga'tii, hansii mrdu uga'tii,
Madhura muskara'tii, laja'tii sudha'tii.

197. Ma'ha' ma'nasa * 321/28.05.09 (Bangla)

Maha' ma'nasa utsarjiye, cetana dhara' gar'ite ja'ya;
Maha' ma'nava prakrti niye, navya ma'nava gar'ite ca'ya.

Tumi eshe, nikat'e boshe, madhu mane va'nshii ba'ja'o;
Madhurata' shudhu d'hele phelo, spandana nava manete ja'ga'o.

Prakrti na'ca'o, gagana sa'ja'o, shobhita mane pheliye ja'o;
Ma'nasa hiya'ya thirakiya' ja'o, shubhra madhu jyotsana' ja'ga'o.

Ta'n'd'ava veshii karo tumi na' ko,
Pa'n'd'ava mane madhurata' a'no;
Da'navata'ya dhvasta karo, dharin'ii dhara dhvaja' phahara'o.

Navya ma'nava ma'navata' niye, prakrti sa'yujye sahajata' niye;
Jar'a cetana ke sange niye, toma'ra 'Madhu' te ma'khiya' ja'ya.

198. Sakala ma'nus'a bha'i * 323/28.05.09 (Bangla')

'Madhu' dhara' ra'ungiye calo sakala ma'nus'a bha'i,
Prema tarunge bha'siye calo, dhara'te saba'i.

Sara'ye da'o sakala a'pada',
Baha'iya' calo sada'i sudha';
Mana ke kiye suhrda brhata,
Ma'navata' ke d'ha'liye mahata.

Piichane kabhu' ta'ka'o na' tumi,
Ma'nava hiya'ya ra'khio cu'mi;
Dharme karme udyata tha'ko,
Maner ma'jha're shubha shubha ta'ko.

Ghrn'a' ka'ro karo na'ko, avahelita karo na' ko;
Chande ta'le saba'i na'co, surete ga'iya' tha'ko.

Sudha' tarunge ma'tiye calo basudha'te saba'i,
Na'ciye calo ga'iye calo, sakala ma'nus'a bha'i.

199. Ogo Madhu tumi a'o * 31/08.04.08 (Bangala')

Ogo 'Madhu' tumi a'o, mora mana madhu niye ja'o!
Tumi mora pa'ne ca'o, more nija pa'ne niye ja'o.

Tumi eshe, mora pa'ne bose,
Tumi kichu kichu kare ja'o, ja'ha' kichu mananete ca'o;
Kichu kichu katha' kaye ja'o, kichu kichu byatha' sune ja'o.

Mora sancita madhu a'che,
Shudhu madhu a'che, kha'nt'i madhu a'che;
Kichui to bence a'chi, sei toma'ya dete ca'i, tumi a'o.

A'mi toma'ri madhurima' ca'i, a'mi toma'ri ma'dhurii dekhii!
A'mi toma'ri shobhanii dekhii, toma'ra mananei d'olii.
Tumi a'o, mora mana madhu niye ja'o.

Mora more bole ja' kichu a'che, se saba tora'i to a'che;
Tumi eshe bha'lobese, a'ma'ke niye ja'o,
More nija pa'ne niye ja'o.

200. Mora tana tora * 38/09.04.08 (Bangala')

Mora tana tora sura laharii, mora svara tora mana laharii;
Tumi a'ma'tei ga'ite ja'o, a'mi sura sedhe cale ja'i.

Tumi a'ma'ya viin'a' mata ba'ja'o, mora ta'ra ta'ra cher'e ja'o;
More ta're ta're cher'e ja'o, tumi nijera dhvani ja'ga'o.
A'ma'ra hrdi tantriite, tumi nijera ra'ga suna'o;
Ja'ha' kichu ca'o kare ja'o.

Tumi a'ma'ra pra'n'era sa'rathii, a'ma'ra mananerai sa'ks'ii;
Mora surerai rathii, mora ra'gerai pa'rakhii;
Mora pa'ne ca'o, a'ma'ya nijetei misha'iya' na'o.

A'mi na'cichi torma'ai ta'le, ga'ibo toma'rai sure;
Ma'tibo toma'rai laye, gunagunie toma'rai ga'ne.
Tumi eshe a'ma'ra sura sedhe da'o, Tumi mrdu 'Madhu' hese;
A'ma'ya dhya'ne ca'o, a'ma'ra dhya'ne a'o. A'ma'tei ga'ite ja'o.

201. Sakala pra'n'era parashaman'i tumi
* 557/08.10.09 (Bangala')

Sakala pra'n'era parashaman'i tumi, sakala ra'gera a'dha'ra bhu'mi;
Sakala hiya'ra parasa kha'ni tumi, sakala viin'a'ra tantrita dhvani.

Brajera Gopa'la tumi eshe   ja'o, a'ma'ra hiya'ya va'nshii ba'ja'o;
Sakala jagate a'ma'ke na'ca'o, jagata ke a'ma'ra hiya'ya na'ca'o.

Jiivane a'mi ya'ha' kichu bha'vi, saba kichu toma'tei seje a'chi;
Toma'ra binu na'him' dhenu ven'u,
Toma'ra bina' na ren'u trasaren'u.

Udayagiri te udadhi jalete, hima shikhirera prati parama'n'u te;
Asta'calerai tapana da'hane, tumi sushiitala suhrda nayane.

A'ma'ra jiivane krpa' kare ja'o, dhya'nera ma'jhe nija pra'n'e ca'o;
Nijerai va'nshiit'I suna'iya' ja'o, nijerei caran'e 'Madhu' ke sa'ja'o.

202. A'ma'ra hiya'ya Tumi eshe ja'o
* 646/09.12.09 (Bangala')

A'ma'ra hiya'ya Tumi eshe ja'o, a'ma'ra mane va'nshiit'i ba'ja'o;
A'ma'ra nikat'e tumi base ja'o, nijera caran'e a'ma'ke bosa'o.

Ama'ra mane parashiya' ja'o, a'ma'ra tane haras'iya' ja'o;
A'mara jiivane na'ciya' ja'o, a'ma'ra darshane thirakiya' ja'o.

Muraliya' Tumi suna'iya' ja'o, dhvani vyanjane saba'ike sa'ja'o;
Pratit'i hrdaye spandana ja'ga'o, prakrti ke niye sam'ge na'ca'o.

Toma'ra va'n'iit'i sunite ca'i, Toma'ra hansit'i dekhiye ca'i;
Toma'ri ca'hanii a'nkhi dekhe ca'i, lakut'iya' tora citte rakhe rai.

Sakala pra'n'era Tumi parashaman'i,
Sakala jiivera Tumi prema kha'nii;
A'ma'ra hiya'ya bhagati ja'ga'o,
'Madhu' ma'nase ma'dhurii na'ca'o.

203. Tumi kii kare raciya' ja'o
* 647/09.12.09 (Bangla)

Tumi kii kare raciya' ja'o, Tumi kii kare kariya' ja'o;
Tumi kii bha've ma'tiya' rao, Tumi kii kii ma'nase ca'o.

Tumi a'tura Tumi ka'tara, Tumi brhatera ma'jhe ca'tura;
Tumi gatira ma'jhe ka'npana, Tumi ha'sera ma'jhe thirakana.

Tumi hiya'ra ma'jhe gopana, Tumi banera ma'jhe siharana;
Tumi citavana ma'jhe citta vana, Tumi bha'vana' ma'jhe bha'vana.

Tumi a'ma'rai mane sa'jo, Tumi a'ma'ra hiya'ya ra'nco;
Tumi aka'tara haye tha'ko, Tumi sacetana sada' tha'ko.

Tumi 'Madhu' mane madhu d'ha'lo, Tumi ca'ndera mata ha'so;
Tumi jagata ke madhu ba'na'o, Tumi sankrti madhu ja'ga'o.

204. Ogo modera pra'n'era sakha'
* 752/01.01.10 (Bangala')

Ogo modera pra'n'era sakha', a'mi tomarai preme ma'kha;
A'mi shudhu ca'ii bha'laba'sha, tumi bheve theko ei a'sha.

Jalasa'ghare a'mi tha'ki, tumi Oder gharete a'chi;
Kan'e kan'e sudha' dekhi a'mi, sudha' jhare bhese theko Tumi.

Veshii tumi a'ma'ke ja'no, tumi bha'lova'shite ja'no;
Na' ja'nii toma'ra bha's'a', tumi ja'no mora abhila'sha'.

A'mi tomara manetei bha's'i, tomarai mananete ha'si;
A'mi toma'tei shudhu ya'ci, toma'kei a'mi niye a'chi.

A'mi tomara sure geye ya'i, toma'rai ga'ne nece ya'i;
Veshii a'mi kichu ca'i na', ca'i ekatu bha'lava'sha'.

205. A'pan'ii Su'rata na' purana' svaru'pa
* 136/12.08.08 (Gujara'tii)

He Satpur'a' mam' mot'ii bhayelii Ta'pii!
A'pan'ii Su'rata na' purana' svaru'pa,
Tu' bhula'vii pa' shake che?
Jyave tu' ku'datii chalaka'vatii thanaganatii,
Potana' kina'ra' tor'ii na'khatii.

Ta'ra' u'para shraddha'no banelo pula,
Tya're eka'kii pa'tar'ii rekha' la'ge che;
Tara' kina're banela' bahu ma'lii maka'no,
Ta'ra'mam' d'uba'yela' dekha'ya che.

Ta'ro pravala prava'ha sa'garane malava' la'ga che;
Kham'bha'tanii kha'r'iinii pu'namanii bharatii,
Tane at'aka'vatii la'ge che.

Ta'ra' vadha're par'ata' prava'ha ne,
Sa'gara pala sviika'ra karato la'gato nathii;
Tane siima'mam' rahava'nu'm'
Kahi rahyo hoya la'ge che.

Ta'ra' pu'ra pachii mot'ii biima'rio a've chae;
Bhu'taka'lana' ket'ala' kha'sa sa'thii,
Ta'ra'thii du'ra cya'lii ja'ya cho.

He Betulamam' janmelii Ta'pii, tu' shanta bahii,
Pota'nii sa'the badha'ne pharava' de;
'Madhu' bastiyom' ne basela' raheva' de,
Ba'dar'o ne varasava' de.

206. Laodhra phullam' tom' vadhada' phu'lada' *
91/12.06.08 (Panja'bii)

Laodhra phullam' tom' vadhada' phu'lada' Ludhia'n'a',
Saon'e bhangar'e na'la nacada' hae;
Pam'ja a'va'n taom' vagada' Pam'ja'ba,
Guru dii kirapa' na'la a'nam'dita hae.

Bha'khar'a' Nam'gal Bha'rata dii sha'na hae,
Govim'da Sa'gara   vad'd'a' visha'la hae;
Ropar'a dii Satalaja dii gahara'ii,
Ma'nava mana dii am'gar'a'ii hae.

Vya'sa da' visha'la bia'sa, adhia'tmika vishava'sa na'la bharia'
hae;
Guruda'sapura taom' Mukeria'm' da' nika'sa,
Vya'sa da' kudaratii pula ati sum'dara hae.

Sangaru'ra de hare bhare kheta'm' vica killa',
Mananu'm' chu'han'a va'la' hae;
Ahmadagar'a ' Madhu' a'nanda   na'la bharia' hae,
Cand'iigar'a da' vika'sa yojana' vaddha hae;
Ba'ga bagiicia'm' viccom' mahakadii hava' vicaradii hae.

Jalandhara via'pa'ra vica magana hae,
Pat'ia'la' A'lla' sim'ha dii sha'na hae;
Hushia'rapura loka giita'm' de rasa na'la bharia' hae,
Amritasara a'nanda va'n'ii vica ram'gia' hae.

207. A'baru' hae to sirfa terii hae * 440/24.07.09 (Urdu')

Abaru' hae to sirfa terii hae, na' hii merii hae, na' kisii kii hae;
Jisakii bhii hae d'hakii tu'ne hae, rakhii jaese bhii rakhii tu'ne hae.

Krodha kii a'ga ho jala' dete, kucha bhii bande se tuma kara' dete;
Palom' mem' usako tuma laja' dete, jagata se saza' bhii dila' dete.

Ma'dhyama jiiva saba tumha're haem',
Isha're naza're naga'r'e haem';
Sam'va're nikha're sam'joye haem',
Sikha'ye saja'ye bad'ha'ye haem'.

Ot'a mem' tuma sada' chipe rahate, kara'te rahate khudii jo cahate;
Indriyom' ko tumhiim' naca' dete, du'ra se baet'ha kara kara' lete.

A'damii kaesii bevashii mem' hae,
Reshamii d'ora mem' bandha' sa' hae;
Chora eka jisaka' pakar'a' 'Usane' hae,
Chora du'ja' 'Madhu' ke mana mem' hae.

208. Ru'ha kii roshanii nira'lii hae * 554/08.10.09 (Urdu')

Ru'ha kii roshanii nira'lii hae, pahelii bujha'tii sujha'tii hae;
Dvidha'em' mit'a'tii ghat'a'tii hae, sudha'em' sudha'tii pila'tii hae.

Ru'ha d'halatii hae, ca'ha d'halatii hae,
Roshanii khuda va khuda hii bad'hatii hae;
Jindagii samajha a'ne lagatii hae, vandagii dhiire dhiire a'tii hae.

Ruha'nii roshanii suha'nii hae, vira'na' vishva apana' karatii hae;
Vira'ne madhura mukhara hote haem', jindagii sajaga sukhada hotii hae.

Pahelii mata bujha'o he priyavara, khuda va khuda a'hii ja'o aba diigara;
Jagata kii rava'nii bata'nii hae, jugati kii ba'ta saba bata'nii hae.

Shakhshiyata merii saba dikha'nii hae, Ruha'nii roshanii dikha'nii hae;
'Madhu' ko ra'ha madhu bata'nii hae, Apane ko ru'baru' dikha'na' hae.

209. Ca'ha kii a'ha mem' * 508/09.09.09 (Urdu'/Hindii)

Ca'ha kii a'ha mem' ra'hem' nikala hii a'tii haem' ,
Ha'rate harate viharate baha'rem' a'tii haem';
Vyatha' katha' vica'ra pa'tii haem',
Vyastata' shuddhi 'Madhu' bar'ha'tii haem'.

Va'hanom' kii kamii vica'rom' kii,
Kamii khushii kii kabhii darda kii sii vechaenii;
Ca'ha ko urvara' kara'tii haem',
Ra'ha khuda hii bana'ye ja'tii haem'.

Jarjarita trasita tana tran'om' se bhii,
An'u u'rja' liye bhuvana se hii;
Na'cata' phirata' ghuma'ta' jiivana,
Jyoti lekara jaga'ta' jaga jiivana.

Pra'n'a mana jaba kabhii jise ca'he,
Srs't'i kara samarpan'a calii a'ye;
Samarpita mana svayam' jabhii hota',
Prakat'a Prabhu pra'n'a hae vahiim' hota'.

Samarpan'a siddhi kii jaru'rata hae,
Vikars'an'a buddhi kii hakiikata hae;
Preran'a' shuddhi mem' samarpita hae,
Es'an'a' Prabhu se prakampita hae.

209 R. Madhu Chanda * 412B/11.07.09 (159 R)

Prakrti sajatii rahii, vikrti bikharii rahii,
Sukrti sajatii rahii, ra'ha banatii rahii;
Saomya sam'sa'ra mem' sa'myata' d'hala rahii,
Sabhyata' pala rahii, shis't'ata' sadha rahii.

210. Srs't'i kii hara ada' * 510/11.09.09 (Urdu'/Hindii)

Srs't'i kii hara ada' nira'lii hae,
Sanva'rii nikha'rii dula'rii hae;
Sam'tulita suhrda sabhii siharita haem',
Sabhii sa'nanda sura mem' shobhita haem'.

Pus'pa hara kiit'a ko bula'te haem',
Giita hara miita ko bula'te haem';
Priiti kii riiti sabhii calate haem',
Diipa d'halate hue bhii jalate haem'.

Phalom' kii khushabu' sabhii ko bha'tii,
Haza'rom' makkhiyom' ko madama'tii;
Madhu kii mahaka ciim't'e le a'tii,
Phu'la kii hara ada' hae madhuma'tii.

Yuvatii hiran'ii hae sada' muska'tii,
Khilatii kaliya'm' haem' gazala ga' ja'tiim';
Shishu kii suha'nii mrdula ha'nsii,
Brddha kii ruha'nii suhrda ha'nsii.

Va'lapana kii vicitra prashna jhar'ii,
Brddha kii vivekii vishuddha ghar'ii;
Sabhii to srs't'i kii vidha'em' haem',
Sabhii 'Madhu' drs't'i kii ada'yem' haem'.

ENGLISH

PLEASE READ ORIGINAL ENGLISH
POEM NOS. 211-225
IN PART 3

PERCEPTION OF BLISS (A'NANDA   ANUBHU'TI)

Spiritual Management Poetry
(A'dhya'tmika Prabandh – Madhu Giiti)

Part 3
ENGLISH VERSION

Introduction, Author Biography,
Theme of Book, Forewords,
Chapters and Prologue

By
GOPAL BAGHEL 'MADHU'

Multilingual Poetry in
Hindi, Sanskrit, Braj, Bengali,
Punjabi, Gujarati, Urdu & English
With English version

PERCEPTION OF BLISS
(A'NANDA   ANUBHU'TI)

Spiritual Management Poetry
(A'dhya'tmika Prabandh – Madhu Giiti)

Part 3
ENGLISH VERSION

INDEX

Page Nos.

DEDICATION
***
Supreme Consciousness
All Incarnations, Whole Cycle of Creation, Nature,
5 Fundamental Elements and whole mobile and immobile Cosmos.

Omni father and Omni Guru **Sada' Shiva**, mother **Pa'rvatii,**
Yogeshvar **Shri Shri Krs'n'a**, affection manifest **Ra'dha' ji,**
Esteemed Guru **Shri Shri A'nandamu'rti ji** and all others
With prostrated touch in their lotus feet.

Paternal & Maternal family:
Grand father late **Dharma Singh ji**
S/O. All late Sukh Ram ji, Grand S/O. Rambal ji
Great Grand S/O. Khushala' ji

Father late **Dal Chand ji**, Mother late **Jai Devi ji**
D/O Late **Sukh Ram ji**
All late G. uncle **Kishan Lal**, G. aunt **Jagani**,
F. in-law **Yad Ram**, M. in-law **Savitri,**

Childhood Inspirers :
All late Jagan Pd. Gupta, Basudev, Charan Singh,
Chhidda Singh, Manohar Lal, Murari Lal, etc.

Spiritual & Literary:
Spiritual Researchers (Rs'ii), spiritual teachers, scientists, spiritual
books, Four Vedas, Tantra, Shrimad Bhagawad Giita,
Shri Ram Charit Manas, Yoga Vashis't'ha, Maha'bha'rat,
Raviindra Sa,m'giita, Subha's'it Sam'grah, Prabha't Sam'giit,
Mahars'i Veda Vyas, Pa'n'ini Muni, Mahars'i Patanjali,
Adi Shankaracharya, Swamii Vivekananda,
Laks'hmi Bai, Ahilya Bai, etc.

Ancient Poets Maharshi Valmiki, Mushana, Goswami Tulasidas,
Suradas, Kabirdas, Bihari, Rahim, Mirabai and others.

ACKNOWLEDGEMENT

Family:
Wife **Asha**, Son **Chaitanya**,
Daughters **Shweta, Richa and Pragya;**
Grandsons **Aranya &   Reyansh**
Domestic dog **Jet**, late **Guffii**, cat **Mam'u'n** &
Squirrel **Gillu**), Birds, trees and others

Whole family & relatives and residents of place of birth
Cousins (Late Bhikam Singh, late Sunhari Lal,
Mr. Om Prakash & Mr.Hardev Singh)

All past, present and future creatures of places of birth, residence,
visits, bhukti,district, province, country, continent, world & cosmos.

Co-travellers in life, teachers and affectionates
In Education, spirituality, meditation, family,
profession, service, business & travel and observers.

All Shri Ganapat Ram Mistry, Udaiveer S. Rawat, Ramaji lal,
Pramod Baghel, Pankaj Baghel, late Gopal P. Gaur, Devidas,
Mr. Balulal, Mrs. Lilavati, etc.

Foreword & Prologue writers
And all who sent/will send suggestions & comments
Inspirers: Poets, singers, writers, readers, listeners,
friends and colleagues known unknown
Publishers, distributors and organizers

Newspapers, magazines, books, radios, televisions
and all persons of all countries in world.
All readers, singers, listeners and philosophers,
All persons enjoying and vibrating bliss,
Interacting & suggesting.

AUTHOR INTRODUCTION

Gopal Baghel 'Madhu' was born in India at Rampur, Aring near Govardhan, the divine sport place of Lord Krs'n'a in district Mathura, U. P. in 1947. He received National Merit Scholarship and regional prizes in singing. He graduated in Mechanical Engineering from National Institute of Technology, Durgapur, West Bengal, India in 1970 with honors which is recognized equivalent by University of Toronto, Ontario, Canada. He completed his AIMA Diploma in Management from All India Management Association, New Delhi, India in 1978.

He has undergone training in Industrial Engineering, Materials Management, Preventive Maintenance, Financial Management, etc. through National Productivity Council and Delhi productivity Council, India during 1972-75. He has been a Chartered Engineer and Govt. approved Surveyor & Loss Assessor in India. He has been member of Delhi Management Association, All India Management Association, Delhi Productivity Council, IPPTA, TAPPI, etc. He has taken training in SAP - Business Warehouse (BW) and Application Security in Canada in 2007-2008.

Professional: He was associated with Paper, Packaging, Sugar, Textile, Food, Woollen and other industries as Mechanical Engineer, Management Analyst, Superintendent PPC, Corporate Materials Controller, Development Manager, General Manager, Vice-President and President in U.P., Rajasthan, W. Bengal, Punjab, Uttaranchal, Gujarat, Haryana, Delhi, etc. in India during 1970-1997. He has travelled all over north, east, west and south of India.

Present: He lives now with his family in Toronto, On., Canada. He is President of Global Fibers, an import export business of Paper and Steel in Toronto, Ontario, Canada since 1997 and has frequently travelled in Canada and USA while interacting with India, China, Far East, Europe, Middle East and South America. He is also associated with various industries, marketing organizations and TAPPI in Canada and USA. He also works at Pearson International Airport, Toronto, On., Canada since 2007.

Spiritual: He got good spiritual environment, inspiration, encouragement and bliss of sentient persons from his childhood. By grace of Guru, he was initiated into Yoga and Meditation in1968. He was blessed with meetings with Guru in 1984. He was deeply associated in meditation, spiritual meetings and interactions and service during 1984-2000. He got an opportunity to focus on special meditation w.e.f. 2000. Stream of life continued to flow with special blessings of Guru, spiritual teachers, literary and poetic persons engaged in physical, spiritual, family, social and literary fields.

Literary: During 1981-84, he composed few poems (Some of which are included in this book) and articles on science and spirituality. March 2008 onwards, he has composed 7000+ poems so far in themes of Spiritual Management, Spiritual Management Research, Devotion and Grace, Compassion, Nature, etc. in Hindi, Braja Bha's'a', Bengali, Sanskrit, Gujarati, Punjabi, Urdu and English, 225 of which are published in this book with Roman Sanskrit and English version. Poems are lyrical and video versions are also available for thousands of poems.

His poems are deeply appreciated and enjoyed by everyone including poets, friends and public and have been published in various Poetic Collections, news papers, magazines, etc. He regularly sings poems in Poetic conferences in Canadian, Indian and USA   and is member of many literary associations. He organizes regular poetic programs and annual functions of Akhil Vishva Hindi Samiti and Hindi Sahitya Sabha, Toronto, On., Canada . He also participates in AVHS New York, USA programs. He sang at Shikshya Yatan amidst global poets in New York. Regularly participate in poetic programs of Hindi Writers Guild, Vishva Hindi Sansthan, etc. in Canada and innumerable organizations in India and world. He organizes and conducts 'Hindi Day' function at Consulate General of India, Toronto. His poems are broadcast on YouTube, radio and television.

He is Founder, Director and President of Akhil Vishva Hindi Samiti and Spiritual Management Foundation, Toronto, On., Canada. He is also member of various literary organizations of Canada and abroad.

THEME OF BOOK

Cycle of Creation and Management of Creation:

Cosmos (Brahma'n'd'a) is fundamentally a creation of
un-manifested (Nirgun'a Brahma) supreme entity. Whenever that
un-manifested cosmic entity, out of desire of divine play gets
expressed or manifested as supreme (Sagun'a Brahma), nature
(Prakrti) gets manifested having three attributes of sentience,
mutability and stativity. As long as these 3 attributes maintain an
equilibrium and equipoise, balance or status quo is maintained. As
soon as this balance gets destabilized, nature starts moving in its
extrovert cycle of creation and cosmic Mahat (I exist), Aham (Doer
I) and Chitta (Done I) get created. With more clash & cohesion
within Chitta (Done I), ethereal, aerial, fire, liquid and solid
fundamental factors get created and come into flow while
preserving within these all earlier subtle stages of extrovert cycle.

When solid factor passes through an extreme clash within, subtle
entity happens to activate dormant Chitta (Done I) whereby creating
unicellular and then multi cellular organism or plants thereby move
into an introvert cycle of creation. Under further clash and cohesion
at every stage in introvert cycle of creation, animals, humans,
intellectual and spiritual human beings get created and evolved. In
the final phase of introvert cycle of creation, the spiritual humans
merge with manifested and help in management of creation.
Depending upon need and situation of management of creation,
manifested entity at times becomes un-manifested and
un-manifested again becomes manifested and supreme entity
manages and controls creation eternally. All stages created in cycle
of creation during extrovert and introvert cycles keep evolving
eternally under overall or individual management of manifested or
un-manifested entity. Cycle of Creation is shown in Annex.

Cosmic Entity, Guru, Yoga, Tantra, Bhakti & Krpa':

Manifested cosmic entity on its own gets expressed as Guru
depending upon desire, situation, need, devotion or grace. Cycle of

creation is cosmic organization of creator i.e. manifested supreme. Created entities are organized, administered and managed by Him. Time, Place (Space) and Persons (Entities) are His domains and dimensions. Creatures keep on developing or promoted while being directed and controlled in creation while being assessed through performance appraisal. Theoretical knowledge, practice and experience of management of creation is Yoga or cosmic management.

On getting developed deep into working and practice of Yoga, one gets established into Tantra. Tantra (Spiritual Technology) is Applied Yoga. On being established and getting approved in performance appraisal of knowledge (Jina'na), devotion (Bhakti), work (Karma), Yoga   & Tantra and devotion having become firm and well established, creator may shower grace. Effort of movement of creatures towards cosmic entity is Bhakti. Efforts of cosmic entity to move towards or help creature is His grace (Krpa'). Mission of creator is to develop every microvitum or entity to make it an expert or deepest possible in cosmic management and ultimately bring it to cosmic controller stage. Only the one, who is able to understand creation well, is able to serve creation properly. The one who is greatest entity in management of creation is Brahma (One who is Brahata Brahata i.e. great great or greatest or supreme).

Spiritual Management:

The cosmic controller keeps on developing creation physically, mentally and spiritually by mutual coordination and exchange of subtle and crude. To make crudest the subtlest is objective and vision of management skill of cosmic management. Yoga is skill of doing the Karma efficiently. Knowledge of cosmic management, Karma (Full of rationality & logic), devotion (Bhakti) & grace (Krpa'), Yoga and Tantra of creator is management expertise.

Time, Place and Persons (TPP):

Cosmic controller manages management of events in creation by controlling time, place and persons (TPP). If any entity acquires a stage of controlling TPP, that entity can then control chain of events in creation. If one of TPP is changed, other two get themselves changed and this events or chain of events get changed. Place (Space) pervades in body of creation or in bodies of its entities. Time is perception of distances in place (Space). Persons are entities pervading in cosmos or creation and their degree of consciousness may vary from zero to infinity or from crudest to subtlest.

Creation or Enhancement in Creation:

Creation or enhancement happens when an entity withdraws from its present time, place (Space) and person (Entity) and gets integrated or associated with creator or manifested entity. Larger the void or vacuum within that entity, larger or better will be the creation or enhancement. Conception of new creature i.e. Conceiving in womb, scientific discoveries, socio political changes, processes of nature, fructification of determination, uprising of reactive momentum (Sam'ska'ra), changes in creation, etc. are all dependent on void or vacuum (Shoonya) created by individual and collective waves of time, place and persons.

Perception of Bliss:

After understanding creator, creation, cosmic management, spirituality and we, our living and serving in creation becomes blissful. Meditation is technique, science, art, process and practice of integrating a person with supreme. Meditation becomes a possibility after manifested cosmic entity expressing as Guru Graces someone. Guru is the one who takes us from darkness (Gu) to light (Ru). Guru guides or rather goads humans on this path. Knowingly or unknowingly, directly or indirectly, Guru remains with everyone at every place at all the times through Ota & Prota (Direct or indirect involvement) Yoga. Guru Himself continuously develops thrills, vibrates and makes us blissful through his styles of cosmic management. He alone establishes creatures in aesthetic science of spiritual management saying," Let all good and great happen!" and He alone gives them awesome perception of bliss.

The pleasure we get by remaining in closeness of creator or supreme is Bliss. He is sharing this bliss with everyone on planet but all creatures are not able to perceive bliss at all times. He wants that all His creatures may enjoy this bliss as early as possible and help manage creation while imparting bliss to creation and themselves. As bliss cannot be enjoyed without experiencing by one oneself, creator desires that we should keep our physical body, mind and consciousness continuously clean, get connected with creator through meditation and while observing, understanding, interacting and managing world (That which moves) with the vision of supreme, we keep it eternal and forever developing. The experiences we have in that stage is what 'Perception of Bliss' is.

When we share our perceptions of bliss, we get more perception of bliss and creator also gets bliss. Creator may get bliss, He may grace us more and we may be able to better serve His creation, is desired objective of every one. May bliss be infinite, perception of bliss may become eternal and whole cosmos may get vibrated! Whole creation, creator, created creatures, nature, five elements and cosmic mind may get vibrated, thrilled and blessed by this cosmic perception of bliss, is what is internal desire and plan of creator. Why not we take this deep desire of His as a grace on us, we let Him shower devotion and bliss so that we may dive deep into perception of bliss along with everyone.

When we perceive flow of His bliss, He may also pat our head with His hand and embrace our heart. All our agony, impediments, intricacy and uneasiness quickly gets removed by His nature. What appears at doorstep is devotion, grace, Karma (Work), effulgence and perception of bliss. Drenched in warm and hearty eternal fondness of creation, human heart happens to sing perceptions of his subtle love after finding sweet expertise in sweet panoramas of bliss of perception. He happens to thrill in its eternal bliss, cosmos starts dancing in his heart and he happens to start singing in an eternal infinite tune in his own privacy perception of bliss on chaste heart violin of creation.

Bliss vibrates from internal union of creature with cosmic controller. Its source lies in passionate stream of creation. The interaction and meeting of creature with cosmic cognition emanates a mysterious vibration. Creature, creation and cosmic controller Himself gets vibrated out of this integration. The perceptions occurring in this stage beyond passion are perception of bliss. It is neither easy to express this nor it is easy to enjoy this bliss without experiencing. Every creature, however, has a comprehension of same. Every creature has sometimes tasted this vibration in its journey in cosmic cycle. He has sometimes enjoyed splendid glimpse of infinite form of supreme entity. He is interested in his bosom to eternally acquire this supreme bliss.

The divine play (Liila) of introvert and extrovert plays of creation keeps creatures knowingly and unknowingly occupied in management stream of creation. It is duty and Dharma of Supreme Consciousness to keep in flow continuous infinite multi dimensional development of creation and creatures forever. He wants that every creature should make optimum contribution in management of creation. This bliss alone establishes them more in Karma and Dharma. This alone makes them more complete. This only manifests and establishes every particle and every creature. This makes flow Ganges of bliss and development of every entity at all times at all places in creation. The bliss of perception may flow, grow, thrill and bliss is inner desire of Cosmic Consciousness, creation and every microvitum.

***

Akhil Vishva Hindi Samiti, New York (All World Hindi Society)

108-15 68 Drive, Forest Hills, New York 11375, USA
Tel.: 718 793 4579
Founding President: Late Rameshvar Ashant

International President: Dr. Dauji Gupt
President: Dr. Vijay kumar Mehta

English Passion of Foreword in Hindi

Perpetual flow of life is like continuous flow of Ganges. Similarly, poetry is spontaneous expression of flux of mind. Its expression is natural and it takes form of a lotus of poetry by lotus hands of poet. Shri Gopal Baghel 'Madhu' is believer and follower of devotional path and according to his philosophy, source of creation is one and only one the greatest of great's supreme controller.

Own personality and belief of poet is important in creation of poetry. Poet or writer is only a tool through the medium of which passion acquires form.

Shri Krishna told Arjun in Shrimadbhagvadgiita-

"There is right to work but there is no right on the fruit of work. One should work without attaching mind with the associated fruit or result of work."

In the creation of poetry, public poet Gopal Baghel 'Madhu' has taken a form of Arjun and Shri Krishna in the form of an inspirer has made him his medium. As and when whatever directions he received, creation happened accordingly. As public poet Gopal 'Madhu' is follower of lord creating creation, he is not worried about what will result from his compositions. Neither he desires fruits of his karma nor he wants to remain without work; rather he wants to become one while merging with lord-
"Kavirmaniis'ii paribhu' svayambhu' "

The public poet has not taken birth to get fruits of karma or creation; not he wants to remain without work. He only believes in his right of creation - karma and he surrenders to lord whatever gets created through medium of his writing because poet and philosopher or researcher are paribhu or beyond domain of creation and they become one with svayambhu or one who is self created i. e. Lord.

The creative world of Shri Gopal Baghel 'Madhu' is not limited, it is multifarious. His poems are divided in 7 chapters- Spiritual management, Spiritual management -science- research- social, Spiritual devotion and grace, Perception of compassion, Perceptions of poet, Natural and Multi-lingual literature in Sanskrit, Braj, Bengali, Gujarati, Punjabi, Urdu and English besides Hindi.
The poet who was born in Mathura (India) came in the form of realization of consciousness of Shri Krishna. Meera had said-

"Mere to giridhar Gopal du'sara' na koii"
(Only Gopal, the up- holder of mountain is mine; no one else)

And who was this up- holder of mountain? That is Shri Krishna, who upheld the mountain on his index finger, protected creation from devastating rain and defeated Indra (The controller of senses.). Those who remained safe in shadow of mountain got "Ananda Anubhuti" or "Perception of Bliss". That same Shri Krishna(Gopal) in His graceful shadow,   giving vibration to public poet Gopal ' Madhu', integrating Braja soil of Mathura to the Braja soil of whole world, is helping people have perception of bliss through his poems.

When Bharat i. e. India emerged after getting free from shackles of dependence, same year, just before that, Gopal Baghel was born in 1947. Gopal himself became 'Bha'rat' (Arjun); he also became Gopal (Shri Krishna), both became one and got integrated together. Shri Krishna reared cows and was called Gopal. Gopal 'Madhu' reared poems born in the form of cows and becoming Gopal, he dissolved ' Madhu' or 'spiritual honey' in the milk of cow like poems; the sweetness of which is bound to give "Ananda Anubhuti" or "Perception of Bliss". Therefore-

"Madhu tum a'ja'o to"
(O honey, if you come by…)

Public poet Gopal has become poet of ' Madhu' tradition. He is not merely a poet of books or readers. Whatever, he writes, he says straight forward; he does not orient or distort poetry. That is why, as a public poet, he says:

"Manavata' shos'it ... Tandava jaga mem' Prabhu kama karado..."
"Humanity is exploited and perturbed…"

Analysing Time scientifically, poet raises question:
"Samaya kya' sras't'i ka'...."
"Is the time relative dimension of creation?"

The reply to all these questions and multifarious problems lays in time related poems of public poet Gopal 'Madhu'. There is no doubt that Momentum and flow of conscious expression of poet in his poems will simply make every poem effectually affectionate.

Dr. Dauji Gupt.
Lucknow, U. P., India

Padmshri, Dr. Shyam Singh Shashi

Ph. D (Sociology), D. Lit (Anthropology & Literature),
P.G. in Management (England)

Senior Poet & Writer, Social Scientist, Anthropologist & Academician

Director General, Research Foundation International, New Delhi.
Visiting Prof.: Indira Gandhi National Open University, New Delhi
Ex Director General, Govt. of India, Publication Division (I&B)

Safdarjung Encl., New Delhi- 110029, India
<drshashi9@rediffmail.com>

Svasti Pam'tha': (May the path be blissful!)

Supreme entity is expressed mainly in two forms- manifested and un-manifested. The visible world manifests through extrovert cycle and integrates through introvert cycle in His manifested form. However, the un-manifested remains real original controlling entity. It's not easy to understand Him in full perspective on the basis of His attributes. While remaining omniscient in whole universe, He remains astonishingly awesome and un-manifested from underlying point of view. Even while remaining established in two forms of Ram - Rahim, he gets spiritual luminosity in faith of one Om'ka'r or Omni Godliness. This is the only truth which has been enlivened and articulated in spiritual expressions (Va'n'ii) of saints through their minds, discourses and actions or karma. Guru Na'naka also liked saint poets Kabiira, Da'du', Raida'sa, Malu'kada'sa, Ba'ba' Fariida, etc. As a result, their contributions got a place in Guru Granth Sa'hib. Much more has been written on Su'rada'sa, Tulasiida'sa and saint poets of manifested entity as compared to saints expressing as regards un-manifested in Hindi saint literature. Kabiir is an exception, whose Va'nii was fully recognized by Dr. Haja'rii Prasa'da Dwivedi and he widely & vividly appraised Kabiira Va'nii. Su'fii faith is emblematic balanced profile of Alla'h and Ra'm and hence both Hindus and Muslims embraced it.

While enjoying spiritual poems of Canadian poet Gopal Baghel 'Madhu' who has immigrated from India, it appeared that whereas, at times, at places, Indian culture appears to be becoming alien in India, few writers of Indian origin have not only enshrined, evolved and expressed it in their consciousness, but they are also sprouting, blossoming and vibrating it in whole world after immigrating to other places on Earth.

I have closely shared, familiarized and envisioned pleasures, pains and blissfulness of Indian progeny and other immigrants and have read and listened to their literary creations in my global journeys inclusive of Europe, USA, Canada, South America, Mauritius, Surinam, Guyana, Fiji, and Trinidad. At times, I have heard their melody in melancholy music stimulating inner bliss of that Roma' clan of Indian origin who had moved to Egypt and other countries a thousand year ago. Even today their offspring overwhelmingly enjoy calling Bha'rata as 'Ba'rotha'na'. Their mother tongue is Roman, whose literature is agonizing article of humanitarian struggle. Their 'Paganism' could survive only after braving tortures of 'Holocaust' and at places, it got associated with worship of nature of Rig-Veda and at other places it flourished in Christian, Muslim and other faiths. It is preserving is existence in message of peace of "Vasudhaeva kut'umbakam" meaning "Whole Earth itself is our family". Roma's have, though, fully amalgamated in western culture; even today one can hear in their Roman language many words of Hindi, Punjabi, Marathi, Gujarati, Marwari, etc.

In my literary journeys of 2003 on invitation of Vishva Hindi Samiti (World Hindi Association), New York & London, Giita'njalii Birmingham and others also, I found Indian progeny excited or overflowing in spiritual love of their own, Indian people in general and Indian reactive momentum. They have been making efforts to move forward forever carrying cosmic expression in their consciousness, moulding themselves in new environment and continuously developing, adjusting and balancing with culture of global human, while giving it a Indian and cosmic melody and tune. The inner realization of cosmic mind of immigrants flows through their compositions and cosmic agony, administration situation, diversity and experiences are converted into 'Perception of Bliss'.

Some poets and writers appears attached to "Chha'ya'ba'da" (Upsurge of subtle, human love, nature & mystic) and others get associated with "Pragativa'da" (Progressive-socialistic). They create ever new literature moulding their reactive momentum in end matching (Tuka'nt) or un-matching (Atuka'nt) meters.

Reactive momentum of spiritual faith, experiences and perceptions have found a blissful flow in compositions of Gopal Baghel 'Madhu', a Canadian poet born in Mathura (U.P.), graduated from Durgapur (W. Bengal), brought up and grown up in India, He has utilized Tatsam (Same words as in Sam'skrta) vocabulary for same. He appears to be submerging, floating and flowing or vibrating and resonating his firm Indian culture and reactive momentum in Milky Way of cosmic fervour in his poetry. Following quote from one of his poem looks to be the fascination of his creation:

" A'nanda umangom' mem' bharakar, Maim' tumara' giita suna' ja'u'm' Maim' ta'raka brahma liye man mem', Tarata' ja'u'm' varata' ja'u'm'."
    (Flowing into exultations of bliss, I may keep singing Your song; Beholding liberating cosmic consciousness in mind, I may keep liberating and integrating.)

While blessing Madhu's writings, I hope that along with flow of spiritual poetry, if he also composes in themes of pure literature that will surely be proved more helpful in upholding and perpetuating Indian culture. May his writings naturally find their own path and spring with even more vigour, perception, bliss and grace of God in next compilation, while buttressing path of revolution of philosophy and spiritual management science. May his path be blissful!

Dr. Shyam Singh Shashi

Poet and Writer of over 400 Books on Encyclopaedias, Nomads of the Himalayas', 'Roma- The Gypsy World', 'The Encyclopaedia of Social Sciences and Humanities (50 Vols.), 20 Poetic collections,etc.

Umadutt Dubey 'Anjan'
Senior Poet, Editor and Writer

Ex Dy. Director; Chief Educational Officer,
Defence Deptt., Govt. of India, New Delhi

Mississauga, On., Canada, eMail: dubey_amit10@yahoo.com

Affectionate Welcome

A flow of limitless bliss was perceived on reading and listening spiritual poems of "Ananda Anubhu'ti or Perception of Bliss" composed by Shri Gopal Baghel 'Madhu'.

Congratulations for pouring awesome melody of Braj in all language, influence of meditation in art & style with amazing sweetness of honey of presentation while analytically expressing spirituality as subject. Compositions are colourful. Its credit goes to his duet pace of literature and music.

His creation will surely look like nectar to evolved readers, it will attract passionate ones and it will   make its special   status in literature.

With affection, blessings and good wishes.

Umadutt Dubey 'Anjan',
M.A. (Hindi), Founder, Rajasthan Forum

Author: Ikkiishaviim' Shata'bdii mem', ' Maim' Jo Kahta Hu'n, Pahli Ba'r, Abha'r,etc.

HEARTILY TO YOU

How Supreme Consciousness makes our life stream flow, is only known to Him. By trying to know Him, we are able to somewhat understand ourselves. Only He knows, when, why, where and how, He will start our life excursion   by giving birth in which family, society, faith, country, continent, planet, star and galaxy. He only knows, when He will like to utilize us else where. We are familiar unfamiliar partner of His Devine sport, plan, project, objective and organization.

If we can involve in work or Karma, while understanding His plan, even while enjoying bliss in His plans, we may start enjoying beauty of every time, place and person. Every action and reaction of His, play of every creature, look and splendour of nature, grandeur of every place or country, footstep of every instant, tune of time and behaviour of persons and creatures, appears to be objective of His plan and project. In that state, language, fervour, idea, behaviour, experience, mind, body, outlook of creation and all that appears to have immersed in perception of bliss.

Creation of presented poems got suddenly sprouted at the doorsteps of pleasures & pains, at the airport of life bound by fetters of work, in the passionate shadow of pleasure, pains and bliss of welcoming or departing hearts of their own persons, in the accelerating or retarding flow tunes of thought- planes ascending & descending in between Earth and skyline amidst thrilling waves of passions of life river.

The effort of bestowing avid chattels of Supreme to His beings with the infinite support of many evolved poets, listeners, evaluators, advisors, and family and foreword writers is dedicated to you. Owing to lots of my personal limits, there is every likelihood of leaving many errors and shortcomings in this effort. You are very kindly urged to indicate inadequacy to enable enact enhanced presentation in future.

Out of 1510 Madhu Giiti composed so far, 225 are included in this collection in their original and Hindi form along with their Roman

Sanskrit and English versions. The remaining Madhu Giiti will be published in future collections as soon as possible. Interested persons may contact author for new poems.

To give bliss of original language to those who are not so good   in Hindi (Devanagari) script or other languages used, Roman Sanskrit version is created as Part 2. English version in Part 3 will be convenient for those who are not aware of Hindi and other original languages used in book. Hindi readers will also enjoy added bliss while reading Madhu Giiti in English version. Effort is made to create English version of poems as sweet as original ones.

Original English Poem Nos. 211 to 225 are available only in Part 3 in English. Pictures and 'Madhu Chhand' or 'Madhu Couplet', which are part of poems composed later, are given with poems. Every part has its own unique bliss with different pictures, Madhu Chhand or Madhu Couplets and Forewords. Illustration of 'Cosmic Cycle' is given in Annex to indicate Chakras or plexuses and various stages and dimensions of creation.

Table of Madhu Giiti nos. and Poem nos. is given in annexure to enable you view Madhu Giiti no. Sl. No. and date of composition of Madhu Giiti are indicated with every title of poem in order of date, month and year (DDMMYY). Almost all Madhu Giiti are lyrical and their Audio and Video versions may be obtained by contacting author. Your valuable guidelines and suggestions and ideas for improvement are heartily welcome and appreciated. With thanks and gratefulness in your tune:

Gopal Baghel 'Madhu'

PerceptionOfBliss@gmail.com
www.GopalBaghelMadhu.com

Toronto, Ontario, Canada

PERCEPTION OF BLISS
Spiritual Management Poetry

Part 3 - ENGLISH VERSION

Chapter 1: Spiritual Management

1. In the blissful landscape of cosmos
* 601/ 15.09.09

A conscience was created in blissful landscape of cosmos,
That conscience was full of flow, liveliness and effulgence;
It poured sweetness in roving universe,
It pleased creatures with its thrill and loveliness.

He bound humans in affection by giving conduct rules,
Giving sweetness to nature, He danced in Lalit dance;
Thrilling in sweet melody, He balanced ethics,
Giving consciousness to conscious, He awakened conscience.

After vibrating subtle stream of culture, He went,
He eternalized wall of degeneration by piercing it;
He decorated and organized subtle human heart,
After composing songs, filling affection and cordiality,
filling friendship in heart, He left.

The heart of cosmos remained in flow in stream of bliss,
He could bear velocity of cries with ease;
Scene changed, trees blossomed, clouds liked Him,
Filling eyes with tears, flowing hearts with love,
He became fond of everyone.

He went after blooming all sources of 'Madhu' sweetness,
He left after illuminating lamps of fresh splendor in cosmos;
I unconsciously kept singing sweet songs of consciousness,
He went after making all dance on tune of His flute in cosmos.

2. Perceptions of Your subtle affection * 132/ 08.08.08

Should I call the perceptions of Your subtle affection?
The 'Aspirations of bliss' or 'Wave of Bliss' for accession!
Should I name these, 'Perception of Bliss' or 'Bliss of Perception'!
Should I call these 'Melody of Cosmic Management"
Or 'Spiritual Management' in action!

Whatever I call them, they are arts of Your grace,
These are garlands made for You O matchless!
Their fragrance and beauty is Yours,
Bliss of putting them onto thread is my providence.

You set your feet on every petal of their pineal gland;
You touch their lily like hearts by Your lips indeed.
Give them bliss by keeping on podium of Your heart so sweetened.

You immerse in their every pour, you thrill every creature;
You sing in every body and intellect,
You inhabit every 'Madhu' heart pulsation.

3. Nectar of bliss sprinkles * 286/12.04.09

Nectar of bliss sprinkles in skies,
Three cosmic echelons and humans are in bliss;
Air thrills in bliss, fragrance of life is in intense bliss.

Human minds are in happiness,
Flowers have fragrance, sky dances in bliss;
Sweet Moon is in tune and melody,
Earth is thrilled in sweet melody.

Sky has blue eye salve, new clouds are thrilling over the moon;
Thrilled in bliss of sea, stars are flowing with pole star.
Delicious in gush of bliss, meteor got illuminated;
All stars are thrilled, Earth is in love overflowed.

Melodious waves flow in Sun; Planets stay amused in reason;
Blissful Guru showers grace, poles are in 'Madhu'* adherence.

4. Deep bliss pervades * 328/30.05.09

Deep bliss pervades, sky is as per penchant of mind;
Gratification is in pride, 'Madhu' Sun has arrived.
Birds are roaming spread, human mind is profusely amused;
Breeze leaps in aspirations, sky is chanting poems.

Some sweet melodies have started playing,
Eternal hearts have started speaking something;
Some ones have started singing in joint melody in bliss,
Some ones are overwhelmed in liking and fondness.

Attracted Earth is in sweet bliss, sweet flower is in magnificence;
Sanctity of nature is momentous, universal Om sound prevails.
Lips are disconcerted, sweet mind is in singing mood;
Flame of meditation is gracious and attuned.

5. Wave in tune * 330/30.05.09

With wave in tune, pain of atrocity in brain,
'Madhu' she-cuckoo looks bonbon;
Meditating within bosom, working with hands,
Integrating intellect, filling smile in heart alliance.

Elated in mind, evaluating environment, observing beauty of spirit;
She explores fragrance in sweet firmament,
While occupied in eternal conduct.

Looking at amazing grand beauty of Earth full of wealth and grains;
She kept singing a sprouting mysterious sweet melody in soft tunes.

Exhilarated in mind, jubilant in body, Looking at unperturbed nature;
Looking at flame of soberness, Evaluating sparrow hawk's chasteness.

Keeping abreast fragrance of bosom, looking at fragrance of tune;
Amused in instant, blemished in time flash,
She keeps singing on 'Madhu' lips.

6. Anticipated excited wave * 191/26.11.08

Anticipated excited wave of life in existence,
Ever new experience and prick of bliss;
Thrilled mind of sweet court space,
Glee lamp of glow of existence.

Sing sweetly dance delightfully,
Life stream may illuminate three worlds wholly;
Meditate charming Krs'n'a* in temple of conscience,
O Onlooker of Radha*! Come to three worlds.

Enshrining in every pour of Radha,
Rehabilitating in forest of Barasa'na'*;
Intermingling in yogurt of Gopii's* conscience,
You are eternally confidential nectar of existence.

In the spiritually playful mind of Gopii*,
In the elated body of Gopa*, in the naughty look of Radha,
In the Madhuvan* like forest of mind of Shyama'*.

In the youthfulness of human mind, in the charming look of bird;
In the sweet look of mother, in the enthralling thrill of devotion.

The life garden of decked 'Madhu' heart,
Mind charming tune of Krs'n'a's flute,
Attractive sound of brown cloudiness,
Om sound of Lord's vastness.

6 E. Madhu Couplet * 469A/01.08.09

O Sun! Climates change just with
Little change in you or your planets;
Days and nights shape with tour of your planets.

A little anger of yours may banish a planet;
A little love of yours may entangle a planet.

7. There is enough base ground * 192/26.11.08

There is enough base ground, creatures are articulated,
And Sun in nature is eagerly enthused;
Vigorousness & ancientness is blissful, human melody is elated.

Proceed profusely penetrating precincts,
Touch sky standing on terrains;
'Madhu' flower* is vibrated by terrains,
Enlightened like Milky Way are skies.

In the melody and tune of bliss, in the hierarchy of creation,
In the auspicious conduct of coordinated cooperation,
In the reflection of every sunbeam;
There is sweet expectation and trance, mind is full of confidence,
Exhale is full of firmness, sky of heart is without pretence.

There is focussed participation, resolution,
Resourcefulness and capability to mend,
Simplicity of adorned mind, brilliancy of irrigated heart;
Uneasiness of flickering heart, quickness of Chan'akya@ mind,
Whiteness of illuminated mind, newness of nectar of bliss in mind.

----

* Flower = Enlightened mind;
@ Chan'akya= A highly evolved innovatory king.

8. Elated, thrilled and awesome * 193/26.11.08

Elated, thrilled and awesome is body,
Like nimbus of gem it is in ecstasy of bliss;
Blissful mind is thrilled by existence,
Fragrant are flowers and bliss is intense.

My mind is in Om* bliss, in auspicious tune is life's fragrance,
It is vigorously driven by reactive momentum of past lives,
It is served by reactive momentum,
It is satiated with 'Madhu' sweetness.

Air flows from Malayaj* hills, clouds echo melody,
There is adequate nectar in clouds body;
Perception of bliss is sweet,
Body is sinuous, ever put and pubescent.

You are yourself adorned by bliss,
Earth is blessed by enormous bliss;
You are yourself Soham*, You are fearless with blissful boon,
Your heart is full of nectar, You look like Shiva*.

You are Goaded by Dharma*, engaged in Karma*,
You roam drinking poison,
You uphold Earth, the base of elements,
You uphold creation becoming Soham'* in bliss.

9. Flowers are magnificent * 195/26.11.08

Flowers * are charming, pleasant and beautiful,
The realized mind is sweet and simple;
Eyes in deep trance are blissful,
The conscious pinch liberates survival.

Mind is elated, body is thrilled,
Earth rushes and breeze is excited;
Sky surrounded in bliss catches
Dream with eyes closed.

Cosmic mind is thrilled in bliss,
Integrated mind is free from doubts;
Human mind is vibrated with hopes,
Sentient human is enthralled by bliss.

Yogi* engaged in sentient work is busy,
Chanting melody, stream is uneasy;
Mind surrendered in faith is steady,
Moments without sufferings are full of glee.

Cosmos sings, universe dances,
Elegant sun eagerly envelops;
Glittering moonlight triggers horns,
'Madhu' night dances becoming congenial.

10. How many centuries have passed * 308/20.05.09

How many centuries have passed,
neither You arrived nor I reached;
How much have stars glittered, how much Earth has rushed round.

How many skies have gazed me,
How many waters have irrigated me;
How many birds have chirped, how many lions have roared.

How much is humanity spread, how much demons have refined;
Body of many a stones have become blossom
In extrovert cycle of creation.

You didn't come in my heart,
I couldn't find tunes, I couldn't reminiscence;
In this jangle of breathes, I couldn't relish weather cycles,
I didn't acquire swiftness.

Master of ocean of love appears to have become restless,
Melody is emanating with fragrance;
In the illusion of body, Mohan* is looking at
Ra'dha'* in 'Madhu' mind.

10E. Madhu Couplet * 469DE/01.08.09

Is space not part of You?
Is time not a component of Yours?
Is every entity not part of You?

Is every time place person not You?
Is space not an entity? Is entity not a space?
Is time not a space? Is space not a time?

11. O beloved, I remained as if adoring * 312/20.05.09

O beloved, I remained as if adoring,
'Madhu' sky kept like raining;
This garden remained as if desiring,
This flower kept like longing.

Creature could not get awakened yet,
Slumber is not going out of heart;
Fear is in heart, affability is not coming in heart.

O beloved, you sing new succulent tune, craft a fresh creation;
Color this colourful brain, affection may spread on terrain.

I kept like dancing all through life;
I kept trembling through out dream;
Sun kept rising unobserved in life,
Night kept weeping without outcome.

O beloved, fill fragrance in blossom,
Evening may happen to sing sweet poem;
Breeze may dance on music of waves clapping,
Dawn may get tune in breathing.

12. Adorned pearl of dust of Earth * 163/23.09.08

You are adorned pearl of dust of Earth!
You are eternal sound of evolved life!
You are sweet crystal of diamond
Of bottom of ocean of life;
You are blissful boat of life.

You are self-conscious ray of bosom of sky,
You are new drop emerging from heavens;
You are a frozen, introverted,
Sobbed and thrilled wave of blissful Ganges.

You are flowered, enlightened, fragranced,
Showered and blissfully sung majestic tune;
You are a thrilled wave of melody;
You are a fragrant dream of continuation.

I don't know and I don't believe,
I only know listening to tune of life;
I only go on saying, hearing and singing
Melodious stories of life.

You come, O honey, you come!
You give flow to springs of life;
You give bliss on Earth!
Take along nectar of bliss of life.

13. O 'Madhu' if you come by! * 28/03.04.08

O 'Madhu'*, if you come by!
We may fill color in lives!

We may fill melody, rhythm and songs in all three worlds;
We may fill beauty, flow and fragrance in every conscience.

Thirst and hunger may get banished,
World may get glittered;
Bodies may get spirited,
Minds may integrate in 'self' to get established.

We may work, meditate and fill devotion in lives;
We may fulfill hopes and aspirations
In world and its persons.

The languages may get filled with passions,
Every life may be able to speak what is in conscience;
Every mind may be able to listen and notice;
Every heart may be able to bear the confines.

Inferiority complexes may get eradicated,
Bitterness may get shared;
Minds and consciousness may not get traumatized,
They may become blissful and vibrated.
The love of creator may get manifested
In every particle of world!

Every particle of Earth may get pleased,
Every flower may get bloomed;
Animals may happily tread,
Every fibre may get vibrated.

You come! Come now candid!
You be there in full in whole world;
Majestically move and roam in cosmic mind,
In mind of atom, in world and lives.

14. You are potency of manliness! * 29/04.04.08

You are potency of manliness; I am bounded by nature's dutifulness;
Adorned by cloud, you are kindliness; I am she peacock's sweetness.

I am freakish fluctuating deftness,
You are deep obscure charismatic Shya'ma*;
I am attached or detached goaded by Karma*,
You are detached to mind goaded by Dharma*.

You naturalize nature; I am goaded by nature's action;
Nature, to me, looks like a creation of some one,
It springs in you like Your own configuration.

Worried, scared, offended and agonized, I move in this world;
Drinking poison, smiling strangely, You roam in cosmos in freedom!

You move carrying dust of Earth; I keep collecting flowers of Earth.
Blend my flowers in your earth;
Taking nature in your lap, O Lord! Make it sleep!

15. You sing 'Madhu' sonnet * 53/08.05.08

You sing 'Madhu' sonnet, O kind hearted! Take mind in Your heart.
You sing a deep melody; take me now in blissful delight.

Taking mind in sky, you flow far off;
You make melody of my heart, the Milky Way.
You go on and flow in tune of bliss;
Take me closer to beloved, You take me close by.

You make me flow in World River;
Making me sweet bee, make me foxtrot.
O kind hearted, you see my heart!
You make me dance on sweet tune of flute.

Making me your medium, You sing songs;
Becoming Ganges, You sink me in sweetness.
Take my mind while vibrating it;
You take me engrossed in sonnet?

16. You make peacock dance in cloud
* 30/04.04.08

You make peacock dance in cloud, O Lord!
Thrilling the nature You mould new world!

May sweet languages flow in every throat ravine!
May throats remain in bliss in heaven!

May every flower bloom with fragrance and pollen!
May mind be free & fearless, may conscience be clean!
Make nectar flow on terrain!

Minds may dance; humans may remain in blissful mood;
Beauty of creation may remain unique and un-deteriorated.

Creatures may thrill in life's splendours;
Nectar may rain in monsoon month from dark clouds.
River of Ganges may again flow from Shiva's* matted hairs.

Remove pollution of mind and body;
Adorn water and forests, make air flow in thrilled sky.

In crude, creatures and world let liberated streams flow;
Make buds blossom by melody of female crow!

Take away dogma from human race,
Save faiths from whims;
Make world broad and behave nice.

Allocate apt wealth to all 'Madhu's,
Becoming cosmic watercourse;
You make every one gush, O Lord!

17. Macrocosm thrives with credence
* 586/ 02.11.09

Macrocosm thrives with credence;
'He' alone gives open and overt conscience.
He fills variety in universe;
'Self' itself on dispersing becomes cosmos.

In the roving features of cosmos,
In the opening caves of life breathes;
In enthralling over-flowing intense clouds,
In amiable thrilling gestures.

The creator of cosmos permeates in;
He controls it all on His own;
He keeps revolving stars and moon;
He alone vibrates atom and microvitum.

The consciousness intuitively teaches
In ever chirping life, how to always move on;
In evolving experiments of nature,
In re-treating peep- holes of degeneration.

The cosmos disseminates and rises every flash;
It accelerates with unique swiftness;
'Madhu' always remains witness,
While keeping liberator of creation
In his conscience.

18. Grace gets showered on doves
* 575/22.10.09

Grace gets showered on doves;
Dense cloud gets brightened in light of moon;
Weakened body gets bloomed in,
Benign mind gets wave of devotion.

On cheeks surrounded by imagination,
Compassionate body blooms young children;
Golden lotus like body of Krs'n'a removes all pain,
It liberates from mirage of mind soon.

The crow is not able to tell his
Painful and bitter story of forests;
In the hesitant eyes of deer,
There are so many stories in kohl of her eyes.

Pressure of sufferings is acrid,
Care taking of sandals is hard;
Effusion of fetters may be restricted,
Liberation comes through vibration of Lord.

Drop of Shvati* at times gets dropped,
Conch shell blooms becoming pearl;
The cheeks get bloomed in
Buds get blossomed in 'Madhu' garden.

19. You are stretch of infinity
* 21/28.03.08

You are stretch of infinity;
I am 'Madhu' depth of world in mobility.
Time, space and entities are Your dimensions;
Sentience, mutability and stativity are
Exhale of Your nature's existence.

Mahata*, Aham* and Citta* are
Waves of Your management attributes.
Five elements are Your assets;
Creatures created by nature are Your descendants.

After dissociating creature from time, place & persons,
Whenever, You merge them in Yourselves;
You create Yourself in void of creatures,
World gets garlanded with glitter of five elements.

You create in each of Your styles & attributes,
You create mysterious creatures in every layer of five elements.
You create within You forests, animals, humans and sentient ones;
All move & develop in and out of people in cosmos.

You create introvert after creating extrovert cycle of creation;
Merging sentient in Yourself, You get creation done.

In every moment, every place and
Every entity of creation, You create;
New creation, new passion, new melody,
New wave & new profundity.

20. In your effulgence, O Lord!
* 42/22.04.08

How many glows came in your effulgence, O Lord!
In your noiseless night, how many stars glittered!
Sitting in corner, my mind could not see and understand.

How many sparks got ignited while getting put out?
How many souls got up from void of funeral or vault?
How many insects got liberated in love of light?
How many creatures got enlightened in keeping others alight?

How many creatures you create in your nature!
You take care of their thirst and hunger.
You give blood and fluid to each cell of creature;
Still you let one creature take life of other.

Some time, I feel, why don't you do
This play of Yours by some other process!
Why You make dance so many unique hapless souls?
Why You time and again give pain of
Expiring and shrinking to every consciousness.

You, probably, evaluate perception and activity of
each life of consciousness;
You again sow that life spirit in creation afresh.

You grow crop of Tantra* of consciousness in Yantra# of body,
Sowing seed of 'Madhu' Mantra in mind's perception, at times,
You keep emancipated seeds in your heart fortitude!

21. Traveller of infinity
* 11/27.03.08

O Lord!   I am traveller of infinity;
You are my witness, my co-traveller!

How many agonies voyage in world?
How many flowers are dispersed over your head?
You give compassion to so many buds?
Many thorns, You get removed?

You keep moving, let all moving,
Make smile, laugh and motivating;
At times, You make them weep,
At other times, You make them sleep.
You make tremble in love
And at times, You make them laugh in wrath.

Your divine play sometimes gets understood;
At times even when it is known, it turn out to be weird.
Sometimes, you look ever kind;
At times you look alone, wayfarer and unkind.

Sometimes, You let creatures roam unconditionally;
At times, entangling their each sense closely,
You let the life and mind drift away obscurely.

Some times, you take away all their effects
and while keeping it all safe in Your heart;
You let them beg and bizarrely approach
For a gracious gift!

At times, sitting on their pineal gland upfront,
You shower 'Madhu' grace and
Make them great for ever!

22. Un-manifested entity
* 56/13.05.08

The un-manifested entity creates creation while manifesting;
The nature emerges as its organization managing.

A balance is established in trigonometric attributes of nature;
Sentient, mutative & static attributes maintain equilibrium.

Whenever, equilibrium in three attributes get un-stabilized;
The nature gets activated in extrovert cycle of creation
To improve management of created world.

The manifested entity takes form of Mahat*,
When the created organization develops more;
Mahat* creates Aham*.

As per need of situation, Aham creates Chitta*,
Mahat, Aham and Chitta control cosmic establishment;
The nature keeps improving in art of management,
The manifested becomes duet and then infinite.

The control of nature of manifested
Increases development in creation;
The manifested Himself gets evolved and emerges
In infinite positions and dimensions of administration.

The expansion of creation of manifested gives
'Madhu' velocity to extrovert cycle of creation;
The style of management of His nature gives
Growth to creation in making.

23. Infinite creator * 14/27.03.08

You are infinite creator of time, space, entities, conscience;
Nature of three attributes* and manifested
Cosmic consciousness.

Your solid, liquid, fire, air and ether factors
Are adorned by five elements.
The mind stuff of Yours after getting grieved
By bang of solid particles;
Gradually creates plants, animals,
Humans and sentient ones.

Yogi interacts with Your manifested;
Your manifest cosmic entity integrates
With cascade of creation.

Yogi merges in cosmic entity un-manifested
While being amused and thrilled.
Un-manifested again becomes manifested,
And a new nature gets created.
The creation while heartening and flowing creates
New creation, Internal & external creation.

Our creation creates entities in space at times;
Time, place & persons happen to dance
With this play of Yours.
Amazed nature becomes blissful
And three attributes get set in gestures.

The depth of un-manifested creates attributes;
It happens to get every entity endeavour in
Each space & time coordinates.

The qualities on expanding and evolving extreme,
Happen to understand quality of un-manifested supreme;
You enjoy nectar of bliss of your Devine sport
While sitting in 'Madhu' conscience.

24. Mahat of Manifested * 57/13.05.08

Mahat of manifested became Aham,
Aham became Chitta;
Every Chitta created its own sky around.

The air flew in each sky, air became fire,
And fire became liquid, liquid became solid;
The world of five fundamental factors was created.

When solid particles of earth vehemently clashed,
Chitta in some solid particle of earth got invoked;
Plants were created out of   clash of solid particles,
The clash in plants created animals.

Animals developed, clashed and created human;
The humans through development and clash
Became intellectual human.

The intellectual human with clash and cohesion,
Became spiritual human,
He recognized Manifested, un-manifested,
Nature and cycle of creation.

Ultimately, spiritual human merged
His mind in manifested;
After deep meditation he surrendered
In manifested and un-manifested.
Manifested developed this newly surrendered
Man to manage created world.

He again created creation of manifested,
Mahat Aham, Chitta, five elements, plants, animals,
Humans and ones spiritually evolved.

Cycles of cycles of creation were created,
Entities became manifested, un-manifested.
Many 'Madhu' streams of bliss flew,
Some Godly entities manifested.

25. When You will do what? * 13/27.03.08

When You will do what? Why You will do what to whom?
My mind   bounded by time, place and persons,
Is not able to comprehend and stand Your divine game.

I am not able to see time of place and persons;
Place of time and persons, persons of place and time;
You are able to see time place & persons,
You shake and vibrate them in Your tune.

You create place and persons at some 'Madhu' time,
Place in place, person in person, time in time.
Or You merge them all in Your own theme!

26. On getting established in yoga * 61/13.05.08

On getting established in yoga, one feels like
Getting opportunity to go deep into knowledge of Tantra;
The practice of accelerated experiment with yoga,
And gracious direction of creator brings close to Tantra.

On being established in Tantra,
One gets capacity of general management of creation;
By regular practice and devotion, one gets more bliss in serving creation.

On getting established in Yoga and Tantra,
Devotion becomes more strengthened,
Faith and confidence in creator gets more amplified;
Wisdom and work remain tuned to Yoga wholly surrendered.
Devotion vibrated by Tantra, remains solely capitulated.

When Devotion, wisdom, work, Yoga and Tantra attain stabilization,
Creator may grace or merge one in Him;
He may give him more responsibility in His creation;
He may take consequences of all his reactive momentum on Himself.

At appropriate time, later, He may grant 'Madhu' man emancipation*;
Some time, He may give him, sweet work of controlling
His cycles of creation.

27. Appraiser and examiner * 12/27.03.08

How amazing an appraiser and examiner, You are!
You are vital, established and experimenting
Observer, manager and entrepreneur.

Though Yoga, You create retreat and union,
By utilizing nature, You arrange situation;
While, appearing non-observer, non-creator & unknown,
You impart acceleration to vistas of creation.

Some times, You let creation sleep in Your lap in tune,
At times, while letting it sit in Your heart,
You synchronise tone.

Some times, You smile in subconscious mind in tune,
You thrill 'Madhu' created beings of creation with exultation.
Some times, transcending with Your sharp vision,
You sprout conscience of Your progeny in line.

28. Is time relative dimension of creation! * 68/21.05.08

Is the time relative dimension of creation!
Is the time sibling of place and person!

Is the time path wave of probability!
Is time a line in between eternity and infinity!
Is time tune of creation!
Has the time emerged from manifested consciousness!

While merging in manifested, can humans pierce time!
Can humans peep into time of place!
Can he see past and future of entities!

Is manifested controller of time! Is cosmic mind visionary of time!
Can 'Madhu' human freely walk in place, persons and time;
By integrating his mind to Cosmic mind at any time!

29. Waves of time, place and persons * 69/21.05.08

Tune waves of time place and persons,
Are vibrated by Cosmic consciousness.

Infinite entities are in play in
Infinite places at infinite times,
They are in rhythm, vibration,
Thrill and bliss.

The path of satellite orbiting Earth,
Appears to be a straight line from space;
Time of creation is similarly organized,
In between eternity and infinity
In consciousness.

Cosmic mind can assess, measure and leap,
Movement of cycle of time;
It can peep into, jolt,
Accelerate and vibrate time.

Cosmic mind well organizes 'Madhu' creatures,
Organizes and expands spaces;
Relative movement of time, it organizes,
In management of creation,
It infuses progressiveness.
***

29 E. Madhu Couplet * 470B/01.08.09

Is He not the only one in every one?
Is He not the only one
In their actions and creations?

Is He not in their motivity of actions?
Is He not in the space of their minds?

30. Subtle action of Cosmic mind * 70/23.05.08

The subtle action of dynamic
Cosmic mind gives bliss to cosmos.

Like, the ball thrown by a child
In a moving train gives pleasure to passengers;
After emerging out of windows,
Same ball may give pain or bliss,
To travelers walking on their pathways.

The same ball on exiting out of Earth's orbit,
Can damage a vehicle situated in space orbit;
Or it may cause to set it in some other orbit.

The subtle movement of ball
Thrown in moving train,
On going out in atmosphere,
Emerges at velocity more than that of train.

Same ball on exiting to space
Emerges at a velocity greater than
That of Earth in space.

The subtle 'Madhu' action of
Cosmic conscience,
Similarly, vibrates and thrills
Five elements and creatures;
It controls and vibrates cosmos,
It gives thrill and bliss to creatures.

31. Capacity of management of creation * 76/28.05.08

Awesome is capacity of Your management of creation!
Mysterious is your efficiency of control and administration!

Your creating creation by becoming manifested,
From un-manifested and then becoming infinity yourselves;
Creating Aham Citta and five elements in Mahata.

Making unicellular and then multi cellular creatures from solid particles;
Merging into your own self even complex minds of humans.

Motivating every creature in extrovert cycle of creation towards progress;
Your encouraging entities at every time and space.

Listening to story of mind of every creature;
Giving direction to every 'Madhu' heart centre.
Understanding clandestine of death of every creature;
Giving birth after birth to every creature.

32. Management training of creation * 77/28.05.08

How mysterious is Your training
Every conscience in management of creation!

Your teaching humans for ages knowledge, science, languages,
Arts, spirituality, life style, social administration & politics;
Educating and training in communication, travel,
Space journey & management of cosmos,
Developing and controlling static
and conscious powers of humans.

Establishing and making expert the individuals and societies,
In social cycles of exploited, warriors, intellectuals and merchants;
Taking science to spirituality, making spirituality scientific.

Giving good situation and opportunity to every 'Madhu' creature,
For full development and fulfillment for developing creation;
On their being or not being keenly interested
In development of creation,
Merging them in Your configuration.

33. Attraction of gravity * 86/05.06.08

Attraction of gravity is naturally built-in,
Gravity determines consequence,
Movement and disposition;
Creation moves due to gravity,
Universe progresses due to gravity.

Gravity of Earth binds
Five fundamental factors aspect,
Plants, animals, human and sentient;
Strength of movement is bound by gravity,
In control of it remain mobile creatures,
Humans and sentient.

Multiplication of masses, mutual distance,
Proportionate gravity's attraction;
Every traveller moving from darkness to light,
Struggles with static, worldly
And sentient attraction.

Spaceships moved by human intellect cross over
Field of gravity at proper angle and velocity;
They return in spaceship after fulfilling their mission,
Coming across 'Madhu' gravity.

34. Gravity of Guru's grandeur * 87/05.06.08

Attraction of great is full of grandeur!
Gravity determines importance,
Movement and disposition.

Guru's grandeur and value motivates,
Surrender of disciple, his movement towards Guru;
Offering and devotion to Guru helps disciple
Beget grace and bowing for Guru.

Guru and disciple attract each other,
Depending on quantum,
Disposition and state of perception;
They attract universe by passion,
They also vibrate and thrill world by devotion.

Aim of discipline is Guru,
Uprising and profound gravity
Of discipline becomes grandeur;
Guru's gravity becomes plain attachment,
While becoming subtle, innate,
Compassionate and grandeur.

Gravity is 'Madhu' truth of creation;
Gravity is grandeur of creation;
Guru is great while having gravity,
Disciple becomes progressive
Owing to gravity in action.

35. Gravity * 88/06.06.08

Attraction of grandeur is gravity.
Coming back of ball thrown up amidst Earth's lap;
Is like home coming and lying in lap of mother
Of a child returning after play.

Playing of insects with source of flood light in fervour;
Continuous gazing of moon by moon bird* in love tender,
Turning of sunflower towards Sun forever.

Coming back of young generation to uphold
Family values after worldly influence;
Coming back of disciple to Guru
After lack of attachment towards Guru's vehemence.

Sleeping on earth in sentient pursuits,
Prostrating to Guru by disciples;
Mother's breast feeding in childhood,
Childlikeness of old after understanding existence.

Goading from darkness to light,
Prompting from crude to subtle stage point;
Is administered by 'Madhu'* peek of Guru,
Like organization of cycle of creation
By cosmic manifested entity*.

36. Mutual love of microvita * 89/06.06.08

Mutual Love of every microvitum of creation is gravity;
Quantum of gravity of entities,
Mutual disposition distances and conditions
Are parameters to measure force of gravity.

Pervading conscience in every microvitum
Attracts all conscience;
They motivate encourage and vibrate
Their vibrated movement in resonance.

Self qualified manifest in creation
Observes and oversees his creation.
It gives and takes eternal bliss
To and from his own organs,
By his own organs in pervading creation.

While calling and catalyzing,
Manifest attracts all conscience,
By his own body, mind and consciousness;
All creatures also attract manifest by their
Physical, mental and spiritual feelings.

Responding to clarion call
And expression of manifest,
Five fundamental factors, plants,
Creatures and great humans happen to dart;
While dancing in their orbits over their axis
Or breaking or changing limitations.

Physical mental and spiritual quantum of entities,
Their physical mental and spiritual distances;
Equilibrium of physical, psychic
And spiritual forces of creation,
Control position, movements
And 'Madhu' values of entity.

37. Every moment of mine is rhythm * 117/27.06.08

Every moment of mine is rhythm of infinite,
my existence is bliss of infinite;
My every part is abode of infinite,
my personality is poetry of infinite.

I am inseparable existence of all pervading,
I am eternal form of Omnipresent;
I am eternal link of infinite relations of
Beginning-less infinite,
I am inseparable existence of Omniscient.

Consciousness is witness of
Continuity of time and space,
Conscience measures distances of relations
Of observer and observed by space.

Consciousness measures
Difference of experience by time.
Time is, however, only an idea,
Its perception is realized or expressed
By bliss of consciousness.

"Cosmic consciousness is truth;
World is relative truth";
'Whatever is in body is in Cosmos' is truth.

Whatever is in creature's conscience,
Same exists in Cosmic conscience;
'Madhu' consciousness which is mine,
Is just one of His infinite.

38. O king of Braja* * 52/08.05.08

O king of Braja* invigorating my intellect,
You keep hovering 'Madhu' heart;
Becoming air You keep flowing out,
You keep ignorance busking out.

You are gracious, You are wisdom,
and You are tune and melody of bliss;
You are colourful sweet appearance and reflection of bliss.
You are science full of optimism, You are spiritual wisdom;
You are catalyst of bliss, You are glow of meditation.

You are fondness of gracious, You are fortune of wisdom;
You are controller of fervour, You are melody of charm.
You are fragrance of flowers, You are bliss of wisdom;
You are wisdom of science, You are science of insight.

39. Am I not perception of bliss! * 123/28.06.08

Am I not perception of bliss! Am I not a form of bliss!
Are my moments not incorporated in creation!
Don't I occupy a place in cosmos!

Does not polar star thrill my conscience?
Am I not in bliss in cosmos!
Are my plexus not blissful with touch of Guru!
Is my serpentine coil not blissful in love of Lord!
Does not Guru bless me at my pineal gland
with boon and fearlessness!
Does not Guru grace my consciousness!

You fill me with effulgence;
You yourself attract me unto you and fill me with bliss.
You merge 'Madhu' mind in You and put in trance.
Did You not bliss me by immersing my mind and consciousness?
Was it not Your un-contemplated unparallel grace?

40. Creation is His! * 8/19.03.08

Creation is His, yours and mine,
it is of all, in all and all are in creation.
We inhale what others exhale, We exhale which others inhale;
We throw our inner pollution away,
Every other creature picks it up considering life array.

This play of breathes, creates creation,
Experiment of five elements makes a good union;
'Madhu' grouping in nature creates great amalgamation,
Union of creature with Supreme is
creation's enormous incorporation.

41. Inseparable organ of infinite * 116/26.06.08

Are we not inseparable organ of infinite existence!
Is our physical body not integrated with cosmos!

Is our mind not in contact with cosmic mind!
Is our body not united with mind!
Are parts of our body not linked to system of flow & immune!
Are our heart and body parts not associated with brain!

Does n't our consciousness vibrates every moment!
Is n't that affected by changing situations of cosmic establishment!
Does not that vibrate like oceanic droplet!
Does n't cosmos care for consciousness every moment!

Each part of our body smears history of creation.
Each part of our body changes every instant.
Cells of our body are expert in self protection.
Cosmos comes, stays & goes as breath in our body every instant.

Our mind maintains balance in every motion of cosmos.
Our mind maintains equilibrium with every situation of cosmos.
Is n't our body form of mind!
Is n't our 'Madhu' mind authority of   cosmos!

42. Advait, Dvait, Advait! * 129/11.07.08

O Lord! Are you Dvait*! Are you Advait*!
Or you are Advait Dvait Advait!

Did you manifest into Dvait and
Then to infinity from un-manifested?
Did the entities of Your infinite creation merged in You
And became Advait or one with you again in end?

Realization of humans "I am the great & gracious",
Is their recognition of their own existence;
It is natural to get ego which then gets
Dissolved in Your conscience.

Fundamentally, humans happen to understand,
That mobile and immobile existence is Yours indeed.
Beyond "I am the great", they soon get realized;
That whole cosmos is like organs of the grand.

Like, we are able to some what understand;
Our father only after becoming father in world.
Similarly, creatures may be able to
Some what understand God;
Only after realizing, "I am great" indeed.

However, just as authorities and responsibilities
Get increased on becoming father or mother;
Authorities and responsibilities of humans get increased,
As soon as one realizes Your 'Madhu' grandeur.

----

* Dvait= Dual, Advait= Non Dual
(Refer Wikipedia for more information)

43. Perception and wisdom * 130/11.07.08

Perception and wisdom are
Stage of developing consciousness;
Unawareness and ignorance are
Natural stage of development oriented conscience.

Ignorance struggles with perception and bliss;
Spiritual knowledge adjusts with ignorance.
Ignorance increases vanity and impurities;
Spiritual knowledge brings devotion and grace.

We are not able to understand father
Without becoming father;
On becoming father, our own off-springs
Are not able to understand us.

This relative ignorance or spiritual erudition,
Is natural in management of creation.
'Madhu' wisdom does not come without ignorance;
Ignorance does not get understood
Without spiritual awareness.

44. Supreme consciousness * 115/26.06.08

The supreme consciousness is
Absolute existence all pervading.
He is the one and only creator,
Who enjoys and remains gratifying.

To observe Himself, the creator
Sometimes, becomes conscious observer;
Creator creates methods of observation,
Creates mind and intellect.

Body and world become prospect;
Observer, observed and backdrop become manifest.
Observer and observed create a mutual relation,
These relations get expressed as space;
Movements in relation create events,
Events show and illustrate time at instance.

Time, place and persons
Are localized eternal existence of consciousness;
Persons become prisoners of intelligence,
They start enjoying limited time and place.

Liberation of intellect is the only 'Madhu' key
To get liberated from world mobility.
Rather than, seeing reflection of reality,
Seeing reality is emancipating.

45. Creature is aware in heart
* 131/11.07.08

Creature is aware in his heart within,
That he is part of supreme one;
Perpetual struggle and progress time and again,
is his effort to meet supreme one.

First he feels lonely and is not able to
Interact with Cosmic Consciousness;
Later on after realizing," I am supreme",
He is not able to say it to others.

All in creation are indeed part of His own consciousness;
'All are supreme' is every one's own factual stance;
After realizing Him, why one may have fear or disgrace,
As all are His own like us.

He gives direction, showers affection and blessings,
On every one in whole creation like relatives;
He makes available our contributions
To every one in apt ways.

May we understand ourselves and all beings in creation!
May we engage in appropriate work, knowledge and devotion!
May we become 'Madhu' strong in Yoga Tantra and meditation!
May we understand and serve creator of creation!

46. Intimate vibration
* 135/11.08.08

O Lord! After receiving your intimate vibration,
Why some of your devotees are not able to remain plain?
Why do they start considering cosmos to be static,
While getting entangled in dogma or doctrine?

Why a little perception of Your management
Of creation makes their mindset poles apart?
Why they are not able to perceive & make out
Subtle play of your higher state?

Why they get entangled in sentient self-esteem?
Why they want to become liberator of creation?
Why they try to take Your authorities?
While forgetting You remain supreme?
Why they start considering Your creation
To be their paternal possession?

Probably, You also keep utilizing every one optimum!
You keep every one engaged in Your play until finale time;
You can pause play of life of any one at any time,
You can get started another play at the same time.

You can make king a begger;
You can give 'Madhu' responsibility of king to a begger;
You may reduce faith of some one who is believer,
A non believer may get full faith and realization.

47. Magnanimous Great! * 50/08.05.08

How magnanimous you are O Great!
How sweet are you O munificent!
How kind- heart you are O munificent!
How heart touching you are O Sweet Heart?

Becoming grandeur of universe,
You remain spread in cosmic sky!
In roving cosmos, You become Milky Way!

You move in sky full of creations carrying ray of day.
You keep irrigating Earth while raining from dense cloudy spray.

You keep moving in this universe, in cosmos;
You are in bliss of eternity, You are in this rhythm of bliss.

You become dream of world,
You become language of universe;
Come, if You can come by,
Sing a 'Madhu' song for me O munificent!

48. Sweet & Gracious! * 51/08.05.08

How sweet you are O gracious! How innate you are O gracious!
You are in the hopefulness of a sweet psyche;
You are in comedy and hobby.

You are in dance of peacock, You are in craving of moon bird;
You are dream and bliss,
You are sweet rhythm and 'Madhu' melodious.

Flowing Ganges of wisdom,
You started flowing from matte of Shiva;
Creating spiritual dance of Krs'n'a,
You happened to control Ka'lia' cobra .
Becoming sweet and coloured in shades of bliss,
You remained inhabited   every heart, becoming Ganges of bliss!

49. Creation organized by manifested * 58/13.05.08

The creation is organized by manifested;
Cycle of Creation is its organization.
The organization of time, place & persons
Is classification of its management administration.

Nature is executing passion of its management in-corporations;
Knowledge, work and devotion are
Performance measuring parameters of His persons.
The measure of mobility of action is time;
The creatures emerged out of clash of five elements are its person.

Cosmic conscience of manifested in body of space;
Utilizes Mahat Aham Chitta of persons to manage creation.
Time place persons are creation's dimensions;
Wisdom, work & devotion are dimensions of persons.

The manifested brings ongoing growth and creation's attributes;
He gets executed his organizational objectives
Through 'Madhu' persons in unison.

50. Ever new plays * 235/06.02.09

What all ever new plays You commence,
You give expression to conscience.
You give grandeur to skies, You mobilize airs.

You awaken creatures, give language to human conscience;
You turn conscious into subconscious,
You make subconscious express.

You give tune to spirituality, You liberate intellect;
You make seeds out of consciousness, You scatter those in cosmos.

In the illusion of cycles of creations,
In the tender body of sweet conscience,
You keep moving becoming seed of consciousness,
You 'Madhu' amuse natural cosmos.

51. In how much agony You are!
* 49/06.05.08

In how much agony you are O travelling being!

How many dawns came and went missing?
How many nights kept running?
You did not get bliss,
You kept moving and moving!

On this path of bliss, in body of your aspirations,
In the knot of quiet pains;
Will you be able to give a tune,
In the void of Lord's conscience?

On how many Earths you moved?
In how many waters you drifted?
How many flames you faced?
How many velocities of air you abided?

How many skies came and went off?
How many skies have seen you off?
How many skies silently watched you off?

Surrender in Lord's meditation,
Your knowledge, your Karma,
Your strength and your devotion;
Come near Lord in this tide
Of bliss, if you can!

Listen to song of my heart, O traveller of supreme!
Sing songs of His heart, O traveller of supreme!

Your agony is His, give it to Him,
Just give it to Him!
Bow your head in feet of Him,
O 'Madhu' traveller being!

52. Appraisal of wisdom, work & devotion * 60/13.05.08

The creator takes decision after measuring and assessing
Wisdom, work and devotion of creatures.

If it is excellent, He graces and promotes,
He gives control of five elements
And other beings to those upright creatures.

Before getting into middle level management of creation,
It is necessary to have wisdom and experience of Yoga.

Yoga is wisdom and experience
Of comprehensive management of organization;
Of acumen of Creator, nature, five elements,
Time, place and persons of creation.

Creature should not have attachment of positions and authorities,
When he gets opportunity of management of creation;
In a propitious situation, in administration of director of creation,
Only the serving of creation should be the object of action.

The creature involved in Yoga of management of creation,
Establish their knowledge work and devotion;
In 'Madhu' direction of creator, depending on sector of creation,
Manages entities and places during that time & circumstance.

53. Pronouncing before incarnating * 78/30.05.08

Hey Krs'n'a! Your act of informing the world in advance through
Ethereal pronouncing before incarnating;
Was that like inviting difficulties for you?
Or it was to ease Your work on coming?

By giving prior intimation to exploitative ruler,
You inflamed his propensities of fear;
And then after getting invoked his anger,
You goaded him into endeavour.
Showing his actions at world floor;
You let everyone know his real stature.

Tolerating and bearing attack of exploiter,
Over You and Your own persons;
Making exploiter unsuccessful and
'Madhu' controlling his actions.

Encouraging sentient ones,
While controlling crude forces;
Gradually getting exploitation crushed
Or surrendered in Your supreme spring.

54. Strange is Your coming * 78A/23.05.08

Strange is O Lord, Your coming, going and staying!
Extremely subtle remains, Your listening, saying and doing;
Special is as usual Your attraction,
Your repulsion, meeting or merging.
This is uniqueness of Your cosmic management playing.

Mysterious is Your cosmic play, Your development and
Control of creatures through intro and extrovert involvement.
You 'Madhu' direct creation in highly accelerated haste;
Your perpetually sprouting well managed entity
Always remains cognizant and waking.

55. Freedom from reactive momentum
* 79/30.05.08

Is it possible for creature indebted by
Reactive momentum of life,
To get free without grace of Lord!

Is the property inherited by
Rights of birth not that of Lord;
Is it not liable to be given to
Offspring in the end!

Our mind, conscience, body and breath
All is His indeed!
Our parents, village, country, world,
Our bringing-up, education, work;
Is all of that society indeed!

Love, relations, 'Madhu' situation and
State of time place and persons,
Are all apparatus bestowed to us by God!
To take work from us in creation of Lord.

56. Stage of human consciousness
* 71/23.05.08

Stage of human consciousness, situation of its place and time,
Situation of place, time and consciousness of other entities,
Stage of situation of humans in cycles of creations;
Gets work done from different entities,
At different times at different places.

'Madhu' Human can control time place & persons,
In well established stage of consciousness;
Amid convenient time, place & persons.
And in developed management stage of creations,
He can peep into time and attain all pervading consciousness;
He can acquire omniscience and spiritual authorities.

57. Available creatures in creation * 80/30.05.08

Creatures, status, money, and materials available in creation,
Are all first His and then afterwards
These are so called ours.

We ourselves are not ours, we are His,
Our breaths and faiths are all His.

Whatever we give, we may give to Him,
Whatever we take, we may take from Him;
We may try to give after taking.

After giving, we may ask for after conceding in Him,
If we can't give or take, we may give in to Him.

We may become link
And not the bitterness of 'Madhu' creation,
We may not get attached to inheritance,
We may organize and manage this donation of His.

Time changes, money comes and goes,
Good & bad time comes and goes;
Only behaviour remains in remembrance.

58. O Cosmic Manager! * 133/08.08.08

O Cosmic Manager!
Are the management systems of Your people,
Not yet vibrated by Your
Supra intuitive technology of management?

Are Your 'Madhu' humans
Still not freed from eight bondage?
Have they not understood art of Your management?

Are your humans, while immersing in ethics,
Still not bound by Your cosmic systems and traditions?

Have they still not become experts
In cosmic management science?
Could they not get established in
Devotion, karma and intelligence?

Why even the capable persons
Elected by people some time before,
Get diverted from their path after acquiring posts?
Why those promising ethics after a while forget ideals,
And start following path of greediness?

Why Your democracies are still entangled in nature?
Why Your ruling systems are mutative and static in nature?
Why sentience gets lured on acquiring a status?
Why statistic ones deflect sentience?

Now, You do not experiment with
Waned dust sprayed human race,
You free the Earth from
The corrupt and Hippocratic managers.

You support and make capable the sentient humans,
Vibrate and develop spiritual management technology, at once
While keeping Earth in Your heart.

59. Your inseparable dominance * 122/28.06.08

I am Your inseparable dominance; infinite is our province.
We are infinite from eternity; we are beginning of boundless.

We are traveller of infinite, we are special person of cosmos;
We are strength of infinite,
We are expressed 'Madhu' form of Godliness.

You are mine, I am Yours, all are ours, all are our own forms;
We're infinite, we're manifested and un-manifested forms,
We're five elements, forest, animals, humans, sentient ones.

60. Even while having wisdom   * 59/13.05.08

Even while having wisdom and doing Karma,
Devotion is dominant;
Even while having wisdom and devotion,
Karma is necessarily important.

Effort of creature to move
Towards Creator is his devotion;
Effort of creator to move towards creatures is
His grace sophistication.

Without devotion, fructification of wisdom
And work may not happen;
It is not necessary to be able to get grace,
Even while having devotion.

Whether creator may be able to
Shower grace depends on His situation.
He may be able to shower grace on 'Madhu'
Even without devotion;
It may take time in getting grace,
Even while having real spiritual attachment.

61. Horizon of my body * 121/28.06.08

Does the horizon of my body
Not mingle with that of cosmic world!
Does my mind not unite with cosmic mind!
Does my consciousness not comprehend Lord!

Doesn't the Sun make me bath! Doesn't the water make me bath!
Doesn't the air thrill me? Doesn't sky overwhelm me!
Doesn't my mind merge in your mind!

Doesn't my mind go beyond horizons of Your conscience!
Doesn't my mind go beyond horizons of cosmos!
Doesn't my mind perceive pain of Your pains!
Doesn't my 'Madhu' mind express Your bliss in world!

62. How many tunes I have articulated * 225/01.02.09

How many tunes I have articulated?
How many bosoms I have envisioned?
How many impediments I have pierced
How many agonies I have shared?

Why do you get aggrieved and perturbed?
Why don't you become blissful and dedicated?
Give sweet melody to humankind,
Why don't you emanate nectar of life hood?

In life, whenever, you get entangled and desolated;
You changed your sweet vision and you got better posed.
Whenever you came close to God,
Stream of life got crossed.

Why don't you get set in subtle vision,
Setting spirituality in mind?
Mould this cosmos in your heart and mind,
You 'Madhu' mould humankind!

Chapter 2.
Spiritual Management Science & Research

63. Contemplation and Plane * 521/21.09.09

All planes fly with contemplation,
Lives attached with plane get uplifted upon;
All planes get landed in contemplation,
Lives attached with plane get landed in.

The plane goes from ground through contemplation,
It goes while stopping and sparkling illumination;
Passenger gets vibrated in proficient sitting position,
They contemplate while flying and enjoying vibration.

All get surrendered while reaching the skies soon,
They are able to watch glamour of clouds by then;
They are able to take a glimpse of terrain,
They happen to taste authorities' of plane.

They are able to roam a bit in plane,
They are able to view horizons from windowpane;
They are able to see golden shimmer of Sun,
They smile seeing stars and Moon.

He happens to do same thing in plane of contemplation,
Conscience moves while consciousness is in observation;
Creation can be witnessed from space in isolation,
Savouring 'Madhu' of contemplation, life gets liberation.

64. Creation and Vision * 520/21.09.09

Creation does not get seen from environs,
Vision does not get focused on surroundings;
It is possible to see more after rising from terrains,
It is possible to see more from the skies.

Aeroplane appears huge on ground, it looks tiny in skies around;
The scene looks small from Earth,
From sky scene appears mammoth.

Whole Earth is visible from outer space,
creation is view-able in small appearance;
All precincts of space and persons
Are visible close piercing time in instance.

By going in vacuum of contemplation themselves,
creatures can pierce every space;
They are able to merge entities in their hearts,
They are able to themselves see what lies ahead in times.

Grandeur of creation then looks lovely,
Vision always focuses on sweet world amiably;
Earth appears awesome, capable and auspicious,
Creation pervading in space then looks 'Madhu' melodious.

65. You are eternal * 138/14.08.08

You are eternal, ever new and gorgeous,
Come and sing melodies of existence.
O blissful creature of Lord! Come and sing songs of your conscience.

You come in splendid form, sing while full in vehemence;
Show source of life, give life to source.
O witness of 'Madhu' adorned peacock! Don't go out of dreams;
Show today affection full of scientific aesthetics to humans.

Fill blissful aspirations in spirit and language of Earth's grace;
Flow blissful nectar in the eternal Om* sound of cosmos.

66. O beloved consciousness
* Madhu Giiti 1/ Comp. 1983

O beloved consciousness! Get up and awaken! Get up and waken!
Awaken O beloved consciousness! Get up O beloved
consciousness!

Both of us went to sleep in His lap,
And we got glided in that dreamlike creation.
How pragmatic used to appear that unreal dreamlike creation!
False & willpower created were whose viewer and vision!

We also once met in that dream,
We loved, built abodes, made and broke home;
And due to our reactive momentum,
We also happened to attack each other.

Once, I cried due to pain of your persecution!
'He' loved and patted me but then I could not sleep!

After awakening, I observe you are still asleep,
You are fearful, captivated and devoid of memory in sleep;
I pat you to awaken but you are afraid of even my embrace.

And you think that I may be retaliating to your attack of dream!
You, however, do not realize why any one
Will attack after awakening some one who attacked in dream.

Love or attack of dream is sweet perception for only rejoicing;
Every corner of awakened life is full of awakening.
It is cheerful, vibrating, blissful and thrilling.

This is why I chat and pat you,
Open your eyes, O 'Madhu' conscience!
Get up and awaken O beloved conscience!
Awaken O beloved conscience! Get up O beloved conscience!

67. Row of lamps is ablaze on earth * 566/16.10.09

Row of lamps is adorned on terrain,
Uncountable stars are cheery in heaven;
Flame of life breath is aflame in heart,
Wave of flame is vibrated in body and spirit.

O Lord, You come and ignite all lamps,
Initiating meditation glow make them conscious;
Diwali is friend of divine radiance,
Diwali is delight of all minds.

Lamps are lightened in homes,
Everyone awakens flame in hearts;
Minds of people of world get vibrated,
Consciousness of world gets piped.

Lamps give peace and bliss,
They give liveliness, yearning and ray of flash;
The flowers get exhilarated and pollinated,
Gardens get exulted budded.

Garland of lamps is offered to Lord,
Row of lamps is warmth of world;
Flame of living beings is grandeur of creation,
Glitter of 'Madhu' is flame of travelling terrain.

68. I ignite light in heart * 567/16.10.09

I ignite light in heart, I awaken melody in tone;
Why don't You ignite eternal light,
Why don't You sing in tune of water fall attune.

My festival of light is in You,
My festival of colors is with you;
My red color and secret thread is in your intellect,
My thread of protection is in your heart.

You are ever new master of play O Virtuous!
You are ever present, eternal and conscious;
You are vigorous source of bliss;
You are vivacious permeating all three Lokas.

I am lamp of Your bosom,
You are promoter of my tune;
I am glow of your reactive momentum;
You are eternal flame of my continuation.

Your lamps are in every one's heart,
Your tunes are in every one's heart;
I simply sing in Your tune,
All happen to listen in their 'Madhu' heart.

69. Creation of Lord * 6/19.03.08

How sweet and great is creation of creature in creation of Lord!
Is planning of creature not part of project of Lord?
Is the effort of creature not part of effort of lord?

Why some creatures want to break boundaries
Of time, place and entities?
Why don't they serve His entities
During His bestowed time in His cosmos?

Why do they create walls within
His affectionate unfathomable void?
Which get scattered on the bank of ocean
By blow of His air like sand?

By creating walls out of His five fundamental elements*;
He obstructs flow, down flow and uprising of five elements.
Making configurations in His universe,
They try to reduce dimension of His compositions.

They attempt to differentiate one
From another consciousness and get pains;
They face thrust of His nature on their creations,
They hurt their own minds, they agonize all in world.

Lord still aptly administers management,
Engineering and development of cosmos;
He 'Madhu' attempts to keep
All creatures elated and thrilled at all times;
While Himself remaining involved from
Within and without in creation widespread.

70. How many colors You have filled * 509/10.09.09

How many colors You have filled in existence,
You are filling 'Madhu' waves in every conscience;
You live in every inhale and exhale, You take along unknown trail.

Your wealth is beautiful, Your agonies are inimitable;
Your manifestation is unimaginable, Your gloominess is spiritual.

How much You knock over, How much relief You volunteer;
How many desires You inspire, How much entreaty You explore.

Every color is in wave of its own, waves are in colors of their own;
Everyday You fill aspiration, You always remain with every one.

You keep longing in every bosom,
You keep us singing in Your own tune;
In 'Madhu' amusing majesty of creation,
You keep pouring poems in every conscience.

71. Mysteries of mind * 26/02.04.08

Mysteries of mind are inimitable;
These are known & unknown, desirable & undesirable.

Peeping in eyes of every known and unknown creature;
We search our 'Him' in them, or search them in depth of our conscience.
All appear to have been met or interacted upon sometime somewhere;
We find relations, develop love, and share heartaches with each other.

We make relations and happen to do some thing together;
And at times, knowingly or unknowingly happen to squabble together.
We are not able to sleep few nights,
After returning from our own or foreign land;
We appear to be 'Madhu' affected by jet-lag, as believed.

However, is it not reaction of passions of our loving persons abroad!
They remember us in their days;
Our sleep goes off in our land in our nights even if undesirable.

72. Why don't you become unadorned! * 7/19.03.08

O being, why don't you become unadorned!
Why don't you get engrossed in His mind!
You do remain in creation in His mind,
Why don't you just play in His created world?

You will make home, plans and friends,
        If   they are irrigated with ego,
If they are not synchronous with created world;
They may get scattered, harmony will remain maintained,
We may   not be able to do any thing or say a word.

All our plans are His programming, our minds,
Conscience and bodies are as per His planning;
If these are not as per His plan, He may alter our planning.
His creation, five fundamental factors and nature
        Will playfully execute His planning.

Why don't we cooperate with Him!
Why don't I engage in Yoga* and attach with Him.
Why not we liberate myself and others through Tantra* of Supreme.
Why not we focus on Him in our meditation and prefer Him;
        Why not we prefer Him in our plans and
Get executed our own and His plans through Him.

Why not we prefer Him in Samadhi*;
And establish life in supreme stance?
Why not we enliven death and make bodies eternally marvellous;
        Why not we make His plans ours
And see Lord in 'Madhu' creatures so vivid?

73. Creatures in love * 27/02.04.08

The creatures become subservient in love,
They happen to cross boundaries of time, place & persons;
'Madhu' creature happens to get conceived in those instants,
The creation moves one generation ahead in those moments.
Loving creatures after becoming parents;
Happen to love hitherto unknown new one,
More than they love themselves.

Every new upcoming creature might be our ancestor,
He may grow big beholding our finger;
At times, however, behaving like grandfather, he can show us
finger.
Whatever pains or medicines we gave him,
He may react in same vein;
Becoming our own, he may give us pain,
An unknown may come and give medicine.

Some of his reactive momentum could be pure;
Some could be better or worse.
Some reactive momentum could come,
From pause in journey of his conscience;
Some new reactive momentum could come,
From his other experiences in this existence.

Whatever creatures we associated with in our infinite lives,
Who so ever creatures we got, came and gone,
Will come in future lives;
All vibrate our conscious waves,
Change our fervour, nature and lives.

That is why, world looks our own,
And at times it looks strange & alien;
All are our own, everyone is like dream person,
All are in mind, all are known.
Any one or all may come again, all are to go again;
All are some what familiar, all are some what mysterious.

74. Probability * 20/28.03.08

Probability is creation of harmonious passion;
Probability is shower of sentient passion.

Harmonious passion is possible by exchange of meditation,
Sentient passion gets created by engrossing into penance;
Meditation balances mind in body and spirit,
Tapa* cleanses body, mind and spirit.

In balanced mind, evolved body,
Conscience moves amidst people & world;
All become harmonious, sentient and possible in created world.
Creation happens in internal and external world.

Harmony comes from simplicity, by meeting of infinity and void;
By merging conscience with all, by merging of creator and created.
And then, all harmony and all sentient, crystallize creation of
Probability, success and 'Madhu' creation.

75. Attachment * 45/24.04.08

Attachment is propensity of love in creatures.
That may, however, be bounded by
Bondages of time place & persons.

A mother may sacrifice every thing in attachment of her child;
However, same mother may be ardour-less,
Unattached or cruel to other beings, persons or child.

In over attachment of country a person may even
Praise inferior products of one's country;
He may, however, not be able love all persons
At all times of that country.

With speedy tireless efforts and meditation;
Humans can free propensity of attachment from oppression.
One can transcend boundaries of time place & persons;
By making attachment sweet, one can become super human.

Becoming super human, one can love every time place and entity;
'Madhu' human can integrate attachment
Into tenderness of supreme stance.

76. When and how you do what * 72/28.05.08

I am not able to understand, when and how you do what.
I am not able to see sensitivity of your judicious clout.

You happen to see busy seller negotiating with buyer,
Holding apparatus in right hand at a shop or
Cart at railway crossing over;
While getting approved unaware bird held in left hand in care,
You are able to assess agony of innocent creature.

Probably, she does not know or stipulate that,
She will not remain alive after few moments later;
Busy and experienced seller is shy of seeing creature in eyes of her.
Probably Buyer only qualifies bulk and beauty of body of her;
Mind and consciousness of creature is irrelevant to buyer.

Seller gives packing her body devoid
Of consciousness to buyer aside;
Her wings, fingers, blood only left behind.
Her living conscience in moments becomes life devoid;
The conscience & body created and served,
By supreme father and nature get lost in void.

You see this cruel, unkind and barbarous act
Of human as 'Madhu' observer.
Probably after getting upset with that,
You get something done somewhere that moment.

77. Sensitivity of Your justice * 73/28.05.08

O Lord!   Sensitivity of Your justice!
Some what I am able to understand;
Some what I am not able to understand.

The deep silence of families of helpless innocent birds and animals,
Being brought in cages in vehicles arriving in city entries.
The clearly visible shadow of death in their eyes;
Their despair from human beings.

Fear of unknown future,
Their desolation from their elders departed earlier;
Their failure to understand what happened to their elders,
It all makes them hurt and heart-rending creatures.

Sitting in a vehicle at the back,
You understand their pains, you read death in their eyes.
However, in helplessness, you are also unable to do
Or say anything in those circumstances.

You just convey the pain of
Their 'Madhu' mind to supreme consciousness;
And You get some swift justice done to creatures around.

78. Your capacity of managing   cosmos* 74/28.05.08

Your capacity of managing cosmos is matchless;
Proficiency of your 'Madhu' administration is mysterious.

When even, great managers of your world,
Become silent and opposed to even fundamental calls of progeny.
When their matter and self centered minds do not listen to,
The demonstration, exile and requests of progeny
And request of Earth's tormented progeny.

Then Your managing nature may probably get terrain shaken;
It may happen to get air blown,
Rain precipitated and consciousness awakened.
To get their slumber removed,
Some thing awkward   may happen for instance.

79. In galaxy of eyes gazing us * 92/14.06.08

On spearheading road of city,
Every human being is absorbed in self;
He is busy in his mind somewhere,
He is somewhat alone in solitude,
Even amidst whole crowd around.

Every human traveling in bus
Is mysterious and alone in oneself;
He is in sort of meditation closing eyes,
Or is busy listening on ear phone.

Every one is unique, expressed, busy,
Expert and renowned in one self.
Still in crowd of unknown ones,
Every one is absorbed in one's own self.

Mind is absorbed in reactive momentum,
It is filled with flow of ideation.
Consciousness is in run aspiring for someone;
It is detached with soul sitting aside one.

Why not we consciously look at
'Madhu' creation napping within us,
We may see through mind, through eyes;
We may say or listen something and pour love,
Get free, give and take bliss.

Why not we look at consciously unknown ones
While getting attached;
Why not we see creator in galaxy of
Eyes gazing us and get   awakened?

80. Is n't Your every creature mysterious * 134/11.08.08

O Lord! Isn't Your every creature mysterious?
Are n't their form, nature, passion and language matchless?
Is Earth's human not awesome like alien of other planets?

Are all the elements of Earth not parts of cosmos?
Is continuous movement of human mind not amazing?
Is unfolding of human mind in so many layers not surprising?
Who molds and adorns us every day in new forms?
Who always keeps vibrating and motivating our thought waves?
Does every atom of countless galaxies
Play a Divine 'Madhu' sport with us?
Do all mobile and immobile entities
Make us smile and dance all the times?

81. Democracy * 75/28.05.08

Some of Your administrative domains
Running in the name of democracy and religious waves,
Become fearless because of apparent faith and firm credence;
Inappropriate selfish persons become rulers
In their narrow perimeter of time, place & persons,
You quickly uncover their concealed character,
Morality, mentality and conscience.

Their peripheral ad of affection for persons
Of family, caste, society and religions,
Their inner wrong notions of selfishness, money pilferage,
Exploitation, immoral character, corruption and atrocities;
Their thought of confusing cosmic breath in caves
Of country, states, districts & villages,
Their foul intention to ill rule by disquieting spiritual humans
Loving time, place and persons.

Momentous allurement of static enjoyment,
Attachment of posts, dogma & self centred powers,
May even astray good rulers
And You then awaken & catalyze good managers.

By motivating every one's 'Madhu' conscience by your nature,
You get the election done confusing mind of ruler;
You then change management of administration and ruler,
You vibrate good management of cycles of social plexuses.

82. Collective Decision * 152/04.09.08

Importance of collective decision in society is utmost valuable.
Getting personal decision approved by
Society is enormously appreciable.

Personal decision is resultant of state of our mind,
Body and consciousness.
The social blessings mature, reinforce,
Recognize & vibrate our conscious conclusions.

Decision of person and society made after mutual exchange,
Makes it balanced, well organized and well managed reality.
The collective decision taken in life,
Brings wave of bliss, success and spirituality.

More the decisions are simple and conscious
Together with consensus,
More the social success and spiritual progress are in pace.
The family and social decisions are usually mutually nice,
Appropriate, effective, beneficial and harmonious.

Consciousness may evolve, understand grace
And know value of grandeur.
It may recognize Supreme, understand value of blessings ??
And decide together.
It may bestow devotion & grace and fill
'Madhu' creation with bliss eternal.

83. Tandava * 141/15.08.08

Humanity is perturbed and exploited;
It's suspicious, fearful and terrorized.
O Lord! Reduce Tandava* fragment in the world;
Make minds of people and controllers heavenly wide.

May Human mind thrill, smile and enthuse!
May every one have education, food and house!
May there be no shortage of medicines and clothes!
May minds and conscience be sentient!

All faiths may have spiritual fondness,
Politics may learn good ethics;
Businessmen may have spiritual progression,
And perform with service passion.

Human beings may remain engaged in sentient career,
All may get perpetual purchasing power,
Inflation and bribery may expire;
Administrators and administered may remain in order.

O Lord! Awake every person, initiate their minds in meditation;
Make 'Madhu' Earth blissful, spiritually evolve and vibrate world,

84. O Bha'rata! You keep cosmos in bosom *
411/10.07.09

O Bha'rata! You keep cosmos in bosom,
Becoming Ganges you liberate cosmos;
Fill beauty and culture, being Bha'trat you prefer cosmos.

Let every one sing in tune and rhythm, let all dance in new melody;
Let every single one smile, let all give flow;
Let each one give pleasure, let every one give tune.

Pour current on Earth, eradicate hunger, give nectar to angst mind;
Keep demoniacal in their nerves, keep humanity in steadiness.

Help cosmos sing spiritual tune, make passions spiritual;
Move while integrating minds, move taking every one together.

Keep singing in 'Madhu' melody,
Take along minds of people and controllers;
Make Earth a family, make cosmos Bha'rat, the illustrious.

Bha'rat = One who fulfills= India, Arjun,
Bha'rat= offspring of Bharat

85. The speedily running aeroplane * 146/25.08.08

The speedily running aeroplane on its small wheels on runway,
Suddenly rises up and disappears in air, spearheading to sky way.
Tunes of aspirations of many a passenger gets thrilled,
While becoming doubtful, fearful, shaky and mystified.

The hopes of many onlookers get illuminated,
Hearing news of upcoming, many hearts get thrilled.
Observing planes frequently flying,
Aspirations of 'Madhu' mind appear flying;
Resolutions rushing incessantly from Earth to sky,
Appear to be shaking living and passing away.

86. Looking at persons coming to airport * 147/25.08.08

Looking at persons coming to airport to see off,
Seeing passengers being seen off;
Looking at minds of persons who came to welcome,
Seeing minds of passengers who came.
My mind suddenly gets touched by emotions
And bliss of their conscience.

However, at airport of life, 'Madhu' has to always witness,
Arrival and departure of planes and passengers;
While observing them like a witness,
I have to take care of their safety and convenience.

I have to see eternal in their hopes and despair,
I have to affectionately smile while occupied in service stir;
I have to 'Madhu' serve best possible and surrender,
Giving charge to some one at the end of the day & hour,
I have to go back to my 'own house' to restore when I take off!

87. In the seed of pears * 148/31.08.08

O Lord! Your keeping the seed in sweet fruit of pears so carefully;
Keeping original seed obscured in soil under huge tree so deeply!

Seed is sprouted under soil giving apt ambience
and it is made big tree gradually;
The original seed gets mingled with dust
and gets almost decayed invisibly,
The plant grows into big tree beating winter,
summer, snow and rain perpetually.

In spring, big tree begets leaves and flowers,
Many a lives and humans enjoy its shadow and fragrance;
By offering infinite fruits to birds animals and humans,
It makes them live sentient and conscious.
Even while suffering from so many pleasures and pains,
It remains in flow and bliss.

The tree becomes leave less at the knock of falls,
Enduring storms of snow, it looks for arrival of springs;
On arrival of suitable time, it again gets full of leaves,
White flowers bloom and fruits get manifestations.

Mysterious is the life of your seed, O Lord!
It goes underground and when time comes it grows into tree
upward;
It keeps offering optimum 'Madhu' fruits to creation continually,
The seeds within fruits get sprinkled in creation dexterously.

88. Heart touching history of seed? * 149/31.08.08

How heart touching is history of seed in fact?
How conscious pricking is its prospect?
Mystery of emergence of seed within fruit,
Eternally developing and becoming countless in many a fruit.

Could branches, leaves and fruits of the tree recognize seed?
Could those enjoying bliss and abode know
The grandeur, vastness and subtlety of seed?
Could the fruits also know future of seeds hidden inside?
Could flowers know the history of seed hidden underground?

Perpetual incarnation of seed into infinite manifestation,
Serving creation, while remaining engaged in creation;
While remaining unknown and invisible in organization,
It's engaging in infinite production.
It is like becoming creator in creation,
And go on playing 'Madhu' divine sport.

89. Blessing is Prasad of bliss * 151/04.09.08

Blessing is Prasad of bliss; blessing is exhale of confidence;
Blessing is invocation of pineal plexus,
Blessing is invitation to reliance.
By assuring expressly under sweet bliss,
The gracious consciousness envisages our pathways;
Our movement is accelerated and vibrated always,
By spiritual momentum of his consciousness in many ways.

May Lord make us capable of enjoying and imparting blessings!
May Earth be full of devotional passions!
May eternal stream of grace flow in cosmos!
May passion of grace full of grandeur keep showering us!
Passion of blessings is realized only after becoming gracious;
Passion of grandeur is able to bless
'Madhu' only on acquiring infinite bliss.

90. By experimenting on Big Bang * 155/10.09.08

By experimenting on Big bang,
Our scientists want to know God particle;
Is God, however, not Himself always eager
To make it known to all.

By keeping particles in accelerator up to two years,
By keeping temperature of   one hundred billion degrees
centigrade;
The particle physicists want to observe
Fundamental particle undivided.
However, will this experiment of humans
Spending dollar eight billion,
Be able to discover mysteries of matter, atom and God?

Is it possible to have existence of any organizational structure,
Even for a moment without its inherent creator?
Does n't every creature articulate cosmic particle and creator?
Don't we eternally witness
Cosmic management in each act of creator?

Can't the mystery of creation be visualized
Without big bang of particle?
Are the creatures not already experimenting
Every moment through psycho spiritual science,
Intuitionally perceiving mystery universal?
Are they not 'Madhu' administering
The management of creation overall?

91. By creating big bang on matter * 156/10.09.08

By creating big bang on matter, the scientists want to envision,
Undivided power of creator in particle subdivision;
However, is it not the same conscience?
Which is expressed and inherent in creation?

Source of psycho spiritual power is cosmic mind in action,
Black hole may exist in void of cosmic mind quiescent in action;
Sprouting of cosmic mind may cause big bang in particle or proton,
Resolution of cosmic mind may activate inauguration or dissolution.

The big bang experiment of scientists
May not be able to hurt creation;
Human blending or research and conscience
Every instant at each location,
Remain under control of cosmic mind managing creation.
The subtle holes or visible activities in void and dimension,
Of time, space & entities in creation are all His experimentation.

The human experiments with matter are undertaken,
To enhance physical psychic and spiritual wisdom
And cosmic co-ordination;
Capacity of human mind is limited and safeguarded in creation,
Every 'Madhu' experiment of science & spirituality
Reduces his distance from Supreme one.

92. Cosmos is manifestation of cause and effect
* 157/10.09.08

Cosmos is manifestation of function of cause and effect;
Theoretically, we should be able to make out
Complete through any of its component.

Just as we can recognize a tree by its original seed,
By its root, stem, branches, leaves, flowers and evolved seed;
It may be easier to recognize it by seed,
To grow and develop it through seed.

It may be easy to understand creation and creator's deeds,
Through age old & new human seeds;
It may be costly in terms of time, cost and efforts,
To understand it through matter or five elements.

Just as by trying to understand, work velocity and effect of humans,
It may not be easy to understand his mind, soul and resolutions;
Similarly, by trying to understand matter's velocity,
Situation and properties,
It may not be easy to comprehend creation and creator's deeds.

Easy approach may be to dissolve conscience into cosmic mind,
Sitting in mind and conscience of creator instant;
It may be possible to easily understand,
'Madhu' mysteries of creation and creator inherent.

93. God particle * 158/10.09.08

Conducting an experiment by scientists,
To recognize God particle created fifteen billion years before;
Trying to understand cosmic particle by accelerating particle;
Is it not their being so much behind schedule by particle physicists?

Only making this much effort by our science in so many years;
Our merely trying to understand ectoplasm and
Cosmic element through particle of creation;
Not being able to observe vastness of
Five elements and cosmic mind!
Science not being able to understand creator,
Creation and cosmic project!

Are there not enough cosmic managers in creation,
Who have understood it thousands of years back?
Who understand every particle, every mind and heart wave;
They excellently execute plans and projects of creator.

Can the creation be run without awakened and vibrated,
Exchange of creator, managers and organization!
Can the big bang our black hole get created or disabled
Without 'Madhu' knowledge of management of universe!

94. Emergency Phone * 185/13.11.08

Usually, we don't use emergency phone while having it;
However, supreme entity wants us to always remember it.
Whenever needed, we must use it.

To test us at a gate of our life, He may Himself happen to run over;
He may expect us to call Him on emergency phone, thereafter.

If we do not call Him, He may punish us;
He may send us for retraining for few days.
He may not utilize us in daily work for some days.

We do not talk to Lord daily while performing good work.
We don't feel need of telephoning or calling Him when we work.
Management of creation goes on
With every one doing excellent work.

However, He may Himself come to
Interact or evaluate us whenever;
We may go on awaiting and expecting Him within for ever.
'Madhu' must remain in contact with Lord for ever;
While remaining awake at the gate of meditation infinite.

95. Heartlessness of Your creatures!   * 201/19.12.08

O Lord! Heartlessness of Your creatures,
Painfulness of Your heart hurt by that;
Your uneasiness arising out of hurt by paucity of their passion,
Is perceived by serenity of 'Madhu' heart.

Their wrongdoing hurting creatures pinches human conscience;
Their crudeness deep-set in ego, ignorance
And decadence; terrorises cosmic sentience.

When Your greatness perturbed by unending torture,
Is unable to tolerate their demonic activity;
When your request and expression is unable to change their dogma,
You are compelled to call upon your cosmic control capability.

When Your service, work engagement,
Kindness and saneness of fervour,
Is not recognized by mind-set of every creature;
The footfall of Your Ta'nd'ava*, fire power of your cosmic anger;
Eradicates their demonic slumber and dust.

96. Vibration of your Ta'nd'ava! * 203/19.12.08

Vibration of your Ta'nd'ava,
Fills created cosmos with thrill, O Lord!
Causticity and torture of creation gets annihilated;
Every heart beat gets vibrated.

Whenever, human mind,
Absorbed in ego and disgrace, sinks in slumbering;
When it hurts mind of sentient, when it perturbs Lord's planning.

Sentient minds and conscience then get awakening;
They happen to surrender while singing,
Meditating and contemplating.
Intensive Lalita, Kaoshikii and Ta'nd'ava   start happening,
Lord enthrones and expresses through minds of sentient beings.

Lord does management reshuffling for improving values in creation,
He invokes extensive shaking and change in that instant;
He destroys deep slumber and darkness of creation,
Lord illuminates and thrills 'Madhu' mind.
***

96 E. Madhu Couplet * 85A ABC/03.06.08

Our science is not fully aware what anger of a microvitum can do!

We often observe expression of anger of microvitum over terrain;
By way of thunder, Katrina, Tsunamis, Earth quake and inundation.
Only the balanced and just action,
In the universal spirit is key to recognition;
That is what universal guideline is
For every person and organization.

97. Remaining in touch with creator * 186/13.11.08

It is odd for supreme entity to all of a sudden
Test management administration.
However, to test sensibility of a situation or someone;
It is His necessity to pass 'Madhu' creature through odd situation;

Every one should remain awake, dynamic and alert;
Every one should properly and carefully work and exert.
Even in the situation of supreme
Himself trying to breach management;
He expects us to inquire, stop and complain to top management.

It is not enough to merely work and serve creation of supreme,
We are expected to immediately report all odd befall to supreme;
We should call for all inappropriate actions
Undertaken by anyone or Him,
Remaining in touch with creator is
Need of creation directed by Supreme one.

***

97E. Madhu Couplet * 84A D/03.06.08

Your supervision is under His supervision,
Every action is controlled by cosmic vision;
Surrender mind, intellect, devotion and all your action,
Offer all your effects to all pervading cosmic Super Vision.

98. Your vastness * 202/19.12.08

O Lord! Your vastness, greatness and enormous heartiness;
Is not comprehensible by cosmic human beings.
Your kindness, charisma and saneness
Is not perceivable by crude mind of creatures.

Your ever vibrated compassionate kindness;
Human mind's unending infinite inappropriateness.
Your grandeur full of conscience, Karma and passion;
Their narrow outwardly self dissipation.

Your spontaneous sensitivity and eternal affection;
Their mentality of finding fault in Your cosmic vision.
Serenity of 'Madhu''s heart is hurt by their intellect;
Looking for dirt in Your Karmas infinite.

Unwillingly, You are compelled to activate;
You are made to experiment Your need and right.
You vibrate cosmic management from within and without;
Undertaking fusion and dissolution in creation,
You happen to pronounce.

99. My agony * 23/02.04.08

My agony, my story, my feature!
My dilemma, my hunger, my nectar!
You are redness of my heart; You are tears of my eyes;
You are aerial plexus of one in distress,
You are yourself tune of aerial plexus.

'Madhu' you sing songs, agony may move out;
Tune of eternal may resonate,
Aerial plexus may get tuned to pituitary plexus upbeat.
I go to sleep in your lap profound;
My mind gets lost in creation of your mind.
You come and caress my head,
Pineal gland of thousand petals gets awakened;
Ethereal plexus brings nectar spirited.

I get awakened, mind sprouts; agony gets dispersed, bliss overtakes.
My hunger becomes extraneous; dilemma becomes convenience.
My story becomes verse; my attributes become lore.

100. Fragrance * 322 AE/28.05.09

Elating in love, smiling sweet,
Fragrance swiftly kept surging sprinkled;
Affectionate, honourable, amiable,
Cool, watery, milky, patient and bold.

Fragrance profusely flowing from awakened consciousness,
Familiar fragrance of neo-humanism;
Fragrance emitting from consciousness of supreme cognition,
'Madhu' like fragrance of impetus of natural world.

101. Fluidity youthfulness * 320/28.05.09

In fluidity, youthfulness, sharpness and swiftness,
Dancing on rhythm, observing and assessing;
Amused mind of creature keeps nature peeping,
While measuring, testing, thrilling and trembling.

Amiability, research fullness, balance and equilibrium,
patience, depth, grandeur and sweetness;
Nature keeps moulding fragrance and liveliness,
profuseness, eloquence, breath poundings.

Dancing, jumping, alluring, tripping,
Man keeps moving moulding sweetness;
Roaming, amusing, and looking in skies,
Jumping on Earth, thrilling in fondness.

While dancing on peak, thrilling like snow, raining,
Scattering, craving, and agonizing;
Amused in mind, tormented in body,
Dancing on tune, observing new nature closing eye.

'Madhu' mind is able to realize depth of meditation
in grandeur of loving nature in peaceful brain;
Humanity tweets witnessing consciousness,
Cosmic man molds magnificence in universe.

102. Your remaining like a seed? * 150/31.08.08

O Lord! Your remaining like a seed in soil of cosmic acumen,
Sprouting, flowering, fructifying and developing creation;
While Your remaining hidden in creation,
Giving attributes and spirit to creation;
Flowering and fructifying every one,
On arrival of right time and situation.

Creating infinite seeds in infinite fruits,
Offering fruits to feed created creatures;
Getting seeds sprinkled all over creations,
Through creatures and five fundamental factors*,
Getting seeds sprouted in right environment and making trees.

Eternal is development of Your creation,
Mysterious is Your direction of conception;
Keeping most creatures engaged in
Enjoying bliss of life activity in creation;
Letting some creatures attempt to know within,
'Madhu' outline of Your causative cognition.

CHAPTER 3.   DEVOTION & GRACE

103. Take me along O beloved * 118/27.06.08

Take me along O beloved, take me!
Keeping my bosom in your heart, take me.

Keep singing song, if you can! Move on, keeping heart resonating;
Do some thing, while producing affection & liking,
Keep moving, considering world as play amusing.

Keep flowing in bliss of gracious,
Take me while flowing in sweet watercourse;
Expand cosmos and immerse it in my conscience,
Take me close to you and submerge in your consciousness.

O Lord! Make me flow, merge my moments in your moments;
Carry me seated over Your eyelets,
Carry my mind crafting 'Madhu' psyche.

104. Pour rhythm and melody of bliss * 119/27.06.08

O Lord, pour rhythm and melody of bliss!
O Lord, make me flow in bliss!

Expand my intellect, make Your conscience!
Make me flute and murmur in soft voice;
Come close to me and compose poem, O gracious!
You sing ample in my sweet tune!

You make me meet all in world making Your own,
You make all in world my own;
You make me serve Yourself,
Making 'Madhu' Your heart, engage in meditations.

105. Engulfed in zeal of bliss * 127/10.07.08

I keep singing Your song engulfed in zeal of bliss.
I keep liberating and singing, keeping Lord in my conscience.

I prefer your feet; I keep listening to You in my conscience;
I may fill world with Your Karma, I may keep singing in bliss.

You are eternal, beautiful and ever new,
I sing in You, I get Your grace;
I may get ocean of bliss,
I may become ever new 'Madhu' cavernous.

You are quiet ocean of wisdom;
I may become Yogi in your devotion so warm;
You are vibrated, Tantra thrilled and occupied in Karma,
I may become instrumental affectionate in bliss.

106. How many melodies have flashed
* 651/09.12.09 (Braj)

How many melodies have flashed today in mind?
How many tones have come in serene mind?
Body is uneasy in sweet melody of void,
Breathes and mind are left behind as if thrilled.

Pure mind is in confines of compassion,
Shivering subsists in swift stream of gratification;
There is liberation in sweet glow of sheen,
There is vibration in neo effulgence of liberation.

How many songs are being sung by this terrain?
How many breezes are being seen by my brain?
Awesome grandeur of sky charms conscience,
The beauty of water searches for reminiscence.

My heart awaits for ever,
It gives base to music of eternity so sober;
It gives nectar to every atom of terrain here,
It sees off diminishing desire of hunger.

Stirred mind in 'Madhu' meeting of departure,
Infused mind in selfishness of departure;
Is engaged in weaving of melody and tune.
It is composing melody in tune and tones of creation.

107. I sing in tune of lily! * 126/10.07.08

I sing in tune of lily, for whom do I intone?
In whose abode I get 'Madhu' hymn? On whose lily I get my tune?

In whose mind, I keep smiling? In whose heart I keep hearing?
Through whose lips I keep singing?　In whose body I keep living?
My mind is His body, His mind is my body;
My heart is His tune in harmony, My tune is His melody.

What do I sing? What I should not sing? I only keep hearing.
I keep doing only as per His motivation;
I keep living with His stimulation.

108. The lonely cowherd daughter Gopi * 2/19.03.08

I, the lonely cowherd daughter Gopi lived at bank of Yamuna river.

I realized tide of youth and felt a pain in my heart;
I felt like meeting my beloved as per uprising wave of my heart.
Sweet & cool breeze was blowing,
Yamuna water was nice & sweet;
Peacock danced under Kadamba tree,
Great Sun was rising in firmament.

Seeing a girl friend near banyan tree at Yamuna bank,
I moved towards Yamuna water intuitively intending to soak;
I became blissful, thrilled & amused
As water started touching from within.
My agony of mind and worldly pain was taken away
By Yamuna water in moment;
I did not feel any physical, psychic or bodily hurt.

With mind enlightened, soul in bliss,
Gopi was amused while mingling with water;
Her mind & body became relaxed, calm & bloom y like honey dear.
Keka and Indian cuckoo were singing
And amusing Gopi's heart centre;
Her mind and body became 'Madhu' like,
As if she became one with God for ever.

109. O Lord! You have stolen my clothes! * 3/19.03.08

O Lord! You have stolen my clothes!
I, the lonely cowherd daughter of Gopa,
Lived near bank of Yamuna watercourse.

As Gopi plunged in blissful Yamuna waters;
Her mind became enlightened after enjoying company of devotees.
One who protects clothes stealing heart,
Playingly stole clothes sitting in conscience!
Krs'n'a* picked up clothes from bank of Yamuna
And set high on Kadamba* branches;
When she pondered about clothes,
She saw pretty Shyam with clothes.

Did Gopi loose her heart or clothes?
Her heart was lost from before and now she lost clothes;
One, who eternally sits within heart, also sits outside us;
He happens to play so well with creatures.
It was as if a deep devotee surrenders in devotion
Plunging amid water of sentient persons;
Devotee dissolves his problems amid sentient ones,
Enlightened persons also become blissful and thrilled in spirits.

With whom to have feelings of shame, fear, bareness?
With one, who makes us play or who plays with us?
Clothes, body, mind, shame & fear are all His!
He is inside, as well as outside us!
He was here before giving clothes, He remains with us
Even after taking our 'Madhu' clothes!

110. I may happen to dance! * 120/27.06.08

I may happen to dance in your heart!
I may happen to get showered in Your thought.

Mind may merge in bliss in your heart centre;
Sky may get merged in your colour.
I may smilingly dance in Your melodic verse;
Sky may get submerged in Your conscience.

Mind may get merged in Your meditation,
Cosmos may get merged in Your manifestation;
Moments may get merged in Your heart;
'Madhu' may get merged in Your feet.

111. Gopi gradually started moving across * 4/19.03.08

Gopi gradually started moving across,
Away from sentient company of Yamuna waters;
While hiding body parts by her hands,
Still feeling shy and nervous.
Krs'n'a, however, looked only in her conscience,
And in her devotion embraced eyes.

Gopi's self confidence increased,
Her surrender evolved, meditation clarified.
Her devotion merged in infinity, bliss overtook her mind.
Gradually, Yamuna water was left behind,
Her mind got attached to bank side,
Her body got submerged in mind.

Her eyes became consciousness,
And finally eyes surrendered themselves.
Krs'n'a walked away, she got her clothes.
The meeting became full of bliss,
Meaning of clothes disappeared, thrill filled bliss;
Her 'Madhu' consciousness aroused enormous.
Gopi became Radha in consciousness.

112. Why Krs'n'a may not steal my clothes! * 5/19.03.08

Why Krs'n'a may not steal my clothes every moment!
Why the body may not become incessant!
Why should I worry about garment?
Why not I give Him clothes every moment!

Why not I come out of lap of Yamuna of sentient persons!
Why not I get laid and lost in His lap while enjoying bliss!
He may see me, may give me blessings of boon and fearlessness!
I may sleep keeping my head in His base!

Why not I get Him seated
On my pineal gland on thousand petal lotus!
And I then recline in His eternal lap timeless!
He may massage my body, mind and consciousness!
And I may merge in His heart plexus!

Why not I give Him affection and massage His plexuses!
May be He is weary of eternally giving away to us!
Why not I give Him His own
'Madhu' conscious creation direct!

113. My existence is infinite * 17/28.03.08

My existence is infinite, I am traveller of infinity.
Some times, I look for beginning of infinity,
At times, I search for end of infinity;
Some times, I get my existence, at times, I loose my existence.

Some times, I find you in middle,
At times, You keep me anxiously waiting until end;
Some times, You get understood,
At times, You make me understand.

My existence lays only in You, I meet my own self, if I meet You;
Only after You caress me, I may be able to caress You,
If you appear in sight, I may be able to prostrate you.

You remain near me, keep closeness,
Don't be miser, don't keep bitterness;
You are busy in controlling created consciousness,
Still, you should remain in touch instantaneous.

In regular company of Yours, in Your existence;
I shall find my path, my existence.

114. How many celebrities came? * 159/14.09.08

O Lord! How many celebrities came to light in your radiance!
O honey! How many 'Madhu' songs descended in your elegance!

How many attributes became attainment?
How much majesty came to manifest?
How many pleasures and pains surged becoming elation?
How many agonies started singing becoming violin?

Vastness of cosmos came to heart as essence;
Essence of life coloured inner conscience.
How much effectual was Guru's grace!
How much congenial became dust particles!

How many demons became humans!
How many humans got liberated from intelligence!
How many reactions became inspirations!
How many lights became conscience!

115. Passion is emotional * 18/28.03.08

Passion is emotional in vortex of ideas,
Black bee is full of passion, Earth is full of bliss;
'Madhu' if you come by, we may fill passion in languages,
We may sing some songs; we may get some friends.

Stars will come, they will bring Moon sideways,
Wagtail with echo, will entertain minds;
May you not get lost in your own melodies!
You mingle your melody in melodies of others.

Fifth note in music will sprout, Papiihara* will converse,
Moon will smile, Moon bird will sing verse;
Emotional water will start flowing after emerging from snow shiver,
Sun will give tune while associating with atmosphere.

Sky will be over head, mind will move express,
Passions will speak through minds,
After flowing from Pituitary plexus.
You also listen and resonate that, Earth will sprout, Moon will
blush;
Passion will speculate arrival of beloved,
Lord will smile and out stretch becoming beloved.

116. O controller of life, give me a base * 140/14.08.08

O Controller of life, give me a base,
Take 'Madhu' blissfully across while giving a tide of bliss;
It is clarion call of my conscience
That you take me away from ocean,
Fill my life stream so that it becomes like an ocean.

O source of stream of life, give stream in life Divine;
Open gates of life, sprinkle garland of emancipation.
Take away problems of Earth, remove clashes, fill passion;
Emancipate every one, O master of cosmos!

117. Journey of Perfect * 25/02.04.08

Journey of Perfect from Perfect to Perfect;
Is complete, fulfilled, was Perfect, will be Perfect.

Every moment and breath of mine is festival of Perfect;
Every step of mine is rhythm of Perfect.
My journey of life is project of Perfect;
Every obstacle of mine is pause of Perfect.

My plans are organized by Him;
My strength and resolves are His breathing exercise.
My sorrows and pains are treatments of Perfect;
My achievements and successes are gift of His grace.

My incomplete story and agony are desired positions of Perfect.
My decoration is future's asset,
All my desires are propositions of Perfect.

Why should I get fearful, worried or pained?
By ever changing momentary future period?
I am His 'Madhu' song, I am His adornment;
I hear His songs on His violin of my body upbeat.

118. When I sing melody of Lord! * 55/08.05.08

When I sing melody of Lord, I get inundated in bliss!

You come in my heart and mind, in tune and song of suppleness;
You dance delightfully in my courtyard in tune of fondness.

You take my intellect to blissful terrain;
You come, now you come, take me amid inundation.

Taking me into invigorating Ganges, make me take a dip in it;
Fill me with subtle ecstasy; give me 'Madhu', fill me with gush.

119. Flowing into oceans of passion * 37/ 08.04.08

Flowing into oceans of passion, O 'Madhu'! You sing song elite;
Sing such a sweet song, that Earth may elate.
Sky may start singing, sweetest perceptions may vibrate.

You come floating in air, burning in fire,
Dissolving in water, sing some soft sweet memory;
Earth may smilingly run, may produce new affection in every person.
The path may become melodious, full of delight,
New and new perceptions may sprout.

Alighting from sky, adorning heart,
You become blissful ever new perfect;
Automating body, vibrating mind with chant,
You become humming of black bee sweet.
While singing, achieving, and amusing heart.

You are sweet, sweetest honey, you are in sky,
And you are also in hearts;
You are in me, You are in all, of course.
Only because you are I am, whole world is,
Body mind and people' life is.
Come, let us all dance and sing, honey emanating 'Madhu Giiti'.

120. You are sweet song of Gracious * 128/10.07.08

You are sweet song of Gracious, You are melody and tune of bliss;
You are tide of my compassion, You are expression of mine.

You are bliss of universe; You remain engrossed in space;
You are evolved human of cosmos, You are melody of bliss.
You please do come in cosmos now in realization of humans;
You have been giving love in creation,
Come to world, You are bliss.

Pouring nectar in every one's brain,
You give knowledge, focus, melody and tune;
Becoming sweet, You sing my verse,
Making these 'Madhu', give tune and melody of bliss.

121. I am heritage girl Of Gokula * 46/01.05.08

I am heritage girl Of Gokula*, You are Nandla'la'* of Madhupur*;
I am Ra'dha'* of sleeping coil,
You are great Shiva* of pineal gland.

Amused by tune of your flute, I am honey-bee hungry of honey;
How many honey bees tasted honey? How many protected honey?

How much play is there in play of honey?
How much attraction is there in this city of honey?
There is deep attraction in sweet honey,
There is excellent management and protection in honey.

I am 'Madhu' teenager of base plexus;
You are abode of honey of Guru plexus;
I am ever new teenager, a new flame,
Pouring new honey, You are heavenly fire.

122. This lovely body created by Lord * 47/01.05.08

This 'Madhu' body created by Lord is
Sweetened musing of many lives;
Subtle configuration of serpentine coil is
Manifestation of many a light years.

The story of affection of Gopi of base plexus is
Krs'n'a flute's Om sound;
The agony of Gopi until she meets Krs'n'a is the touching legend
Of heart of great Shiva of pineal gland.

This journey from base plexus to pineal gland;
This journey from creature to Lord is quite undersized.
But, why does it appear so long and takes so much time indeed?

Probably, Lord allows every life of every creature to let it get ready.
To let it adorn and meet; He gives bliss, takes bliss.

123. What shall I sing? * 54/08.05.08

What shall I sing! Now, you sing.

Becoming nectar you arrive, becoming bliss you besiege.
Come and sing in my heart, come and sing tone of flute.

I beget bliss when I sing your high note melody.
I get filled with rhythm and melody; I get ecstasy.

You come, come now; O master player of life!
You come, come now amidst ocean of Earth; take my mind off.

Allow me to massage your feet;
You pat my forehead.
You keep singing 'Madhu' song,
Let me ecstatically perceive song.

124. You are life! * 137/14.08.08

You are life, you are tune of existence!
You are ever new, sweet melody of human race!

You go on singing 'Madhu Giiti', the songs of consciousness,
While flowing in blissful 'Madhu' sweetness;
Go on imparting sweet bliss,
Keep on revealing some perceptions.

I come and sing, You just do not remain listening to my songs;
While enjoying infinite bliss, You become inquisitive amorous.

Now you sing songs of planet,
Spread aspirations of heart;
You sing songs of His heart,
Sing while entering every one's conscience.

125. Honey bee rushes to every petal * 160/23.09.08

The honey bee rushes to every petal of flowers;
She creates honey collecting pollinated particles.

Herds of flowers are hesitated, fragrant and elated;
Tune of black bee is alluring aptitude, fragrance of Earth is so
sweetened.
Flower scatters cuteness day and night in many ways.
My mind gets smiled and sprouted in new ways.

O 'Madhu'! You get smiled, get thrilled in body, sprouted in mind;
Get vibrated, excited & adorned, become blissful in consciousness.

126. How do I sing melodies of terrain! * 139/14.08.08

How do I sing melodies of terrain!
I am getting entangled in Your tune!
I am getting dyed in your shade!
I am able to hear less of life indeed!

What shall I be able to see and hear?
What will you be able to say or utter?
What shall I be able to give You?
What will you be able to take from myself?

Your melody is sweet and awesome full of glee,
It's attractive, ever new and sweeter than black bee;
You listen to bosom's tune, take tune in bosom,
Give me a new harmony.

I am fragrant blissful tune,
I am 'Madhu' attracted by perceptions;
I am thrilled, amused and in-attracted by illusions,
Of spiritual authority and realization.

127. My amiable mind is adorned by * 161/23.09.08

My amiable mind is full of honey, it is tasted by honey bee;
It has been protected by thorns, it is sweetly adorned by flowers.

Sweet attainment full of sweet affection,
Fills sweet attributes in mind;
God's grace keeps 'Madhu' bound,
Devotion keeps its mind balanced.
The focused is stream of Dha'ran'a'*,
Earth is organized by Pra'n'a'ya'ma*;
' Sama'dhi'* radiates realization, Yam & Niyam* control Earth.

Pratya'ha'r* removes allurements,
Yoga'san* and Mudra* are sweet doors;
Meditation* gets surrendered and lost in Supreme,
The vibration of collective meditation is unique.
Elegance of fasting body refines affection of mind & consciousness;
The flow of Kiirtan* is lovely, God's stream flows blissfully.

128. I used to flee becoming honey bee * 164/23.09.08

I used to flee becoming honey bee; from flowers,
I used to bring pollen's of honey.
I used to go on keeping honey in honey house;
I used to keep surrendering it to lord of honey.
I used to rush, come and go every day while collecting honey;
However, a day used to come, when some one would come
And take away sweet adorned honey.

I used to again fly from honey house,
I used to blissfully collect honey;
I used to expect 'stealing of honey',
I used to look at lord of 'lord of honey'!
My small bee-mind used to get enlarged,
Passion of possessing used to get sprinkled;
I used to adorn sweet-life by sweetness,
Giving honey to 'Madhu', I beautified bliss of honey.

CHAPTER 4. COMPASSION

129. Story of Particles of Pebbles * 153/05.09.08

Story of particles of pebbles is full of feelings,
Submerged in 'Madhu' bliss,
It is, however, full of features;
Though its heart is some what perturbed by screams,
It is in harmony and thrill in its bosom indoors.

How much beautiful history is concealed within pebbles'
Multicoloured, muti-configured & innocent appearance!
Multi storey s of its expectations have seen countless
Prosperity, attributes and administrations.

Meteorites of many ethereal bodies came to meet pebbles,
Many pearls of oceans became dust particles;
Many peaks of mountains got frozen in snowstorms,
They got strewn on terrain bathing in bliss of glaciers.

Pious hill stones also get worshiped by humans,
Stones flowing in streams also glee getting glamorous;
We have observed many stones and pebbles
After bringing from other planets and sub planets,
Many of our spacecrafts have become dust particles
After reaching other planets.

130. The heart particle of pebble * 154/05.09.08

The heart particle of pebble of pathways,
Is little lonely, hurt and apart these days;
In sweet memory of golden olden blissful days,
It's uneasy, upset & agonized in mind in many ways.

Its body is of forms and colors infinite,
Dust decorated Earth is its mother inherent;
There is umbrella of sky, water, air and sun over it,
It has shade of white snow sprinkled over it.

Heart beat of Earth is due to of stiffness of pebble,
Vanity entangles pebbles to pebble;
Reciprocal keenness keeps them connected and capable,
Road of humans is made possible due to patience of pebble.

Density of pebbles is because of their internal attraction,
Base of their minds are bathed and purified by
Five elements of creation;
What doesn't it absorb & tolerate with its
Weight and porous passion!

It habitats 'Madhu' colonies of ectoplasm
Even in desert of its compassion;
Letting human vehicles move over their heads,
They make human beings reach their goals.

131. This brownness of my brainpower * 176/13.11.08

This brownness of my brainpower,
This mascara appearing in my figure!
Has been molded by only You, it has surely been shaded by You!

Why do You create mind in organism?
Why do You color it in your Karma?
Why do You engage it in work? Why do You sidetrack psyche?

All alacrity of creation, all coyness of vision, You have given;
All sensibilities You have given all brownness You have taken.

Why do You become ever kind?
Why do You become somewhat hard, O Lord!
Why do You get done from 'Madhu'!
Why You get scattered from me!

My heart is fair and brunette;
It is reactive momentum's   dust of twilight.
It's spontaneity of prior lives' reactive momentum;
It's language of Your nature.

132. Move on to Madhuvan * 182/13.11.08

Move on to Madhuvan, O mind of mine;
In ever moving every lonesome occasion;
Come in blissful Yamuna's rhythm, in monkey's soft scream.
Come in madhu banquet of honey bees, in sweet bird of eyes;
Come in stars' Omni filled sound;
In 'Madhu' thrilled melody of my mind.

I may sing in melody of Soham'*; flame of life, I may gleam;
I may enjoy pleasure of beloved; I may flow in melody of world.
Overflowing wave of awakening is
Ever new, sweet, eternal and gorgeous;
In each ever new, mind charming tune of existence,
In each melodic resonance of chasteness.

133. O Lord! What did you do? * 175/13.11.08

O Lord! What did you happen to execute?
Why did You color my mind this way out!
How much flame did You inflict? Of what nature You made my intellect?

O beloved, you give how much anxiety,
You give your mind to my anatomy;
You squeeze me to boundary, You entangle me in mental staticity.

You make me move at your will power,
You make me pause whenever you desire;
You make me speak whatever whenever,
You get some works done howsoever.

Why should I nurture worry and fear,
Let me do whatever I can endeavour;
Let me leave whatever is left undone for you,
Let me surrender my mind unto you.

You are catalyst of my acumen, O beloved! You are server of creation;
You are sole upholder of attendant;
You are saviour of 'Madhu' enthralment.

134. You are smile of my grandeur * 179/13.11.08

You are smile of my grandeur, Are you able to recognize me?
You are shower of my vastness, Are you able to observe me?
You are vastness of obstacles of cosmos,
You are glory of infinite effulgence;
You are laughter of comprehensiveness of cosmic face,
You are magnificent vision of cosmic appearance.

Why you are directionless in dissonance?
Why you are terrified in impasse?
You are exhale of brilliant wish, You are emblem of rosiness of cosmos.
You are mystery of sacred flame, you are friend in life's gloom.
You are lamp of 'Madhu''s life gleam,
You are vortex of awesome stream.

135. O mother of creation, silence! * 178/13.11.08

O mother of creation, silence!
The amusing grandeur of human conscience!
The sensitive adeptness of observers awakens!
The catalytic rejuvenation of divine!

Bring heartening source of Lord!
Come in sight in convoluted woodland!
While appearing in body, you get thrilled!
You stay put close to my mind.

I am not able to understand your grace,
I am not able to observe your closeness;
I am not able to recognize your fondness,
I am not able to realize Your assistance.

You are mystery of infinite values,
You are soul mate of vastness of cosmos;
You are fearfulness of infinite pleasures,
You are fragrance of many melodies.

You are Lalit dance catalyzing affection in creation,
You are Ta'nd'ava dance penetrating all obstruction;
You are vast stream of existence, You are 'Madhu' glow of bliss. ?

136. You are manifestation of my grandeur *
180/13.11.08

You are manifestation of my grandeur, You are profusion of nature;
You are loveliness of my humankind, You are quiet limelight elated.
You are modesty of peacock of mind,
You are hierarchy of melodic natural world.
You are aircraft of my fortune, You are my heart's meditation.

What shall I call and tell you! Where and how do I look for you!
How do I keep You in my heart! How do I make it all clear and straight!
You are 'Madhu' state unified, I am pure, alone and exhausted;
Looking to ancestry of nature, I am ever innovative, melodic and tender.

137. O 'Madhu' bird! What do you look at *
183/13.11.08

O 'Madhu' bird! What do you look at? What do you smell and evaluate?
What do you hear and crave? Why do you come and leave?

You search for and think of some thing; You speak and chatter something.
You somewhat swing and shilly-shally; You get shy and then you fly.
You have an old relation with humans, your treasure lies in thorns;
In short while, you fly away, with the swipe of air, you go away.

Your mind and consciousness is filled with caring eagerness,
You are full of bravery of journey of continents;
You have drunk juice of grandeur of existence,
You have tasted nectar of creation's magnificence.

138. Elated, enthralled, thrilled & taciturn * 84/13.11.08

Elated, enthralled, thrilled and taciturn
Mind of mine is afflicted by reservation;
Brushwood of bosom is full of obstruction,
Songs of mind are full of vision.

Efforts of life full of probability,
Language passionate illustrious morality;
Perceptible efforts of humanity,
Sweet value of affection in spirituality.
Gleaming illuminated observer, burning desire of divine fire.
I give up my mind's desire, let His desire be my desire.

In sacred surrender of submission,
In sacrifice of mind charmed by meditation;
Why should I worry and imagine,
Let me offer myself to Him and depend upon.

How do I know, what does He yearn?
I don't know what He may get done;
Let me give up my all to Him,
Let me take 'Madhu' ocean of affection.

139. Void of my mind! * 162/23.09.08

How and from where has arrived void of my mind!
How and who brought serenity of my mind!

What did I pick up, what did I drop?
What did I disseminate, what did I hope?
Why am I fond of, why did I weep?
Why am I awakened, why did I sleep?

How my nature got sprouted? How agony aroused in mind?
How my prudence got worsened? How my desires got deserted?

Why do you come and sing? Why do you unwillingly go away?
You give tune to violin of mind, You thrill and cheer me away.

O smiling colleague of human mind!
O observer of adorned grandeur of mine!
O overseer of engulfed mind!
O sweet witness of blissful 'Madhu' mind!

140. Depths of my horizons * 226/03.02.09

Don't peep in depths of my horizons,
Engross in waves of my heart's high seas;
Squeeze in depths of my conscience,
Spread in waves of ocean of my bliss.

Don't mislay in laughter of ridicule of my conscience,
Find me in source of my heart's Ganges;
Witness me in solitude of my conscience,
Get immersed in stream of my bliss.

You glance at glory of my bosom's seas,
Glitter in splendour of my loveliness.
Get laid in melody of my tunes,
Get thrilled in 'Madhu' cave of my bliss.

141. What a delight I give to humanity? * 236/06.02.09

What a delight I give to human race!
What displeasure I give to inhuman ones!
Let me flow in waves of pains and pleasures,
Let me fill my heart with nectar of bliss.

Why should I thrill the world!
Why do I enthuse and enlighten living world!
Why do I wake up or sleep amid, why do I come and go around!

You are the cause and sustenance of every one,
You are the inducer and illuminate of every one;
Why am I angry and tainted, why am I enthused and elated!

Why do I get filled with songs! Why do I bear sadness!
Why do I take fire to conscience! Why do I give nectar of bliss!

Why do I come and sing! Why do I fly becoming big bee and bang!
Why do I bear flame of fire becoming stream of water!

Why should I give my heart to airs! Why should I stretch skies!
Why should I create such a creation!
Why should I disperse 'Madhu' conscience!

142. Will you like to let me sing! * 238/06.02.09

Will you like to let me sing!
Will you own 'Madhu' as Your offspring!
Will you remove my blemishes!
Will you give me your chasteness!

What could I do coming and going daily!
I kept singing ecstatically;
I lose awareness and intellect of human mind,
I remain in melody of your heart and mind.

Looking at dense, deep and dark cloud formation,
And attractive three layered
Matted configuration of your bosom;
I wobble and amuse in my mind,
My body gets untangled, band of hairs get entangled.

You may now come and peep in my conscience,
Have a look at scenery of sweetness;
Prevent and admonish, sing and dance,
Thrill in mind, smile in heart in song.

143. Agony amid heart * 319/28.05.09

Agony amid heart, tale in tune,
Traits in body device, nectar in conscience;
Passion pervades nectar of bliss,
Inhalation fills liveliness.

Spotlight in Your base,
Aptness full of inquisitiveness;
Adoring easiness of immediacy spiritual,
Sweet deepness of venerable.

Amiably desired vibrancy of
Spirituality exploring humans;
Amused in blissful splendour in sweet posture of
Reactive momentum of past lives.

Fragrance is fortunate, ocean exists in intellect,
Sky is sweet, annoyance is innocent;
Action is enthused by environment,
Firefly is in sweet chant.

Lips are soft, nectar is chaste,
And brook of bliss is well bent;
Heart is co-ordinate d and decked out,
Cultured is conduct, melody is sweet.

Grandeur of gentle glimpse,
Prominence of   'Madhu' showers;
Loveliness of Om elated terrains,
Sparseness of expanding universe.

144. I have been into dreams
* 327/30.05.09

I have been into dreams in macrocosm,
I have been afloat in secretion of scene;
I am enunciated and expressed in new creation,
I am doing Karmas in new affection.

Vision of my human is agonized and suspicious,
Mind of demon is confident delimited by fear;
Amused in pursuit, humankind is gravely divided,
Owing to narrow vision of creation.

Tale is tired, traits are desolated,
And Earth in slumber is extroverted;
Skies are amused, water is sweet and unmoved.

I kept moving scattered, desolated, attached or detached,
I kept preferring expression of bliss in my heart fortitude.

Creature is young and free of debt,
Body is adaptable and compassionate;
He is delighted, decked and unbound
By emancipation of infliction.

His mind is not tired, body is vibrated by rest,
And humans are free in brain;
Earth is besieged in 'Madhu' calm,
Sky is rushing in heaven.

145. You didn't arrive, You didn't hasten * 260/29.03.09

You didn't arrive, You didn't hasten!
How much pain You aroused in heart!
How much ache is grown up in bosom!
How much agony is awakened in intellect!

I kept on crying in crude world,
People kept laughing in world;
I remained irksome trying in world,
Mercy did not arise in creatures' mind.

People kept doing as per their mood,
No one thought of my body and mind;
No one thought of   gracious in mind,
I could not receive hearty affection of beloved!

You come now, come now,
Don't distress creature so much for now;
Sing a song in my mind, show your love in world.

Take care treating me your maid, teach liberation to human;
Make liberated consciousness dance with 'Madhu' man,
Awaken creatures and pour spiritual attachment.

146. I have seen white swan in dream
* 188/14.11.08

I have seen white swan* in dream,
I have seen him flying at the crack of dawn;
He was decorated in sweet glow in light,
He was moving in slow & sweet gait.

In awesome grandeur, white swan was flying,
He was walking, flying, pausing & charming;
A brown bird later came near him,
He sweetly smiled after meeting him.

He again came strolling, swinging and flying,
He met nearby birds and went flying;
I took pictures getting enthralled,
I became elated, exhilarated and thrilled.

Did you come in form of swan, O Lord!
Did you come to meet 'Madhu' in world?
After meeting living beings, You nicely smiled,
Emanating bliss, You ran airborne.

Chapter 5.
Poetic Perceptions

147. My Sonnet
* 15 / 27.03.08

Whose creation are you, my sonnet!
In which creation, will you get spread out!

Sitting at heart of paper,
Are you juice of blackness of pen!
Or are you lily of desolation!
Or you are affluence of expanding creation!

Expressed in emotion, gratified in spirit;
Are you asleep amid paper surface!
Manifested in mind, engaged in body;
Crawling in heart, motivated by conscience.

Will you like to live!
Will you be able to live for ever in book's creation!
In conception, cadence and dissolution of creation!

Or you will like to live in conscience,
Consciousness and void of my 'Madhu' creation!
In vibration of every life;
In compassionate story of every particle of terrain!

Will you meet every stream of water,
Every spark of fire, every wave of air!
With every melody, tune and poem
Living in void of   firmament!

148. O Poet! You may not belittle * 224/20.01.09

O Poet! You may not belittle the delicate body of poem!
Give a 'Madhu' blissful visage to poem born out of passion.

Wrap it in austerity, make world passionate with devotion;
Make everyone elated and rhythmic,
Compose invigorating and apostle tune.

Give gesture and fragrance of Earth, fill radiance of stars;
Give splendour of sunrise, pour surge of moon rise.

Bind yourself in Yama and Niyama,
Keep doing yoga postures and meditation;
Engage in Pra'n'a'ya'ma, give dedicated soul to Supreme.

Give flow of supreme to world, accredit bliss to Lord;
Flow in waves of bliss, proffer elated poem.

149. My spiritual verse * 22/02.04.08

My spiritual verse, when you will get spiritually established!
After sprouting on thousand petals at pineal,
When you will get awakened!

In which direction you will flow?
In what situation, you will survive?
In which melody you will thrill?
In which rhythm you will dance?

In which tune you will sing?
On which music you will enjoy trance?
Based on which expectation, you will be controller of senses?

You are eternal, always new, ever new, eternal sound;
You are my tune, you are 'Madhu' mind,
You are verse of Veda and you are "I am That" sound.

150. Whose shower are you, my Poetry!
*16/27.03.08

Whose shower are you, my Poetry indeed!
In which creation, you would like to get unfolded!

Will you look for each poem which is still asleep in human wisdom!
Will you like to express feelings of all minds composing poem!
Will you extend flow to every agony!
Will you make bliss even more heavenly!

Every breath and conscience of mine is in affliction;
Some are in bliss in ignorance; some are not in bliss in acumen.

You lovingly massage their heads,
Shower flowers in their feet & head;
Massage their hearts in such a way, that their minds get elucidated.
Their tears get dispersed, their hearts get thrilled;
They get briskly respired,
They happen to sing and get bliss enthused.

Don't express pains of your heart, you only listen,
Learn to tolerate, understand weeping, teach smiling & irrigation;
Keep smiling, make others laugh and get bliss contain.

You don't look for prize, don't think of prestige or price;
You simply move from 'Madhu' heart to hearts.
From the wave of pleasure and pains to flow of bliss;
From creatures to creator, from creator to created.

151. Subtle wave of poetry
* 43/23.04.08

O 'Madhu'! How did this subtle wave of poetry
Arise in your heart centre;
Why your heart started flowing like glacier!

Beholding pot on your head,
How could you become full of fervour!
Why your passion got showered!
How you started singing over!

Did someone ignite you!
Or some spark ignited you!
Did you get ignited looking at some spark!
Or you got vibrated by 'perception of bliss'!

Did you perceive movement of moving creation!
Or you understood secret of father of creation!
Did you understand song of operation of creation?
Or you came to know source of consciousness of creation!

What did you start composing!
For whom you started composing!
What did you start murmuring!
Whose tune you started liking!

Why you started practicing tune!
What melody you started singing!
For whom you started singing!
To whom you started listening!

Your poetry became wave of bliss,
Water flute started playing in fervour of river;
He started singing some thing on flute of His heart centre,
Flute of your heart started singing,
Resonating and vibrating with His heart centre.

152. Your Poetry gives bliss * 44/24.04.08

'Madhu'! Your poetry gives bliss
To supreme consciousness,
His wave of bliss gives you added bliss;
You keep composing poems, you give life to lives.

Your melody, rhythm and tune are revolutionary;
Spark of consciousness is beauty of your poetry.

It's rhythm of life, it is tone of Shiva;
It is tune of Earth,
It is melody of echo of eternal Shiva.

You don't wait for each one to enjoy bliss;
You just compose and freely sing.
That will give pace to movement of orb;
It will bliss several beings.

With spark of your poem,
Some one will get ignited;
His mind will get illuminated,
Light will reach you unimpeded.

He will also enlighten some one,
The world will get illuminated.
As you proffer poems,
God will be elated.

You only ignite, spark, awaken,
And spread awareness and sing;
Extend enlightenment,
World will eventually get enlightened.

Conscience will get illuminated,
You will get vibrated;
All will enjoy bliss,
Guru who initiated you will also enjoy bliss.

Chapter 6.
NATURAL

153. Your arriving every day with Sunrise!
* 48/05.05.08

Your arriving every day with sunrise!
Bringing along new ardour and existence.
Bracing all with bliss is fortune of Your grace!

Musical predawn chirping of birds;
The echo of collective meditation of family of birds.
Gift of cuisine of 'Madhu Giiti' to world;
Are blissful greetings of Sun to Lord!

Current of cool, slow & fragrant morning wind,
Roving of white flower petals in backyard;
Humber River's surge sound, deer's free roaming speed.

Greeting of dedicated dog at abode,
His looking for loving touch of hand;
Request for fresh water by mew
While tenderly touching her body and tail end.
Sudden awakening of unconsciously sleeping ant
In wash room bend,
Request for seeds by birds and squirrels in back yard.

Mind's getting absorbed in   predawn meditation,
Getting set in breathing exercise, meditation,
Self study and Yoga'san;
Mind's becoming suddenly subtle,
Sprouting of 'Madhu' songs on its own.
Filling of every one with bliss is fortune of Your grace.

154. Amid shower of white snow flurries
* 240/18.02.09

Amid shower of white snow flurries,
You have come with 'Madhu' loveliness;
You are manifested in all three worlds, carrying garlands of flurries.

In sweet bosom of brownish cloud, in language of mind of Krs'n'a;
You keep singing 'Madhu Giiti' in chaste abode of supreme.
World is lake of your love, I am your loving one, O Supreme!
I come and go within You, O beloved!
You remain within my bosom!

Human mind reads you through language of your nature;
In winter summer snow and rain, in charming fervent desire.
Human minds smile, while reading and understanding You;
You mingle with your own creation
And rush becoming snow flurries.

155. O mother Earth! Your revolving around Sun *
81/02.06.08

O mother Earth! Your revolving around Sun,
Carrying all of us under direction of God divine!
Being so adventurous and busy!
How mysterious and blissful is this!

You revolve in your axis, while carrying us over your knees.
Overwhelmed by mystery of days and nights,
We're not able to see your swiftness.

You move in vast space around Sun,
Some times, in this or that side of Sun.
At times, you are able to see
'Madhu' stars of Milky Way from close-in.
The planets of solar system, sometimes, come close to you,
While revolving around Sun; at times,
They happen to go to the other side of Sun.

156. O mother Earth! We play in your lap * 81A/02.06.08

O mother Earth! We play in your lap day and night;
We're not able to still understand your pain and plight.

How many proper and improper deeds we do in universe;
We do not comprehend your passion and unhappiness!
Your extreme affection towards us,
Your moving in two motions without giving any pain to us,
enables us keep in eagerness and bliss.

You keep moving in year in days and nights;
O mother! You are so kind and patient!
Moving for ages, you have made us developed and proficient;
You have made us 'Madhu' human
While sprouting us every moment.

157. O mother Earth! Facing Sun * 82/02.06.08

O mother Earth! Facing Sun,
By not allowing light to enter back side of your hemisphere,
You make the night happen.
Taking your creation in night in your lap, You make it sleep.

That too you do in such a way that, this process runs continuously,
Some may see morning & evening,
Some sleep and some remain awake;
So that your creation runs smoothly.

All creatures, awoke or sleeping, remain balanced and happy.
How systematic is your movement, How balanced is your yawn;
Pulling and nurturing every one   in eternal love is
'Madhu' depth of your gravitational brawn.

158. How planned is your revolving * 82A/02.06.08

O Earth! How planned is your revolving on poles!
Gradual disposition of poles,
And resultant change of weather conditions.

How splendid is your figure, blue water,
White snow & green forests;
Moving creatures, animals and humans,
Satellites, airplanes and space ships
Created by human intelligence.

Your revolving while facing Sun,
Filling every one with 'Madhu' brightness,
Making stars and Galaxies invisible to our eyes;
Presenting again in night seven coloured beauty of stars,
Awakening every one in morning with singing of bird songs.

159. O Earth! Keeping everyone * 83/02.06.08

O Earth keeping everyone on surface of your body, you move on!
You do not show fire of your stomach to any one.

Human could see your bluish pearl 'Madhu' splendour,
Only while going away from you to Moon in space;
Greatness of your gait, desire of your infinite movement,
Makes me love you, O mother.

Your undiscovered plants, multifaceted creatures & animals,
Ever developing human beings are all dancing in keenness;
Imbalance in Your creation gets balanced in due course of time.
Many difficult circumstances come
And get changed with movement of time.

O mother Earth!, you move and make others move around,
You go on dancing in universal 'Om' sound;
You go on moving 'Madhu' creation,
You keep gratifying creator of terrain.

160. Passionate land of India * 24/02.04.08

Passionate land of India is confidence of cosmic terrain;
Cosmic passion of India is potentiality of creation.

Ideal life of Ra'ma, Shiva's proliferation of Yoga,
Tantra, Tandava, marriage and Ayurveda,
Attraction of   sixteen arts of Krs'n'a, complete surrender of Arjuna;
Realization of Buddha, Neo humanism of
A'nandamurti, Pa'tanjali's philosophy of Yoga,
Bravery of Bharat, Nam Mantra of Guru Nanak,
Path of Kabiira & sentient life of Jaena.

Dedicated devotion of Miira Soor Tulasii Chaitany
Viveka'nand & Raviindra,
Glory of Shiva' ji, focus of Laxmiii Baii
And sentience of Ahilya Baii Holkar;
Dedication of Ga'ndhii to truth,
Sacrifice of   Subhash Bhagat Patel and Tilak,
National dedication of Ra'jendra, Ra'dha'krs'nana,
Nehru, Nanda, La'la Baha'dur & Atal.

Yoga of all Yogis, wisdom integration of spiritual researchers,
Great blending of devotees of Dharma;
Sacred place of realization and Karma for all Dharma,
Spiritual experiment of human Dharma.

Creator of spiritual science, 'Madhu' seer of affection of Cosmos;
Researcher of void to infinity, experiment maker of cosmic passion.

161. O cloud of my mind! * 144/20.08.08

O 'Madhu' cloud of my mind!
At times you appear spread over the skies!
At other times, you appear no where in silent sky of my conscience!

At times, every one sees you, at other times, you see every one;
Some times, you thunder and rain, becoming black & brown,
At times, you thrill becoming white and quiet shrine.

Whenever, I come to meet you sitting in plane of meditation,
You play in fun like a teen, you move together, up or down;
Some times, you come close to me,
At times you go far away from me,
Some times, I get lost in atmosphere, at times,
You get lost in my conscience.

162. Where are you going, O cloud! * 258/12.03.09

Where are you going, O cloud! Carrying melody of my conscience?
You are moving in blue sky, acquiring seven coloured loveliness.
You keep flying overhead every one, in brown sweet form & design;
You start moving in your own tune, in elated and thrilled passion.

You start rushing at dawn every day,
What all you go on doing whole day!
You fly like birds, singing sweet and attractive songs.
Carrying group of coloured clouds,
You play Holi* amid bosom of skies;
What kind of ever-new colors you smear,
You excite people of Earth here.
You shine, sparkle and swing; you rush like monsoon in spring;
You sing 'Madhu' Holi* song, you rush in cluster and groups.

163. Every particle of Canada * 93/14.06.08

Every particle of Canada is filled with Kan'a'di*'s thoughtfulness;
Mind and breathe of Canada is full of innate gorgeousness.
Natives' austerity, visitors' depth of mind
And immigrants' relevance;
Molds Canada's global society's sweetness.

It's laboratory of human values,
It's place for studying, thinking and openness;
It's expansion of knowledge, actions and devotions,
It has Yoga and Tantra's accelerated acceptance.

Mutual sweet behaviour of humans
And their equal respect for birds and animals;
Takes our civilization to introvert guidelines,
It helps in development of sub-conscience mind of humans.

Here, we have 'Madhu' junction of global civilizations,
We have exchange of intermixing cultures;
We are goaded from selfishness to benevolence;
We are world's gleaming radiance.

164. River after deluge * 563/15.10.09

River gets small after deluge,
Stream becomes small and sand gets huge;
River gets silent after emerging from mountain;
It flows in broad stream with acceleration.

It becomes silent after flood; it fills serenity in sand;
Flowing currents get patient,
They happen to bear distance from embankment.

River becomes large at the time of deluge;
It destroys villages, trees and edge;
It moves broadening its way; it drifts whatever comes in way.

Travelers have to move enough to cross over;
They take a look at horror of downpour.
They cross stream sitting in ferryboat;
They look at infinite heart of sand a lot.

The scene of flood is passionate; the later scene does vibrate.
Many streams flow out of 'Madhu' heart cage;
The distressed sand tells a lot of huge deluge.

165. What does horror of flood say * 564/15.10.09

What does horror of flood say?
Hearts of how many trees get elated in a way?
How much agony river banks speak out?
How many hills get razed to environment?

How many villages get devastated and scattered?
Where do the creatures and lives go in flood?
How many new escarpments get created?
How many new streams get born in flood?

How many stones become sand?
How much branches of trees bear all around?
Grandeur of how many crops gets lost? How many lives get lost?

You move broadening your breast
While encompassing all within your bosom.
You shake and relocate house of nature,
You destroy and submerge bosom of fiber.

I get lost in your integrated mind;
I sleep amid your bosom becoming sand.
You happen to say a lot to me in your way;
Why don't you move carrying my 'Madhu' mind away.

166. You came out of bosom of cloud * 588/04.11.09

You came out of bosom of cloud
While assuming an awesome glimpse;
How many fabulous pictures you made
O Sun before your appearance!

You showed many forms of clouds;
How many oceans you spread in skies?
How many streams of glows rushed taking multifarious forms?

At times you came hidden, at times you showed your effulgence;
Sometimes, you came out of veil of clouds feeling self-conscious.

While spreading light, the rays smilingly saw whole cosmos;
You over-flooded eyes of all and then you hid in dense clouds.

On arriving, you awakened everyone who slept covering minds;
Showing 'Madhu' effulgence in space,
You awakened every one's conscience.

167. Cluster of bushes on bank of Humber * 62/14.05.08

Cluster of bushes on the bank of Humber watercourse,
Hustle bustle of squirrels
While going up and down over the trees;
Sound of wings of chirping birds,
Sprouting of white flowers on decorated trees.

Swimming of cool white seagull in watercourse,
Drinking of water in hurry and worry by forest creatures;
Jumping of dog while walking in river waters,
Fly jump of birds in Humber from trees.

O Humber! You have shown the pathway to so many generations,
You have founded many a businesses;
You have inhabited Toronto city while adorning with lots of
flowers,
You have flown and dipped in lake of Ontario many cute streams.

I always remember your momentous swiftness;
Your 'Madhu' knocking of my mind to subserviently come close.

168. O Humber! How many forms of yours I have seen
* 63/14.05.08

O Humber! How many forms of yours I have seen!
How many tides and shortages of your water, I have seen!

Some times, you want to overflow jumping your interface,
At times, you get contented within stones in your base;
Some times, you yourself become snow,
At times, you quietly flow underneath snow.

How many times, I have walked far off along with you in summer,
How many times, I have seen you trembling on parting in winter;
Many times, you have offered me sweet mulberry and apples,
Many times, you have let me meet your hesitating deer's and hares.

Many a time, I have walked in silent caves of your bushes,
Many times, I have watched your surge, sitting on scattered stones;
Many times, I have talked to your trees beside boundary,
Many times, sitting with you in your jingling melody,
I have practised 'Madhu' meditation on creator Devine.

169. At the knock of fall * 65/14.05.08

At the knock of fall, leaves of trees change colors,
Their orange, Pink, lemon or yellow,
Shades express agony of their minds;
However, looking at their changing shades,
Human mind takes pleasure considering that as their prettiness.

Leaves get scattered in agony of arrival of fall in infinite colors;
They move on earth after alighting from trees,
Flying with velocity of air, they run in all places.

Probably, to exhaust reactive momentum of
Remaining up on the trees;
They roam every Earth corner to meet 'Madhu' dust of surrounds.
They go and prostrate each and every one and sentient ones.

170. Water fall of blue lake of Niagara * 94/16.06.08

Water fall of blue Lake of Niagara,
Is thrilling vibrating and full of sweetness;
Sudden fall of water columns,
Forms excellent rare rainbow in the skies.

Uprising of suddenly falling water drops of water streams,
Rising in sky, manifesting in infinite showers;
Makes human minds thrill and dance,
Every human being gets vibrated by water waves.

Feelings of unwanted fall of unwilling water-run,
Takes mind of water to sky free of pain;
Emotional gets mind of human,
It moistens conscience of 'Madhu' filling inner ambitions.

171. Existence of water particles * 97/16.06.08

Existence of How many water particles
Got uplifted from Niagara's water falls!
How much air got filled with water,
How many Sun-rays became cooler!

How many skies got reverberated!
How many birds and animals got chirped!
How many Human minds got vibrated!
How many hearts and conscience got awakened!

How many water drops merged in streams and became sinuous!
How many drops made rainbow after merging with Sun-rays!
How many drops strayed after meeting air waves!
While beginning to get merged in human breathes!

How many water particles rushed to skies!
And came back to caress forest gardens and paths!
How many hearts they strengthened in 'Madhu' fondness!
How many couples they balanced in tenderness!

172. Prior to water fall of Niagara * 96/16.06.08

Prior to water fall of Niagara, blue water of Ontario Lake,
Is soft and dreamy in 'Madhu' depth to great extent.
But then, after flowing on series of pebbles, it gets smart,
Seagull, looking at it, starts ballet.

Moving on pebbles with accelerated velocity,
Noiseless water thrilled with velocity;
The glittering water thrilled in mentality,
Becomes more bluish sensing destiny.

Sudden losing of base of thrilling and thriving waters,
Patient water becoming upset by shaking of its existence;
Observation of this happening by universe,
Seeing this, galaxy's becoming soundless.

It is made to jump in strange depths, its heart & breath gets rapture;
This heart rendering incidence of fall, becomes its life's nightmare.

Out of collective clash of this fall,
How many water drops made electrical power!
How many water particles flew with air!
How many flew to sky and became 'Madhu' rainbow in air!

173. Silent drops of Niagara * 98/16.06.08

Silent water drops of Niagara Fall,
Are closing their eyes in suspicion of sudden fall;
The drops which became serious due to slow speed,
Try to assess depth of dam while keeping their eyes closed.

Some drops try to associate with base of water under stream,
Some want to remain in same side of dam
And try to understand grandeur of dam;
Looking towards drops ahead and above them,
Being driven by flow to the other side of dam,
They are awestruck, fearful and some of them,
Are free from pain even in turbulent stream.

Tormented by momentum of water flowing from rear,
Shaking by streams flowing under;
Forced to remain flowing up, water drops are moved by sore.

Water stream of suddenly arrived momentum of water,
Takes them to other side of barrier
Taking their sub consciousness no where;
'Madhu' sub consciousness of astounded drops of water,
Make humans loose their sub consciousness later.

174. Vigorous dance of water of Niagara * 99/16.06.08

Sudden fall of water drops to so much deepness,
Trembling of accompanying water drops;
Rising up of some drops out of ensuing collective clash,
Flowing down of some drops in stream of lakes.

In this collective Tand'ava* dance of water drops,
In this untimely collective downfall of drops;
In destruction of some drops and rise of some other drops,
Air gets moistened, sky gets soft hearted with tears.
Moved by waves of waters, 'Madhu' observers of Niagara Falls
Happen to vibrate mind waves and look for angelic creator in Falls.

175. Thrilled by Niagara Falls * 95/16.06.08

Thrilled by Niagara Falls,
Conscience of some water particles fly to skies,
They become rainbow, mincing with Sun rays;
While singing, the birds touch 'Madhu' skies,
Wearing blue jackets, humans' boat underneath falls.

Uprising hills of five elements*, thrilling water,
Flying breeze, spearheading sky, pleases human mind;
Five elements engulfed by cosmic mind become pleased,
Astonished humans, animals,   birds and flowers,
Start dancing after getting happiness.

176. Onlookers of Niagara Falls * 100/16.06.08

The on looking men and women of Niagara Falls;
Are thrilled and enthralled by charisma of rain of drops.

Perpetual flow of spellbound water stream
Flowing over dam echelon;
Rainbow created up in sky, fills minds with infatuation.

Uprising of water drops from clash of falls,
Their getting sprinkled far and wide in all directions;
They inundate human minds and bodies,
And make them meekly soak in flow of love & tenderness.

Collective watching of fall by families,
Getting wet in slowly falling drops which had risen up in skies;
Soft mind's getting amused and enlightened,
It appears as if drops are in bliss after meeting the Lord!

The amused group of men & women
In blue jackets enjoying boating below dam;
Got thrilled and elated while seeing
'Madhu' waters falling from up the streams.

177. **Brown cloud in blue sky** * 142/20.08.08

Brown cloud in blue sky creates and weaves movies,
Every moment in the heart of heavens;
How much play is there in thunder of clouds!
How quiet is bosom of the skies!

How many islands you form?
How many oceans you keep in your bosom?
How many languages of minds you read?
In how many adornments you adorn?
You manifest in mountains, animals and birds,
You become hero in drama of skies;
You get manifested in many dimensions,
You get vibrated and thrilled in heavens.

When you remain perturbed, scattered and rootless,
When you get alone, departed, unconscious and mindless;
Swinging waves of air arrive across,
You start moving while smiling and thrilling in space.
Merging mind in creator, looking at observers;
You come at the courtyard of Earth conscious,
come in courtyard of 'Madhu' conscience.

178. Splendour of charismatic clouds * 143/20.08.08

Splendour of charismatic clouds looked gracious!
Their art of adornment looked 'Madhu' nice,
Their beauty delighted conscience.

Whosoever water drops could liberate,
Whatever air could become cloud innate;
Whatever fire could purify in it,
Earth smiled within mind looking at it.
Flame of life gives garland of achievement,
New sky girl makes you forget;
Sweet teenage takes you from the start,
Drinking sweet cup, you start movement.

You saw many affectionate persons,
You saw hesitating, paused and vibrated minds;
You have looked at lonely minds,
You curiously peeped at your own ones.
Whenever your mind gets saturated,
Wherever your affection with sky gets accomplished;
Come home to meet mother terrain,
Come out of cosmos rushing as showers.

Chapter 7
Literature in Various Languages

179. You are my source of bliss * 189/17.11.08 (Sanskrit)

You are source of my bliss,
You are ship of my safe havens;
You are glow of my consciousness,
You are Guru of my conscience.

You are source of our conscience,
You are flame of consciousness of cosmos;
You are my bosom, You are my tone,
You are my only sustain.

You are eternal flow, You are my substratum,
You are my path, You are my accelerated stream;
You are attainment, You are gleam of my wisdom,
You are voice & violin, You are Yourself passion.

Melody of my life rushes to Your bosom,
It sings enthralled in Your mind;
Tide of my life comes to Your ocean,
Cloud of 'Madhu''s mind then flows unto You, O Gracious!

180. You are my melody * 190/17.11.08 (Sanskrit)

You are my melody, O violin Player!*
You are my own self,
You are sweet bliss and gleam Yourself;
My mind is thrilled, enthralled & blissful;
You are flame of our life.

Stream of my life has lost tone,
My mind has lost tune in your mind;
You are sweet flow editing life,
You have sweet resolve in proximity of spiritual guide.

You are trio-flow at junction of tone,
In melody of life, You are offshoot of tune;
You are saviour, You are source of tune,
You are driver of my life stream.

Earth flows in elation a midst inundation,
All are thrilled in source of Your meditation;
For life of 'Madhu', You are catalyst of acceleration,
You are blissful eternal source of emancipation of life.

181. You are supreme veneration * 194/26.11.08 (Sanskrit)

You are my supreme veneration,
You are my lone aim of meditation;
I bow before you O Omniscient! I submit all my attachment.

You are my fervent delight in dream & despair,
You are my shelter in slumber;
You are vigorous flow in my survival,
You are assurance in my exhale.

You are my rational mind in riches,
You are my patience at terrible times;
You are discipline in management,
You are enthroned in posture of my heart.

You dwell in entire cosmic establishment,
In garden of my mind, in brush woods of my heart;
You are in five elements and in flow of intellect,
O virtuous, You are in Mahata* and Aham* sprouted afloat.

You are ever new, awesome and 'That is I',
You are my beginning and end in infinity;
You are inner conscience of 'Madhu' man,
You are sweetest Omni mobile consciousness of mine.

182. O friend, Shyam has not arrived * 329/30.05.09 (Braj)

O Friend, Shyam* has not arrived in forest!
Creepers and leaves are getting faded,
Cuckoo* is getting confounded;
Minds of Gopiis are getting mislaid, mind of Haladhar is hesitated.

Yamuna water rushes with jiggling sound,
It hurts heart of restless Radha;
Children of cows go on looking for,
Uncomfortable are friends of Shyam.

All adolescent girls of Braj want to see
Amazingly decked garland at bosom of Shyam;
Tree branches appear beautiful and well formed,
Young girls of Braj move a midst vine.

Teasing body, pleasing mind, we could not know, when He arrived;
In beautiful tune of flute, He sang a melody in 'Madhu' heart.
O beloved, Shyam has arrived today in forest.

----

* Cuckoo= Cha'tak= A bird which only drinks drops of rain
Shyam= Krs'na= God, Haldhar= Name of a friend of Krs'na
Radha= Krs'na's beloved spiritual friend
Braj= An area around Mathura in Uttar Pradesh in India where
Krs'na was born and did His Divine play in young age.
Yamuna= A river flowing through Braj and other areas in India

183. O friend, I don't live here any more!
* 40/17.04.08 Braj

O friend, I don't live here any more!
I live with son of Nanda* now, forgetting all pain and pleasure!

My body lives here, mind does not, my soul lives in Braja#;
I take food, live in house,
I keep walking & bathing in Yamuna water.
I keep playing with children of Braja#.
Early morning, I rush to Yamuna bank,
I play flute with cowherd children;
I go from Gokula to Vrindavana,
To graze the cows, I go to Govardhana .

I see beauty of sweet Madhuvana, I want to see beauty of Krs'n'a;
My mind goes in trance, body moves in cosmos,
I subserviently keep moving in Gokula parish.
I do not feel pangs of winter and summer, in rain, I immerse;
My mind gets pleased when you come,
Love for son of Nand*, it enhances.

He does not come when I play with you someway,
He comes and adores me as you go away;
'Madhu' mind has become affectionate of Krs'n'a,
I am in affection with Him for ever.

184. Flute beholder has arrived * 281/09.04.09 (Braj)

O friend, flute beholder* has arrived, He rushed in my courtyard;
He has seen my churning pot, He has gazed at my pot.

He didn't take apart churn,
He rushed some where taking butter again;
He played at Yamuna' shoreline,
He is obsessed in mind of everyone.

He came walking on foot lane, He looked with charm & passion;
I have not been able to forget Him,
He is very much liked by my brain.

My mind somewhat thrills in, He appears to be of my own;
He has eaten my lovely butter,
He helped put on my head my pitcher.

I am cherished and heart-string, I am thrilled with sweet bliss sting;
I appear to have lost some thing,
I have acquired blissful nectar of   sweet spring.

He appears to have touched middle of my brow in His mind,
He appears to have waved 'Madhu' hand over my head;
He appears to have taken my head in His lap in His mind,
He has probably sung a melody of new kind.

He has danced in Vranda'van of my mind,
O friend, flute player* has arrived!

185. He plays flute in Gokul * 600/14.11.09 (Hindi/Braj)

He plays flute in Gokul,
Gopies are listening in every heart;
Cuckoos sing in Braj forests,
Tinkle of ankle trinkets thrill in Madhu forests.

When did Krs'n'a come on Earth!
He rushed enthralling Radha's sweet conscience;
He fulfilled dream of devotees,
He emerged with sweetness in cosmos.

Birds are spread in life and ambition;
creepers are strewn with awe;
Dense clouds arise in affection,
scenery is speckled in thrill.

He remained occupied in Shyam gardens;
He huddled in secret minds.
He came to articulate weak bodies;
He came to flame weak consciousness.

My mind appears to flow in affection;
world seems to have lost a bit.
Yamuna water is frisking every moment;
'Madhu' heart dances in new tune.

186. O Lord, You take care of Dharma
* 263/31.03.09 (Braj Bha's'a')

O Lord, You take care of Dharma of my life!
I have been wandering in life without sparkle, I don't get espousal;
I want to move with You for ever, You improve my attire.

I am not able to serve, I am not able to touch your holy foot wear;
I keep thinking some what in my mind,
I am not able to understand what is in God's mind.

I keep singing and meditating on Lord,
Devotion and Yoga is not so much understood;
Caste and groupings get some what mislaid,
Human Dharma gets some what understood.

Dharma holds life, essence of human mind is Dharma;
All humans are of one caste, all humans have one clan and Karma.

World's glow of life is one, all traditions of life are one;
Affection of human minds is one, 'Madhu' song of humans is one.
Now, You come and take care of all in life!

187. Bird of 'Madhu' mind
* 429/17.7.09 (Braj)

Bird of 'Madhu' mind keeps running, flying,
Descending and ascending in Lord's skies;
At times it gets weary, at times it is uneasy,
At times it smiles, at times it recalls.

I am not able to realize, I can't figure out,
I don't tune in, I don't get clarified;
At times I get tune, I get gratification,
I don't make out when morning turns around.

At times I tweet, at times I blaze,
At times I topple and at times I succeed;
I am not able to contemplate much,
I remain busy in act of Lord.

I am neither satisfied in this world,
Nor I am asleep in awakening;
Neither I am getting lost,
Nor I am getting much involved in it.

Loveliness lives in my body,
All instruments are there in my body;
As Your Tantra, I keep flying,
As Your Mantra in world, I keep roaming.

188. Smiling in her heart !
* 239/11.02.09 (Braj Bha's'a')

Smiling in her heart, aggravated in mind,
Jasumati@ is hesitant in head;
Ka'nha'* is going to forest for a promenade,
Mind of Gopiis is getting elated!

She talks peeping in eyes,
She disciplines indicating her index finger;
Her body feels good, mind is enthused,
Heart is smiled, foot steps are thrilled.

Murmuring in enlightened body,
Mohan+ smiles in mind;
Mana Sukha% has some thing to say in his mind,
Shya'ma'** is delighted in her mind.

Shya'ma^ remains in Ra'dha''s# heart,
She wants to listen melody of Krs'n'a$ flute.
Looking Krs'n'a $ affront,
She gets upset and hidden in climbing plant.

Krs'n'a moves with his friends,
Ra'dha'# walks amidst her friends;
The cow keeps listening to flute,
She-crow tastes 'Madhu' cascade.

@ Jasumati= Mother of Krs'n'a who brought Him up in Gokul
* Kanha'= ^ Shya'ma= + Mohan= $ Krs'n'a,
# Ra'dha'= Beloved devotee of Krs'n'a
% Mana Sukh = Friend of Krs'n'a; ** Shya'ma'= Friend of Ra'dha'

189. When grace of Lord gets showered
* 41/17.04.08 (Braj)

When grace of Lord gets showered,
My mind gets profusely delighted;
Braja blooms, cow sings,
Flute gets tuned without being played.

Cowherd children start running unknowingly,
Yamuna water gets sweetened;
She crow happens to sing her melody,
Peacock starts dancing keeping wings on head.

Body free from dirt, gets disciplined, my heart gets elated.
My plexus sing their own tune, mind dances, spirit gets amused.

Base* plexus scatters incense,
Fluidal* plexus reduces hunger & thirst sense;
Navel* plexus spreads red brilliance,
Heart* plexus runs advancing to skies.

Throat plexus pours spiritual authority & wisdom,
Brow* plexus motivates Dharma and Karma;
Guru graces bestowing devotion,
I surrender my blissful 'Madhu' mind.

190. O friend, beloved has arrived
* 434/17.07.09 (Braj)

O friend, beloved has arrived on terrain,
To liberate passion, to awaken devotion;
To engage in affection, to eliminate apprehension,
To give a direction, to teach Yoga & meditation.

O friend, you dance, sing and meditate,
Grow vine of sentient amity about;
You try to stay Him put through fasting out,
Try to thrill Ka'nha's* heart.

I am very passionate, I am rapt in untainted love,
I keep desiring Him so much in heart centre;
Swiftness of sentient, ethics of Yogiis,
Make me dance, thrills my conscience.

Peacock points out to me by dancing, I don't realize in illusion;
Skylark looks at wings of peacock at His head,
Sky is decked looking at His yellow garb.

Why are you blissfully singing?
Why are you standing and not even blinking?
Have you also seen 'Madhu' idol?
Are you also attracted looking at Mohan*?

----

* Ka'nha'= Mohan= Krs'n'a= Lord

191. My mind gets strewn at times
* 645/05.12.09 (Braj)

My mind gets strewn at times;
It gets strayed at times.
My mind gets cleared up at times;
It gets entangled at times.

It opens out and takes off some times,
It runs in pace of dream at times;
At times, it likes Yamuna water while overflowing,
At times it goes to clouds while gyrating.

Mind runs radiantly at times,
It crawls from hills at times;
It is perturbed at terrain at times,
It sings in melody of mud at times.

It dances with a kite at times;
It runs to terrain in moments.
At times mind is very elated;
At times mind is very terrified.

It speaks earnestly at times;
It smiles within mind at times.
Mind is in good spirits at times;
'Madhu' gets omniscient at times.

192. Let me keep dancing O Giridharii!
* 656/11.12.09 (Braj)

Let me keep dancing O Giridharii*!
Why do You put me to quandary?
Why don't You bestow me lovely Bhakti@?
Why do You keep me balancing, O Mura'rii#?

I enjoy loving You, my mind likes to dance with You;
Never aloof Your vision never upset creation.

You uphold motion of all creatures,
You balance wits of all creatures;
O Lord, You uphold all life breathes,
You liberate motion of all minds.

May everyone dance with You O Omni conscience!
They may not make creatures dance!
They may not get entangled in reactive momentum!
They may be able to serve, devote and esteem!

While purifying affection of all conscience,
While looking at amity of all creatures;
While keeping lotus feet on head in crisis,
O Shiva, You habitat 'Madhu' conscience!

Giridhari= Murari = Lord Krs'n'a
Bhakti= Spiritual devotion, Tripurari = Lord Shiva

193. You are caretaker of cosmos
* 668/13.12.09

You are caretaker of cosmos,
Why do I keep thinking in ways of woodworms?
You are conscience of moving and non-moving beings,
You are coordinator of whole cosmos.

No one can destroy any one as long as You protect one;
You keep an eye on destructive force,
You destroy their mind whenever You wish.

Age of all creatures is because of Your grace,
Every moment is under Your embrace;
Whosoever look creatures by unclean vision,
You plan and control their motion.

May no one expire at unripe age!
May human not be able to destroy any one!
O Giridhari, You take spiritual care in such a way,
That no creature may suffer at the hands of others.

Whenever, it sees destroying creatures,
When someone thinks like this by mind and actions;
'Madhu' mind overflows and gyrates,
It only appeals to Yourselves.

194. When my mind gets resolute
* 669/13.12.09

When my mind gets resolute,
It is able to bear cosmic sun and heat;
Whenever, it remains soft,
Cosmos at times makes it dance a lot.

It meditates moderating conscience,
It likes Tandav, Lalit and Kaoshiki dance;
It envisions Guru based on Guru Plexus,
It sees cosmos within conscience.

It dances loving gracious, it makes drill devils;
It dances keeping entire cosmos in bosom,
It keeps on surrendering all to bosom of supreme.

The cosmic management gets serene,
Equipoise and equilibrium emerge and bring us near supreme;
Intellect gets purified and clarifies Karma,
This brings surrender, service and affection.

That makes creature get consciousness of world,
Mind gets dedicated in feet of Lord;
My mind gets blissful in effect,
'Madhu' creation gets adorned in firm heart.

195. O Shyam! Upholder of hill! * 700/21.12.09 (Braj)

O Shyam#! Upholder of hill#! Do liberate me!
Night is incredibly murky; it is not easy to see.
Do not make any delay, recollect and dash to me,
O upholder of Chakra@! You rush, take away calamity.

My breath is getting obstructed, mind is getting sidetracked;
My spirit is quivering, heart is getting shattered.
Neither intellect reveals, nor is patience in place,
I am not able to comprehend what should be done.

You come close to me, give me patience,
Bring some movement; tell me an easy way out;
Mind is heavily laden, I have got sadden,
O upholder of mountain#, You come and take away pain.

No one is with me, You forgive me,
Give some vim, give some devotion;
O loving one! Affectionate of eyes! Come fast,
Take away predicament, habitat in my heart.

Come in my heart, O Lord! Holding Chakra@ in hand!
Look at my heart! Keep me within Your heart;
O habitant of 'Madhu' heart, speak sweet,
Impart soft smile, let lovely dawn permeate!

Shyam= Giridhari= Upholder of hill= Lord Krs'n'a
@ Chakra= Sudarshan Chakra used by Lord Krs'n'a
= Wheel of enlightenment= Spinning disc with sharp edge

196. I keep writing compassionate note
* 701/22.12.09 (Braj)

I keep writing compassionate note to my darling#,
While softly smiling, thrilling and amusing;
While weeping, fuming, amusing and teasing,
While contracting, surrendering, hiding and concealing.

Whatever pains I have in heart, whatever smarting stayed put,
I write whatever lies in heart, whatever I want I write;
My beloved is a Yogi, my mind is lonely,
He keeps conducting experiment and integrating in self spirit.

I write thoughts of my mind, my nights get passed,
Memory does not fade away, beloved does not come by;
No news arrives, mid day does not pass,
All moments do pass, evening comes alas!

I do not apply kohl, I do not deck garland in head,
I keep writing to beloved and amuse in mind;
My eyes are sweet; my girl friends keep looking at;
My bosom vibrates hearing tune of anklets.

'Madhu' is affable of beloved, Shyam is my beloved,
Note is 'spiritual management poem' I keep writing daily to adored.
It awakens sweet tinge, it keeps soft smile triggering,
While I smile sweetly, get shy and outpour nectar amusing.

Darling= Beloved= Lord = Shyam= Sanvariya'

197. Supreme subtle mind * 321/28.05.09 (Bengali)

While elating, supreme subtle mind
Wants to build conscious Terrain;
Utilizing nature, Supreme human wants to create neo human.

While arriving and sitting beside, You play flute in melodious mind;
You simply pour kindness, initiate new vibration in mind.

You cause nature dance, adorn skies,
Stretch amidst magnificence of conscience;
Thrill in human heart, awaken sweet white gleam in conscience.

You don't do too much Tandava,
Bring sweetness in mind of Pandava;
You destroy cult of demonists, You unfurl flag O Earth upholder!

Remaining plain with cooperation of nature,
Neo human is taking humanity together;
You may get integrated with your 'Madhu',
Taking crude and subtle as one.

198. All human brothers * 323/28.05.09 (Bengali)

O all human brothers, keep coloring 'Madhu' terrains!
You keep infusing every one with wave of love on terrains !

Remove all distress, move on flowing nectar for eternity;
Keeping minds gracious and generous,
Keep moulding magnificent humanity.
Don't look behind, keep embracing human conscience;
Keep enthused in Dharma and Karma,
Look for only good amidst conscience.

Don't hate any one, don't disregard any one;
Let every one dance in melody and rhythm, stay tuned in tune.
Let every one on Earth get engrossed in wave of nectar of bliss;
Keep singing and dancing, O human brothers!

199. O honey! You come! * 31/08.04.08 (Bengali)

O 'Madhu'* you come by, take honey of my conscience away!
You look at me, take me closer to you tenderly.

You come and while sitting close to me,
Go on doing some thing, whatever you feel like in your conscience;
Go on saying some thing, hear some stories of woe.

I have my accumulated honey, It is pure honey, very pure it is;
Only a little is left out, I want to give this to you. You come!
I want your sweetness, I see your charm, and I see your grandeur;
I move in your heart, You come, take honey of my heart.

Whatever is so called mine that is all yours!
You come and while loving, you take me along.
Take me closure to you and your way.

200. My body is wave of Your tune * 38/09.04.08 (Bengali)

My body is wave of Your tune, Your mind bestows me tone;
You keep singing within me Your tune, I go on balancing tune.

You play me as your violin, play with each nerve wire of mine;
You touch and play in my every nerve wire, You awake Your tune.
You sing your melody on instrument of my heart,
You do whatever you covet.

You are co-chariot of my consciousness,
You are witness of my conscience;
You are chariot of my tune, You are appraiser of my composition.
You look to me in conscience, You get me merged in Yourselves.

I dance in your rhythm, I shall sing in your tune.
I shall become barmy in your composition,
While murmuring your hymn. You come and set my tune.
Smiling 'Madhu' softly within, You adore me in meditation;
You come in my contemplation. You keep singing Your tune.

201. You are touch jewel   * 557/08.10.09 (Bangla)

You are touch jewel of all life breaths;
You are base ground of all melodies.
You are touch mine of all hearts;
You are liberated sound of all violins.

O Gopal of Braj! You come by and play flute in my heart.
Make me dance in whole cosmos; make cosmos dance in my heart.

Whatever I envision in life is adorned within You O sweet heart!
Without You are not cows and flute,
Without You are not dust and micro dust.

In Udaigiri mounts, in water of oceans, in each atom of snow hills;
In sorrow of suffering of Sunset,
You are sweet cool in sweet-hearty eyes.

You shower grace in my life,
You see me in own breath in meditations;
You go on making me hear your flute,
You adorn 'Madhu' in Your base.

202. You come in my heart * 646/09.12.09 (Bangla)

You come in my heart, You play flute in my intellect;
You sit beside me, You make me sit in your feet.

You touch my psyche, You cheer in my body;
Keep dancing in my life, keep thrilling in my belief.
You keep playing flute, adorn every one in cuisine of tune;
Awaken vibration in every heart, taking nature along, You ballet.

I want to hear Your guideline,   I want to see Your smile;
I want to see your peep in eyes, I keep your stick in my conscience.
You are touch jewel of all breathes, You are love mine of all beings;
You awaken devotion in my heart,
Thrill sweetness in 'Madhu' spirit.

203. How do you create? * 647/09.12.09 (Bangla)

How do you create? How do you act?
In what passion You elate?
What all You want in Your intellect?

You are impatient, You are upset, You are talented amidst great;
You are tremor amidst motion, You are thrill amidst smiley sight.

You are secret amidst heart, You are chill in forest;
You are forest of conscience in sight,
You are favorite in passion delight.

You deck in my mind intact, You create in my heart;
You stay bold, You stay ever awakened.

You pour honey in 'Madhu'mind, You smile like Moon behind;
You make world sweet, You awaken sweet cultural taste.

204. O beloved pal of my breath verve * 752/01.01.10

O beloved pal of my breath verve; I am decked in your love.
I am only looking for your love; I hope you perceive.

I live in a house of spectacle; you live in His domicile.
I look for nectar in every particle;
Showering nectar on all, you comprehend it all.

You know me much better; you know how to adore.
I do not understand your language; you know my yearning.

I am observable in your mind; I merely smile in your mind.
I only seek from you; I only survive embracing you.

I keep singing in your tune; I keep dancing amid your song.
I do not look forward for anything additional;
I do crave for your irresistible love diminutive.

205. O Tapti*! * 136/12.08.08 (Gujarati)

O Tapti* grown up on Satpur'a'!
Can you forget that form of your flood of Surat?
When you cross limit,
While jumping, spreading and enjoying conceit?

The bridge of ethics made overhead at that time,
Looks like a lonely weak line;
The high rise buildings established on your shoreline,
Appear to have been submerged in your inundation.

Your forceful flow looks like ocean in sight;
Tide of full moon of Bay of Khambat appears to hold you out.
The ocean is not accepting your sudden pour out,
It is asking you to remain within your limit.

The pestilence comes after your torrent;
Many close colleagues of past go far off from your sight.
O Tapti! Born in Betul, You flow quiet,
Let every one move or stay put;
Let 'Madhu' dwellings remain inhabited at their site,
Let clouds keep pouring out.

* Tapti: A 742 km long river of western India takes birth in Betul in
M.P., grows in Satpur'a' and flows in Gujarat. It merges in Bay of
Khambat in Arabic ocean. It gets flooded in Surat in Gujarat.

206. Punjab * 91/12.06.08 (Punjabi)

Ludhiana groomed by Laudhra* flowers,
Is thrilled by mind blowing Bhangr'a'* dance;
Punjab in flow of five waters, is under bliss by Guru's grace.

Bhakhar'a' Nangal is gracious, Govind Sagar is enormous;
Depth of Satalaj of Ropar is stretch of human intelligence.

Pervading Bias of Vya's is full of spiritual confidence.
Natural bridge on Vya's at the passage,
From Gurudaspur to Mukerian is very gorgeous.

Jallandhar is busy with business,
Patiala is full of A'la' Singh's honours;
Hoshiarpur is full of flow of folk songs,
Amritsar is in Guru Vanii's bliss.

Fort amidst green fields of Sangrur touches minds;
Ahmedgarh is full of 'Madhu' bliss.
Development of Chandigarh is organized with excellence;
Breeze flowing through gardens is in fragrance.

207. If there is any honor, it is only Yours * 440/24.07.09

If there is any honor, it is only Yours,
Neither it is mine, nor it is of anyone else;
Whosoever has it is covered by you,
In whatever way it is kept, it is kept by you.

You ignite fire of anger; You get anything done from creature.
You get him ashamed in moments;
You get him punished by worldly beings.

All creatures are your mediums;
They are Your beckons, vista and music drums.
They are all cared for, clarified and arranged for,
Taught adorned and grown so far.

You always hide behind; You get done whatever You need.
You make senses dance, sitting afar You get it all done.

Man is in a kind of helplessness; he is tied with a silky rope alas.
One end of this rope is held by Matchless,
Other end is in 'Madhu' conscience.

208. Effulgence of consciousness * 554/08.10.09

Effulgence of consciousness is unique;
It suggests and solves many mysteries.
It reduces and removes dilemmas;
It makes explore and offer nectars.

Longings diminish as consciousness moulds;
Effulgence on its own enhances.
Life starts getting understood in flash;
Offering tribute gradually comes.

Spiritual effulgence is benign; it makes strange world our own.
Bizarre become sweet and open; life becomes alert and fine.

O beloved, do not play conundrum; do come close on your own!
Explain cycle of creation; tell me how to wisely get along on own.

You have to show my real traits;
You have to show me spiritual brightness.
You have to tell 'Madhu' sweet course;
You have to show Yourself in imminence.

***

208/173 E. Madhu Couplet * 469C/01.08.09

Is ultimate some one there?
Is He here and every where?
Is He within and without you?
Is He within and without every one?

209. In the passion of ambition * 508/09.09.09 (Urdu/Hindi)

In the passion of ambition, we get pathways,
Bloom arrives roving while depriving and mislaying in many ways;
The agonies get stories and thought ways,
The busyness improves purity of 'Madhu' in various ways.

The lack of vehicles and passion,
Lack of happiness and casual uneasiness of pain,
Make desires fertile; they keep making ways on their own.

Taking energy from weakened besieged bodies & fibres,
While also taking energy from cosmos;
Atom keeps dancing, moving and spiralling life,
Fortifying flame, it awakens cosmic life.

Whenever consciousness and conscience desire whom so ever,
The creation comes conceding then and there;
Whenever mind surrenders itself,
The cosmic consciousness appears there itself.

Surrender is necessity of empowerment;
Deflection is actuality of intellect;
Inspiration is surrendered in purity,
Will is vibrated by supreme entity.
***

209/168E. Madhu Couplet * 470C/01.08.09

Is He not in void! Is He not in crowd!
Is He not in shroud! Is He not in blessed or less- blessed!

210. Every style of creation is unique
* 510/11.09.09 (Urdu/Hindi)

Every style of creation is of its own kind,
It is reared, purified and loved;
All balanced good hearted are smiled,
All are adorned in blissful tune and mood.

Flowers tempt every insect, songs prompt every friend;
All walk on tradition of love, lamps keep burning around,
Even while fading, lamps stay lightened.

The fragrance of fruits is liked by all in world,
Thousands of flies are mesmerized;
Fragrance of honey brings ants,
Honey like is every style of flowers.

Youthful she deer always smiles,
Sprouting Lilies happen to sing songs;
The pleasant soft smile of a child,
The spiritual intimate good hearted smile of an aged.

The odd shower of questions of childhood,
The cognitive pure moments of old,
All are of course attributes of created world,
All are styles of 'Madhu' vision of mind.

ENGLISH – ORGINAL

211. My I is yours
* 168/04.10.08 (English)

My I is yours, His and of every individual;
My I is of infinite and infinitesimal.
My I is in you, Him and every one;
You are in me, Him and every 'Madhu' one.

He is in you, He is in all, He is infinity;
His I is universe and His uni-verse.
His I is innovative, inquisitive & inherent;
It is ideal and unique universe.

His I is intimate, instinctive & intangible;
It is interesting and intelligible.
It is immense, impartial & illumine;
It is immortal and immutable.

His I is incessant, incredible & indisputable;
It is industrious and inevitable.
It is identity, idea & ideology;
It is idiom, ignition and identifiable.

His I is intact, involuntary & irresistible;
It is introvert, extrovert and invisible.
It is interface, inventive & invincible;
It is intended, intrinsic and invaluable.

His I is relevant, religious & sensible;
It is sensitive, secure and rational.
It is consistent, decisive & hospitable;
It is sincere, scientific and spiritual.

212. O Sun! You come every day
* 468/01.08.09 (English)

O Sun! You come every day! O Sun, you love all day!
O Sun! You greet every day! O Sun, you meet all day!
You do not delay; you do your duty everyday.
You do not play; you do not take holiday.

You are unique; you are source of energy & strength.
You are inspiration; you are upholder of Earth.
You are clouded by clouds; you are eclipsed by Moons.
You are encircled by planets; you are surrounded by stars;
You blaze within eternally while outshining stars on Earth;
You shine externally while remaining a small star in space.

You are busy in revolving around Milky Way;
You keep planets busy in revolving around your way.
Moons revolve around planets like grandsons their way,
Meteors flash around in 'Madhu' space losing their way.

213. I remain in ocean
* 461/ 01.08.09 (English)

I remain in ocean a midst sea of solitude;
You are silence of sub conscience indeed.
I am presentation of profile in need;
You are brightness of 'Madhu' much-loved.

I am unlimited resource, You are beautiful outsource;
I am outcome of utmost, You are utopia of support.
I am ever evolving creature, You are ever upholding father;
I am growing generosity, You are source of enormous beauty.

You behold and hold within, I call and cry without reason;
You counsel and console, I count and collect your jewel.
You work and plan for me, I enjoy and ponder;
You protect and shelter, I slumber and thunder.

214. When an alien arrives at our Planet
* 167/23.09.08

When an alien arrives at our Planet and looks at our Paper Mills;
He may wonder why do we really call them Paper Mills.

They look like Waste Paper Mills full of raw materials;
Finished products get quickly shipped out of Mills.

There is less finished paper,
More raw materials & packing materials;
It has machines processing materials
With humans operating machines.

It is not easy to see supervisors, managers,
Chief executive and clients;
Directors may only be coming for
Few hours a day or once in years.

In our Cosmos, similarly,
We may have more raw elements & consciousness;
More of in-process & processing infrastructure
And less of evolved conscience.

Every in-process microvitum may be
Under the multiple development process;
Every entity may be ever evolving through
Multidimensional cycles of creations.

The management plans, organizes & observes,
It evaluates reviews and directs;
It incorporates, employs & appraises,
It communicates, coordinates and controls.

Sprouting silently in subtlety,
Supreme consciousness may manage cosmos;
It may rarely be realized amid st management of
'Madhu' projects and equipment s.

215. O Time! * 463/01.08.09 (English)

O Time! Are you measurement of motivity of action?
How do I capture you? How do I possess you?
How do I pierce you? Can I see within you?

Can I see what really lies within you?
Can I see what lies beyond you?
Can I see what all went through an entity?
Can I see what all happened at a place in eternity?

Are you like entropy ever increasing?
Are you a dimension over space and entities ever unfolding?
Do you know what you will do at a space over time?
Do you know what you will do to an entity over time?

Is entity afraid of your unfolding event?
Is space fearful of what you may implement?
Is some one happy to welcome you?
Does Some One control you?

Do you love to watch 'Madhu' space?
Do you love to live every entity in a person?
Do you tangentially touch every one?
Do you passionately love every one?

216. O Time! Are you innocent?
* 464/01.08.09 (English)

O Time! Why do you make every one run?
Why every one cares for you while on run?
Why every one works with you?
Why every one happens to leave you?

No one knows what you may do after a while?
Is there some one who is easy with you for a while?
Is there Sun to welcome you? Is there Moon to relish you?

Do you dance in rhythm in consistency?
Do you trance in trajectory?
Do you enhance in eternity? Do you enjoy affinity?
Do you like to love space? Do you survive space?
Do you limit life? Do you observe life?

Are you transient? Are you transcript?
Are you imminent? Are you 'Madhu' innocent?
Do you simply pass over? Do you barely cross over?
Do you linger on? Do you carry on?

217. O man! My dear * 658/12.12.09

O man! My dear, Is your heart so clear!
Are you not in despair? Are you all that clear?

Do you not hurt lives? Do you not touch vibes?
Do you not crush nature? Do you not thrust pressure?
Do you respect your body? Do you love your buddy?
Do you think of others? Do you really serve others?

Do you know your conscience? Do you recognize consciousness?
Do you know your history? Do you know your geography?
Do you know your owner? Do you have your honor?
Do you love 'Madhu' creator? Do you love creature?

218. O Time! Are you perpetuity
* 465/01.08.09 (English)

O Time! Are you measurement of eternity?
Are you management of infinity?
Are you perpetuity?

Are you revelation? Are you realization?
Are you part of crystallization?
Are you phenomenon?

Are you preconceived? Are you Polaroid?
Are you oscillating, organizing and operating?
Are you commanding, calculative and cooperative?
Are you inspired, versatile and creative?

Are you universal, original and imperative?
Are you innovative and imaginative?
Are you controlled? Are you in control?

Are you reality of cosmic continuation ever present?
Are you intuitive, reminiscent and buoyant?
Are you obvious, influx, ever emergent?

O Time, do you dwell in cosmic conscience?
Do you enjoy nature? Do you evolve in His bliss?
Do you monitor 'Madhu' space and entity?

219. O Time! Do you uphold space * 466/01.08.09 (English)

O Time! Do you uphold space in entirety? Do you behold entity?
Do you unfold 'Madhu' eternity? Do you bolster affinity?

Can you continue for ever? Can you stop wherever?
Can you stop whenever? Can you do whatever?
Will you inspire space? Will you survive space?
Will you evolve entity? Will you engross creativity?

May you enlighten entity in space! May you brighten bliss!
May you highlight happiness! May you crystallize progress!
Do you tour and detour space, Do you cheer up creation,
Do you sprout meditation, do you enlighten enlightened creation.

Can you sing over in dignity? Can you swing over in calamity?
Can you shrine here in proximity? Can you shine over infinity?

220. Tree is like a space colony * 467/ 01.08.09 (English)

Every tree is like a space colony; it has its own community.
It has home for 'Madhu' birds; it has melodic music of birds.

Birds rest there in night, they return after work in daylight.
They have their nests; they have kids to look afterwards.

Branches are hidden, greenery is in shine.
Flowers are booming, fruits are sprouting.

Birds and squirrels have food on trees,
It is play ground for squirrels.
Raccoon s visit trees, humans love trees.

Trees look cool; they vibrate with breeze keeping cool.
They like company of trees; they like birds chirping songs.

They inhale carbon dioxide, they exhale oxygen in nighttime.
They inhale pollution daily; they exhale nectar of life every jiffy.

221. Evolution of Grass
* 471/01.08.09 (English)

O grass! You are amazingly splendid!
You are green and sweetened.
You are leveled and humbled;
You are flowered and showered.

You live close in family; you do not keep any fissure.
You stand small together, you flower altogether.

You inhabit insects; you attract butterflies.
You tolerate intrusions; you bear torments.

You lie low, you aspire high and you beautify space;
You enlighten human intelligence, you enthuse babies.

You love every one seeing you;
You observe every one observing you.
You enjoy butterflies and bees,
You like dogs and cats.

You enjoy getting grazed by goats & cows;
You enjoy visiting their digestive systems.

You become milk to enter human systems;
You enter brains to enjoy intelligence.

You comprehend 'Madhu' civilization;
You grow to enjoy deep realization.

You evolve to cosmic conscience;
You acquire your supreme stance of mind.

222. Are we really loving nature? * 661/12.12.09

Are we really loving nature? Are we really keen to creator?
Are we intimately our own? Are we akin to creation?

We are busy in corruption, we are increasing pollution;
We are playing with nature, we are exploiting creation.
Our focus is merely on us, our momentum is lost in crisis;
Our plans are to squeeze others; our motto is to live on others.

Unless we improve ourselves, until we serve others;
Unless we love and help live others,
We don't remain vivacious ourselves.

Why can't we integrate our heart?
Why can't we integrate to cosmic spirit?
Why can't we become 'Madhu' operator?
Why can't we come close to creator?

223. By prematurely putting off one * 666/12.12.09

By prematurely putting off one,
Aren't we removing one of our own?
If there is supreme in us,
How will He allow putting off one from us?

Who are we to put off life of one, if we cannot create that one?
Creator does transfer life after exhausting reactive momenta in time.

By eliminating life of even one,
We spoil cosmic equipoise & equilibrium;
It may even trigger accumulated reactive momenta to quake terrain.

Spirit never dies, it only evolves; the way it goes matters.
The way it goes affects; one who affects it, gets affected of course.
O Man, be beware of persecution! Beware of hurt and humiliation!
You will face consequence of every act undertaken in creation.
Don't set out any of His 'Madhu' creature hurt you in creation!

224. O Earth! Are you still not evolved! * 662/12.12.09

O Earth! Are you still not evolved? You still remain revolved!
O Earth! You still have man not fully evolved,
You still love and nurture creatures not evolved!

You keep revolving, keep evolving,
You keep loving, evolve loving;
You bear pains of misdeeds of man,
You forgive them for contamination.

What may happen, if you punish man, the way it troubles creation;
What may happen, if you humiliate man,
The way it ravages creation.

Let love and compassion evolve, let service and passion evolve;
Let awareness and wisdom grow, let devotion and evolution grow.
O Earth, you touch every one's heart, you make them nonviolent;
You enhance their 'Madhu' mind, you swiftly get them evolved.

225. Am I not a citizen of cosmos? * 665/12.12.09

Am I not a citizen of cosmos? Am I not citizen of every conscience?
Am I not occupant of whole space? Am I not resident of all times?

Is the space enjoyed by me not enjoyed by others?
Do the birds, trees and insects not reside freely in my space?
Is the space I live in, is not occupied at other times by others?
Is my space not part of generous Milky Way and cosmic space?

Is the space I own is really mine?
Was it always mine and will remain mine?
Can I remove microcosm out of it?
Can I send waves of consciousness out of it?
Is space in my consciousness limited?
Is the space at large not integrated?
Can I not enjoy my space in His cosmic space?
Can I not let others enjoy my 'Madhu' space?

*GLOSSARY OF SPIRITUAL TERMS USED
(SANSKRIT/ HINDI WORDS)

Madhu= Honey, Honey of consciousness, Gracious, Pen name of Author
Madhu Giiti= Spiritual Management Poetry, Sweet spiritual songs
Karma= Work or action, Jina'na - Karma= Bhakti=   Spiritual devotion
Dharma = Fundamental attributes which hold creatures
Lord Shiva = He incarnated 7000 years ago in Indian subcontinent and
initiated systems of marriage, Yoga, Tantra, Ayurved, etc.
3 Properties = Sata (Sentient), Raja (Mutative) and Tama (Static)
Nirgun'a or Nira'ka'r Brahm= Un-manifested supreme consciousness
Sagun'a Brahm= Sa'ka'r Brahm= Manifested cosmic consciousness
Srs't'i cakra= Cycles of creation consisting of Sam'car (Extrovert) and
Prati-Sam'car (Introvert) stages of Cycles of Creation, Manifested,
Mahat, Aham, Citta, 5 elements, Plants, animals, humans, intellectual
& spiritual humans and integrated beings with Sagun'a or Nirgun'a.
Mahat = Cosmic I Exist, i.e. whole existence is of singular cosmic stance
Aham = Cosmic I do, i.e. I ego manifests within cosmos creating duality
Chitta = Cosmic Done I, i.e. whole existence   now also has a mind stuff
which moves at   high frequency every moment amidst   cosmic entities.
Sam'ska'r = Reactive momentum
Dagdhabiija= Emancipated = Becoming free from reactive momentum
Sahodar = Brother = Emerged from same entity
Chakori = Moon bird, who keeps looking at Moon.
Ganges = Holy Indian river flowing from Himalayas to Bay of Bengal
Ka'liya' mardan = A python living in Mathura pond conquered by
Krs'n'a
5 fundamental elements of creation= Solid, liquid, fire, air and ether
Om = Eternal sound of cosmos, Ham'+ So= Om, An initiation Mantra
Krs'n'a= Lord Krs'n'a born 3500 years ago in Mathura, U.P., India who
established a rule of Dharma in Indian subcontinent by supporting sentient
persons and helping   them win through a Dharma Yuddha
(Spiritual war) named Maha' Bha'rat. Brownish Lord Krs'n'a, One who
interacts and attracts all in universe spiritually
Braja = Region around Mathura, U.P., India where Lord Krs'n'a
undertook His childhood activities and spiritual plays
Ma'nava Dharma= Human Dharma= Characteristics which hold humans
Yoga = Spiritual management of cosmos = That which integrates with
Supreme consciousness
Tantra = Spiritual technology, Applied Yoga (Spiritual Management) with
special practices

Yantra = Spiritual instrument, spiritual figure or design with or without Mantra inscribed

Mantra = Vibration that instils contemplation, personally given by Guru to competent spiritual aspirant as per his/her reactive momentum,few Siddha(Empowered) syllables

Brahm= That who is greatest, Supreme consciousness, God, Lord

Sagun'a or Sa'ka'r Brahm= Manifested supreme consciousness, Supreme in cosmic management mode, Ta'rak Brahma (Liberating God) in tangential stage in cosmic cycle

Nirgun'a= Un-manifested supreme consciousness, Supreme consciousness in introvert phase or mode relaxing or contemplating, Active in other spiritual domain or dimensions

Shree = Eternally alive, Evolution of Siddhii (Spiritual authority)

Tapa = Self disciplined and dedicated efforts to keep body, mind and consciousness pure   through sentient food, company, Yoga, Tantra, Karma, service, meditation, etc.

Kadamba tree = A large tree in Braj near Yamuna river where Krs'n'a used to play flute.

Keka'= A Braj bird who sings sweetly and silently

Gokul = Town near bank of Yamuna' in Mathura', India where   young Krs'n'a grew as a child

Tand'ava = Vigorous spiritual standing dance introduced by Lord Shiva which vibrates and exercises brain & body, boosts self confidence and creates fearlessness, etc.

Nandla'la' = Son of Nanda, Krs'n'a

Madhupur = Sweet city, Mathura.

Gokula = Mu'la'dha'ra cakra or Base plexus;

Ra'dha' = Beloved of Krs'n'a, deep spiritual devotee of Krs'n'a, Nature,Kulakund'alinii

Dha'ran'a' = Focussing mind on Supreme Consciousness, Contemplation in meditation

Samadhi = Stance of interacting or merging unit consciousness with cosmic consciousness

Pra'n'a'ya'ma = Yogic breathing, regulation of inhale and exhale

Yama Niyama = Penance & observance, 5 external & 5 internal disciplines

Pratya'ha'ra= Making senses introvert, withdrawal of senses

Yoga'sana = Yogic postures to streamline glands, nerves & plexus of body

Kiirtan = Chanting Mantra while uplifting hands, dancing, focussing on Supreme overhead

Mudra' = Yogic postures to activate subtle centers through hands, fingers, body & mind.

Meditation = A physical psycho-spiritual process or initiation given by authorized yoga teacher (Guru) by practicing which one can integrate consciousness to supreme stance.

Soham' = So (That) + Ham' (I) = 'I am That',   an initiation Mantra

Ham'sa = Swan, a white bird, A soul enveloped in Maya(Illusion), vital air

Pa'nchajanya = Predawn meditation practiced immediately as we   get up.

Kan'a'di = An ancient Ris'i (Researcher) of India

Holi = Festival of colours celebrated at onset of spring in India or abroad

Holika' = Burning a collection of dung and wood symbolic to evil burning

Saraswatii= The Goddess of learning & attainment who plays violin

Sujan= Sentient persons, whose minds are integrating with Supreme .

Suman= Sentient minds, flowers

Vanshii va'rao= Muralii va'rao= Beholder of flute, Krs'n'a

Jasumati= Mother of Krs'n'a who brought Him up in Gokul

Devakii = Mother of   Lord Krs'n'a who gave Him birth in Mathura prison

Kanha'= Shya'ma'= Mohan= Nanda Lal= Krs'n'a

Devakii Nandan= Kanhaiya'= Krs'n'a

Mana Sukh = Friend of Krs'n'a

Shya'ma'= Friend of Ra'dha'

Cakra's= 7 Main plexus across back bone (Mu'la'dha'r, Sva'dhistha'n, Man'ipur, Ana'hat, Vishuddha, Ajin'a, Guru and Sahasra'r or Pineal) which control human entity.

Ma'nava deha= Human body, an instrument able to integrate with supreme

Mana pra'n'a= Mind and consciousness, Conscious breath

Tapti: A river of western India flowing from M.P. to Gujarat

Laudhra flowers= Wild flowers named Laudhra were earlier popular in Punjab and name of city Ludhiana is said to be evolved from Laodhra – Ludhi over the time.

Prabha'kar= Creator of glow, Sun , Supreme consciousness

Chan'akya = A spiritually evolved highly diplomatic king of India

Malayaj = Himalayan hill having sandals releasing fragrant blissful breeze

Barasa'na'= Native place of Ra'dha' toward north of Mathura

Gopii= Cowherd girl; devotee of Krs'n'a

Gopa= Cowherd boy, devotee of Krs'n'a

Madhuvan= A garden in Vranda'van, Maholi, Sweet garden in Braj

MADHU GIITI (MG) & POEM No. (PN) INDEX
मधु–गीति व कविता सं. तालिका

MG-PN	MG-PN	MG-PN	MG-PN	MG-PN	MG-PN	MG-PN	
मधुगीति – कविता सं.	मधुगीति – कविता सं.	मधुगीति – कविता सं.	मधुगीति – कविता सं.	मधुगीति – कविता सं.	मधुगीति – कविता सं.	मधुगीति – कविता सं.	
01- 066	43- 151	78A- 054	128- 120	162- 139	240- 154	521- 063	
02- 108	44- 152	79- 055	129- 042	163- 012	258- 162	554- 208	
03- 109	45- 075	80- 057	130- 043	164- 128	260- 145	557- 201	
04- 111	46- 121	81- 155	131- 045	167- 214	263- 186	563- 164	
05- 112	47- 122	81A- 156	132- 002	168- 211	281- 184	564- 165	
06 - 069	48- 153	82- 157	133- 058	175- 133	286- 003	566- 067	
07- 072	49- 051	82A- 158	134- 080	176- 131	308- 010	567- 068	
08- 040	50- 047	83- 159	135- 046	178- 135	312- 011	575- 018	
11- 021	51- 048	86- 033	136- 205	179- 134	319- 143	586- 017	
12- 027	52- 038	87- 034	137- 124	180- 136	320- 101	588- 166	
13- 025	53- 015	88- 035	138- 065	182- 132	321- 197	600- 185	
14- 023	54- 123	89- 036	139- 126	183- 137	322- 100	601- 001	
15- 147	55- 118	91- 206	140- 116	184- 138	323- 198	645-191	
16- 150	56- 022	92- 079	141- 083	185- 094	327- 144	646- 202	
17- 113	57- 024	93- 163	142- 177	186- 097	328- 004	647- 203	
18- 115	58- 049	94- 170	143- 178	188- 146	329-182	651- 106	
20- 074	59- 060	95- 175	144- 161	189- 179	330- 005	656- 192	
21- 019	60- 052	96- 172	146- 085	190- 180	411- 084	658- 217	
22- 149	61- 026	97- 171	147- 086	191- 006	429- 187	661- 222	

23- 099	62- 167	98- 173	148- 087	192- 007	434- 190	662- 224	
24- 160	63- 168	99- 174	149- 088	193- 008	440- 207	665- 225	
25- 117	65- 169	100- 176	150- 102	194- 181	461- 213	666- 223	
26- 071	68- 028	115- 044	151- 089	195- 009	463- 215	668- 193	
27- 073	69- 029	116- 041	152- 082	201- 095	464- 216	669- 194	
28- 013	70- 030	117- 037	153- 129	202- 098	465- 218	700- 195	
29- 014	71- 056	118- 103	154- 130	203- 096	466- 219	701- 196	
30- 016	72- 076	119- 104	155- 090	224-148	467- 220	752- 204	
31- 199	73- 077	120- 110	156- 091	225- 062	468- 212		
37- 119	74- 078	121- 061	157- 092	226- 140	471- 221		
38- 200	75- 081	122- 059	158- 093	235- 050	508- 209		
40- 183	76- 031	123- 039	159- 114	236- 141	509- 070		
41- 189	77- 032	126- 107	160- 125	238- 142	510- 210		
42- 020	78- 053	127- 105	161- 127	239- 188	520- 064		

प्राक्कथन

* आपकी नववर्ष की कविता पढ़ी; बहुत अच्छी लगी– **कुँवर बेचैन**, वरिष्ठ कवि, गाजियाबाद, उ. प्र., भारत

* आपकी न्यूयार्क में गायी कविता "विश्व विश्वास से भरा रहता" बहुत ही अच्छी रचना है. आपने भाव विभोर कर दिया. शब्दों की उतनी अहमियत नहीं होती जितनी भाव की. कवि वही है जो अपने भावों को कविता में ढाल सके और आप अपने इस प्रयास में पूरे कामयाब हैं. ईश्वर से प्रार्थना है कि आप और आनन्द बाँटें और साहित्य में एक नया आयाम स्थापित करें– **श्यामा सिंह**, कवियित्री व लेखिका, किचनर, ओन्टारिओ, कनाडा.

* आपकी उच्च स्तरीय कवितायें कविताकोश में आपके वार्ता पन्ने पर पढ़ीं. आपके जैसे अच्छे कवि का कविताकोश में सदस्य बनना, निसंदेह कुछ अच्छी दुर्लभ रचनाओं का कविता कोश में जुड़ने का शुभ संकेत है. मुझे बेसब्री से आपकी रचनायें पढ़ने का इंतज़ार रहेगा. धन्यवाद. – **श्रद्धा जैन**, सिंगापुर.

* ब्राम्प्टन, कनाडा में आयोजित कवि सम्मेलन में गिल्ड के सदस्य श्री गोपाल बघेल 'मधु' जी ने अपने प्रेरणा पूर्ण गीत 'भारत भुवन को उर रखो' के मधुर गान से सब को मुग्ध कर लिया– **हिन्दी राइटर्स गिल्ड**, कनाडा, www.Hindiwg.blogspot.com

* आप जैसे साहित्यकार की कृतियां प्रकाशित कर हम गौरवान्वित हैं– **महेन्द्र प्रताप सिंह 'राजा'**, मुख्य उप संपादक, राष्ट्रीय सहारा/ सहारा समय, लखनऊ, भारत.

* शिक्षा यतन, न्यूयॉर्क में जुलाई ७, २००९ को हुए अन्तर्राष्ट्रीय कवियों के कवि सम्मेलन में टोरोन्टो, कनाडा से आये कवि गोपाल बघेल 'मधु' ने अपनी कवितायें गाकर समां बाँध दिया– संवाददाता – **देवी नाँगरानी**, संयुक्त राज्य अमेरिका – **'कुतुब नुमा' हिन्दी पत्रिका**, मुम्बई, भारत.

* आपकी कविताओं में मधु ही नहीं प्राकृतिक मकरन्द भी है. अब जहाँ प्रकृति स्वयं निवास करे वह कृति सुन्दर तो होगी ही – **डॉ. के. एल. पाल**, संपादक, पा. समाज वाणी, पटियाला, पञ्जाब, भारत

* आपकी कवितायें आपकी मधुर आवाज में प्रत्यक्ष व विडिओ पर सुनकर बहुत आनन्द आया. आपकी आध्यात्मिक कविताओं में सहजता, सरलता और सुकोमलता का परिचय मिलता है. आपके अन्तर्मन में छिपी आनन्द की अनुभूति, आस्था और संवेदना इनमें झलकती है. मुझे विश्वास है कि इन भक्ति भाव से ओत प्रोत कविताओं की महक बहुत दूर तक फैलेगी. मैं हृदय की गहराइयों से आपको शुभ कामनायें देती हूँ– **डॉ. सरिता मेहता**, अध्यक्ष, विद्या धाम, न्यूयॉर्क, सं. रा. अ. www.Hindi4us.com

* आपने सभी के हृदयों में उठते हुए भावों को इस प्रकार से अपनी कविताओं में स्वाभाविक रूप से प्रकट किया है जैसे कि आप सभी के मनों से मिलकर आये हों और सबके हृदयों में रहते हों. सभी कविताएं प्रेरणा स्रोत हैं और आध्यात्मिक भावों से ओतप्रोत हैं. उनकी रचनाओं में एक आकर्षक चुम्बकीय प्रभाव है. भावों को समझना सुगम है. कवि ने ८ भाषाओं में लिखकर भाषाओं में स्नेह की मन्दाकिनी बहाई है. उनकी सब भाषा भाषियों व उनके भावों से तन्मयता है. उनकी कविताएं 'प्रबन्ध स्वर' लगती हैं. वे सच्चे शान्त प्रेम भाव से मन को मुग्ध करती हैं. वे जीवन जगत की सच्चाई और वास्तविकता से परिचय कराती हैं जिससे जीवन और सुन्दर व मधुर दीख पड़ता है.– **प्रमोद कुमार,** एम.सी.ए.,भारत

* आपकी मधु गीति अध्यात्म व जीवन से जुड़ी हुई कविताओं का संग्रह है जो आपकी काव्यात्मक प्रतिभा व आध्यात्मिक स्वरूप को दर्शाता है– **किशोर चन्द्र व्यास**, पूर्व विंग कमाँडर, भा. वायु सेना, ब्राम्प्टन, कनाडा

* आपकी कविताओं में आध्यात्मिकता और जीवन के यथार्थ के दिग्दर्शन होते हैं– **डा. दिनेश पाठक शशि**, साहित्यकार, प्रवर अभियन्ता, भारतीय रेल, www.dineshpathakshashi.blogspot.com

PROLOGUE

* Your New Year composition is heart-warming and very good- **Dr. Onkar Dwivedi**, Order of Canada, Ph.D., LL.D. (Honorary), Dr. Env.S. (Honorary), FRS(Canada), University Professor Emeritus, Department of Political Science, University of Guelph, Guelph, On., Canada.

* We all, your Mechanical Engineering classmates, appreciate your effort and devotion in learning Bengali in NIT, Durgapur to enjoy the original creations of Giitanjali and now transforming yourself to an able creator in this language too. May everyone draw inspiration from your untiring work and disciplined approach to life. We wish you the very best - **Dileep Chatterjee,** Hyderabad, India.

* I am elated to read your Bengali poems and realize my limitation of not composing even a line in Bengali to match your composition.   Please keep it up. - **Dipak Basu**, Kolikata, W.B., India.

* It is blissful to be in the presence of the celestial music sung by you in the intensity of depth that leads to oneness - **Devi Nangrani**, Poetess and Editor, Chicago, IL, USA.

* It will be a pleasure to see you and listen to your divine poetry when you are here in New York – **Dr. Sarita Mehta**, President, Vidya Dham, USA.

* Ananda Anubhuti/ Perception of Bliss' is an exemplary, exquisite and unique effort to give impetus to literature in 8 languages. This collection has compositions each one of which is exceptional and highly appreciable. **Dr. Dauji Gupt**, President, P.E.N., India ; International President, Akhil Vishva Hindi Samiti, New York, USA.

* When I need to unwind and contemplate the beauty of all creation, I read Gopal jii's poetry to get me in a blissful vibration. Sheer Devotion. -   **Tom Lavrih (Prashanta)**, Professional Engineer , Toronto, On.,Canada

* Gopal Madhu ji has made remarkable expedition into spiritual poetry, consciousness and philosophy. I appreciate his devotion to human society and for composing "Madhu Geeti", a series of spiritual poetry which is creating a wave of difference. We all need his creation; universe applauds him to continue it. - **Tanvir Sayed**, President, Banijjika, Mississauga, On., Canada.

* I enjoyed glimpse of 'Ananda Anubhuti' in Hindi, English & other languages. Your talent has gone afar to create an additional chapter in Poetry. This is amazing and unique. I appreciate your skills and literary conceptions -   **Ram B Gautam**, President, International Hindi Association, New Jersey, USA.

* I enjoyed your 'Ananda Anubhuti' poems at You Tube, websites and ones sent by mail.   These are amazing and fantastic. I appreciate your word power, composing skills, knowledge of literature and concepts of spirituality - **Nishi Pal**, Editor, P.K. Samachar, New Delhi, India.

* I am so happy to   listen and read your poems and comprehend that   each of   your word   and sentence is amazingly attractive. I enjoy every song. These are truly spiritual poems after listening which I happen to go in trance and get real peace. Deep imprints of philosophy, freshness, originality, innovation, novelty and uniqueness of thoughts are avidly & vividly observable in your poems. - **Pramod Kumar**, MCA, Gwalior, M.P., India.

* Your poems are rich in spiritual thought and content and carry a very high level of philosophy. They are sweet, melodious and lyrical. I spontaneously start reciting while reading them.- **Dr. J. P. Baghel**, Senior Poet, Mumbai, India.

* I have read your poems in Hindi, Punjabi, Roman and English. They are awesome. - **Dr. Balwant Singh Chandan**, Retd. Prof., PAU, Ludhiana, Pb., India, Mississauga, On, Canada. .

* It is great work you have undertaken. It is like another 'Gitanjali' in making- **Er. Uttam K. Banerjii**, Mississauga, On., Canada.

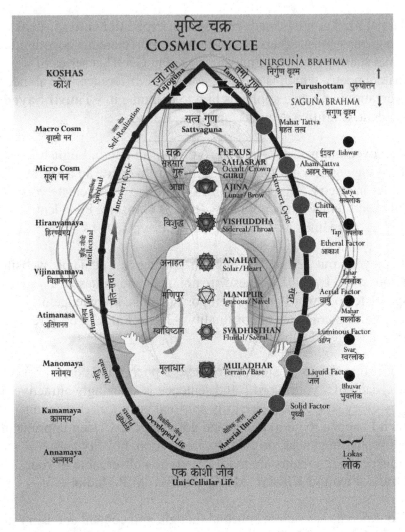

Graphic Design of Cosmic Cycle is created by Shweta Baghel

ॐ तत्सदिति 'आनन्द अनुभूति' ॐ मधुः ॐ मधुः ॐ मधुः

Om tatsaditi 'A'nanda Anubhu'ti',
Om Madhu:, Om Madhu:, Om Madhu:

O Supreme! Here it gets accomplished 'A'nanda Anubhu'ti'
O Supreme Sweetness! O Supreme Sweetness! O Supreme
Sweetness!

सर्वङ्गं ब्रह्म मयङ्ग जगत

गोपाल बघेल 'मधु'

अध्यक्ष व निदेशक

अखिल विश्व हिन्दी समिति

आध्यात्मिक प्रबन्ध पीठ
टोरोंटो, ओन्टारिओ, कनाडा

www.GopalBaghelMadhu.com

AnandaAnubhuti@gmail.com

एक संभ्रान्त भारतीय किसान परिवार में जन्मे, इंजीनीयरिंग व प्रबंध शास्त्र में शिक्षित, एस. ए. पी. – बी. डब्ल्यू. में प्रशिक्षित, पेपर व अन्य उद्योगों के प्रबंध व व्यापार में व्यस्त रहे, आयात निर्यात इत्यादि में रत, विश्व को विलोकते, आध्यात्मिक साधना में प्रवृत, ग्रहस्त जीवन के सुख दुख भोगते गोपाल बघेल 'मधु' के भाव भरे हृदय से यकायक विभिन्न भारतीय भाषाओं व अंग्रेजी में 'मधु गीति' काव्य धारा निःसृत हुई जो इस संकलन में समाहित है।

सुधी पाठक इन गेय गीतों की माधुरी व आध्यात्मिक तरङ्ग में भूमा की भाव गङ्गा को स्वयं में बहते देख अपनी 'आनन्द अनुभूति' में निज प्राण मन को उल्लसित, प्रफुल्लित व आत्म विभोर पायेंगे। यह अनवरत आनन्द प्रवाह पृथ्वी के प्रति प्राण को तरङ्गित कर प्रति देश काल पात्र को नव स्फूर्ति व भाव उत्प्रेरणा दे, सद्कर्म, ज्ञान व भक्ति में उत्तरोत्तर प्रतिष्ठित कर अनन्त कृपा धारा बहाये व मानव मन कला, संस्कृति, विज्ञान, अध्यात्म, परस्पर स्नेह, सेवा, कर्म, त्याग व आनन्द की आकाश गङ्गा में उत्तरोत्तर मग्न रहे, यही मेरी लालसा है।

44 Barford Road, Toronto, On., M9W 4H4, Canada

Phone:+1-416-505-8873, AkhilVishvaHindiSamitiToronto@gmail.com

Gopal Baghel 'Madhu'

President and Director

Akhil Vishva Hindi Samiti,

Spiritual Management Foundation,

Toronto, On., Canada

www.GopalBaghelMadhu.com

PerceptionOfBliss@gmail.com

A limitless lyrical flow of 'Madhu Giiti' suddenly sprang up in various Indian languages and English from passionate conscience of Gopal Baghel 'Madhu' born in a valued farmer family in India. He is B.E. (Mech.) with P.G. Diploma in Management and trained in SAP - B.W. He has been occupied in management & business of Paper and other industries in India and Canada. This poetry collection is compiled while observing world, practicing spiritual meditation and while enjoying delight and twinge of family life.

Evolved readers will find their minds & conscience gleeful, elated and enthralled in their Perception of Bliss while finding themselves flowing in fervent cosmic Ganges of melody and spiritual wave of these lyrical songs. This incessant blissful flow will vibrate every conscience, it may give renewed vigour and passionate eternal rejuvenation to every entity at every place at all times. It may help out pour unlimited streams of grace while endlessly engaging and establishing in sentient Karma, devotion & knowledge while human mind may remain continuously enlightened in Milky Way of arts, sciences, spirituality, Karma, penance and bliss, is my yearning.

Printed in the United States
By Bookmasters